RUSSIA'S ORIENT

RUSSIA'S ORIENT

Imperial Borderlands and Peoples, 1700–1917

Daniel R. Brower and Edward J. Lazzerini, editors

INDIANA UNIVERSITY PRESS   BLOOMINGTON & INDIANAPOLIS

This book is a publication of

Indiana University Press
601 North Morton Street
Bloomington, IN 47404-3797 USA

http://iupress.indiana.edu

Telephone orders 800-842-6796
Fax orders 812-855-7931
Orders by e-mail iuporder@indiana.edu

The paper used in this publication meets the minimum requirements of American National Standard for Information Sciences—Permanence of Paper for Printed Library Materials, ANSI Z39.48-1984.

Manufactured in the United States of America

Library of Congress Cataloging-in-Publication Data

Russia's Orient : imperial borderlands and peoples, 1700–1917 / Daniel R. Brower and Edward J. Lazzerini, editors.
p.   cm. — (Indiana-Michigan series in Russian and East European studies)
Includes bibliographical references and index.
ISBN 0-253-33274-5 (alk. paper). — ISBN 0-253-21113-1 (pbk. : alk. paper)
1. Russia—Ethnic relations. 2. Minorities—Russia.
3. Russia—History—1689–1801. 4. Russia—History—1801–1917.
I. Brower, Daniel R. II. Lazzerini, Edward J. III. Series.
DK33.R88   1997
323.1'47—dc21   96-39473

3 4 5 6 05 04 03

For Alexandre Bennigsen

CONTENTS

Preface ix

Introduction xi

Note on Transliteration and Terminology xxi

❀

PART ONE   Empire and Orient   1

1. "Ignoble Savages and Unfaithful Subjects": Constructing Non-Christian Identities in Early Modern Russia / *Michael Khodarkovsky*

9

2. Naturalists versus Nations: Eighteenth-Century Russian Scholars Confront Ethnic Diversity / *Yuri Slezkine*   27

3. Empire and Citizenship / *Dov Yaroshevski*   58

4. Nineteenth-Century Russian Mythologies of Caucasian Savagery / *Susan Layton* 80

5. From Savagery to Citizenship: Caucasian Mountaineers and Muslims in the Russian Empire / *Austin Lee Jersild*   101

6. Islam and Ethnicity: Russian Colonial Policy in Turkestan / *Daniel Brower*   115

7. Russian Orientalism at an Impasse: Tsarist Education Policy and the 1910 Conference on Islam / *Robert Geraci*   138

Contents

PART TWO   Frontier Encounters   163

8. Local Accommodation and Resistance to Colonialism in Nineteenth-Century Crimea / *Edward J. Lazzerini*   169

9. Representations of Russia in Central Asian Jadid Discourse / *Adeeb Khalid*   188

10. Historical Memory, Cultural Identity, and Change: Mirza ʿAbd al-ʿAziz Sami's Representation of the Russian Conquest of Bukhara / *Jo-Ann Gross*   203

11. Crossing Boundaries: The Trading Frontiers of the Terek Cossacks / *Thomas M. Barrett*   227

12. Barïmta: Nomadic Custom, Imperial Crime / *Virginia Martin*   249

13. Constructing an Islamic Identity: The Case of Elyshevo Village in the Nineteenth Century / *Agnès Kefeli*   271

14. Empire and Savagery: The Politics of Primitivism in Late Imperial Russia / *Bruce Grant*   292

Conclusion   311

Bibliography   317

Contributors   333

Index   335

MAPS

Map 1: Russian Empire circa 1900 / xxii–xxiii

Map 2: Crimea and Caucasia / 100

Map 3: Kazakh Steppe circa 1860 / 136

Map 4: Kazakh Steppe and Central Asia, Early Twentieth Century / 137

Preface

This volume is a product of the collective labors of people within and around the academic community having a scholarly interest in the oriental borderlands of the Russian Empire. It began in 1990 as a collaborative and impoverished research project, which was soon generously funded by the National Council for Soviet and East European Research. In that early stage our only clear objective was bringing together scholars daring or foolhardy enough to judge Russian imperial history in need of revision. A struggling "Borderlands Research Group" (BRG) took on new life and momentum thanks to a grant from the council, whose support continued for the entire period of the project.

As it gained focus, the BRG concentrated on organizing a research conference dedicated to the discussion of essays proposing new approaches to that long-neglected area of Russian history. The two-day conference, held in September 1994 at the University of California–Berkeley, gave its twenty-five participants the opportunity for an intensive and extremely fruitful exchange of concepts, theories, and information spread unevenly over two centuries and covering even more unevenly the enormous territory of the Russian Empire. The conference received additional financial backing from the Social Science Research Council, supplementing funds from the National Council. Thanks go to the staff of Berkeley's Slavic Center, who ensured that the conference ran smoothly and that the participants had ready access to everything from hotel rooms to sharp pencils, while discreetly placed microphones and a reliable tape recorder retained for posterity those two days of animated discussions. Guest moderators Ronald Suny, Thomas Metcalf, and Mark von Hagen ably and enthusiastically presided over the sessions.

The ultimate mark of the conference's success was the general agreement among participants to seek publication of revised conference papers. The editors were further gratified to find that each of their universities was prepared to provide subsidies to ensure the generous inclusion of illustrations and maps as well as the appearance simultaneously of both paperback and hardbound editions. For this we wish to express our thanks to Alan Olmsted, director of the Institute for Governmental Affairs of the University of California–Davis, and to two colleagues at the University of New Orleans—Shirley Laska, Vice Chancellor for Research and Sponsored Programs, and Philip B. Coulter, Dean of the College of Liberal Arts. Ultimately, our greatest thanks must go to the authors for their commitment to the project and their readiness to put up with periodic demands and pleas from their editors.

Introduction

The collapse of the USSR and the increased access to its former regions (and their local archives) have opened up exciting opportunities for scholars long accustomed to reliance on published materials and, at best, glimpses of places to which they may have devoted years of study from afar. While they have not been the sole beneficiaries of these developments, those who years ago staked a claim to recovering the multiethnic character of the Tsarist Empire can be excused for feeling that they have been reborn as scholars. Being able, as seldom in a long while, to visit the erstwhile borderlands, see the material remnants of local history, tread paths that previously had to be conjured from the travels of others, and experience what only being there can provide may be likened to a smorgasbord for the famished. Events have made the possibility of "revisioning imperial Russia," as the title of a recent article proclaimed, real indeed.[1]

But not events alone. Later in this introduction we shall suggest some of the fresh approaches, research methodologies, and conceptual modeling, often from disciplines other than history, that have helped shape the thinking of all who have contributed to this volume. Much of this rethinking has been late in coming to students of Russian history. But the turn to different kinds of analysis, the most recent and challenging fruits of which can be found later in these pages, was emerging long before the demise of the Soviet Union and was establishing a foundation for what could be done under the changing circumstances of the past decade.

Commensurate with anything that French, English, or German scholars have produced, oriental studies (*vostokovedenie*) in the Russian academy has a long and justifiably proud history of sound research, superb textual analysis, and substantial contribution to the archive of information about the peoples and cultures along the empire's southern and eastern borderlands. Whatever their involvement, direct or indirect, in the creation of a Russian orientalism, in the sense captured by Edward Said's critique,[2] old-regime specialists such as B. A. Dorn, A. E. Krymskii, V. R. Rozen, and V. V. Bartol'd made oriental studies a pursuit in the best European intellectual and scholarly traditions. The collapse of the tsarist system and the birth of the Soviet did little to undermine interest in vostokovedenie or the skillful training of succeeding generations of researchers and teachers. The political purposes to which the effort was put may have been more blatant, and Soviet administrators certainly shaped it in ways that tsarist bureaucrats could only have dreamed of, yet work of good and even great quality continued to emerge from the labors of many scholars.[3]

Elsewhere, interest in Russia's Orient has been understandably less pronounced and compelling, except insofar as concern for Great Power politics drew attention to the region and those who controlled it. A few small centers of activity, often energized by Soviet or East European émigrés, cropped up in Paris, Munich, Cologne, London, and New York, and an equally small number of academic institutions (Harvard, Columbia, Indiana, Washington) offered hospitable settings for scholars to pursue what most believed to be an arcane, exotic, and impractical field of study.[4] The commitment to area studies, especially in the United States in the 1950s and 1960s, certainly bolstered the modest expansion of these activities, but the critical development that ultimately transformed the study of Russia's Orient was generated in Paris through the efforts of Alexandre Bennigsen and his small cadre of colleagues and students.[5]

The major contributions of the Bennigsen *collectif* were several: first, it discovered and recovered published materials, especially of the regional periodical press, that unlocked previously unheard voices and unexamined insights from among indigenous peoples themselves; second, it tapped into archival documents in Turkey and, to a lesser extent, Iran that added another dimension to the study of parts of Russia's Orient, particularly before the Soviet period; third, it drew attention away from the center of the Russian/Soviet empires to the southern and eastern peripheries, assisting thereby to broaden the range of perspectives about events and developments that helped shape the borderlands and the heartland; and fourth, it began weaning scholarship on the subject from its fruitful but limiting philological and literary roots onto a broader-based enterprise that drew increasingly upon the social sciences and their evolving methodologies. At the same time, those working in the social sciences were made to appreciate more than before the importance to their research of the local languages. Bennigsen's "Centre Russe," as it was popularly called, was an integral part of what became the École des Hautes Études en Sciences Sociales, France's most esteemed research-oriented institution of higher education, and was housed on its "campus" along the Boulevard Raspail. It eventually served not only as an extraordinary research collection, but as a mecca for scholars young and old from across the world, where they found an eminently congenial setting to pursue their work, imbibe an afternoon *café turque,* and contribute in separate and collective ways to the development in the West of a fuller study of Russia. The conscious expansion of France's premier specialized journal in the field, *Cahiers du monde russe et soviétique,* to include scholarship on the Russian Orient was one more reflection of Bennigsen's influence.

To his French base, Bennigsen added other European and Turkish and especially American colleagues and students—some who worked directly with him at the University of Chicago, where he held a joint appointment in the 1970s and early 1980s; others who made the pilgrimage to Paris; and still others who either heard him lecture or read his publications. We do not need to exaggerate his influence, or deny the controversy he at times engendered with his interpretations, to note that from under his guidance and encouragement emerged a small but innovative and productive generation of scholars who in turn have helped shape some of the best of the newest. We like to think of Bennigsen as a pioneer of sorts whose vision for vostokovedenie in the West included, above all, a fundamental respect for the viewpoint from the borderlands and the development of an ability to interpret it effectively, a sensitivity to the realities of interaction among peoples and cultures as a formative force itself, and a willingness to wrestle with the social as well as the political, the local as well as the imperial or international. Directly or indirectly, echoes of that vision reverberate in our own volume of essays, the authors of which are all beneficiaries of Mikhail Gorbachev's political gambit and Bennigsen's intellectual opening.

Our collection carries forward the work of scholars such as Bennigsen while reframing the subject of imperial history. Though the eastern and southern borders of the empire appear clearly defined on historical maps (those, at least, that include the territories beyond European Russia), inquiry into the evolution of imperial rule and its influence on the peoples inhabiting those regions remains meager. In part, this shortcoming results from scholarly preoccupation with the Russian autocracy. The power of the tsar and the St. Petersburg ministries, the focal point and center of the empire, drew attention logically to the process of policy formulation and to administrative actions, but inevitably away from events and developments in the outlying regions. Yet this reluctance to investigate the eastern and southern borderlands also stemmed from a lack of vision.

Much of the literature produced about the Russian imperial experience has focused on policy as defined from the center, along with generalizations and conclusions from "official" statements that pay little heed to, first, the unarguable tension between theory and practice; second, the influence on policy implementation of local circumstances—whether geographic, economic, or cultural—that varied enormously across a huge territory; and third, the role of regional/local authorities and populations in actual policy formulation and application. Even at the centers of power, debate over policy choices among and within ministries or other institutions remains essentially unexamined, as do the arguments and counterarguments in and beyond governmental circles about causes, goals, and consequences of administrative decisions. Is it language or religion, for example, politics or culture, invidious discrimination or raison d'état that explains the pursuit of Russification, its absence or increased intensity? For that matter, can one so easily explain policies such as Russification without acknowledging some interaction between the arbiters of power and their presumably obliging subjects?

The debates that went on within Russian elite groups, both secular and religious, have barely echoed in the historiography, as is true for questions of how indigenous peoples conducted their individual and communal lives under colonial conditions. For all the writing on Russia as empire, we have been left a remarkable legacy of significant silences. With its presumption of Russian superiority, the influence/response paradigm that had colored discussions of colonial relations for so long is much to blame. By implicitly accepting the universal and fundamentally determinist future proposed by modernization theory, that paradigm proved especially minimalist and one-sided. All influence, it effectively insisted, flowed from the outside (advanced and progressive) into the native settings (backward and traditional), making colonial domination an apparently necessary stage along the path to the modern. Missing from the discussion were cultures and their fragments, authentic voices from below and on the margins, indigenous ethnographers who could act as cultural mediators of a different kind, and iconographies of the "other" that were self-generated rather than imposed. Narratives about ethnic groups reflected, however innocently, neocolonial assumptions that for all their sympathy reduced the subjects' involvement in the making of history to a shadow of its logical extent. Even when recorded, the drama of insurgency, for example, too often meant the story of colonial administrative efforts at suppression and control, leaving us little understanding of the insurgents themselves. In fact, the equation of insurgency with criminality effaced its significance as a fight for social justice.

For now, histories of imperial Russia cannot claim the distinction of the many recent studies of the French and British empires that have enlarged and enriched their topics by redefining the very notion of imperial history. The essays in our book, however, do suggest ways by which the study of the Russian Empire in its turn can become the source of new insight into the history of that vast land and its peoples, begin to overcome the ethnographic travesties of the past, and make so many stereotypes, by contemporaries as well as historians, less compelling. Our rethinking of this imperial past uses what might appear to be a conventional vocabulary to explore a variety of themes that emerge from the interdependent concepts of empire and colony. Implicit in our approach to the Russian Empire is the idea that the relations between eastern and southern regions and the state were those of colonial lands and empire. Their peoples were dominated politically and militarily by an imperial center and were considered backward as gauged by the customary eighteenth- and nineteenth-century Russian (Western) measures of civilization. Their status resembled that of the peoples in the overseas colonies of the French and British empires. European rulers distanced themselves from these peoples by emphasizing their exotic, oriental character. By analogy, St. Petersburg ruled its own Russian Orient.

Our rethinking of the empire's history is not the product of one conceptual paradigm; on the contrary, readers will discover a diversity of approaches in the pages that follow. Still, our project is grounded in general agreement among the authors—who collaborated first in a working conference and then in the preparation of this volume—on the benefit of viewing that history through new, unfamiliar perspectives. Consequently, certain conceptual issues are of particular importance to our undertaking.

Our approach to Russian imperial history builds on the insights of cultural anthropologists and ethnographers regarding the concept of ethnic identity. Out of their discussions has emerged an understanding of ethnicity as a socially constructed bond of group identification. Frederic Barth suggests that the vital factor in studying ethnic groups is boundary maintenance, that is, the criteria established by one group for distancing itself from others to maintain its own integrity. In his theoretical construct, ethnic boundaries are subject to alteration, since in his view the markers of group identity are not the product of a primordial, unchangeable essence. These boundaries are permeable, for individuals can and do change their ethnic identity, leaving one group to join another.[6]

This theory has several important conceptual implications. First, Barth's approach affirms that social interaction is key to ethnicity, which in these terms requires mutual agreement about who is excluded from and who belongs to the group. Second, the process of interaction depends upon the perceptions and practices of a population choosing the elements that constitute their key markers of ethnic identity. In Manning Nash's terms, the "building blocks" of ethnic identity, such as language, shared history, and religious practice, "are virtually the same all over the world," but the ingredients in each case are historically specific and unique.[7]

Third, the process of boundary formation and maintenance is a product of particular historical circumstances. Imperial conquest and rule of subject peoples elevated ethnicity to a position of political prominence in modern history. The naming of peoples became a major project of nineteenth-century ethnographers, whose investigations extended from Western populations into the most distant imperial domains. Recent studies have revealed that their criteria of ethnic identity strongly influenced their observations and selection of data. Their conclusions, which claimed the objectivity of dispassionate observation, seem to one contemporary ethnographer to have been a kind of "cultural representation" of ethnic groups. Yet these representations were also "social facts."[8]

Ethnicity acquired special significance when imperial administrators concluded that knowledge of their subject peoples could help them formulate policies for effective, progressive rule. Benedict Anderson points in particular to the use of ethnic labels in censuses, maps, and museums to divide the populations into knowable groups. In his words, these institutions "profoundly shaped the way in which the colonial state imagined its domination—the nature of the human beings it ruled, the geography of its domain, and the legitimacy of its ancestry."[9]

To emphasize the importance of the colonial experience suggests the need to explore points of contact or "encounters," imagined or lived, among the empire's peoples and between the tsarist regime and its subject communities. It underlines the need to understand the response of subject populations to colonial rule. These peoples play a major part in our story of the empire; their accommodation with and resistance to the empire constitute in many respects the real imperial history of Russia. Their response entailed refining, redefining, and codifying their own markers of identity, and in the process shaped their own history as a people.

The contacts across the social and cultural boundaries separating colonizers and colonized, Westerners and non-Westerners, extended far beyond the realm of imperial administration and ethnographic expeditions. Missionaries, traders, doctors, and teachers sought, at times successfully, to penetrate the domain of the colonial "other." To "go native" was yet another mode of infiltration, undertaken not to convert or improve but to escape. Taken all together, these contacts created the immediate context for direct encounters between empire and colony, between colonizers and colonized.

They also produced invaluable records of the impact of colonial rule. The ethnohistorian Greg Dening found that beaches became arenas of exchange and border crossing when Western sailing ships approached Polynesian islands in the late eighteenth and early nineteenth century. He presents convincing evidence that beachcombers, both figuratively and literally, were key actors establishing communication across these cultural barriers. Their records were indispensable to his search to uncover the vanished culture of the Marquesas islanders. Though their testimony could never escape the cultural bias of their origins, he is convinced that "one can see beyond the frontier only through the eyes of those who stood on the frontier and looked out. To know the native one must know the intruder."[10]

This judgment is relevant to our inquiry into the imperial borderlands. It stresses the importance of a close reading of the documents left by the colonizers, for their records remain the principal account of interethnic relations under imperial rule. They viewed the colonial world through blinders created by ethnic and historical stereotypes, and by clichés built of their own sense of ethnic and national identity and their conviction of moral superiority. Their records are a story of Russian self-representation, official and popular, through the centuries when Russians became increasingly engaged in encounters with non-Russians. At the same time, the information derived from a critical analysis of their observations is a key ingredient in our revised history of the empire.

In the same manner, the records and writings of the colonized present the colonial experience from a vantage point that is essential to our story. Those who sought to "cross the beach" to collaborate in one manner or other with the colonizers have as much to tell us of the encounter as officials whose imperial mission included learning native languages and studying native cultures. This arena, more than any other imperial site, became the location where elements of tolerance and mutual understanding were likely to emerge alongside the intolerance and domination that imperial rule cultivated. Historical hindsight suggests that these moments may have an important lesson for our postcolonial age of ethnic conflict.

This cultural and social encounter was inherently unequal. Although, as one cultural semiotician has recently suggested, the boundary between two cultures resembles a "zone of cultural bilingualism," communication occurs in the colonial context in conditions of what he calls "semiotic inequality."[11] As a result, those who held the instruments of political power also controlled the terms in which that communication took place. This form of imperial hegemony found expression in symbolic imagery and verbal stereotypes, which language embodied and to which it gave voice.

To investigate these forms of imperial domination greatly enlarges the scope of the topics relevant to imperial history. The cultural symbols that embodied colonial inequality appeared in national histories, travel literature, popular newspapers, art, and even exhibits at world's fairs. One historian has investigated what he terms the "rhetoric of empire," that is, the peculiar literary devices that proclaimed the legitimacy of imperial domination.[12] The images that characterized "primitive" and "savage" peoples were the simplest and arguably the most powerful labels to confirm cultural inferiority. They appeared not only in popular literature but in the works of social anthropologists as well. They emerged out of a theory of primitive society, which, as one recent scholar argues, "is about something which does not and never has existed."[13] When colonial empires recognized ethnic differences, they also constructed their own scale of cultural superiority, extending from savage natives to their own self-image of civilized nation. As a result, approaching the history of the empire from this cultural angle opens up new perspectives on the Russian homeland itself.

Probably the most influential study of the textual records of Western imperialism is Edward Said's examination of French and English literary images of the "Orient." In his work this term covers a vaguely defined area extending from North Africa to India. But Said is concerned only with Western literary images, which he describes as a "system of knowledge," of the peoples of these lands. "Orientalism" signifies the Western point of view, or "discourse," that created an imaginary, exotic picture of eastern peoples and lands. For Said, it captures the pervasive, demeaning nature of Western global domination.[14]

Said's perception of the significance to Western imperialism of degrading images of eastern peoples has proved a fruitful foundation for new studies of imperial history, including our own. But it hides a serious weakness. The ethnographer James Clifford has pointed out that Said's literary analysis lacks any allusions to, or even any basis on which to understand, oriental judgments of the West. The West is privileged to the extent of silencing any other, contrary voices. Said's method, in Clifford's opinion, is gravely flawed for want of a conceptual position from which to evaluate "the ways in which distinct groups of humanity imagine, describe, and comprehend each other."[15] This observation is a timely warning. The success of the literary contribution to imperial history must depend on allowing a multiplicity of voices to be heard—Westerners and non-Westerners, colonizers and colonized.

The parallels are numerous between French and British images of Muslim lands and Russian cultural representations of the peoples in the empire's southern and eastern territories. The "Orient" in our title alludes both to non-Russian borderlands extending from the Crimea to Sakhalin and to the various textual portraits and stories of the colonial experience that these borderlands produced. Acknowledgment of a border separating the Russian "West" from its "Orient" emerged repeatedly throughout the long period of Russian imperial rule, yet it fluctuated from place to place, and from one period to the next. Just as no one geographical site could claim to be *the* Russian Orient, no simple line on a map separated Western and Eastern peoples within the empire. Some Russians discussed in this volume even used oriental imagery to express their distaste for political or cultural aspects of their own people and state, placed outside the civilized West. In this respect, too, the Russian Empire occupied a unique place among Western states.

In many ways, our manner of writing the history of the empire is a study in comparative history. Along the borderlands of the Russian Empire, imperial policies and interethnic relations varied from one region to another, each with its own peculiar mixture of language, religious practices, and cultural traditions. Our essays propose a comparative approach to regional developments on the edges of the empire. Without denying the importance of separate histories of different peoples and regions, this

Introduction

volume seeks to uncover those historical processes common to some or all of the subject peoples.

On a broader scale, the Russian Empire evolved in ways that are comparable to those of other Western empires. The experience of these empires passed into Russian policies and practices of imperial rule beginning with the reign of Peter I. It remained a point of reference, to be condemned or emulated, to the very end of the empire's existence. Yet the Muscovite origins of the Russian Empire continued to influence imperial practices, both at the center and in the borderlands. The empire's historical tradition and geopolitical context set it apart from the other Western states. By keeping in mind these comparative perspectives, enriched by the abundant postcolonial studies of Western empires, we hope to widen the range of relevant issues and conceptual approaches, and expand the place of the imperial experience in Russian history.

The Russian Empire and its successor empire, the Soviet Union, have vanished, leaving behind political borders drawn to isolate ethnically distinct peoples first recognized and represented within imperial borderlands. One heritage of this history is the transformation of ethnicity into the cornerstone of current ethnoterritorial nationalism. The history of the successor nation-states must pay particular attention to the imperial period. Our essays on peoples and borderlands speak to conditions of a very different age, but that age prepared the way for the Soviet project of national territorial divisions and, ultimately, the independence of the republics. We do not demonize that imperial past; we seek, rather, to throw light on the little-known history of those peoples under imperial rule and to make understandable the historical background of the new, post-imperial age of the former imperial borderlands.

NOTES

1. Jane Burbank, "Revisioning Imperial Russia," *Slavic Review* 52, no. 3 (1993): 555–567.

2. See Edward Said, *Orientalism* (New York, 1979).

3. The legacy of Russian/Soviet vostokovedenie has been the subject of extensive writing within its native setting but has received little attention elsewhere. In fact, even among those who, like Edward Said, have attended to the ideological dimension of "Orientalism" in something of a comparative perspective (at least within the European community), the Russian variant might just as well have never existed. The marginalization of this legacy by the dominant Euro-American academic discourse is testimony to both the linguistic handicaps of non-Russianists (very much like that affecting Americanists who seek to contribute to the historiography of the Cold War) and, contrarily, the indifference of Russianists, though with important exceptions. The most significant publications of the latter may be found listed in the bibliography accompanying this volume.

4. In this context, the careers of Edward Allworth, Michael Rywkin, Alan Fisher,

Omeljan Pritsak, Halil Inalcik, Kemal H. Karpat, Yuri Bregel, Denis Sinor, and Peter B. Golden stand out, as does Serge A. Zenkovsky's pioneering study *Pan-Turkism and Islam in Russia* (Cambridge, Mass., 1967).

5. Bennigsen published more than two hundred articles and at least a dozen books during his career, but the two that he wrote with his longtime collaborator, Chantal Quelquejay, stand out in our minds as most reflective of the character of his accomplishments: *Les Mouvements nationaux chez les musulmans de Russie: Le "Sultangalievisme" au Tatarstan* (Paris, 1960) and *La Presse et le mouvement national chez les musulmans de Russie avant 1920* (Paris, 1964). Perhaps more than any other book, the former awakened attention to an aspect of Bolshevik history and the October Revolution that had been unappreciated in its significance *because* it involved bringing in the margins of those subjects, while the latter served to expose the virtually unknown yet extraordinary array of published material— periodical and nonperiodical—produced in the borderlands and by natives themselves.

6. "Introduction," in *Ethnic Groups and Boundaries*, ed. Frederic Barth (Boston, 1969), pp. 4–5 and 9–10.

7. Manning Nash, *The Cauldron of Ethnicity in the Modern World* (Chicago, 1989), pp. 5–6.

8. James Clifford, "Introduction," in *Writing Culture: The Poetics and Politics of Ethnography*, ed. J. Clifford and G. Marcus (Berkeley, 1986), p. 13.

9. Benedict Anderson, *Imagined Communities: Reflections on the Origins and Spread of Nationalism* (New York, 1991), pp. 163–164.

10. Greg Dening, *Islands and Beaches: Discourse on a Silent Land, Marquesas, 1774–1880* (Honolulu, 1980), p. 43.

11. Iurii Lotman, *Struktura dialoga kak printsip raboty semioticheskogo mekhanizma* (Tartu, 1987), pp. 10–12.

12. See David Spurr, *The Rhetoric of Empire: Colonial Discourse in Journalism, Travel Writing, and Imperial Administration* (Durham, N.C., 1993), esp. chap. 4 ("Classification: The Order of Nature").

13. Adam Kuper, *The Invention of Primitive Society: Transformations of an Illusion* (London, 1988), p. 8.

14. Said, *Orientalism*, pp. 2–8.

15. James Clifford, "On Orientalism," in *The Predicament of Culture: Twentieth-Century Ethnography, Literature, and Art* (Cambridge, Mass., 1988), p. 266.

A Note on Transliteration and Terminology

The personal and place names, the terminology, and the notes and bibliography that help fill this book bear witness to the complex issues of transliteration with which we have had to wrestle. For the sake of as much simplicity as possible, if not necessarily consistency, we have adopted the following rules to handle Russian, Turkic, Arabic, and Persian-rooted words:

1. Transliteration from Russian in text, notes, and bibliography follows the Library of Congress system.

2. Transliteration of Turkic, Arabic, and Persian terms, geographical sites, personal names, phrases, and bibliographic entries is generally left to the discretion of the contributors, who come to this project from different disciplines and cultural contexts. We have tried to compensate for this diversity in the index, where cross-references and alternative spellings are indicated.

3. For a select few terms that have long been in use across Russia's largely Turkic Orient and that derive from Arabic, we have adopted the Arabic form in transliteration. This list includes *Qurʾan, madrasa, maktab, ulama, Shariʿa, mulla,* and *amir.*

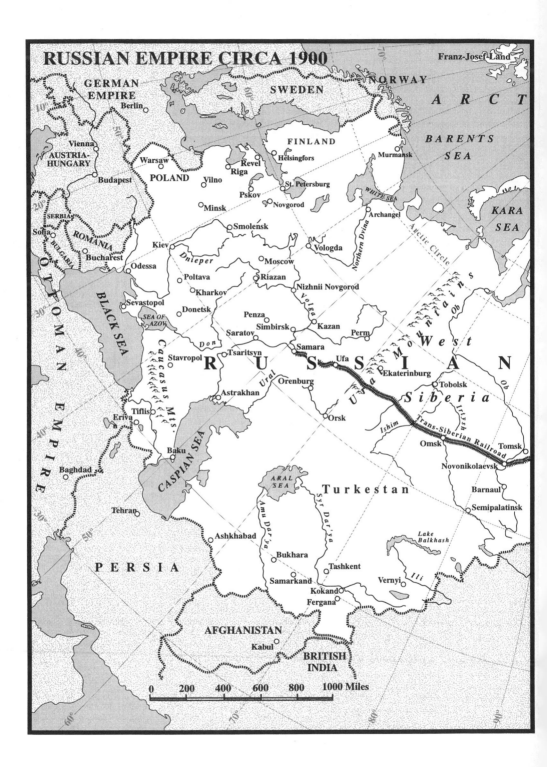

RUSSIAN EMPIRE CIRCA 1900

Franz-Josef Land

GERMAN EMPIRE

SWEDEN

NORWAY

A R C T

Berlin

BARENTS SEA

FINLAND

Vienna

Murmansk

AUSTRIA-HUNGARY

Warsaw

Helsingfors

Revel
Riga

St. Petersburg

KARA SEA

POLAND

Vilno

Pskov

Budapest

Minsk

Novgorod

Archangel

SERBIA

Smolensk

Vologda

Sofia

Kiev

Dnieper

Moscow

BULGARIA

ROMANIA

Poltava

Riazan

Bucharest

Odessa

Kharkov

Nizhnii Novgorod

Volga

Sevastopol

Donetsk

Penza

Simbirsk

Kazan

Perm

SEA OF AZOV

BLACK SEA

Saratov

Don

West

Caucasus Mts.

Stavropol

Tsaritsyn

Samara

Ufa

R U S S I A N

Ekaterinburg

Ob

Astrakhan

Ural

Orenburg

Tobolsk

Siberia

Ural Mountains

Tiflis

Eriva
a

Orsk

Ishim

Irtysh

Trans-Siberian Railroad

Ob

Baku

CASPIAN SEA

Omsk

Tomsk

Baghdad

ARAL SEA

Novonikolaevsk

OTTOMAN EMPIRE

Turkestan

Barnaul

Tehran

Syr Dar'ya

Semipalatinsk

Ashkhabad

Amu Dar'ya

Lake Balkhash

P E R S I A

Bukhara

Tashkent

Ili

Samarkand

Vernyi

Kokand
Fergana

AFGHANISTAN

Kabul

BRITISH INDIA

0   200   400   600   800   1000 Miles

PART ONE

Empire & Orient

In his entertaining and provocative novel *The Name of the Rose,* Umberto Eco draws the reader through a masterfully orchestrated mystery where, in the end, meaning is found without being sought. Along the way the appropriately Franciscan protagonist, William of Baskerville, is doubly confounded when his enormous gift for observation is rendered irrelevant and his belief that signs can be used to acquire knowledge is sorely challenged. Part of the novel's charm, and certainly one of its "meanings," is that it is a mystery in which very little is discovered and the detective is defeated. Neither is supposed to happen, especially in an age and place (fourteenth-century Europe) in which major intellectual steps were being taken to make the world more intelligible and graspable.

William is an early, albeit fictional, product of Roger Bacon's theorizing about knowledge and science, which became a critical part of the European trajectory into the eighteenth and nineteenth centuries. Its cultural, political, economic, and social influence is still with us, and it has generated a seemingly boundless inclination to order the natural and human, to name so as to *give* and not to find meaning. Out of this came anthropology, sociology, statistics, and positivist thinking habits as well as the extraordinary data gathering and record keeping that so engaged the modern imperial states in their belief that knowledge was power. The mystery of administering vast empires and diverse peoples was to be dispelled by making meaning out of the archive of information available out there, by reading cultures through imperial eyes. William of Baskerville's experiences can be dismissed as a fiction that the real world would never confront, yet the real world of empire produced its own fictions, the meaning of knowledge being one of them.

Discovering who was out there consumed the attention of Russians concerned with their own empire as much as it did others across Europe. Until the eighteenth century, as Michael Khodarkovsky shows in his chapter, steppe neighbors falling under the Russian gaze and/or Russian control were provided various identities, not necessarily consistent, and mostly inaccurate, but reflecting separate political, economic, linguistic, and above all religious concerns. Their construction began after the mid-sixteenth century, and though it drew upon the steppe context, with which Russians had had a long interaction, in the result we can find clear evidence of fantasies about self and other. Khodarkovsky amply reveals the fictive and self-serving quality of Russian definition of empire and peoples by highlighting the countervailing perceptions and interpretations held by those inhabiting the borderland.

By the second half of the eighteenth century, as part of a larger European development ushered in by the deceptively modest classificatory system proposed by the Swedish naturalist Carl Linnaeus, Russian thought about empire began turning away from an emphasis on religion to one on culture. Yuri Slezkine in his chapter lays out in convincing detail how natural history as a knowledge-structuring paradigm offered the emerging Russian scholarly community a means for confronting the empire's ethnic diversity. The ethnographic research that resulted was most interested in the mundane aspects of culture (food, sex, clothing and dwelling styles, economic activity), though there was still room for religion in an increasingly secular perspective. At the same time, as Dov Yaroshevski tells us in his contribution, the eighteenth century produced the beginnings of theorizing about citizenship, a polysemic term, that nevertheless held out the possibility of turning borderland subjects ("rebellious natives") into loyal citizens whose differences from Russians would be minimized by a kind of cultural revolution. Law and order, with the latter flowing from the former, offered for some (beginning with Catherine II) the best hope for a conscious and active citizenry devoted to the public interest of the empire.

Susan Layton turns our attention to the relationship between literature, specifically Romantic literature, and the dynamics of meaning-making. For its part, Russian Romanticism was as important in constructing identities for borderland peoples as was the Enlightenment. In their portrayal of regional natives, Romantic writers may have remained torn between contrasting judgments of their subjects' fundamental character (Are they noble or ignoble?), but they revealed a penchant to adopt an anti-conquest stance commensurate with their alienation from the state. In this respect, the Russian Romantic perspective stands in contrast to European literature's more typical support for imperialism. Romantic innocence vis-à-vis the empire's power game, for all its passion, however, was unable to fully disavow Russian hegemony over peoples in out-of-the-way places.

Going out among native peoples, imaginatively or literally, became a major activity for Russians after the middle of the eighteenth century. The chapters by Khodarkovsky, Slezkine, Yaroshevski, and Layton are testimony to the "traveling" that became so fashionable, but they also remind us of the emergence and evolution of Russian self-consciousness highlighted by vigorous and passionate debates over humanity, reason, and civilization. We can also sense, *pace* William of Baskerville, how confounding the empire became despite all the observation, and how illusive/elusive its meaning remained.

If, as Thomas Richards has written recently, "an empire is by definition and default a nation in overreach," we can appreciate some of the difficulties that Russian imperial authorities experienced in trying to hold on to territories—albeit contiguous and not overseas—and control peoples with very different socioeconomic and cultural characteristics.[1] The administrative challenge was seemingly eternal and is well known to students of Russian history, but less attention has been devoted to the ways Russians have tried over the centuries to merge national and imperial identities in both theory and practice. It was relatively easy to make the empire seem national by adding titles to those long claimed by the tsar, by setting up branches of Russian institutions in colonial settings, and by extending use of the Russian language far and wide. The result, however, was another of those imperial fictions—unity. Through its symbolic play, the "evidence" of unity may have comforted Russians, but it also helped generate a historiographic tradition that typically has meant viewing Russian imperial history through a Russian lens, from a Russian center, and by a Russian agency.

In the several other chapters comprising the first part of this volume, the colonial strategies articulated and implemented from around the 1860s to the end of the Old Regime are revealed to have been more complex and variegated than previously presumed. How to control the empire's peoples and cultures was hotly contested, the more so as the empire was increasingly buffeted by modernizing forces that disrupted what seemed to be organic and normal, whether in social relations, economic activity, cultural creativity, or politics. While each of these chapters differs from the others in its particular subject matter, they are all concerned with the deeper question of the empire's character.

Austin Jersild underscores the growing importance of notions of citizenship (*grazhdanstvennost'*) and civil society in redefining the empire and its peoples. These appear as logical extensions of the Catherinian commitment to toleration, designed to include non-Russians as equals within an empire struggling to make better use of its natural and human resources, and to avoid "militaristic solutions" to ethnic relations as much as possible. Jersild encourages us to recognize that citizenship is, however, a concept subject to multiple definitions, and that part of the complication derives from non-Russians' taking Russian liberality at its word. His examination of the career of the Azerbaijani intellectual and social activist Hasan Bey Zardobi is particularly valuable in picking up on this point and drawing a link with chapters by Khalid and Lazzerini elsewhere in this volume that highlight the unintended subversive aspect of the inclusive colonial strategy.

Daniel Brower focuses on the frontier policy in Turkestan under the administration of Governor-General Konstantin von Kaufman. He reads that policy as an "ethnographic project," that is, as a rekindling of the enlightened perspective regarding non-Russians and their place in the empire first officially enunciated by Catherine II in the later eighteenth century but suffering from criticism in government, military, and church circles by the middle of the nineteenth. For Kaufman, governance of non-Russians required knowing (scientifically) who they were, so that ethnicity became a primary instrument of colonial rule. Knowledge derived from rigorous investigation by cadres of trained observers was coupled with a presumption of the social invention of ethnicity, so that in Kaufman's view the "vestiges of backwardness" afflicting the peoples of Turkestan could be eliminated, and they could become full and productive subjects of a Russian empire.

Subversion is a major theme of Robert Geraci's chapter, which uses a conference convened in St. Petersburg early in 1910 to reveal the thinking underlying a countervailing view of what the empire should be. That gathering of government administrators, orientalists, and Orthodox missionaries, sponsored by Prime Minister P. A. Stolypin, was redolent of fear that Russia's Muslims, epitomized by the Tatars, were taking advantage of what "liberal" Russia had been offering (allowing) in order to satisfy agenda inimical to imperial interests. A contentious spirit animated the conference, whose subtext was shaped by the kind of "orientalism" to which Edward Said did so much to draw our attention.

The Russian Empire, then, like others that emerged from European bases in the sixteenth century and after, indulged a growing and endless need to connect the known and familiar to the unknown and alien. Toward that end it employed representational practices—some confessional or philosophical, but others bureaucratic or literary—hoping in the process to assert convenient truths when facing uncomfortable fictions might have been better. Confronted by the multiethnic character of its own Orient, Russia's elite seemed determined to shape it to fit a Russian self-definition, all the while finding itself saddled with unresolved and unresolvable cultural incompatibilities. Poised between preserving and erasing difference, those elites were "frequent and cunning liars," in Stephen Greenblatt's phrase, "whose position virtually required the strategic manipulation and distortion and outright suppression of the truth."[2] Representational practices were not always ideological, fixed, and unidirectional, but they were productive of empire. Ultimately, however, they were also productive of its undoing, leaving colonial appropriations less than marvelous in their rewards.

NOTES

1. Thomas Richards, *The Imperial Archive: Knowledge and the Fantasy of Empire* (New York, 1993), p. 1.
2. Stephen Greenblatt, *Marvelous Possessions: The Wonder of the New World* (Chicago, 1991), p. 7.

.1.

MICHAEL KHODARKOVSKY

"Ignoble Savages and Unfaithful Subjects": Constructing Non-Christian Identities in Early Modern Russia

By the late eighteenth century, Russia emerged as one of the largest empires in the world. The numerous subject peoples included Jews, Orthodox and Catholic Christians in the west, and, in the south and east, Muslims, Buddhists, and pagans. All the non-Christian peoples were referred to by the generic term *inorodtsy*, i.e., the non-Christian or non-Russian subjects of the empire.

This chapter examines the process of construction of non-Russian, non-Christian identities in Russia. As the Russian state continued to expand from the fifteenth century onward, it increasingly came into contact with the various peoples to the east and south. They were distinctly different from the Russians, for they neither spoke the language nor shared the religious beliefs of their new rulers. What were the official and popular perceptions of the newly encountered peoples? Is it possible to attribute to the Russians a certain conceptual and coherent vision of the "other" and to distinguish attitudes and policies toward these peoples consciously pursued by the government? I suggest that while the perceptions of the non-Christians were subject to change, particularly in the eighteenth century, the government policy toward them reveals consistent conceptual simi-larities.

In the middle of the eighteenth century, Russian officials in charge of the southern and eastern frontier districts frequently referred to the neighboring nomadic peoples, the Kazakhs, Kalmyks, and Bashkirs, as "wild, untamed horses," "wild animals," "wild, unruly, and disloyal peoples," whose khans practiced "savage customs." By contrast, the Russian Empire was proudly portrayed by government officials as "the world's respected and glorious state."[1] Obviously, the political universe of the Russian officials was limited to a clear-cut, bipolar world in which non-Christian nomads represented the savage, the brutish, the unreliable, and the unruly, while Russia stood for civilization, morality, and a stately order, like a "pillar of stability" untouched by the "steppe winds." Revealing more about Russia's self-image than about its neighbors, this description of the "other" reflected the government's newly developed realization of its civilizing mission among the non-Christians. To become Russia's subjects, the non-Christians were to be made "better," they were to become Russians. How was Russia to tame and civilize its unruly neighbors, and otherwise turn them into faithful subjects?

The process of encounter, contact, and incorporation of the non-Christian peoples into Muscovy, and later into the Russian Empire, can be seen as a three-part development. First, their identity as the "other," the stranger and the alien, was constructed, as they were seen and described in opposition to the Russians. Then they had to undergo transitional rites of swearing political allegiance and accepting a separate economic status. By classifying the non-Christian peoples and by creating a special status for them, whether preferential or discriminatory, the government set them apart from others and confirmed their separate identity. Finally, religious conversion ended their "otherness." It served as the ultimate rite of incorporation leading to a change of customs, as well as legal and economic integration. We shall examine below how the identities of the non-Christian peoples in Russia were constructed through official rituals, symbols, and rhetoric.

Political Identity

In 1483 a military band of Muscovites crossed the Iron Gates or the Rocky Belt, both terms used at the time to refer to the Ural Mountains. It was not the first time that various adventurers, mostly from the city of Novgorod, had crossed the Urals to explore the riches of the unknown lands and to establish trade with the local peoples. But when they did so in 1483, they arrived as representatives of Ivan III, the ruler of the rapidly expanding and self-consciously Orthodox Muscovite state. Muscovite officials described one such encounter and the ceremony involved in striking a peace treaty between the chiefs of the Khanty and Mansi peoples and the Muscovites:

> Their custom of making peace is as follows: They put a bearskin under the thick trunk of a cut pine tree; then they put two sabers with their sharp ends upward and bread and fish on the bearskin. We put a cross atop the pine tree, and they took a wooden idol and tied it up below the cross; and they began to walk below their idol in the direction of the sun. And one of them standing nearby said: "He who will break this peace, let him be punished by the God of his faith." They walked around the tree three times, and we bowed to the cross, and they bowed to the sun. After all of this they drank water from a cup containing a golden nugget, and they kept saying: "You, gold, seek the one who betrays."[2]

The same event was registered in the Russian chronicle but was described quite differently: "and the local princes swore not to bear any ill will, nor to exhibit any violence, and to be loyal to the Grand Prince of Muscovy." Obviously, things did not look the same from the banks of the Siberian rivers and from Moscow. What the local chiefs considered a peace treaty concluded with the newly arrived strangers, Moscow regarded as the chiefs' oath of allegiance to the grand prince and their submission to Moscow. Russia's conquest of Siberia unfolded in a climate of mutual misconceptions. From the beginning, Moscow judged the natives to be the subjects of the tsar, while the natives saw in the Russians merely another military and trading partner.

Moscow's attitude toward its neighbors had not always been domineering. The princes of Kievan Rus' regarded the steppe people as equal allies; in the early Muscovite period the grand princes considered themselves subjects of the Mongol khans. This situation began to change in the mid-sixteenth century after Moscow's spectacular conquests of the Muslim city-states of Kazan and Astrakhan. Since both Kazan and Astrakhan were heirs to the Golden Horde, the victory was much more than a mere military success. In the eyes of Russian contemporaries it proved the indisputable supremacy of the Russian Orthodox state over its Muslim neighbors. Moscow's new image was on display when Ivan IV ordered the construction of St. Basil's Cathedral in Red Square and proudly added the title of tsar of Kazan and Astrakhan to those he already claimed.

From this time onward, Muscovite chroniclers as well as Foreign Office interpreters and scribes began deliberately to construct an image of the "other." The Russian state could codify its relationship with the disparate non-Christian and non-state-organized peoples along its expanding frontiers only in terms of a suzerain-subject modus operandi. The government used every possible means to underscore the permanence of this relationship in both its diplomatic practices and its written records.

Russia in Tataria
View of Kazan Fortress, 1837 (*Eduardo Turnerelli, courtesy
of the State Museum of Tatarstan*)

In 1616 the Nogai prince Ishterek wrote to Moscow and, continuing the practice of many Nogai and Crimean princes, addressed Tsar Mikhail as a friend. The response of the Muscovite officials was a sharp rebuke: "A servant can never be the tsar's friend."[3] When the letters of the Mongol ruler Lubsan, in which he addressed the tsar as an inferior local ruler, were delivered to the Russian monarch, they were referred to in Russian terminology as a "petition [*chelobit'e*] of the Mongol prince." While Lubsan offered peace and asked for military assistance, the government praised him for "seeking the sovereign's favor" and encouraged him "not to violate his oath of allegiance."[4] On another occasion, when in 1673 the envoys of the well-known and fiercely independent Galdan Boshoktu Khan of the Oirats arrived in Moscow—the first such embassy to Russia—they probably were surprised to be told by Russian officials that their khan was a subject of the tsar.[5]

Since the fifteenth century, the basis for Muscovy's relationship with the peoples it had recently encountered in the east or in the south had been the peace treaty. Such a peace treaty (*shert'* in Russian, a term derived from the Turkic *şart* or *şärt*, as adopted from the Arabic *shart*—a condition, a clause of a treaty) was conceived, understood, and referred to by a term different from the ones Moscow used in relations with neighbors to the west. In the eyes of Moscow, shert' was not a mutual treaty but an allegiance sworn by a non-Christian people to their Muscovite sovereign. The usual procedure involved one or more local chiefs' pledging allegiance on behalf of their people in the presence of a Muscovite official. Moscow always tried to make sure that such an allegiance of "eternal submission to the grand tsar" was made according to the native customs of its newly sworn subjects.[6]

A Russian official of the early eighteenth century, Vasilii Bakunin, offered his own explanation of what every Kalmyk chief thought of such treaties:

> The Kalmyk *tayishi*s never recognized their former agreements as oaths of allegiance. Its very name, "shert'," is alien not only to the Russian but to the Kalmyk language as well. They [the tayishis] referred only to the agreement concluded with Prince B. A. Golitsyn. It is obvious that they were not aware of [the contents of] those [previous] "sherts." It is clear from the copies found that the original allegiance records were written in Russian, and were only signed in Kalmyk.[7]

Neither Kalmyk chiefs nor numerous other peoples encountered by the Russians in the east and south regarded themselves as Russia's subjects. When, in 1730, Abul Khayir, khan of the Kazakh Lesser Horde, decided to make peace with the Bashkirs, he had to send a letter to St. Petersburg, which was presented as his "petition to become a Russian subject."[8]

The Russian government's attitude toward the newly encountered peoples was most unambiguously expressed by Mehmet Tevkelev, the Russian envoy to the Kazakhs in the early 1730s. When Kazakh nobles explained to him that they had sent an envoy to Russia solely to make peace but not to become Russia's subjects, Tevkelev replied: "The Russian Empire is in high repute among many states in the world, and it is not befitting such an illustrious monarch to be at peace with you, the steppe beasts."[9]

In 1779, even in the face of military retribution, the nobles of Greater Kabarda refused to swear an allegiance and declared that they had traditionally been under Russian protectorship as guests or allies (*kunak*s), but not as subjects. In the end, when the Russian troops marched into Kabarda, the Kabardians had to sue for peace and swore an unconditional allegiance.[10]

Either induced by the offers of gifts and payments or intimidated by the force of the Russian army, Russia's "infidel" neighbors had to be made loyal, to be forced into submission, and eventually to become a part of the Russian state. Their political identity as subjects of the Russian crown had to be constructed and reaffirmed through a peace treaty—a rite which was intended to change their status from independence to transitional. This was the beginning of the long and arduous process of their political integration into Russia.

Ethnolinguistic Identity

Language is much more than just a means of communication; it is also a marker of cultural identity. It was certainly so in the Middle Ages, when often no clear distinction existed between the notions of "people" and "language." The Latin *lingua* denoted both "language" and "people"; so did the Slavic word *iazyk*. A Russian chronicle, describing the Khanty and Mansi peoples in the eleventh century, states: "Iugra zhe liudie est' iazyk nem," which could be translated as either "The Iugra are the people who speak a foreign language," or "The Iugra are a foreign people."[11] Even today, perhaps as a reminder of the older days, the words *iazyk* in Slavic and *dil* in Turkic languages retain the specific meaning of "a prisoner of war captured to obtain information." Language was used as a primary differentiating marker long before other signs such as religion, ethnicity, or culture supplemented or replaced it in isolating group identities.

The recently encountered peoples needed to be given names, to be separated not only from the Russians but also from each other. Wholly ignorant of the peoples they encountered, the Muscovites naturally used the names they heard from others. Thus, they first referred to the Khanty by the Komi name *iugra* and later by the Turkic name *ostiak* (Tatar *ishtek*), while the Mansi became known as *vogul* (a Komi word meaning "wild"). The Oirat people of western Siberia were referred to by the Turkic name *kalmyk,* and continued to be known by this name, even though they did not conceive of themselves as a united people and had no word for a supratribal ethnic affiliation. The same name-giving process applied to many peoples, from the Nogais of the southern steppes to the Yakuts of eastern Siberia. In the nineteenth century, when many of the non-Christian peoples emerged with the sense of collective identity, they began to use as their self-designation those exact terms, which were originally both alien to their language and imposed on them by others.[12]

Projecting its own names onto the peoples it encountered, Moscow attempted to classify the indigenous population into large ethnolinguistic groups. For instance, the peoples of the newly conquered Kazan region were divided according to the six different languages spoken there: Tatar, Bashkir, Mordva, Chuvash, Cheremis, and Votiak.[13] Tribal confusion and Moscow's lack of knowledge of the native kinship-based societies continued to defy Russian attempts at naming and classifying the natives. The Kabardians of the North Caucasus were often referred to as Circassians, the Nogais were considered to be Tatars, and the Khanty living along the

Chusovaia River west of the Urals were referred to at different times as Tatars, Voguls, and Ostiaks.[14]

Separateness or foreignness was defined in Russia through language, territory, kinship, or religion. A well-known example is the Slavic word *nemets* (lit. "one who speaks unclearly"), which referred to an outsider, a foreigner in general, before it acquired the more specific designation of "German." *Inozemets* (lit. "a person of a different land") referred to either foreigners from western Europe or the natives of Siberia.[15] They were attributed an extraterritorial identity and considered foreigners (cf. the German *Ausländer*).

Two other terms, *inorodets* (lit. "of a different kin") and *inoverets* (lit. "of a different faith"), came into usage in the seventeenth century and were reserved for the non-Christian peoples residing in the newly conquered territories in the east and south. The encounter with numerous non-Christian peoples crystallized Moscow's self-image as an Orthodox Christian state, and the choice of terms clearly reflected a change in Moscow's self-perception. Religion became the most important marker separating Russians from the Muslim, Buddhist, or pagan subjects of the growing Russian Empire.

Economic Identity

The non-Christians' economic status or identity also had to be expressed in terms implying subservience to their Russian overlord. Such, at least, was Moscow's belief. The separate economic identity of the non-Russian peoples was constructed through the notion of *iasak* (from the Mongol *yasa*—a law). This term meant different things at different times. For the natives of Siberia, iasak was a levy paid in furs, but the peoples of the Kazan region paid it partly in cash and partly in kind. At all times, however, iasak was a levy imposed by the state specifically on the non-Christian peoples of Russia.[16]

If peace treaties were intended to formalize non-Christians' political subservience to Moscow, the imposition of iasak was supposed to be another and more tangible manifestation of the natives' subject status vis-à-vis the Russian suzerain. In fact, in the minds of the Muscovite officials, the notions of peace and iasak payment were often equated. Those natives who refused to submit themselves immediately to the Russian governors were classified as hostile *nemirnye liudi*[17] (people who were not at peace with Russia), and their territory was referred to as *nemirnaia neiasachnaia zemlitsa*[18] (a territory which is not at peace with Russia and which does not submit iasak).

The non-Christian peoples of Siberia were concerned less with their political status and more with their practical relations with the Russians.

Each time the natives brought their furs to the Russian officials, they were presented with the sovereign's compensation (*gosudarevo zhalovan'e*).[19] And although the Russians distinguished carefully between the iasak paid by the natives and the sovereign's benevolent presents or compensation, there is no indication that the native peoples separated the two notions. What was tribute to the Russian authorities was a trade transaction to the natives.

Each transaction was accompanied by the distribution of compensation, which ordinarily included axes, knives, tin and copper pots, woolens, flints, and tobacco. The most popular item, however, was beads, particularly crystal beads of different colors (*odekui*).[20] In addition, Moscow provided the natives with supplies consisting of rye flour, butter, and fish oil. When iasak was brought, the authorities were expected to throw a feast for the native representatives.[21]

For reasons of its own, Moscow could not and did not deliver compensation or supplies with any regularity, and the natives did not fail to voice their complaints in this regard. On other occasions, the natives considered their compensation unsatisfactory and complained to the authorities that they were obtaining items of poor quality. According to some reports from the middle of the seventeenth century, the natives registered their displeasure by beating the Russian officials, "and they toss the sovereign's presents away, or tie them to the necks of dogs, or pitch them into the fire; and they pay iasak with no courtesy, kicking it with their feet and throwing it to the ground; and they call us, your slaves, bad people."[22]

The government was aware of the quid pro quo nature of its relationship with the natives. The reports from the Russian agents in charge of collecting the iasak stated clearly that the natives submitted the levy only in exchange for the sovereign's compensation; whenever they found their compensation to be inadequate, they did not deliver iasak in full. The agents added that they were running out of compensation and supplies, and without them collection of the iasak would cease completely. In response, Moscow instructed its officials in Siberia to give small amounts of compensation in accordance with the iasak, to explain to the natives that they should not regard this as a trade but as the sovereign's compensation, and to insist that the natives be content with the amount they received.[23]

At times, reality proved to exert a stronger influence on the government's policies than a desire to codify its relationship with the natives in the usual submissive terms. In 1730, local Russian officials were able to extract a promise from the Kazakhs to make an annual delivery of iasak similar to that of the Bashkirs. The government, however, instructed its zealous agents not to demand the iasak payment but to wait until the Kazakhs brought it voluntarily.[24] In 1766, seeking to improve the supply of furs in Siberia, the Iasak Distribution Commission suggested standardizing the long-existing practices. It recommended that in exchange for the iasak, the native nobles should be given presents in the amount of 2 percent of the furs' value.[25]

The non-Christians' separate economic status could be changed only if they chose to become Christian. Upon conversion, non-Christians were given a three-to-five-year exemption from iasak payment and then joined the regular tax rolls. Like other social categories constructed by Moscow to set the non-Christians apart from the Russian Orthodox, economic identity was inseparable from the religious one.

Religious Identity

Religion defined the aggregate identity of the Russians in premodern Russia. To be Russian was first and foremost to be a Russian Orthodox. And it was in these terms that Moscow perceived itself and was so perceived by others. In April 1552, on the eve of Moscow's conquest of Kazan, the Nogai mirza Belek Bulat wrote to his "brother," the Russian tsar, and made clear that "although he [Ivan IV] was an infidel, and we are Muslims, each has his own faith."[26] A few months later, in a much less compromising missive, the metropolitan Makarii blessed Ivan IV and his "soldiers of Christ" against the Kazan Tatars, who were "infidels and enemies of Christ, and who had always spilled Christian blood and destroyed holy churches."[27]

Upon the conquest of Kazan in 1552, Moscow acquired large numbers of new subjects who were neither Christian nor Russian-speaking. The Russian language and Russian administration had to replace Tatar, and Christianity had to replace Islam. Ivan IV banned the construction of new mosques and ordered those in the khanate demolished and churches built in their stead.[28] Religious conversion would become the most important policy tool in bringing the newly conquered people into the Russian state. The non-Christians were expected to shed their previous non-Christian faith.

Before Moscow's dramatic expansion in the 1550s, religious conversion of non-Russians took place only occasionally. In the middle of the sixteenth century, the idea of religious conversion began to enjoy the complete support of a government imbued with a sense of manifest religious destiny. The new missionary spirit of an increasingly self-conscious Orthodox Muscovy was forcefully expressed by the triumphant Russian tsar. In his 1556 letter to Archbishop Gurii of the newly founded Kazan diocese, Ivan IV suggested that converting pagans was a divine duty. He added that missionaries "should teach the pagans [*mladentsy*, lit. "children"] to read and write, and should make them truly understand what they read, and [they], then, will be able to teach others, including the Muslims."[29]

Few conversions occurred during the sixteenth century. The Ottoman threat, a series of uprisings in the Kazan region, and the corruption of local officials served to restrain the zeal of the Russian state to spread the gospel among the natives.[30] The issue was raised again in earnest in the early 1590s by the Kazan metropolitan Germogen, who complained in a letter to the tsar that, as a consequence of the neglect of the local governors, converts did not observe Christian laws and continued to live among their non-Christian kin, while the Tatars built new mosques. In response, the tsar's decree of 1593 stipulated that converts should be resettled near Kazan, be given farmland, and live among the Russians. The Russian officials were to ensure that converts observed Christian law and did not intermarry with Muslims or foreign prisoners of war. Furthermore, children of mixed marriages and slaves of the converts were to be baptized. Those converts who did not follow Christian ways were to be put in chains and thrown in jail to make them forget the "Tatar" faith and become firm believers in Christ. All mosques were to be destroyed.[31]

The combined threat of intimidation, force, and abolition of old privileges was only part of the government's missionary policy. Coercion could be applied only in the territories already under the firm control of the Russian military and bureaucracy, such as the middle Volga region. In addition to the stick, the carrot was no less important in Muscovy's initial appeal to the non-Christians. This was particularly true in the frontier areas, where the government's hold over the new territory remained tenuous and the need for the cooperation of the natives was acute. Here, church officials were instructed to win converts not by force but by "love." Each convert was rewarded with woolen clothing, a shirt, a pair of boots, and cash. Converts were also enlisted as musketeers, assigned to one of the frontier garrisons, and given cash and flour in payment.[32]

Ultimately, conversion was the only means by which the government could ensure the non-Russians' loyalty and their acceptance into Russian society. Their racial characteristics mattered less than their religious affiliation. For non-Russian nobles, conversion meant a fast track to assimilation. Converted nobles intermarried with their Russian counterparts, held high military positions, and often served in the frontier regions as Russia's trusted intermediaries.[33] Within two generations their names often no longer betrayed their non-Russian origin.[34] Assimilation was complete when a family was inscribed in the genealogical books of the Russian nobility.[35]

The fate of converts who did not belong to noble families differed from that of their more noble brethren in that they were designated "new converts" and were regarded as a separate social group, alienated both from their previous pagan, Muslim, or Buddhist kin and from their present Russian Orthodox coreligionists.[36] Their privileges, such as exemptions from taxes or military service, were only temporary, and after three or five years they had to resume their onerous obligations.[37] Moreover, they found themselves victims of frequent abuse by local Russian officials, who took advantage of the converts' ignorance of the Russian language, laws, and customs.[38]

The importance and duty of converting non-Russians was reiterated by Ivan Pososhkov, contemporary of Peter the Great and often referred to as "the Russian Adam Smith." In a treatise written in 1719, Pososhkov contrasted the feeble missionary efforts of the Russians with that of the Roman Catholic Church and chastised the Russian government and the Orthodox Church for their inability to attract non-Russians to Christianity:

> These peoples have been the subjects of the Russian Empire for two hundred years, but they did not become Christians, and their souls perish because of our negligence. The Catholics are sending their missionaries to China, India, and America. [Despite] the fact that our faith is a right one—and what could be easier than converting the Mordvas, the Cheremis, and the Chuvash?—yet we cannot do this. And our pagans [*inovertsy*] are like children, without a written language, without a law, and they do not live far away, but within the Russian Empire, along the Volga and the Kama rivers; and they are not sovereign, but the subjects of Russia.[39]

Inspired by the missionary work of the Catholic Church and particularly the Jesuit order, Ivan Pososhkov was primarily concerned with saving the souls of non-Russians and making them good Christians.

His crusading spirit was shared by the government, albeit for different reasons. Increasingly defined in Peter I's time by a new missionary sense of struggle with Islam, government policies on religious conversion acquired further importance as a policy tool aimed at securing the political loyalty of Moscow's non-Russian subjects. New efforts to convert non-Russians were prompted in part by Russia's strategic interests. The government feared the emergence of an Islamic axis—a united front of the various Muslim peoples under the Ottoman umbrella—against Russia. At various times the Ottomans and the Crimean Tatars attempted to unite the Muslim Kazakhs, Karakalpaks, Bashkirs, and Nogais in a broad anti-Russian coalition.[40] No less important, however, were disturbing reports of a growing number of non-Russian subjects' converting to Islam. The news that some non-Russians were lured by the "disgusting faith of Muhammad" prompted Peter I to order that missionaries be taught native languages and sent to preach among non-Russians.[41]

Although the numbers of converts continued to grow on paper, reports from the field lamented the fact that the conversions were only nominal, and converts remained ignorant of Christianity and did not observe any of its precepts. It was becoming apparent that reliance on sheer force or legislative discrimination to effect conversions was not sufficient.[42]

The government and the church responded by focusing missionary activity on spreading the Gospel among converts and ensuring their understanding of and attachment to Christianity. The idea of civilizing the savage ("wild," "ignorant," "unenlightened") became a major driving force behind proselytizing throughout the eighteenth century. The language of church officials clearly reflected a change of attitude. They increasingly began to refer to non-Russian converts as the "newly enlightened" (*novoprosveshchennye*). The new approach was further spelled out in 1721 in the Synod's instructions to the bishop of the Viatka region. The bishop was cautioned to teach potential converts the Gospel before their baptism and to find out whether they wanted to become Christian out of good will or simply to avoid heavy taxation.[43]

Fifty years later, the feeble efforts of the church missionary activity were summarized by Amvrosii Podobedov, the newly appointed archbishop of Kazan. In his report to the Synod on the state of affairs in his archdiocese, he wrote: "I find that the ignorant [*neprosveshchennye*] non-Russian peoples, the Chuvash and Cheremis who reside here, have not only an insufficient, but not even the slightest notion about the precepts of faith into which they were converted by holy baptism."[44]

Religious conversion in Russia appears least of all religious and spiritual and involved only a nominal redefinition of religious identity. For the non-Christians, conversion promised tangible economic benefits and a hope of social and economic mobility. As in other premodern societies where religion defined not only religious life but also cultural, social, and political norms, conversion in Russia was first and foremost a process of cultural transformation of the "other."

Yet conversion in Russia was not synonymous with assimilation. Shedding one's previous identity and acquiring a new one proved to be a long and difficult process.[45] Conversion was most successful not for communities as a whole, but for individuals both at the top and at the bottom of their native societies. The non-Christian elites were able to make a transition relatively quickly. Upon conversion they retained their privileged status, received additional benefits, intermarried with the Russian nobility, and were fully assimilated within two or three generations. Those who for various reasons found themselves transplanted from their native societies as slaves or serfs in Russian households were also rapidly assimilated upon conversion.

For other non-Christians, however, conversion meant little beyond receiving temporary benefits. Commoners were attracted to Christianity by promises of exemptions from taxes, hard labor, or military service, while the local gentry converted to avoid having their lands and property confiscated. They remained in the transitional category of "new converts" for generations. Even those whose ancestors had converted centuries previously were still referred to as "old converts."[46]

Conversion, for both groups and individuals, was a rite intended to incorporate the non-Russians into the state. Long after non-Christians' initial conversion and despite the government's efforts to introduce them to the Russian way of life, both new and old converts continued to have little or no knowledge of the Russian language, law, and lifestyle, or, most important, of their new faith.

The Russian state constructed images and identities of its non-Christian subjects. The four official identities we have considered were not the only ones intended to define and separate the "other" peoples. Russian merchants, officials, and colonists who initially encountered the non-Christians in the frontier areas used other markers: hairstyles, clothing, smell, food, marriage, customs, lifestyle, language, and race.[47] Yet most of these remained of only secondary concern to the government. Clothing, food, and customs were expected to change upon conversion to Christianity. In and of themselves, as far as Moscow was concerned, they neither served as differentiating markers nor were worthy of being noticed, described, or studied. Nowhere in the written heritage of official Russia can one find before the early eighteenth century the slightest attention to the different mores and customs of the non-Christians.

This lack of curiosity was replaced by official interest in the political, economic, and religious classification of the non-Russians. As the number and the significance of non-Russians within the Russian Empire grew, it became increasingly important to describe them, to ensure their loyalty, and to develop a set of uniform policies to incorporate the new territories and peoples into the empire. One of the earliest attempts at a political classification was made by the eighteenth-century Russian writer and historian Prince Mikhail Shcherbatov. In his 1776 treatise, Prince Shcherbatov suggested that the peoples of the empire should be divided into six categories in accordance with their lifestyle, taxation, military service, and religious affiliation:

1. Russians and all non-Christians [*inovertsy*] who pay the soul tax and provide recruits
2. Russians and non-Christians who pay taxes but do not provide recruits
3. Christians other than Russian Orthodox
4. All kinds of Cossacks and other military settlers
5. Bashkirs and other wild peoples who practice Islam
6. Kalmyks and other nomadic idol-worshippers[48]

It is not surprising that Prince Shcherbatov referred indiscriminately to religious, ethnic, and social identities. The overlapping of categories, typical of premodern societies, was quite common in Russia, where no clear distinction was made between ethnic, economic, and religious identities. For instance, the late-sixteenth-century description of the Nizhnii Novgorod region classifies the residents of various villages as peasants, Mordva, or beekeepers.[49] Obviously, the word *krest'ianin* in Russian parlance meant not just any peasant, but specifically a peasant of the Russian Orthodox faith. Mordva implied not only ethnicity but, more important, the economic and religious status of the iasak-paying pagans.

Likewise, non-Russian pagan peoples considered Christianity a Russian faith and Islam a Tatar one.[50] In Russian official correspondence, non-Christian peoples were referred to by their specific names, such as Chuvash, Bashkir, or Tatar. The Chuvash, however, were often synonymous with the iasak-paying non-Christians and the Mari, the Mordva, and the Cheremis of the Kazan region were commonly referred to as "Chuvash." Tatar meant that a person was a iasak-paying peasant and a Muslim. Those Tatars who performed a military service were known as "military service [*sluzhilye*] Tatars." Often included in this category were other non-Christians who enlisted into the Muscovite military.[51]

The process of constructing the identities of the non-Christian peoples in Russia was not original. In fact, both the names of the newly encountered peoples and the terms in which the encounter was codified were inherited from the Turko-Mongol principalities that preceded the arrival of the Russians (cf. among others the origins of the words *shert'* and *iasak*).

For many non-Christian peoples, particularly those who saw themselves as the legitimate heirs to Chinggis Khan and to the legacy of the Golden Horde, the terms of encounter looked different than they did to the Muscovites. Whereas Moscow regarded all the newly encountered peoples as its subjects, the non-Christians often considered Russia no more than a military ally. What the natives of Siberia often considered to be trade, Moscow regarded as levy that it was due. Moscow's construction of political and economic, ethnic and religious identities for its new subjects was a projection of its own image. For the non-Christians, kinship, language, territory, and local gods remained far more important. Different expectations led to misunderstandings and conflicts. Resistance and violence accompanied Moscow's attempts to convert the natives to Christianity.

The place of encounter remained a place where several different cultures met. One was pagan and shamanistic, allowing for the worship of numerous idols; it was also fragmented and tribal. Two others, Muslim and Orthodox Christian, each bowed to a single God. Islam remained uncompromising until the military-bureaucratic Russian state succeeded in imposing its own victorious rhetoric upon the vanquished. In the end, the Russian Empire was able to appropriate, though only partially, the space, the time, and the terms of the contest. But these different worlds continued to stand apart long after their initial encounter.

NOTES

1. Rossiiskii gosudarstvennyi arkhiv drevnikh aktov (hereafter cited as RGADA), Opis' del sekretnoi ekspeditsii senata, f. 248, op. 113, no. 181, l. 20; *Kazakhsko-russkie otnosheniia v 16–18 vekakh* (Alma-Ata, 1961), pp. 74, 81, 96, and 138.

2. S. V. Bakhrushin, "Ostiatskie i vogul'skie kniazhestva v 16 i 17 vv.," in *Nauchnye trudy,* 4 vols. (Moscow, 1952–59), vol. 3, pt. 2, p. 152.

3. RGADA, Snosheniia Rossii s nogaiami, f. 127, op. 1, no. 2, 1616 g., l. 6.

4. N. P. Shastina, "Pis'ma Lubsan taidzhi v Moskvu," in *Filologiia i istoriia mongol'skikh narodov* (Moscow, 1958), pp. 279–281.

5. E. I. Kychanov, *Povestvovanie ob oiratskom Galdane Boshoktu-Khane* (Novosibirsk, 1980), p. 53.

6. To ensure that the shert' would be adhered to, the Muscovite authorities persisted in finding out whether it was *priamaia,* i.e., performed in accordance with the customs of a given people. Shert' varied from those sworn by Muslim peoples on the Qur'an and by Buddhist Kalmyks on their prayer book to the elaborate rituals of various shamanistic peoples of Siberia (S. V. Bakhrushin, "Iasak v Sibiri v 17 v.," in *Nauchnye trudy,* vol. 3, pt. 2, pp. 65–66; also his "Ocherki po istorii Krasnoiarskogo uezda v 17 v.," in ibid., vol. 4, p. 47).

7. Vasilii Bakunin, "Opisanie istorii kalmytskogo naroda," *Krasnyi arkhiv* 3 (1939): 214–215.

8. *Kazakhsko-russkie otnosheniia,* p. 35, no. 25.

9. Ibid., pp. 53–54, no. 33.

10. *Akty, sobrannye Kavkazskoiu Arkheograficheskoiu komissieiu,* vol. 1 (Tiflis, 1866–83), p. 91.

11. Bakhrushin, "Ostiatskie," p. 86.

12. When it was necessary for military and economic purposes, Moscow was able to take into account various tribal and clan divisions, but it had never been able to translate this knowledge into a political recognition of these societies' disparate nature and their loose confederational structure. (See the precise description of the mirzas and their peoples in RGADA, Nogaiskie dela, f. 127, op. 1, no. 11, 1642 g.)

13. Andrei Kurbskii, "Istoriia o velikom kniaze Moskovskom," in *Russkaia istoricheskaia biblioteka,* vol. 31 (St. Petersburg–Leningrad, 1872–1927), pp. 205–206.

14. Bakhrushin, "Ostiatskie," p. 88.

15. *Akty istoricheskie, sobrannye i izdannye Arkheograficheskoiu komissieiu,* vol. 4 (St. Petersburg, 1841–43), p. 473 (hereafter cited as *AI*).

16. I. P. Ermolaev, *Srednee Povolzh'e vo vtoroi polovine 16–17 vv.* (Kazan, 1982), pp. 72–74; Andreas Kappeler, *Russlands erste Nationalitäten. Das Zarenreich und die Völker der Mittleren Wolga vom 16. bis 19. Jahrhundert* (Cologne, 1982), pp. 102–103. The most recent discussion of the iasak in Siberia is in Yuri Slezkine, *Arctic Mirrors: Russia and the Small Peoples of the North* (Ithaca, N.Y., 1994), pp. 20–32 and 60–71.

17. *Sbornik dokumentov po istorii Buriatii 17 v.,* comp. G. N. Rumiantsev and S. B. Okun' (Ulan-Ude, 1960), p. 360.

18. Bakhrushin, "Ocherki," p. 97.

19. Bakhrushin, "Iasak," p. 71.

20. Ibid., pp. 71–72; *Kolonial'naia politika moskovskogo gosudarstva v Iakutii v 17 veke*, ed. Ia. P. Al'kor and B. D. Grekov (Leningrad, 1936), pp. 239–240, no. 191.

21. Bakhrushin, "Iasak," pp. 72–73; Bakhrushin, "Ocherki," pp. 55–56; *Kolonial'naia*, pp. 92–93, no. 40.

22. *Kolonial'naia*, p. 25, no. 17; pp. 98–99, no. 45.

23. Bakhrushin, "Iasak," pp. 74–75; *Kolonial'naia*, p. 96, no. 43; p. 98, no. 44.

24. *Kazakhsko-russkie*, p. 37, no. 26.

25. *Istoriia Iakutskoi ASSR*, vol. 2 (Moscow, 1957), p. 139.

26. *Prodolzhenie drevnei rossiiskoi vivliofiki*, vol. 9 (St. Petersburg, 1786–1801), p. 251; repr., Slavic printings and reprintings, ed. C. H. van Schooneveld (The Hague–Paris, 1970), p. 17 (hereafter cited as *PDRV*).

27. *AI*, vol. 1, p. 291, no. 160. For a discussion of the Kazan conquest, see Edward L. Keenan, "Muscovy and Kazan, 1441–1552: A Study in Steppe Policy" (Ph.D. diss., Harvard University, 1965); and Jaroslaw Pelenski, *Russia and Kazan: Conquest and Imperial Ideology (1438–1560s)* (The Hague, 1974).

28. Efim Malov, "O tatarskikh mechetiakh v Rossii," *Pravoslavnyi sobesednik* (December 1867), p. 288; Apollon Mozharovskii, "Izlozhenie khoda missioner-skago dela po prosveshcheniiu inorodtsev s 1552 po 1867 goda," *Chteniia v Imperatorskom obshchestve istorii i drevnostei rossiiskikh pri Moskovskom universitete. Sbornik* 1 (1880), p. 25 (hereafter cited as *ChOIDR*).

29. *PDRV*, vol. 5, p. 242.

30. In the late 1560s, population registers of the city of Kazan listed 24 converts (*Materialy po istorii Tatarskoi ASSR. Pistsovye knigi goroda Kazani, 1565–68 gg. i 1646 g.* [Leningrad, 1932], p. 179). Even fewer converts could be found in Kazan province (K. I. Nevostruev, *Spisok s pistsovykh knig po g. Kazani s uezdom* [Kazan, 1877], pp. 67 and 75). I have found no evidence to support Mozharovskii's claims that initially conversions were numerous and, in contrast to those in the eighteenth century, the converts were inspired by true belief (Mozharovskii, "Izlozhenie," pp. 22–23). In response to Russian colonization of the Kazan region, powerful anti-Russian uprisings led by local nobles took place in 1556, 1572, and 1582 (V. D. Dmitriev, "Krest'ianskaia voina nachala 17 veka na territorii Chuvashii," *Trudy Nauchno-issledovatel'skogo instituta iazyka, literatury, istorii i ekonomiki Chuvashskoi ASSR* 93 [1979]: 46–48).

31. *Akty, sobrannye v bibliotekakh i arkhivakh Rossiiskoi imperii Arkheograficheskoi ekspeditsieiu Imp. Akademii nauk*, vol. 1 (St. Petersburg, 1836), pp. 436–439, no. 358.

32. Such were the instructions of Tsar Boris concerning the Vogul converts in Siberia in 1603 (*AI*, vol. 2, pp. 56–57, no. 43). Archbishop Makarii of Siberia and Tobol'sk was similarly instructed in 1625 (*Opisanie gosudarstvennago arkhiva starykh del*, comp. P. I. Ivanov [Moscow, 1850], pp. 253–266).

33. A daughter of Tsar Aleksei was promised in marriage to the Kasimov prince Seyid-Burkhan upon his conversion (V. V. Vel'iaminov-Zernov, *Izsledovanie o kasimovskikh tsariakh i tsarevichakh*, vol. 3 [St. Petersburg, 1863–87], p. 200). Cf. the names of the commanders in Tsar Boris's campaign against Crimea in 1598 (M. M. Shcherbatov, *Istoriia rossiiskaia*, vol. 7 [St. Petersburg, n.d.], pt. 1, p. 23). From the early seventeenth century, the Kabardian dynasty of Circassian princes was extremely important in implementing Russian policies in the North Caucasus (*Kabardino-russkie otnosheniia v 16–18vv. Dokumenty i materialy*, vol. 1 [Moscow, 1957], pp. 73–75, no. 46).

34. The Tatar prince Abul-Khayir of Siberia was the first of his dynasty to convert, in 1591. While his son was known as Vasilii Abulgairovich, his grandson's name, Roman Vasil'evich, could no longer be distinguished from a native Russian name (Vel'iaminov-Zernov, *Izsledovanie*, vol. 3, pp. 54–55).

35. In 1686 the tsar decreed that the dynasties of the ruler of Imeretia in the Caucasus and the princes of Siberia and Kasimov were to be entered into the genealogical books of the Russian nobility (Vel'iaminov-Zernov, *Izsledovanie*, vol. 4, p. 144).

36. "Vypiski iz razriadnykh arkhivov," in *DRV*, vol. 16, pp. 339–345; *Drevnie gosudarstvennye gramoty, nakaznye pamiati i chelobitnye sobrannye v Permskoi gubernii* (St. Petersburg, 1821), p. 79.

37. *Polnoe sobranie zakonov Rossiiskoi imperii. Sobranie pervoe*, vol. 2 (St. Petersburg, 1830), pp. 312–313, no. 867 (hereafter cited as *PSZ*).

38. *Opisanie dokumentov i del, khraniashchikhsia v arkhive sviateishego sinoda* (hereafter cited as *ODD*) (St. Petersburg, 1868), vol. 1, p. 144, no. 157; *PSPR*, vol. 2, 1744–1745 g. (St. Petersburg, 1907), pp. 83–89, no. 608.

39. I. T. Pososhkov, *Zaveshchanie otecheskoe*, ed. E. M. Prilezhaev (St. Petersburg, 1893), p. 323. Pososhkov further urged the government to send missionaries to the Kamchatka peninsula in the Far East, "for if the Catholics find out, they will send their mission" (p. 327).

40. Michael Khodarkovsky, *Where Two Worlds Met: The Russian State and the Kalmyk Nomads, 1600–1771* (Ithaca, N.Y., 1992), pp. 98, 113, and 145–146.

41. *Pis'ma i bumagi imperatora Petra Velikogo*, vol. 1 (St. Petersburg and Moscow, 1887–1977), pp. 694–695, note to no. 227.

42. One of the most striking accounts came from the Kazan metropolitan Sil'vestr in 1729. He reported that 170 years after their conversion to Christianity, the "old converts" (*starokreshchennye*) continued to reside in their old villages far from the churches, remaining wholly ignorant of the Russian language and Christian laws ("Luka Konashevich, Episkop Kazanskii," *Pravoslavnyi sobesednik* [1858], pp. 234–237).

43. *ODD*, vol. 1, pp. 141–143, no. 157; Appendix, no. 27, pp. cccv–cccxiv.

44. Mozharovskii, "Izlozhenie," p. 107.

45. See Yuri Slezkine, "Savage Christians or Unorthodox Russians? The Missionary Dilemma in Siberia," in *Between Heaven and Hell: The Myth of Siberia in Russian Culture*, ed. Galya Diment and Yuri Slezkine (New York, 1993), pp. 15–32.

46. It is instructive to compare the fate of "converts" in Russia with that of *conversos*, the Jewish converts in late-fifteenth-century Spain. Spanish authorities considered *conversos* a distinct and separate group. They were discriminated against, and their purity of blood ("limpieza de sangre") remained a criterion for their advancement until the early twentieth century (Angus McKay, *Spain in the Middle Ages: From Frontier to Empire, 1000–1500* [New York, 1977], pp. 185–187).

47. The Don Cossacks, when describing to Russian officials a man who had come to them with a letter and invited them to join the rebels of the Shatsk district, noted that he "had the mug of a Cheremis" ("a v mordu Cheremis") (*Krest'ianskaia voina pod predvoditel'stvom Stepana Razina. Sbornik dokumentov*, vol. 2 [Moscow, 1954], pt. 1, p. 183, no. 155).

48. M. M. Shcherbatov, "Statistika v razsuzhdenii Rossii," in *ChOIDR*, book 3, pt. 11 (1859), p. 46.

49. G. N. Anpilogov, *Nizhegorodskie dokumenty 16 veka (1588–1600)* (Moscow, 1977), pp. 48, 58, and 71.

50. S. V. Chicherina, *O privolzhskikh inorodtsakh i sovremennom znachenii sistemy N. I. Il'minskago* (St. Petersburg, 1906), p. 4.

51. Ermolaev, *Srednee Povolzh'e,* p. 67.

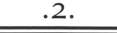

.2.

Yuri Slezkine

Naturalists versus Nations: Eighteenth-Century Russian Scholars Confront Ethnic Diversity

Seventeenth-century Muscovites did not travel. They might escape, migrate, or peregrinate, but they did not view movement through space as a worthy pursuit in its own right and did not encourage wonder at things profane or blasphemous. According to Isaac Massa, the tsar's servitors "saw many curious plants, flowers, fruits, rare trees, animals, and strange birds. But as the Muscovites themselves are not an inquisitive folk they care nothing for such things, seeking only profit everywhere, for they are a rude and negligent people."[1] Because of this negligence, "nothing was enquired into."[2] When Leibniz, the world's most unrepentantly inquisitive polymath, requested some Asian exotica, the Brandenburg ambassador in Moscow explained that some people considered such pursuits "useless": "The Muscovite nation is totally incapable of searching for such curiosities because it does not apply itself to anything that does not smell of money and does not appear to be of obvious practical use."[3]

No one in Muscovy seemed to be in the least defensive about this. Chasing "strange birds" was ludicrous and perhaps even dangerous behavior, and "inquisitiveness" was indeed a bad word. "New rivers" were needed to find—and define—"new lands"; new lands contained little besides new "foreigners" (*inozemtsy*); and new foreigners were useful only if they could provide "profit" (*vygoda*) for the tsar. Profit was usually equal to tribute, while tribute-paying foreigners remained "inozemtsy" and were expected to keep their own names, gods, and oaths. There could be no New Muscovy after the fashion of New France or New England because old Muscovy had no clear borders (in time or space) and because the new lands in the east were being incorporated without being fully appropriated (christened, Christianized, and conquered à la Columbus "by proclamation made and with the royal standard unfurled").[4]

But Peter I's mentors and mercenaries lived in a different world and saw the world differently (because they "observed" it carefully). All creation as they understood it was neatly divided into the "natural" and "artful" (or man-made) varieties, with the recovery of "natural" nature possible only as a result of the elimination of everything "erring" and "altered."[5] "Curiosity" was both a virtue and a profession; "curiosities" were objects remarkably close to the original plan ("primitive") or particularly far removed from it ("monstrous"); and travel was an increasingly well-regarded endeavor to bring curios to the curious. Europe's most assiduous producers and consumers of travel accounts were the Germans, who had been urged by Schlözer to count "love of travel" among their "national strengths." They brought to Russia a long tradition of *Kavalier-stour* and—more important for Peter—a fully developed science of academic fieldwork (*gelehrte Reise*) complete with such trophies as could be housed in museums, cabinets, galleries, libraries, zoological and botanical gardens, Kunst-Kammern, and Antiquitaeten-Zimmer.[6] Soon Peter was demanding to see "live animals and birds of various kinds that are a marvel to man"; his collaborator Tatishchev was offering his own money to local officials for "extraordinarily *kur'oznye* things"; and Müller was trying to reproduce in St. Petersburg the "multicolored paradise of unknown grasses," "the zoo of rare Asian animals," and "the cabinet of antiquities containing pagan burial sites" that he had found in Siberia.[7] By midcentury the Russian Empire was full of "places of interest" (*Sehenswürdigkeiten, dostopamiatnosti*) that were being described by the newly formed class of professional (and mostly German) learned travelers to the newly formed class of "curious" and increasingly Russian "benevolent readers" (*blago-sklonnye chitateli*).

"Curiosity" (*liubopytstvo*) served the double purpose of "entertainment" (*uveselenie*) and "utility" (*pol'za*).[8] The utility of entertainment grew steadily in direct proportion to the size of the reading public (readers minus sponsors), but throughout most of the eighteenth century, utility remained paramount. Unlike the profit of the Muscovite sovereigns, it referred to a common good ultimately based on natural law, and in contrast to the impressions of fin-de-siècle tourists, it strove for strict scientific regularities (also ultimately based on natural law). As Leibniz explained to Peter I, the same cabinets, galleries, and museums would look very different if organized "not only as an object of general curiosity but as a means of perfecting the arts and sciences."[9] The utility of the common good as pursued by the state and the utility of the arts and sciences as defined by scholars were perceived to be identical (unless scholars arrived at an erroneous definition, of course, as both Müller and Schlözer had a chance to find out). In any case, a truly useful activity had to be universalist: no group of people and no group of objects could claim exemption from natural law, and no scholarly or administrative practice could be complete unless it claimed to be natural.

As far as the learned and enlightened travelers were concerned, this meant describing and classifying "everything" (not only curiosities). Since Russia was "a blank slate" in matters of enlightenment, "everything" loomed very large indeed.[10] Called upon to "débarbariser ce vaste empire," as Leibniz put it,[11] the German scholars hired by Peter were given Adam's—or Robinson Crusoe's—job of naming the world in its entirety.[12] The fairly flat lands that used to melt around the edges unless propped up by rivers were now crisscrossed by countless borders at multiple levels, all of them neatly separating distinct but related layers of nature endowed with unique but ultimately transparent names. "The Earth's sphere" was divided into longitudes, latitudes, and "climes of various magnitudes." These constituted the new "mathematical geography" and were invisibly but inexorably connected to the stars and—via the much-used "magnet hand"—to the "innards of the earth." "Natural geography" further partitioned the "Earth's surface" into well-delineated continents ("Is Asia connected to America?" "Where does Europe end?"),[13] islands, peninsulas, mountains, oceans, seas, lakes, and rivers; natural history filled them with minerals and populated them with all creatures large and small; and "political geography" crowned the edifice with such fruits of "human disposition" (*proizvoleniia cheloviecheskago*) as forts, mills, mines, roads, fairs, towns, states, coins, churches, villages, monasteries, cemeteries, chancelleries, family names, artillery pieces, governors' uniforms, infantry regiments, "and the like."[14] The universe, including the woefully underexplored Russian portion, consisted of a prodigious but finite number of objects and phenomena, all of which needed to be named, exhaustively described, and then systematized "under a single point of view" (shape, origin, location, alphabetical order, "vital organs").[15] By the time Catherine II and her French(ified) confrères had begun to doubt Reason (*esprit de système*), question the encyclopedic grasp of the *Encyclopédie*, and cloud the stern scholarly gaze with an occasional tear of "sentiment," the Russian landscape—or "topography," as the systematizers themselves would have it—had changed beyond recognition.[16]

The most visible and uncertain presence in the new scheme of things was Man: the apex of the ladder of Nature, the manufacturer of the system of artifacts, and both the cause and the beneficiary of the state-directed utility enterprise, he straddled the creator/creature divide and was not easily classifiable in the well-ordered universe next to *"Homo monstru-osus,"* angels, gorillas ("in respect of shape"), parrots ("in respect of sound"), elephants ("in respect of memory and understanding"), and bees ("in respect of spirituality and power").[17] But while the final discovery of Adam's "scientific" (that is, genealogical) relationship to the "cattle, fowls, and beasts" that he had named had to wait until the next century, the search for order *within* the family of man was the principal preoccupation of the Age of Reason. People were organized into peoples. All of them needed to be minutely (and thus ever more faithfully) described if the shape of natural society was to be ascertained and the career of the arts and sciences properly traced. Every description of a "people" assumed a certain—rarely examined—structure of human social existence (from birth to death); once all of life's ingredients had been catalogued, the scholar knew "everything" and could move on to another community. As in most other provinces of the eighteenth-century universe, however, the menu of ingredients grew faster than the capacity of the amplest scholarly stomach. The ethnographic instructions that Gerhard Friedrich Müller received from the St. Petersburg Academy of Sciences in 1733 contained only eleven items "for particular observation" during his Siberian expedition. The instructions that the travel-weary Müller prepared for his own successor, Johann Eberhard Fischer, reached No. 923 before proceeding to maps, Kunst-Kammern, and dictionaries. By the turn of the century, most travelers had given up on the idea of devouring "everything" and started focusing on miscellany or "principles."[18]

The search for principles, or what D'Alembert called "the art of reducing, as far as possible, a great number of phenomena to a single one which can be regarded as the principle of them," had, of course, always accompanied the grand inventory of the eighteenth century.[19] "Everything" was not supposed to be a shapeless pile: some of its components were—naturally or artificially—more important than others and served as organizing principles and standards for comparison. Before describing a nation, the scholar had to decide where one nation ended and the other began: in other words, he had to find the ethnic equivalent of Linnaeus's pistils and stamens by constructing a complex but necessarily complete hierarchy of communal traits.

The first such trait was the name, invariably mentioned as the first and most obvious badge of existential autonomy. It pointed to a nomenclature that was preexisting and thus possibly natural; uniquely human in that it was based on the actual *nomen* (no other classifiable item named itself or had its own kinship hypothesis); and eminently convenient because "in our age it has become customary in most of Europe to teach the sciences in alphabetic order through dictionaries."[20] Convenience was not the same as utility, however. The independent (and thus unverifiable) provenance of ethnic appellations in the Russian Empire created more problems than possibilities for "the cautious and unbiased historian" whose principal ambition was to separate "fables" (which "all peoples have" and which "mothers tell their children in times of idleness") from "incontrovertible or at least probable proof."[21] Nothing about ethnic names was probable or incontrovertible: "for example, the Finns call us 'Venelaima'; the Iakuts call us 'Liudi'; the Tatars call us 'Urus'; the Kazak Horde calls the Bashkirs 'Sarnisherek'; and the Ostiaks call the Tungus 'Kellem' or 'Kuellem,' which means 'piebald.'" To compound the difficulty, "we" could call ourselves "Orthodox" ("according to law"), "Slavs" ("according to people"), or "Russians" ("according to territory")—which, among other things, meant that "we" did not exist before a certain people became attached to a certain territory.[22]

Territory, or *obitanie,* as in "habitation" or "habitat," was usually the second item on ethnographic lists. It potentially was the single point of view that might result in a graceful classification (particularly if "Russian" was indeed a territorial concept). There were the steppe peoples and the forest peoples; the peoples of Europe and the peoples of Asia; the peoples of the Indigirka River and the peoples of the Caucasus mountains; the peoples of the Kamchatka Peninsula and the peoples of the Caspian Sea; the peoples of the Turukhansk district and the peoples of the Orenburg province.[23] The main advantage of this arrangement consisted in the inclusion of human communities in the "mathematical," "natural," and "political" worlds that were being simultaneously catalogued by the same scholarly "name-callers" (nomenclators). Peoples were found in certain locales along with animals, vegetables, minerals, cemeteries, and artillery pieces; they were a part of the landscape and could be studied as such—as indeed, they were. The landscape molded in the eighteenth century proved extremely durable, and the territorial principle of ethnic classification turned out to be as useful as it was convenient. The English lived in England; *russkie/rossiiane* resided in Russia; and the Kamchadals inhabited Kamchatka. England, Russia, and Kamchatka were all geographical concepts that defined people found within their borders.

Not completely and not always, however. A truly scientific taxonomy had to rest on traits inherent to the objects in question. Yet it was clear that the English had come from Germany; that some peoples of the Turukhansk district would presently defect to Berezov; and that the various "Siberian" or "steppe" peoples invariably collapsed into the Ostiaks, the Koriaks, and the Kaisaks, whose uniqueness and mutual differences seemed to stem as much from their own nature as from the Nature that surrounded them. And were not the Russians defining the shape of Russia just as they were being defined by it? Did not *russkii* (a Russian) and *rossiianin* (a Russian of the Russian [*Rossiiskaia*] Empire) mean one and the same thing?

The latter question was never posed in this fashion because the answer was assumed to be in the affirmative (and the use of the two terms interchangeable). Still, it was equally obvious that not every resident of the Russian Empire was Russian and that the traditional dividing line was called "faith." In seventeenth-century Muscovy, "Russian" had been equal to "Orthodox" (although not the other way around), and baptism had dispelled foreignness along with darkness. But what did faith mean beyond the act of conversion? What, if anything, did a baptized Ostiak have to do to become a good Russian (Christian), particularly if there were no priests around? And what was the equivalent of conversion outside Christianity or Islam? If the Ostiaks and the Koriaks were different peoples (as they themselves contended and everyone else confirmed), and if "faith" was a universal indicator of difference, then how could an individual Ostiak convert to Koriakness? What did "faith" consist of?

The traditional answer—both popular and official—had seemed to begin with food. Dietary taboos defined one's own community as distinct from "savages" ("raw-eating" Eskimo or "self-eating" Samoed), "foreigners" ("and that fish smells so foul that a Russian person can barely stand it"),[24] or other "nonhumans." One traveler to the Russian Arctic returned convinced that "these people are worse than animals, for even dumb animals [*skot bezslovesen*] do not eat beasts, fowl, or grass that God has forbidden them to eat, while these people, not knowing God who dwells in Heaven and refusing to accept His law from those who bring it to them, are raw-eaters who eat the meat of beasts and vermin, drink animal filth and blood as if it were water, and eat grass and roots."[25]

Another crucial marker of foreignness had been sex. All aliens broke some of the rules of proper procreation, and most forms of apostasy and impiety (*zlochestie*) were accompanied by "lecherous business" and "filthy fornication" (*skvernaia pokhot'*).[26] The third basic component of "faith"— ultimately related to sex as well as sustenance—was a certain relationship to the land. Seventeenth-century Russian frontiersmen had divided all peoples into "settled" and "nomadic" (*sidiachie* and *kochevnye*), and further into "pastoral" or "agricultural" (*skotnye* or *pashennye*) and "walking, horse-riding, or reindeer-breeding" (*peshie, konnye,* or *olennye*). Most non-Christians wandered in the wilderness (the original "savage," *silvaticus,* was a "forest-dweller"), and a baptized nomad had to stop being a nomad because all Orthodox Christians (*khristiane*) were, however indirectly, peasants (*krest'iane*), just as all "Chaucha" were "reindeer people." Finally, an Ostiak who agreed to cook his fish and settle down as both a husband and a husbandman was also expected to adopt the numerous customs that invariably, though seldom conspicuously, accompanied faith: that is, to "live in a household and make bread, and keep horses, and cattle, and pigs, and chickens, and also make wine, and weave, and spin, all according to the Russian custom [*so vsego obychaia s russkogo*]."[27]

Over the course of the eighteenth century, the part and the whole changed places. Custom rapidly grew in importance, acquiring a separate value and gradually congealing into a "spirit of nations" (and eventually "culture"), while faith became one of its elements, still necessary but increasingly divorced from the vicissitudes of eating and mating. Stripped down to ethical and liturgical precepts collectively known as "law" (*zakon*), it usually came toward the end of Russian ethnographic accounts, after subsistence and before festivals: "If they have not been enlightened by Christian Law," observed one learned traveler, "what notion do they have of divinity and of man's duty toward his Creator and his neighbor; what is their idea of virtue; what kind of reward for good and punishment for evil do they expect in future life; and what kind of divine service or law or spiritual rites do they have—in other words, do they have their own idols and worship inanimate things, and what do they hold to be sacred?"[28]

By the end of the century, the answers to these questions could be entirely dissolved in customs, with ethics construed as part of the "spiritual qualities" along with art and temperament, and divine service joined with "nuptial solemnities" and "funereal rites."[29] This seemed especially appropriate because not all peoples of the empire had a clearly ascertainable canon comparable to "Christian Law," and because Christian Law was broader than Natural Law and thus subject to abridgment. The Tungus religion, for example, was "more custom . . . than law," which meant that "they distinguish[ed] between vice and virtue on the basis of the universal natural principle, namely not to do unto others what they would not have others do unto them."[30] Similarly, Novitskii's Ostiaks wallowed in the "abyss of godlessness" and "evil idol worship" but followed "the law of nature" (*zakon estestva*) by encouraging the love of one's neighbor (thus making up in custom what they lacked in religion).[31] Even developed laws were of little significance. As Tatishchev put it, "[Religious] discord is sown by self-interested priests, superstitious pharisees, or brainless fanatics. Among intelligent people it cannot occur because an intelligent person cares nothing about another man's faith, and it is all the same to him whether he lives and trades with Luther, Calvin, a papist, an Anabaptist, a Mohammedan, or a pagan. For rather than looking at his faith he looks at his merchandise, his actions, and his ways, and treats him accordingly."[32]

Thus, while the Russian state continued to classify all imperial subjects according to religion, the state-sponsored scholars and their curious readers (many of them state bureaucrats) wanted to learn the true nature of nations and the true relationships among them. And this involved the multiplying, cataloguing, and ranking of customs—no longer simply *obychai* but *Sitten und Gebräuchen*, usually translated as *nravy i obyknoveniia*, or "mores and traditions." These customs, which were duly isolated and subdivided components of the old faith, were now expected to serve as independent standards of comparison and, taken together, constitute "everything" about a given ethnic group. Usually positioned after name and territory, the mores and traditions included food, dwellings, clothing, economic pursuits, transportation, tools and utensils, cosmogonic beliefs, calendars, social graces, festivals, the arts and sciences, trade and manufacture, childbirth and child-rearing, sex and marriage, war, crime and punishment, friendship and hospitality, disease and medicine, death and burial, system of government, social classes, and, where applicable, political/dynastic history and administrative status within the empire. In addition, all peoples had individual characters known as *Gemueths-Beschaffenheit* (usually rendered as "spiritual qualities"). Fal'k preferred the "sober and clean" Tatars to the "rude and obstinate" Cossacks; Pallas found the Ingushians to be "an honest and brave set of people" while describing the Ossetes as "a barbarous, predatory, and miserable race of men who have always infested the public road leading to Georgia"; Lesseps "was astonished by the solidity of [the Chukchi] understanding" but thought the Koriaks to be "suspicious, cruel, incapable either of benevolence or pity"; and Georgi reported that while the Mordva were "honest, industrious, and friendly," the Izhors "not only led a life of scarcity and dissolution but were also stupid, distrustful, thievish, and, owing to their proclivity for violence and robbery, dangerous." In more ambiguous cases, Lepekhin considered the Tatars "exceedingly amiable, curious, hospitable, but also cunning"; Fischer believed the Moldavians to be as uncertain in their friendship as they were generous in not remembering evil; and Georgi characterized the Baltic "Semi-Germans" (Latvians, Ests, and Livonians) as "extremely obstinate, lazy, unkempt, and given to drunkenness, but notwithstanding sharp of wit."[33]

Indeed, the closer to home and the longer one looked, the less focused the portrait became. The distant Spaniards or Italians might be "jealous," and the Dutch might be "the strictest observers of household cleanliness and neatness." But when it came to the ethnographically processed peoples of the Russian Empire, most had their clothes, economic tasks, and, yes, spiritual qualities calibrated according to gender, while some—most notably Finns, Poles, and Russians—had "national" subdivisions according to class.[34] Still, the adding up of all mores and traditions of a given nation was supposed to result in a true and final representation of that nation (*nation* was a French term occasionally substituted for *Volk/narod* in the last quarter of the century). Fischer, for instance, believed that he could prove the Chinese origins of the Native Americans simply by comparing customs. Both despised virginity, respected couvade, and practiced "the cutting of hair as an expression of the greatest grief"; "the destruction of dwellings after the owners' death"; "the launching of an arrow as a sign of nationwide alert"; "the carving of images on the face and all over the body"; "the scalping of captive or defeated enemies"; and "the killing of old and sick people"—hence they were related, hence only

(From left) *"Bukharan, Khivan Tatar, Orenburg Tatar"* (*T. de
Pauli,* Description ethnographique des peuples de la
Russie [*St. Petersburg, 1862*])

migration (of the Chinese to Peru) could account for so remarkable a
similarity.[35]

The triumph of customs over faith led to a major reshuffle of the seventeenth-century universe. The Muscovite state had formally divided the
frontier population into the Orthodox (also known as Russians) and the
foreigners/infidels, whose otherness had usually been interpreted in
terms of Oriental "perfidy" or raw-eating beastliness. In the meantime, the

(From left) *"Bukharan Woman, Khivan Woman, Tatar Woman" (T. de Pauli,* Description ethnographique des peuples de la Russie*)*

Orthodox frontiersmen themselves had been reporting on their heathen counterparts without recourse to either vocabulary and on the apparent assumption that the world consisted of countless peoples entitled to their languages, faiths, and customs (but not to liberty/*volia*, of course).[36] Perhaps ironically, the scholarly findings of the eighteenth century seemed to vindicate the latter view. The new world discovered by academic ethnog-

"Peoples of the Russian Empire: [from left] Ostiaks, Tungus, Iakuts" (1900
poster, courtesy of the Russian State Library print collection)

raphers appeared pluralistic, decentered, and relativist. Objectivity was a
value applied to scholars as well as nations, and reflexivity grew stronger
as the century wore on. One German learned traveler concluded in
midcentury that "the surest way to find out the spiritual inclinations of a
certain people is undoubtedly the one where we pay the greatest possible
attention to their actions without forgetting to watch ourselves and to note
the thoughts that occur to us when we are discoursing about others."[37]

Natural law presupposed the uniformity of human nature. Customs
could vary, but the "passions" remained the same. Fontenelle and other
Moderns could compete with the Ancients only if "their trees" were "as
great as those of former times," and Schlözer's world history could be
truly universal only if it saw "all parts of the world as equal to each other"
and "passed with equal interest from the Ganges to the Nile and from the
Tiber to the Vistula."[38] Accordingly, the Russians belonged on the same list
as the Izhors and the Ossetes, and it was possible to say—as it had been in
a seventeenth-century fairy tale—that "the muezzin corresponds to our
sexton [*ponomar'*]: our sexton calls people to church by ringing the bells,

and the muezzin by shouting."[39] In the same spirit, later travelers could report that "as much as [the Kalmyks] are inferior to others in the matter of husbandry, so they are superior to them as pastoralists."[40] And perhaps most remarkable, "the reindeer Chukchis deal with the settled ones in the same way that Russian estate owners deal with their peasants: the settled ones must prepare whale blubber for the reindeer ones, while the reindeer ones bring nothing but reindeer meat."[41] On a loftier scholarly plane, the first collection of Russian folklore did not distinguish between Russians and non-Russians, and Klevetskii's textbook portrait of the Russians was no more flattering than that of the Germans, Poles, or indeed Persians and Moroccans: "They are of middle height, sturdy, strong, brave, good imitators; many—especially the gentry—speak foreign languages and engage in the sciences and arts with great success. The common people are rude."[42] Even the second edition of Georgi's ethnographic compendium, which introduced the Russians as "the ruling nation," described them in terms usually applied to the Tungus:

> The Russians are for the most part cheerful, carefree to the point of frivolity [bezpechny dazhe do vetrennosti], keen on sensual pleasures, quick to understand and to do things, expert at reducing the amount of their work, lively in all things, agile, and sociable. They are not moderate in their attachments, quickly lose their sense of proportion, and often go to the farthest extremes. They are attentive, decisive, courageous, and energetic. They have the greatest passion for trade and barter. They are hospitable and generous, often to their own detriment. They are not overly concerned about the future. Their manner is friendly, open, helpful, and unenvious when they lose. They are jocose and capable of keeping a secret. Their naturally simple way of life and cheerful disposition do not engender many needs, and those that they do have are easy to satisfy; this gives them time to relax, free themselves from troublesome chores [zabotlivykh zatei], find joy in all things, keep their health and strength, and enjoy an unburdensome, tranquil, happy, and, for the most part, lengthy old age.[43]

Even allowing for the Arcadian predilections of the age of sentimentalism, this sketch does not make the Russians stand out among their peers. The amount of space devoted to them is in proportion to their "ruling" status, but the specific traits that make up the whole are subject to the same unblinking scholarly stare that scrutinized the Moldavians and the Mingrelians:

> Most [Russian] women have dark hair and fair skin, and many of them are true beauties. Since they do not wear tight dresses or lace themselves up, their breasts are naturally large and their other body parts are quite fat. Their breasts are much larger than those of Tatar women. Girls usually mature by the age of twelve or thirteen, but some of them lose all

their beauty after only two years of marriage. Some naturalists opine that such early maturation and fertility are brought about by frequent baths, while the fact that their beauty is so short-lived results from their habit of rubbing various substances onto their bodies, or perhaps to the heavy chores commonly performed by married women.[44]

And yet there was something about the Russians that made them feel superior to both the Moldavians and the Mingrelians, something that allowed them to dismiss the Buriats as brutes (and occasionally made them uneasy about their own position vis-à-vis the Germans). This was education, or enlightenment, roughly analogous, on the national level, to the development of the arts, sciences, trade, and industry. Education was the reason the learned mercenaries were in Russia, the official cause of Russia's growing greatness, the true meaning of history, and perhaps the only meaningful way of measuring the relative virtues of "naturally" equal nations. According to a German geography textbook that went through three Russian editions and was remarkable for the consistency of its criteria of excellence, the French "apply themselves greatly to the arts and sciences, have excellent and profitable industries and prosperous commerce"; the Germans "diligently pursue the arts and sciences, and their industry and commerce are both prosperous"; and the Dutch "maintain in a prosperous situation not only the arts and sciences, but also their industries and commerce." On the other hand, there were the Portuguese, "who do poorly in sciences, do not apply themselves to the arts and industries, and engage in commerce without having much to show for it"; the Irish, "who do not care about the arts and sciences but engage in cattle-raising and commerce"; and the totally "unenlightened" Africans, who "are not at all diligent in either the sciences or the arts." Perhaps uniquely, the Russians were rapidly moving from the second into the first category: "the sciences, arts, and industries introduced by Peter the Great are in very good [*izriadnom*] condition; commerce is quite prosperous."[45]

Even conversion to Orthodoxy seemed indistinguishable from enlightenment. "For it is self-evident," wrote Leibniz for Peter I's benefit, "that the spread of science can be accompanied, most successfully, by the spread of truth and piety."[46] Proper education involved both piety and "good citizenship," and good citizenship presupposed the adoption of the "Russian language, life's rituals, clothing, and mores."[47] In other words, Christianization was equal to education was still equal to becoming Russian—particularly because, in Georgi's optimistic opinion, "the uniformity of State organization wisely helps to bring this along by leading our rude Peoples by giant steps toward the common goal of general enlightenment in Russia, of a wonderful fusion of all into a single body and soul, and of creating, as it were, an unshakable Giant that will stand for hundreds of centuries."[48]

This was a very distant goal, celebrated in courtly introductions but altogether irrelevant to the work of traveling naturalists trying to classify the existing diversity of strikingly non-Russian customs. If enlightenment was the ultimate measure of nations, how could one measure an unenlightened nation's relative enlightenment? Tatishchev proposed three criteria: the possession of a writing system, adherence to Christianity, and the use of the printing press. His scheme was strictly historical, however (the enlightened peoples of today were first enlightened by Moses, then by Jesus, and finally by Gutenberg), and thus a relatively poor yardstick for the peoples of the contemporary Russian Empire. If illiterate Christians were not true Christians, as Tatishchev argued, and if learned non-Christians were not truly learned, then there was only one criterion rather than three. And if so, how was one to rank the many nations that languished below that line; how was one to evaluate "the numerous peoples still enveloped in the deepest darkness of ignorance and unawareness"?[49]

Perhaps surprisingly, the basics of sustenance, sex, and settlement remained the touchstones of collective identity: enlightenment had as much to do with bodily needs as faith had. On the frontier, of course, the change in scholarly paradigms had not affected the traditional notions of difference. Russian soldiers returning from "the Kirgiz-Kaisak steppe" waxed sentimental about the look of a settlement and the "taste of bread"; while some "rich Iakut" refused to be baptized/Russified/educated because "Christian law forbids having two wives; eating beef, milk, and butter during Lent; and especially partaking of mare's meat, which they consider the best treat in the world."[50] Yet even in academic and administrative discourse, "raw-eating" was still the clearest line of demarcation—except that now it was not a violation of a religious taboo but a sin against hygiene, neatness, and good manners. "I have almost no strength left to go on detailing for my readers the unspeakably filthy state in which these peoples find themselves," writes Zuev about the inhabitants of the Lower Ob', "for it consists not only in their way of life but in their very food, on which all human life depends."[51] Krasheninnikov and Sarychev were similarly impressed by the Kamchadals (Itel'men); Novitskii by the Ostiaks (Khanty); Lepekhin by the Zyrians (Komi); and Georgi by the Izhors.[52] The Archmandrite Sofronii reported that the Chinese ate dogs, cats, mice, "and other animals that other peoples found disgusting"; Lepekhin discovered that the folk etymology of "Samoed" was "eating filth"; and Nesterev refused to consider the Soiot human because "they ate the same food as the fiercest of animals."[53] To convey the physical immediacy of this crucial national difference, most authors resorted to the same stylistical devices. The city of Beijing exuded "such a terrible odor [smrad] that one could hardly walk the streets"; the Vogul (Mansi) huts were so "disgusting" [gadkie] that "spending any time there should be considered a punishment"; "the smell in [Ostiak] tents [was] so revolting [merzkoi] that probably no one would agree to sit there for a long time"; "the infectious odour that exhale[d] from [Kamchadal] fish would suffice to repulse the most hungry being"; and "the air and filthiness occasioned by [Chukchi tents] are insupportable; let it suffice to say that they feel no disgust at seeing their food and their drink close to the most offensive objects, for no words can describe the excess of their indolence."[54]

Food was frequently overshadowed by smell, but smell—no matter how pungent—was not a separate ethnographic item but one ingredient of the increasingly important virtue of cleanliness. The eighteenth-century scholars appropriated a common religious metaphor and made it literal: "unclean living" came to mean "not washing their hands and faces; not cutting their fingernails; eating off the same plates as dogs and never washing them; smelling like fish; . . . and not combing their hair."[55] On the other hand, cleanliness was an attribute of "civility" or "good manners" (*uchtivstvo, obkhozhdenie*), generally synonymous with the ideal demeanor of a "true fine gentleman" (as per Steele and Addison). The Kamchadals, for example, exhibited their lack of "fear and modesty" by "singing and giving themselves up to all the absurdities which their imagination suggests"; the Crimean Tatars offended against the rules of gentlemanly warfare by "fighting more in the manner of highwaymen"; and the Georgians betrayed their "most spoilt ways" and "incorrect upbringing" by not respecting each other's physical integrity, private property, or bonds of matrimony (by the last quarter of the century, many "Christian laws" had passed through customs and entered the realm of manners).[56] Conversely, a Crimean khan did well by forsaking his saddle in favor of an "English carriage," and Tungus comportment (obkhozhdenie) turned out to be pleasantly "direct and without affectation."[57]

Civility was a reasonable artifice because it was ultimately based on natural law and hence on moderation. "Everything done in moderation is useful [*polezno*] and necessary, whereas excess and insufficiency are called sins or damage to oneself."[58] With reference to nations, the two extremes were usually described as joyless, dreary labor, on one hand, and laziness or indolence, on the other.[59] The latter vice was characteristic of all "unenlightened" peoples, including the Crimean Tatars as observed by Pallas: "To sit with a pipe in their hands, frequently without smoking, for many hours on a shady bank, or on a hill, though totally devoid of all taste for the beauties of nature, and looking straight before them; or, if at work, to make long pauses, and above all to do nothing, constitute their supreme enjoyments."[60]

This false (undeserved and unappreciated) paradise was contrasted with the real one, found in the new German agricultural settlements of southern Siberia: "The healthy, strong, and neatly dressed husbandmen that I encountered numbered up to two hundred people. Scattered around the fields like industrious ants, they followed their heavy plows attached to two or four horses and sang joyous songs. In delight, I felt transported to the beautiful Magdeburg plains, sown with wheat for so many centuries."[61] Prosperous industry was unthinkable without "industriousness," so that true enlightenment had to be accompanied by—and be based on— the "love of toil" (*trudoliubie*). Curiously, however, only "husbandmen" and their urban cousins could be industrious, and only agricultural toil could be truly meaningful (that is, ultimately conducive to the flourishing of the arts, sciences, industry, and commerce). The empire's nomads could not be enlightened any more than they had been able to be Orthodox.

The other excess was a matter of gender because, according to eighteenth-century travelers, almost all dreary and ungrateful labor was done by women. Generally closer to natural law and more sensitive to the ideal of moderation, women tended to be represented as less unenlightened than their male partners (the Cossack women, for example, were "as industrious as the Cossack men were lazy and generally improvident").[62] In spite of that, and perhaps for that very reason, they were, according to the Russian observers, roundly and universally oppressed by their fathers and husbands—so universally, in fact, as to make ignorance synonymous with gender injustice. "In China the husband has no less power over his wife than a master does over his slave"; among the Chuvash "the husband has total power in everything, and his wife must obey him without question"; on Kamchatka "women are . . . the slaves of their husbands"; and on the Lower Ob', "the female sex is worse off than the slave of the sternest master."[63] Most forms of traditional gender-based division of labor, avoidance rules, and social intercourse were now considered grossly unfair. As Zuev put it,

> I am not equal to the task of fully depicting just how despised the female sex is among the Ostiaks and the Samoeds, but I dare say that their women live not like human beings but like cattle that men cannot do without. The poor woman spends her whole life working, knowing neither rest nor holidays, and ever trying to please her man. All his fortune rests on her and her alone, yet he never deigns to even talk to her . . . (a funny aside: they do not know how to embrace their wives, do not know anything about kissing, and are generally unaware of how nicely the charming [*prelestnyi*] sex is treated in polite society).[64]

In this fashion, the triad that used to define communities based on faith was now employed to provide the true measure of enlightenment. Just as the seventeenth-century (male) "foreigners" had expressed their foreignness (and the Christian ascetics their asceticism) through their peculiar relationship to food, women, and domicile, so the eighteenth-century "peoples" could—at the very minimum—be distinguished by the way they ate, treated the "charming sex," and related to the land.

As the number of derivatives increased and their mutual relationships became more complex, however, the picture appeared progressively less stark. Civility narrowly construed ("They do not take off their hats and do not bow to each other") could become a dominant variable, and the application of the "scientific usefulness" yardstick to all customs/manners could result in an endless series of collective rationality tests. Lepekhin, for example, surveyed the rural scene in Russia and reported on the unacceptable health hazards posed by the use of folk medicine, the wearing of bast shoes (*lapti*), the soaking of hemp in rivers, the making of soap, the tanning of leather, and the universally inept way of raising cattle, among other things.[65] There were also some brand-new ways of comparing nations. As Russia's own government became increasingly "enlightened," for example, the degree of enlightenment of non-Russian peoples could be measured according to the "fairness" of their government. China's troubles resulted from the "great injustice" of its political system; Georgia's chaotic state might have something to do with the scandalous treatment of its commoners; and the "lamentable predicament" of what used to be "the highest degree of human glory" in Persia was entirely due to government tyranny and corruption.[66]

The inexorable piling up of such criteria, old and new, among Russian scholars resulted in the creation of an ethnic rating system with the "perfection" of enlightenment at the top and, quite literally, "nothing" at the bottom. As most ethnographic lists assumed the absolute normalcy of perfection and formulated their questions accordingly ("Do they have . . . ?"), a great number of ethnographic subjects could respond only with silence. The result was a negative mode of description and a growing collection of absences. The Moldavians, for example, "do not know anything about the arts and sciences"; "the Kuriles have no notion of any eternal being"; the Oliutor Islanders "care nothing about their souls"; the mid-Volga peoples "have no concept of honesty or virtue"; and the Aleuts "have no law at all," including "no rituals such as weddings, funerals, or festive gatherings" and "no authorities—either elected or of any other kind."[67] This state of nonpossession was known as "savagery" (*dikost'*), which was now equal to "ignorance" (*nevezhestvo*) and "stupidity" (*glupost'*). All nations had some ignorant people and stupid (or nonexistent) customs, and some peoples had so many of them as to be totally "blinded by exceeding stupidity and ignorance" (with fairly Hobbesian results).[68] A special calendar (*miesiatseslov*) entry, for example, introduced a translated account of "the stupid and strange opinions" of the Greenlanders on stars and celestial phenomena, in order to observe "the blindness and utter ignorance of that poor idolatrous nation," as well as to ascertain "the well-being of those nations that, while adhering to Christian law, accompany it with the most solid knowledge of the natural sciences."[69]

There were certain advantages to being stupid, as Catherine II's sentimental sojourners occasionally pointed out (with a sigh), but those were the advantages of childhood innocence. While many scholars professed to envy the "utmost harmony" of the Kamchadals or the "heroic spirit" of the Circassians, no one seemed prepared to "barter the polished vices" of enlightenment for the "rude virtues" of ignorance.[70] The underlying question was much larger and much less frequently posed: If "mankind is so much the same, in all times and places" (as David Hume, unchallenged, summed up the conventional wisdom of the Enlightenment), then why were some people polished, and others rude? The most common answer was "climate," meaning environment in general. As Radishchev proposed, perhaps not originally, "the first teacher of invention was necessity. . . . Those who lived by the water invented boats and nets; those who traveled in the woods and roamed the mountains invented the bow and arrow and became the first warriors; and those who dwelled in the meadows covered with grass and flowers domesticated peaceful animals and became pastoralists."[71] Accordingly, "the differences in the color of human skin could be attributed to the differences in climate, way of life, and food"; the "mores" of the Moldavians varied "because the state of the soil and weather was not the same throughout this large province"; and the Samoed tents were "nothing but mobile shelters invented through necessity by a people who wander over the cold and barren steppes of the midnight land."[72] Sometimes environmental determinism led Russian naturalists to cultural relativism. If "those who traveled in the woods invented the bow and arrow," and if this made them stupid, then, in Johann Georg Gmelin's words, "the other peoples are equally stupid from the Tungus point of view" because "in this fashion any person can be called a fool if he is not particularly knowledgeable in things that he has little opportunity to see or hear. The Tungus are, consequently, . . . just as intelligent as those who are good at deceiving but are stupid at hunting, at which the Tungus are so skillful."[73] This point was rarely pursued, however, because no one, including Gmelin, seriously believed that the utility of hunting skills was comparable to that of the arts and sciences. If one unabashedly affirmed the absolute value of enlightenment, the environmentalist position appeared defenseless before the commonly held belief that "the arts and sciences . . . had their origins among the peoples of the Orient, were later transferred from there to Greece, and from there came to us in Europe."[74] In other words—and again in David Hume's formulation—the manners of peoples "could change very considerably from age to age," so that the North Sea coast could be as fertile in "great men" as the now-decayed shores of the Mediterranean.[75] This augured well for Russia's own efforts and generally offered hope for all future competitors of the current champions. "The Greenlander, Lapplander, Moor, Hottentot, and Kamchadal are, in their own way, as reasonable as the frivolous [*vetrianoi*] Frenchman," argued one Russian scholar, "and if they had the same opportunity for purifying their minds and rectifying their will as we do, they would if not exceed, then certainly equal in this respect any enlightened European."[76] It was not the climate, therefore, but a matter of the historical accident of diffusion. There were intelligent people among the Tungus, but most of them happened to be stupid because they believed, for lack of an alternative, "what they had learned from their stupid ancestors."[77]

This view was also vulnerable, however, because most Tungus seemed to prefer the false wisdom of their ancestors even after they had been exposed to a superior Russian alternative. Radishchev, for example, observed that even "the grown-up Tungus who had been raised in Russian households almost always lagged far behind the Russians with regard to intellectual ability."[78] In a similar vein, a Turukhansk policeman named Ivan Bashkurov reported that the savagery of his native subjects was "rooted in their nature" as well as the climate and thus "could not be eradicated"; Tatishchev explained that the Jews were not tolerated in Russia "not because of their faith but because of their evil nature"; and Lepekhin believed that the mid-Volga pagans could not be fully Christianized because of the "darkness of their mind."[79]

All these examples could represent temporary reverses, as Radishchev himself suggested: "Nature needs several generations to equalize intellectual abilities in humans. The appropriate organs will become finer and subtler; blood, lymph, and especially nerves will become improved and pass from the father to the embryo; and insofar as everything in nature is gradual, it should also be possible in this case."[80] Yet the very association of "intellectual abilities" with "physical nature" was as problematic as it was helpful. Along with "government," the most striking innovation of eighteenth-century German ethnographies of the Russian Empire was *Leibes-Beschaffenheit*, analogous to *Gemueths-Beschaffenheit* and usually translated as "physical features." Unlike Muscovy's faceless "foreigners," the empire's "peoples" could be distinguished and classified according to any number of these features—a constantly growing number, in fact, because they kept splitting and multiplying in the manner of "customs" (size, skin color, hair, and "women's beauty" were the most popular categories, with facial features and head shape gaining momentum toward the end of the century).[81] Following Linnaeus's general classification of the human species ("American: copper-colored, choleric, erect. Paints self. Regulated by custom"), Russian ethnographic descriptions combined bodies with souls in still unexplained but potentially disturbing relationships. Complexion, which most people explained in terms of climate or nature; cleanliness, which most attributed to education; and intelligence, which apparently depended on all three, were usually mentioned in the same breath. Witness Klevetskii's Persians ("of middle height, dark complexion, lovers of cleanliness, quick-witted, and as jealous as the Italians") or Georgi's Chuvash ("with mostly pale faces, less agile and even dumber than the Cheremis, and not any cleaner about their persons").[82]

The apparent asymmetry in the architecture of national traits was not the only, and certainly not the most commonly lamented, problem for the eighteenth-century Russian classifiers. The fact remained that none of these traits—including the newly discovered physical ones—could provide the universal axis around which the ultimate ethnic nomenclature could be organized. Too interrelated to survive on their own and too unwieldy as a group, they were unable to replace the no longer tenable unity of faith with D'Alembert's "principle of true rational thought [*esprit systematique*]."

This principle had emerged, almost imperceptibly, from the very source of the confusion—the Tower of Babel itself. In one of the most important and least celebrated intellectual developments of the eighteenth century, language turned out to be the human mind's equivalent of Newton's law of gravitation (in Condillac's formulation), and the human communities' equivalent of Linnaeus's pistils and stamens (as Schlözer saw it).[83] By 1776, when Adam Smith's *Wealth of Nations* came out, most naturalists took for granted, and hence rarely made explicit, the fact that the greatest wealth of nations was their languages.

According to the traditional Christian view, the plurality of both nations and languages resulted from the fruitfulness of Noah's three sons; their diversity stemmed from the Babylonian Confusion; and their wide dispersal was the result of *Völkerwanderungen*. The original *lingua Adamica* might or might not be Hebrew; in any case, it had to be more pure and natural (in the sense of the unity of sound and meaning) than any of the existing languages, and it could probably be reconstructed through comparative word study. By the eighteenth century, the rise of national states, national vernaculars, and national churches had resulted in the nationalization of Paradise (claims had been made that Adam and Eve spoke Flemish, French, and Swedish, among others), and then in the appearance of multiple autonomous paradises (all nations/languages had their own excellent ancestors). In 1610 Joseph Justus Scaliger had divided the European languages into four major families: Greek, Romance, Germanic, and Slavic, all of which were descended from totally unrelated "mother languages" (*linguae matrices*).[84] The biblical genealogy and the metaphor of "human descent" had become science: all languages and hence all nations had parents, siblings, and offspring (dialects); all linguistic elements could be divided between congenital and acquired; hence a correct method of distinguishing between the two would result in flawless genealogy.[85]

This meant that the apparently arcane search for the origins of words was the best answer to the much-publicized search for the origins of nations. Moreover, it so happened that the reputed home of some European languages was "Scythia," and that G. W. Leibniz, the world's most learned and enthusiastic champion of comparative linguistics, was also the world's warmest supporter of Russia's *débarbarisation*.[86] With remarkable persistence, he assured his Russian correspondents that language was "the best means to discover connections among nations"; urged them to translate "Our Father" into all the languages of the Russian Empire; asked them about possible relationships among "les Siberians, les Czirkasses, les Kalmucs, les Mugalles, les Uzbecs et les Lamas de Chine"; and himself suggested that "all peoples from the Laponians to the Tatars, who live beyond the Caspian, are related to each other, and that the Finns, Estonians, Livonians, Permians, Samoeds, and even Hungarians belong in the same category."[87] Stralenberg, Tatishchev, Müller, Fischer, Schlözer, and Pallas applied themselves to the task, and by the end of the eighteenth century the Finno-Ugrian and Turkic "families" had been discovered and described, with the Russian Empire officially consisting of peoples classified first by language and then, within linguistic categories, by custom and physical type.[88] "The main difference" could be reinforced, clarified, and sometimes contradicted by other criteria (there would always be "Russian-speaking Finns" and "Iakut-speaking Russians"), but the consensus was that "the similarity of languages proves the common origin of peoples."[89] To be more precise,

> Although many people regard similarity of mores, customs, and behaviors as a sign of kinship, and, conversely, difference as evidence of different derivations, the majority of authors reject this view with convincing proof, for it has been sufficiently noted that peoples who stem from the same root have very different ways and customs, and on the other hand, peoples who have different ancestors and . . . never had or could have any contact, possess great similarities in both their mores and their rites, religious as well as secular; for which reasons the most reliable sign of kinship between peoples is thought to be their language.[90]

This meant that if the Iakuts spoke a "Tatar" language, they belonged to "the Tatar lineage" (*pokolenie*). Perhaps more significant for future theories of nationalism, this could mean that "as [the Votiaks, Chuvash, and Cheremis] belong to the Finnish lineage, so they live like Finns."[91]

In any case, kinship signified origins. "Related" languages had common ancestors, and all language "families" had their language matriarchs, or *Muttersprache*. This was true of any "basic principle" because, as Condillac explained, "*principle* and *beginning* are two words which originally signify the same thing."[92] It was especially true of languages and nations, however, because the search for origins was ultimately animated by the need to separate the "natural" from the "artificial," and most scholars agreed that none of the existing languages and nations were natural in the sense of having been created by God once and for all. Thus, the great linguistic turn was by definition a turn toward historicism. If the biological taxonomies were essentially static, the linguistic ones were genetic; if the biological species were mutually insulated, the linguistic ones were potentially open to interbreeding (two *Muttersprache* might very well turn out to be cousins); and while Linnaeus had insisted that "every egg produces an offspring identical to the parent," every linguist knew that Old French was different from Latin, and Modern French was even more so.[93] In other words, a difference in language—and consequently in custom, and possibly in physical type—was also a difference in time.[94] Agriculture was not just better than hunting—it was *later.* A tent was not just less comfortable than a building—it was its ancestor. Most non-Russian peoples of the Russian Empire were not just unenlightened—they were "ancient." The Circassians resembled the medieval "German knights in Prussia and Livonia," while some Siberians represented the "crude" infancy of mankind.[95] The Russian Empire did not simply contain "a great number of different peoples"—it embraced "all the stages of transformation from the ancient, simple World very close to its natural condition to the present World, refined and enriched by needs."[96]

Universal history as a sequence of technological and behavioral stages was not the only beneficiary of ethnographic research. Russian history as a professional and imperial enterprise also arose from the study of non-Russian peoples. The reason for this was a paradox: the linguistic quest for the national origins had been based on the presumed identity of languages and nations, yet the most obvious result of this quest had been the decoupling of the two. It turned out that not only had peoples themselves traveled from place to place (this was a truism), but their names, languages, and governments had moved around independently of each other. The scholars brought in to describe the Russian Empire and to bring glory to its name, state, tongue, land, and people had ended up discovering that, in terms of origins and according to the best primary sources, none of these categories had anything to do with each other. The Russian land had not been "Russian" for very long; the Russian state and the Russian name had come from Sweden; the Russian apostle Andrew had never been to Russia; and the Russian language had been—quite recently—brought in by the tribes chased out of the Danube. As Schlözer summed up the scholarly findings, "Russian history begins with the arrival of Riurik in the middle of the ninth century"; whatever had come before was not any more enlightening than the "Kamchadal fables."[97] Moreover, if "history without politics is nothing but monks' chronicles," and if monks' chronicles "did not have the authority to persuade us of something that was contrary to history," then until very recently the Russians themselves had been like the Kamchadals and could be described only in terms of what they did not have—most notably politics, history, religion, and enlightenment.[98]

As far as scientific usefulness was concerned, this was just fine. After all, as Müller insisted, there was a difference "between a historical dissertation and a panegyric," and in any case "the origins of peoples, mostly quite obscure; the beginnings of states, usually humble; and the savage ways of ancestors," among other things, had "absolutely nothing to do with either fame or infamy."[99] Yet from the point of view of state usefulness, they most certainly did. From the point of view of state usefulness, a historical dissertation that was not a panegyric was "reprehensible" [*predosuditel'na*], as well as "annoying" and "unpleasant" to the readers, because a great state should have great beginnings. Besides, great states were now associated with great peoples, which, like states, were now entitled to glorious genealogies. Lomonosov took the Varangian issue very seriously: "If the modern Russian nation is descended primarily from the ancient people who existed before the coming of the Varangians, then the dishonor engendered by contempt for those ancient people affects in very large measure the modern nation."[100]

One solution was to ignore the prehistory and trace Russian greatness from the coming of Riurik, as Boltin chose to do. Another was to insist on greater antiquity but essentially accept the deconstructed nature of past Russianness. Thus, the Russian territory could be praised irrespective of who lived there: "Contemporary Little Russia gave birth to the Goths, who went on to found prosperous states in Italy, France, and Spain. And from the Volga, Ural, and Kama rivers came the Hungarians, Huns, and various other peoples who . . . shook Europe and gave it its present shape. In this way many peoples must look to our Fatherland in order to find their forebears."[101] Likewise, the Slavs could be praised irrespective of where they lived (in fact, "the variety of different lands of the Slavic tribe is the most incontrovertible proof of its greatness and antiquity");[102] the Slavic language could be praised irrespective of where it was spoken;[103] the Russian state could be praised irrespective of the people it ruled (for old dynastic reasons but increasingly for the new reason of "tolerance");[104] and even the name *Rossiiane* could be derived from *razseiany*, "scattered."[105] In this scheme, Russian history tended to begin according to the territorial principle, then shift to the national-linguistic, and finally switch to the state—for good.[106]

Yet it was clear that the Russian Empire was, however uncomfortably, also a Russian nation-state, which presupposed a triumphant and ancient unity of territory, people, language, state, and name. Standard geography textbooks that characterized the states/peoples of the world (and never defined empires as multinational states) described Russians under Russia while placing the Tatars in the Asia section.[107] The greatest challenge, however, was to overcome ethnography by history; to abolish the new ethnographic findings in "our" case; to conflate—once and for all—the various independent components of Russian nationality. The first to set himself this task was Lomonosov, who endeavored to prove that the ancient Russians had been called Roksolans (Russians) and had spoken Slavic (name equals language); that the ancient Slavs had been Sarmatians and hence always inhabited the Russian territory (name equals language equals territory); that the Lithuanians were also Slavs, as had been the Prussians; and that the Varangians had been Prussians and hence Russians (name equals language equals territory equals state).[108]

Few of these claims could be maintained in the long run. Lomonosov himself would have to trace some Russians back to the Finns (and so—*noblesse oblige*—trace the Finns themselves to the "great and ancient" Scythians),[109] while his successors would soon surrender the Roksolans, the Lithuanians, and—for a while—the Varangians. Yet the problem had been formulated, at least in terms of the past. Solving it, and posing it in terms of the present, was a challenge that the nineteenth-century state (known as *rossiiskoe* and identified with "Orthodoxy, autocracy, and nationality" in that order) would have to share with a self-styled "intelligentsia" (known as *russkaia* and identified with nationality as distinct from the state).[110] The enlightenment inventory of internal foreigners conducted by mostly foreign officials for an increasingly foreign (bureaucratic) state had contributed to the disaggregation of Russianness and thus to the predicament of those "foreigners at home, foreigners abroad" who would reshape the world in order to put Russianness back together.[111] The difficulty was quite common, of course: Britain and England were not convinced they were not synonyms, the Franks and the Gauls were still arguing over paternity, and not all Castilian speakers knew they were speaking Spanish. Still, Russia's challenge seemed unusually formidable. Much of its "sacred" heartland seemed to consist of borderlands.

NOTES

I am grateful to Nicholas V. Riasanovsky, to the participants in the SSRC-sponsored workshop "Visions, Institutions, and Experiences of Imperial Russia," and to the fellows of the Doreen B. Townsend Center for the Humanities (University of California, Berkeley) for stimulating discussions. This chapter was previously published in *Representations* 47 (1994): 170–195. It is reprinted here with permission from the University of California Press.

1. John F. Baddeley, *Russia, Mongolia, China,* vol. 2 (New York, n.d.), p. 10.

2. Ibid., p. 8.

3. Vladimir Ger'e, *Leibnits i ego viek,* vol. 2: *Otnosheniia Leibnitsa k Rossii i Petru Velikomu po neizdannym bumagam Leibnitsa v gannoverskoi biblioteke* (St. Petersburg, 1871), pp. 5 and 12. Cf. Daniel Droixhe, "Le Voyage de 'Schreiten': Leibniz et les débuts du comparatisme finno-ougrienne," in Tullio de Mauro and Lia Formigari, eds., *Leibniz, Humboldt, and the Origins of Comparativism* (Amsterdam, 1990), p. 19.

4. For more on this, see Yuri Slezkine, "The Sovereign's Foreigners: Classifying

the Native Siberians in 17th-Century Russia," forthcoming in *Russian History/ Histoire russe*. See also Stephen Greenblatt, *Marvelous Possessions: The Wonder of the New World* (Chicago, 1991), pp. 82–83.

5. See Margaret T. Hodgen, *Early Anthropology in the Sixteenth and Seventeenth Centuries* (Philadelphia, 1971), p. 129 and passim.

6. Rainer S. Elkar, "Reisen bildet," in B. I. Krasnobaev, Gert Robel, and Herbert Zeman, eds., *Reisen und Reisebeschreibungen im 18. und 19. Jahrhundert als Quellen der Kulturbeziehungsforschung* (Berlin, 1980), p. 54; Hans Erich Bädeker, "Reisebeschreibungen im historischen Diskurs der Aufklärung," in Hans Erich Bädeker et al., eds., *Aufklärung und Geschichte: Studien zur deutschen Geschichtswissenschaft im 18. Jahrhundert* (Göttingen, 1986), pp. 279–281. Also P. Miliukov, *Glavnyia techeniia russkoi istoricheskoi mysli* (St. Petersburg, 1913), p. 72.

7. *Rossiia. Arkheograficheskaia komissiia. Pamiatniki sibirskoi istorii XVIII vieka*, vol. 2 (St. Petersburg, 1885), pp. 292–293, 460; V. N. Tatishchev, *Izbrannye trudy po geografii Rossii* (Moscow, 1950), p. 13; V. G. Mirzoev, *Istoriografiia Sibiri. Domarksistskii period* (Moscow, 1970), p. 78; G. F. Miller [Gerhard F. Müller], *Istoriia Sibiri*, vol. 1 (Moscow-Leningrad, 1937), p. 30.

8. The first Russian monthly, published by the Academy and edited by Müller, appealed to both (*Ezhemesiachnye sochineniia, k pol'ze i uveseleniiu sluzhashchie*).

9. Ger'e, *Leibnits*, vol. 2, p. 76. See also Ivan Lepekhin, *Dnevnyia zapiski puteshestviia doktora i akademii nauk ad"iunkta Ivana Lepekhina po raznym provintsiiam Rossiiskago gosudarstva* (St. Petersburg, 1771–1805), vol. 1, p. 90.

10. Konrad Bittner, "Slavica bei G. W. von Leibniz," *Germanoslavica*, no. 3 (1931–32): 227–228; no. 4 (1931–32): 528–529 and 537–539; Ger'e, *Leibniz*, vol. 2, pp. 16–18.

11. Bittner, "Slavica," no. 4, p. 191.

12. See Bernard McGrane, *Beyond Anthropology: Society and the Other* (New York, 1989), p. 48.

13. See Mark Bassin, "Russia between Europe and Asia: The Ideological Construction of Geographical Space," *Slavic Review*, no. 1 (1991): 1–7.

14. For some major compilations, see *Atlas Rossiiskoi, sostoiashchei iz deviatnadtsati spetsial'nykh kart predstavliaiushchikh Vserossiskuiu Imperiiu s pogranichnymi zemliami, sochinennoi po pravilam geograficheskim i noveishim observatsiiam* (St. Petersburg, 1745); Khariton Chebotarev, *Geograficheskoe metodicheskoe opisanie Rossiiskoi imperii* (Moscow, 1776); Ivan Kirilov, *Tsvietushchee sostoianie Vserossiiskago gosudarstva* (Moscow, 1831) (compiled in 1727); Martin Ia. Klevetskii, *Rukovodstvo k geografii s upotrebleniem zemnago shara i landkart* (St. Petersburg, 1773); "Kratkoe opisanie Tobol'skago Namiestnichestva," in *Sobranie sochinenii vybrannykh iz miesiatsoslovov na raznye gody*, pt. 6 (1790), pp. 148–218; Sergei Pleshcheev, *Obozrienie Rossiiskiia imperii v nynieshnem eia novoustroennom sostoianii* , 3rd ed. (St. Petersburg, 1790); Fedor Polunin, *Geograficheskii leksikon Rossiiskago gosudarstva* (Moscow, 1773); V. N. Tatishchev, *Izbrannye proizvedeniia* (Leningrad, 1979), pp. 328–360; Tatishchev, *Izbrannye trudy po geografii*, pp. 36–97; Kh. N. Vinsgeim, *Kratkaia politicheskaia geografiia* (St. Petersburg, 1745).

15. On this activity, see L. A. Goldenberg and A. V. Postnikov, "Development of Mapping Methods in Russia in the Eighteenth Century," *Imago mundi*, no. 37 (1985): 63–64; D. M. Lebedev, *Ocherki po istorii geografii v Rossii XVIII v.* (Moscow,

1957); M. G. Novlianskaia, *I. K. Kirilov i ego Atlas Vserossiiskoi imperii* (Moscow, 1958), pp. 5–6, 9, and 11; A. N. Pypin, *Istoriia russkoi etnografii*, vol. 1 (St. Petersburg, 1890), pp. 95–99.

16. Charles Frankel, *The Faith of Reason: The Idea of Progress in the French Enlightenment* (New York, 1948), pp. 44–45. Catherine's travelers tended to be more sensitive than inquisitive and more impressionistic than systematic.

17. Hodgen, *Early Anthropology*, pp. 418–426; McGrane, *Beyond Anthropology*, pp. 78–81. The quotes are from Carl Linnaeus's *System of Nature* and William Petty's *The Scale of Creatures*.

18. *Russkie ekspeditsii po izucheniiu severnoi chasti Tikhogo okeana v pervoi polovine XVIII v. Sbornik dokumentov* (Moscow, 1984), p. 155; G. F. Müller, "Instruktion G. F. Müller's für den Akademiker-Adjuncten J. E. Fischer. Unterricht, was bey Beschreibung der Völker, absonderlich der Sibirischen in acht zu nehmen," *Sbornik Muzeia po antropologii i etnografii* 1 (1900): 37–99.

19. Frankel, *The Faith of Reason*, p. 44.

20. See Müller's introduction to Fedor Polunin's *Geograficheskii leksikon Rossiiskago gosudarstva* (Moscow, 1773). See also Tatishchev, *Izbrannye trudy po geografii*, pp. 174–183, and Tatishchev, *Izbrannye proizvedeniia*, pp. 153–327.

21. G. F. Miller [Müller], *Opisanie Sibirskago tsarstva* (St. Petersburg, 1750), pp. 27 and 29.

22. Tatishchev, *Izbrannye trudy po geografii*, 88–89. See also Lepekhin, *Dnevnyia zapiski*, vol. 4, pp. 198–199.

23. See, for example, A. I. Andreev, ed., "Opisaniia o zhizni i uprazhnenii obitaiushchikh v Turukhanskoi i Berezovskoi okrugakh raznogo roda iasachnykh inovertsakh," *Sovetskaia etnografiia*, no. 1 (1947): 84–103; Ludwig Adolph Baumann, *Kratkoe nachertanie geografii* (Moscow, 1775); Ivan Gustav Gerber, "Izviestie o nakhodiashchikhsia s Zapadnoi storony Kaspiiskago moria mezhdu Astrakhan'iu i riekoiu Kurom narodakh," *Sochineniia i perevody, k pol'zie i uveseleniiu sluzhashchie* (July 1760), pp. 1–48; (August 1760), pp. 99–140; (September 1760), pp. 195–232; (October 1760), pp. 292–303; Kirilov, *Tsvetushchee sostoianie*; S. P. Krasheninnikov, *Opisanie zemli Kamchatki* (Moscow, 1949); Egor Nesterev, "Primiechaniia o prikosnovennykh okolo Kitaiskoi granitsy zhiteliakh," *Novyia ezhemiesiachnyia sochineniia* 79 (January 1793): 59–82; *Russkie ekspeditsii po izu-cheniiu severnoi chasti Tikhogo okeana vo vtoroi polovine XVIII v. Sbornik dokumentov* (Moscow, 1989), p. 85; Petr I. Rychkov, *Topografiia Orenburgskaia* (St. Petersburg, 1762); Vinsgeim, *Kratkaia politicheskaia geografiia*.

24. "'Skaska' piatidesiatnika Vladimira Atlasova, 3 iiunia 1700," in Ia. P. Al'kor and A. K. Drezen, eds., *Kolonial'naia politika tsarizma na Kamchatke i Chukotke v XVIII veke. Sbornik arkhivnykh materialov* (Leningrad, 1935), p. 31.

25. *Sibirskiia lietopisi* (St. Petersburg, 1907), p. 112. Cf. N. S. Orlova, ed., *Otkrytiia russkikh zemleprokhodtsev i poliarnykh morekhodov XVII veka na severo-vostoke Azii. Sbornik dokumentov* (Moscow, 1951), pp. 83 and 98. For more on this, see Slezkine, "The Sovereign's Foreigners."

26. See, for example, Miller, *Istoriia Sibiri*, vol. 2, p. 276; *Sibirskiia lietopisi*, p. 112. Cf. Hayden White, "The Forms of Wildness: Archaeology of an Idea," in Edward Dudley and Maximilian E. Novak, eds., *The Wild Man Within: An Image in Western Thought from the Renaissance to Romanticism* (Pittsburgh, 1972), pp. 19–22.

27. Orlova, ed., *Otkrytiia*, p. 140; *Russkaia tikhookeanskaia epopeia* (Khabarovsk, 1979), p. 69.

28. Andreev, ed., "Opisaniia," p. 90. See also Johann Gottlieb Georgi, *Opisanie vsiekh obitaiushchikh v Rossiiskom gosudarstvie narodov* (St. Petersburg, 1799), vol. 1, p. 18 and passim; Krasheninnikov, *Opisanie*, pp. 406–413; Müller, "Instruktion," pp. 72f.; Tatishchev, *Izbrannye trudy po geografii*, p. 38.

29. See, in particular, Simon-Peter Pallas, *Travels into the Southern Provinces of the Russian Empire in the Years 1793 and 1794* (London, 1802), vol. 1, passim, and vol. 2, p. 354. Also Khrisanf, Mitropolit Novopatrasskii, "O stranakh Srednei Azii" and "Izvestie o Kitaiskom gosudarstve," in *Chteniia v Imperatorskom Obshchestve istorii i drevnostei Rossiiskikh pri Moskovskom universitete*, kn. 1 (1861), and G. A. Sarychev, *Puteshestvie po severo-vostochnoi chasti Sibiri, Ledovitomu moriu i Vostochnomu okeanu* (Moscow, 1952).

30. "O Tungusakh voobshche," *Sobranie sochinenii vybrannykh iz miesiatsoslovov na raznye gody*, pt. 6 (1790), pp. 286 and 289.

31. Grigorii Novitskii, *Kratkoe opisanie o narodie Ostiatskom, sochinennoe v 1715 godu* (St. Petersburg, 1884), pp. 31–32 and 47–49. See also Georg Wilhelm Steller, *Beschreibung von dem Lande Kamtschatka* (Frankfurt und Leipzig, 1774), pp. 355–358.

32. Tatishchev, *Izbrannye proizvedeniia*, p. 87.

33. Johann Peter Fal'k, *Zapiski puteshestviia akademika Fal'ka. Polnoe sobranie uchenykh puteshestvii po Rossii* (St. Petersburg, 1824), vol. 6, pp. 222 and 233–234; [Johann Eberhard Fischer], "O proizkhozhdenii moldavtsov, o ikh iazykic, znatneishikh prikliucheniiakh, vierie, nravakh i povedeniiakh," in *Sobranie sochinenii vybrannykh iz miesiatsoslovov na raznye gody*, pt. 3 (1789), p. 81; Georgi, *Opisanie*, vol. 1, pp. 21, 23, and 42; Lepekhin, *Dnevnyia zapiski*, vol. 1, p. 138; M. de Lesseps, *Travels in Kamtschatka during the Years 1787 and 1788* (London, 1790), vol. 2, pp. 27 and 84; Pallas, *Travels*, vol. 1, pp. 431 and 446.

34. Klevetskii, *Rukovodstvo*, pp. 52–53, 60, 74, 83, 91, and passim; Georgi, *Opisanie*, vol. 1, pp. 14–19; vol. 4, pp. 69–70, 83, and passim.

35. [Fischer], "Dogadki o proizkhozhdenii Amerikantsov," in *Sobranie sochinenii vybrannykh iz miesiatsoslovov na raznye gody*, pt. 3 (1789), pp. 122–173.

36. See Slezkine, "The Sovereign's Foreigners."

37. Samuel G. Gmelin, *Puteshestvie po Rossii* (St. Petersburg, 1771), p. 209.

38. Hodgen, *Early Anthropology*, p. 448; Miliukov, *Glavnyia techeniia*, p. 74.

39. Lepekhin, *Dnevnyia zapiski*, vol. 1, p. 179.

40. Ibid., p. 213.

41. "Perechen' iz dnevnoi zapiski kazach'eva sotnika Ivana Kobeleva, posylanago 1779 goda v martie miesiatsie iz Gizhiginskoi kreposti v Chukotskuiu zemliu," in *Sobranie sochinenii vybrannykh iz miesiatsoslovov na raznye gody*, pt. 5 (1790), p. 368.

42. M. D. Chulkov, *Abevega russkikh suieverii* (Moscow, 1786); Klevetskii, *Rukovodstvo*, pp. 47, 53, 83, 103, and 114. See also Baumann, *Kratkoe nachertanie*, p. 86.

43. Georgi, *Opisanie*, vol. 4, p. 83.

44. Ibid., p. 84.

45. Baumann, *Kratkoe nachertanie*, pp. 17, 24, 37, 39, 86, and 114.

46. Ger'e, *Leibnits*, vol. 2, pp. 25–26. See also Lepekhin, *Dnevnyia zapiski*, vol. 3, p. 241.

47. Tatishchev, *Izbrannye proizvedeniia*, pp. 103–104; Georgi, *Opisanie*, vol. 1, pp. viii–ix; Ivan Boltin, *Primechaniia na istoriiu drevniia i nyneshniia Rossii g. Leklerka* (St. Petersburg, 1788), p. 146.

48. Georgi, *Opisanie*, vol. 1, p. ix.

49. Tatishchev, *Izbrannye proizvedeniia*, pp. 70–79.

50. N. Rychkov, *Dnevnyia zapiski puteshestviia Kapitana Nikolaia Rychkova v Kirgis-Kaisatskoi stepie, 1771 godu* (St. Petersburg, 1772), pp. 79–81; Sarychev, *Puteshestvie*, p. 41.

51. V. F. Zuev, *Materialy po etnografii Sibiri XVIII veka (1771–1772)*, AN SSSR, Trudy Instituta etnografii im. N. N. Miklukho-Maklaia, Novaia seriia, vol. 5 (Moscow-Leningrad, 1947), p. 36.

52. Krasheninnikov, *Opisanie*, p. 367; Novitskii, *Kratkoe opisanie*, p. 43; Lepekhin, *Dnevnyia zapiski*, vol. 3, p. 275; Georgi, *Opisanie*, vol. 1, p. 23.

53. Arkhimandrit Sofronii, "Izviestie o Kitaiskom, nyne Mandzhuro-Kitaiskom gosudarstvie," *Chteniia v Imperatorskom obshchestvie istorii i drevnostei rossiiskikh*, no. 1 (1861), section 5, p. 71; Lepekhin, *Dnevnyia zapiski*, vol. 4, p. 118; Nesterev, "Primiechaniia," pp. 56–57.

54. See, respectively, Khrisanf, "O strankakh," pp. 48–49; Lepekhin, *Dnevnyia zapiski*, vol. 3, p. 20; Zuev, *Materialy*, p. 29; and Lesseps, *Travels*, vol. 1, p. 91, and vol. 2, p. 41.

55. Krasheninnikov, *Opisanie*, p. 367.

56. Lesseps, *Travels*, vol. 1, p. 89; [V. F. Zuev], "Vypiska iz puteshestvennykh zapisok Vasil'ia Zueva, kasaiushchikhsia do poluostrova Kryma, 1782 goda," in *Sobranie sochinenii vybrannykh iz miesiatsoslovov na raznye gody*, pt. 5 (1790), p. 286; [V. F. Zuev], "Vypiska iz puteshestvennykh zapisok Vasil'ia Zueva ob Aziatskikh oblastiakh k Chernomu moriu prilezhashchikh," in *Sobranie sochinenii vybrannykh iz miesiatsoslovov na raznye gody*, pt. 6 (1790), p. 232.

57. "Vypiska iz puteshestvennykh zapisok Vasil'ia Zueva, kasaiushchikhsia do poluostrova Kryma, 1782 goda," p. 288; "O Tungusakh voobshche," p. 297.

58. Tatishchev, *Izbrannye proizvedeniia*, p. 60.

59. Lesseps, *Travels*, vol. 1, p. 89.

60. Pallas, *Travels*, vol. 2, p. 356. Cf. Lesseps, *Travels*, vol. 1, p. 96: "The greatest happiness, in [the Kamchadal] estimation, next to that of getting drunk, is to have nothing to do, and live for ever in tranquil indolence."

61. G. Berens, "O sostoianii novykh poselenii v Iuzhnoi Sibiri [1776 g.]," *Sibirskii viestnik*, pt. 10, bk. 5 (1820), p. 297.

62. Fal'k, *Zapiski*, vol. 6, p. 54. See also N. Rychkov, *Dnevnyia zapiski*, p. 31.

63. Khrisanf, "O strankakh," p. 86; Georgi, *Opisanie*, p. 38; Lesseps, *Travels*, vol. 1, p. 29; Zuev, *Materialy*, p. 31.

64. Zuev, *Materialy*, p. 59.

65. Lepekhin, *Dnevnyia zapiski*, vol. 1, pp. 16, 64, 69, 73, 84, and 109.

66. Khrisanf, "O strankakh," pp. 35–39; Sofronii, "Izviestie," pp. 25–35; "Vypiska iz puteshestvennykh zapisok Vasil'ia Zueva ob Aziatskikh oblastiakh," p. 227; Gmelin, *Puteshestvie*, pt. 3, pp. 172–173. For "free peoples" see, for example, "Kratkoe geograficheskoe opisanie kniazhestva Moldavskago i lezhashchikh

mezhdu Chernym i Kaspiiskim moriami zemel' i narodov s landkartoiu sikh zemel'," in *Sobranie sochinenii vybrannykh iz miesiatsoslovov na raznye gody*, pt. 3 (1789), pp. 108–117.

67. "O proizkhozhdenii moldavtsov," p. 82; "Opisanie Kuril'skikh ostrovov," in *Sobranie sochinenii vybrannykh iz miesiatsoslovov na raznye gody*, pt. 6 (1790), p. 97; "Kratkoe izviestie o novoizobrietennom sievernom arkhipelagie," in *Sobranie sochinenii vybrannykh iz miesiatsoslovov na raznye gody*, pt. 3 (1789), p. 355; "Opisanie trekh iazycheskikh narodov v kazanskoi gubernii, a imenno cheremisov, chuvashei i votiakov," in *Ezhemiesiachnyia sochineniia k pol'ze i uveseleniiu sluzhashchiia* (July 1756), pp. 42–43 and 54–55; (August 1756), pp. 119–245; "Perechen' puteshestviia shturmana Zaikova k ostrovam mezhdu Azieiu i Amerikoiu nakhodiashchimsia na botie Sv. Vladimira," in *Sobranie sochinenii vybrannykh iz miesiatsoslovov na raznye gody*, pt. 5 (1790), p. 159; *Russkie ekspeditsii po izucheniiu severnoi chasti Tikhogo okeana vo vtoroi polovine XVIII v.*, p. 115.

68. "Opisanie trekh" (July 1756), p. 43; "O Tungusakh voobshche," p. 297.

69. "Ob astronomii Grenlandskikh zhitelei," in *Sobranie sochinenii vybrannykh iz miesiatsoslovov na raznye gody*, pt. 1 (1785), p. 153.

70. Lesseps, *Travels*, vol. 1, pp. 95–97; Pallas, *Travels*, vol. 1, p. 391.

71. A. N. Radishchev, *Polnoe sobranie sochinenii*, vol. 2 (Moscow-Leningrad, 1941), p. 64.

72. Chebotarev, *Geograficheskoe metodicheskoe opisanie*, p. 47; "O proizkhozhdenii moldavtsov," p. 83; Lepekhin, *Dnevnyia zapiski*, vol. 4, p. 226.

73. Quoted in L. P. Belkovets, *Iogann Georg Gmelin, 1709–1755* (Moscow, 1990), p. 89.

74. Chebotarev, *Geograficheskoe metodicheskoe opisanie*, pp. 43–44. See also "Izviestiia o Bukharii," in *Sobranie sochinenii vybrannykh iz miesiatsoslovov na raznye gody*, pt. 4 (1790), pp. 139–140. Cf. Hodgen, *Early Anthropology*, pp. 461–463.

75. Hodgen, *Early Anthropology*, p. 487.

76. Chebotarev, *Geograficheskoe metodicheskoe opisanie*, p. 48.

77. "O Tungusakh voobshche," p. 297.

78. Radishchev, *Polnoe sobranie*, vol. 2, p. 66.

79. Andreev, "Opisaniia," p. 94; Tatishchev, *Izbrannye proizvedeniia*, p. 88; Lepekhin, *Dnevnyia zapiski*, vol. 1, p. 168.

80. Radishchev, *Polnoe sobranie*, vol. 2, p. 66.

81. See, for example, Johann Eberhard Fischer, *Sibirskaia istoriia s samago otkrytiia Sibiri do zavoevaniia sei zemli Rossiiskim oruzhiem* (St. Petersburg, 1774), p. 67; Lepekhin, *Dnevnyia zapiski*, vol. 3, p. 28; vol. 4, p. 212; Müller, "Instruktion," pp. 39–41; Müller, *Opisanie*, p. 21; Pallas, *Travels*, vol. 1, p. 390; vol. 2, p. 345; Steller, *Beschreibung*, pp. 297–303.

82. Georgi, *Opisanie*, vol. 1, p. 35.

83. Frankel, *The Faith of Reason*, p. 52; Miliukov, *Glavnyia techeniia*, p. 89.

84. Hans Aarslef, *From Locke to Saussure: Essays on the Study of Language and Intellectual History* (Minneapolis, 1982), pp. 281–282; Maurice Olender, *The Languages of Paradise: Race, Religion, and Philology in the Nineteenth Century* (Cambridge, Mass., 1992), pp. 1–5; R. H. Robins, "The History of Language Classification," in Thomas A. Sebeok, ed., *Current Trends in Linguistics*, vol. 2 (The Hague, 1973), pp. 7–11.

85. Henry M. Hoenigswald, "Descent, Perfection, and the Comparative Method since Leibniz," in Mauro and Formigari, eds., *Leibniz*, pp. 119–131.

86. Hans Aarslef, "The Eighteenth Century, Including Leibniz," in *Current Trends in Linguistics*, vol. 13 (The Hague, 1975), pp. 391–394; Robert H. Robins, "Leibniz and Wilhelm von Humboldt and the History of Comparative Linguistics," in Mauro and Formigari, eds., *Leibniz*, pp. 85–93.

87. Bittner, "Slavica," no. 4, pp. 199 and 201; Ger'e, *Leibnits*, vol. 2, pp. 41–42.

88. See, for example, Philip Johan Tabbert von Stralenberg, *Russia, Siberia, and Great Tartary* (New York, 1970 [reprint of the 1738 edition]); Tatishchev, *Izbrannye trudy*, pp. 70–72, 173; V. N. Tatishchev, *Istoriia Rossiiskaia*, vol. 1 (Moscow-Leningrad, 1962); Fischer, *Sibirskaia istoriia*, pp. 70–105 (much of the linguistic material was apparently provided by Müller); P. P. Pekarskii, *Istoriia imperatorskoi Akademii Nauk v Peterburgie* (St. Petersburg, 1870), pp. 630–632; Peter Simon Pallas, *Sravnitel'nye slovari vsiekh iazykov i nariechii, sobrannye desnitseiu vsevysochaishei osoby* (St. Petersburg, 1789). For the definitive ethnic classifications, see Georgi, *Opisanie*, and Pleshcheev, *Obozrienie*, pp. 26–38.

89. N. Ia. Ozeretskovskii, *Puteshestvie po ozeram Ladozhskomu i Onezhskomu* (Petrozavodsk, 1989), p. 124. Cf. Müller, *Opisanie*, p. 1.

90. Lepekhin, *Dnevnyia zapiski*, vol. 4, p. 404.

91. Pleshcheev, *Obozrienie*, p. 78.

92. Aarslef, *From Locke to Saussure*, pp. 158–159; Frankel, *The Faith of Reason*, pp. 44–45.

93. W. Keith Percival, "Linguistic and Biological Classification in the Eighteenth Century," in Donald C. Mell, Jr., Theodore E. D. Braun, and Lucia M. Palmer, eds., *Man, God, and Nature in the Enlightenment* (East Lansing, Mich., 1988), pp. 205–214.

94. Bädeker, "Reisebeschreibungen," p. 286; Hodgen, *Early Anthropology*, pp. 433–471; McGrane, *Beyond Anthropology*, pp. 83–85.

95. Pallas, *Travels*, vol. 1, p. 391; Georgi, *Opisanie*, vol. 1, pp. xiii–xx.

96. Georgi, *Opisanie*, vol. 1, pp. xiii–xx.

97. Miliukov, *Osnovnyia techeniia*, p. 86.

98. The first quote is by Schlözer, in Georg G. Iggers, "The European Context of Eighteenth-Century German Historiography," in Bädeker et al., eds., *Aufklärung und Geschichte*, p. 239; the second is by Müller, in M. V. Lomonosov, *Polnoe sobranie sochinenii*, vol. 6 (Moscow-Leningrad, 1952), p. 57.

99. Lomonosov, *Polnoe sobranie*, vol. 6, pp. 67–68.

100. Ibid., pp. 77–78.

101. M. D. Chulkov, *Istoricheskoe opisanie Rossiiskoi kommertsii pri vsiekh portakh i granitsakh*, vol. 1 (St. Petersburg, 1781), p. 4.

102. M. V. Lomonosov, *Izbrannye proizvedeniia*, vol. 2 (Moscow, 1986), p. 52.

103. *Novieishee poviestvovatel'noe zemleopisanie vsiekh chetyrekh chastei svieta* (St. Petersburg, 1795), vol. 2, p. 129.

104. Catherine, Empress of Russia, *Sochineniia imperatritsy Ekateriny II* (St. Petersburg, 1901), vol. 7, p. 55; Georgi, *Opisanie*, vol. 4, p. 66; Tatishchev, *Izbrannye proizvedeniia*, p. 87.

105. *Novieishee*, vol. 1, p. 17.

106. See, for example, "Sokrashchenie Rossiiskoi istorii," in *Sobranie sochinenii vybrannykh iz miesiatsoslovov na raznye gody*, pt. 3 (1789), pp. 1–10.

107. Klevetskii, *Rukovodstvo*, p. 108.

108. Lomonosov, *Polnoe sobranie*, vol. 6, pp. 25–80. For the eighteenth-century origins of Russian nationalism, see Hans Rogger's pioneering *National Consciousness in Eighteenth-Century Russia* (Cambridge, 1960).

109. Lomonosov, *Izbrannye*, vol. 2, pp. 66–72.

110. See, in particular, Nicholas V. Riasanovsky, *Nicholas I and Official Nationality in Russia, 1825–1855* (Berkeley, 1959), and Liah Greenfeld, *Nationalism: Five Roads to Modernity* (Cambridge, Mass., 1992), pp. 190–274.

111. "Foreigners at home, foreigners abroad, idle spectators, spoilt for Russia by Western prejudices and for the West by Russian habits." Alexander Herzen, *My Past and Thoughts* (Berkeley, 1982), p. 66.

·3·

Dov Yaroshevski

Empire and Citizenship

I

In a book published in 1910, former Russian war minister A. N. Kuropatkin retold how he had arrived in Ashkhabad as the newly appointed governor (*nachal'nik*) of the Transcaspian oblast' on 15 July 1890. There was much pomp and ceremony to greet the new governor. The script of the ceremony assigned a special role to the local population's delegations to Kuropatkin at the railway station platform. To his astonishment, recollects Kuropatkin, the first one who spoke to him was a wealthy Armenian merchant. Kuropatkin did not have an attentive ear for him. He vociferously interrupted the merchant's speech, and announced at the top of his lungs to the shocked gathering that the delegations should be rearranged. He put in the first row the delegation of modest Russian *meshchane* (town residents), in the second row the Turkmens and the Kirgiz. Then, according to hierarchy as he perceived it, came other imperial subjects—Christians (among them the delegation of Armenian merchants), non-Christians, and at the end the alien subjects, Persians, and Afghans.[1]

The reshuffling that took place at the Ashkhabad railway station obviously had a symbolic meaning for Kuropatkin. To understand it properly (as it may have made sense in 1890), we have to remember that Kuropatkin arrived as the first civil governor of the newly established Transcaspian oblast', six years after the final military conquest of Turkmenia. His arrival at this imperial outpost, staged as a solemn procession, itself was a mes-

Nicholas among the Natives
Photograph of Tsarevich Nicholas Aleksandrovich on a visit to Buriats, 1892
(Courtesy of Dov Yaroshevski)

sage of a new civil order which the empire brought to a country previously ravaged by disorder.

Kuropatkin may have been hostile toward the Armenian merchants participating in the ceremony, but I am inclined to think that he had another concern in mind, namely, imperial representation.[2] Kuropatkin's theatrics touched the deeper image of Russian domination. Instead of *obaianie russkogo imeni* (literally, "aura of the Russian name"), a metaphor which has been associated with the terror of Russian arms, conquest, and abuse, Kuropatkin proffers a new relationship—a partnership of Russians and the borderlands' native populations. What he signaled was that the public interest of empire, the public good of its entire population, will overrule parochialism and egoistic interests. From this time on, implied Kuropatkin, borderland society should be approached not in terms of visible power constellations, but rather in imagined terms of public good, which he, Kuropatkin, as the highest and legitimate representative of empire at this eastern outpost, established and which the residents should live by. These terms were well known to many Russians of the time as *grazhdanstvennost'* (citizenship). Kuropatkin's performance at the railway station platform should be seen as an introductory public lecture on this concept.

Citizenship is an ambiguous notion. Despite the ambiguity, however, throughout Western history it has served as a crucial and indispensable frame of reference. Going back to Aristotle and the Greek *polis*, citizenship represented citizens devoted to the civic ideal. Laden with universal meaning, the notion contributed to the development of a discourse on public and individual concerns, self-interest, and the public good. It spoke about altruism and purposeful service, and promoted the interests of groups. In various societies, competing public agencies disseminated disparate visions of citizenship and the criteria for receiving it.[3]

Citizenship in modern times has been seen, through liberal historical experience, as the assertion of individual rights, the allocation of entitlements, and the expansion of social positions of various groups previously excluded or marginalized in society. This view of citizenship deemphasizes the notions of civic commitment and moral public order; instead it stresses inviolable rights, limited state involvement in the affairs of individuals, and the consent of various groups and powers participating in public life.[4]

But there has always been another important kind of citizenship, namely, republican citizenship (in J. G. A. Pocock's sense).[5] It places in the foreground the value-oriented activity in joint endeavors of citizens striving for the good of each one and contributing to the good of others, and through this participation aiming at the well-being of the whole. It emphasizes a community of values shared by associations of citizens. One of the basic principles of this sort of citizenship is that private ends should be subjected to the public interest. This kind of perspective on citizenship is concerned with the public good, *res publica*, and therefore it was termed "republican." Republican citizenship highlights the public good as opposed to individual entitlements and views citizenship as virtue. It calls on every citizen to act in pursuit of the public good. For this perspective on citizenship, sociability and its construction and encouragement are a crucial dimension; a penchant for public interests is perceived as a virtue. It dismisses narrow local issues as parochialism and foregrounds national civil aims.

An important thread that winds through the story of republican citizenship is the idea of combating and overcoming corruption, understood as a lack of citizenship. It is a crucial reference point for viewing political and civil experience. The person introducing citizenship and promoting it, whether a legislator or a statesman, was held up as a living paradigm of virtue. Therefore the business of legislation has a central function in this kind of citizenship. Finally, through participation, civil obligations, and virtuous service, citizens and the society of citizens (civil society) become models for emulation for those who are still far from this affiliation.

For historians of imperial Russia, this perspective is like "an eccentric excursion into the byways of history."[6] Scholars have preferred to see citizenship in late imperial Russia through the contest between an autocratic repressive regime and emerging civil society—e.g., voluntary associations, local self-government (*zemstvo*), the middle class. This vista is complemented by a focus on the creation of, and conflict over, elementary civil rights by various deprived social groups (peasants, women, religious and ethnic minorities). Another privileged theme has been the narrative of the constitutional state, the rule of law, and social activism.[7] This attention toward mostly liberal approaches to citizenship does not leave room for research into a citizenship paradigm shared and disseminated by the autocratic state.

This chapter is an attempt to theorize republican citizenship in the Russian imperial milieu, and particularly to investigate how it was imagined, discussed, and enforced in the eastern borderlands. Its name in Russian was grazhdanstvennost'. This was a polysemic concept: it bore the meaning of citizenship as civic virtue, as civil society (community of citizens), civil order (as contrasted to a despotic regime), and a stage of social evolution (after family and clanship).

In Russian political thinking, the idea of citizenship developed in the century between 1767 and 1867. It grew out of the western European political tradition, and its first articulators, educated and privileged Russians, were a tiny group in a sea of voiceless imperial subjects. They perceived the nurturing of citizenship as a great and long crusade. Later, with the emancipation of the serfs, the idea of citizenship took the shape of a rejuvenated civil order, with networks of civil associations emerging through participation in self-government, and a reconstructed judicial system.

The appearance of grazhdanstvennost' coincided with the end of the eastward territorial expansion of imperial Russia. It became part of the search for new foundations of social control in the eastern parts of the empire. The limits of military repression became evident during the last stage of the Great Caucasian War. Therefore during the Great Reforms period there was a serious effort to conceive of an alternative strategy for the eastern borderlands. The grazhdanstvennost' option was discussed and elevated to the rank of imperial strategy, reified and reinforced through everyday politics in the borderlands—until the collapse of the empire in 1917.

In the eastern borderlands the strategy of citizenship took three basic directions: to undermine the kinship-based aristocracy, to promote local self-government, and to establish a reformed native court. The process of passage to citizenship in the borderlands was imagined as a kind of cultural revolution which would form a new social order and would turn rebellious natives into loyal citizens. With the introduction of the strategy of citizenship in the eastern borderlands after the 1860s, the Russian imperial establishment aimed at firmly reproducing their social power. What they created, however, was a rather precarious balance of negotiated power—of Russians and newly arranged native political elites. Thus the hoped-for cohesion of the empire on new bases was not realized, and the frustrated imperial officials had to continuously revise their politics and their vision-of-citizenship strategy.

II

Historically, the concept of republican citizenship—perceived vaguely as the citizen's contribution to the positive public good—served as a productive frame of reference for public discourse on governance in imperial Russia during the century between 1767 and 1867. This period can be divided into four stages: 1767–1800, 1801–1825, 1826–1855, and 1856–1867. The first stage sees the elaboration of the basic vocabulary of the relationship between the ruler and the imperial subjects. The second stage introduces basic semantic innovations and ties them to alternative political forms of governance in imperial Russia. The third stage witnesses a semantic proliferation accompanied by a cautious approach toward citizenship within the empire. Finally, the fourth stage redefines citizenship both semantically and politically and transforms it into one of the constituents of governance in post-reform Russia.

There was no other European country in the mid-eighteenth century so distant from the Aristotelian republic of citizens as the Russian Empire. In the citizenship vocabulary of the century, it could be equated with despotism and corruption.[8] But Catherine II's lasting fascination with legislation, in particular with Russia's spectacular Legislative Commission bringing together delegates of all races and ranks, and her endeavor to create status categories (estates) demonstrate that the concept of citizenship was familiar to the empress.[9] Beyond the imperial court, the image of the citizen and the idea of citizenship interested many Russians who were educated abroad and learned in the classics, and attracted foreign experts temporarily in Russian service.[10] Their views on the role, aim, and place of the citizen in Russia varied greatly, however.

For August Ludwig Schlözer, an outstanding representative of the German *Aufklärung* and a self-styled expert on government, statistics, and Russian history, the monarch was a demiurge and citizens constituted a non-entity, or in his metaphor, "the dead mass." In a panegyrical preface written in Moscow in 1767 for a book on Catherine's accomplishments, Schlözer compared Russia of the time to a huge machine which the empress puts into motion through her laws, while the dead mass is brought back to life and harnessed to the majestic machine.[11] Through this representation, Schlözer foregrounds the legislator (another standard theme of republican citizenship discourse) and relegates the citizens to the status of a working tool. Later he counsels the citizens that eventually they will become "enlightened, many, and laborious." Nevertheless, in his rhetoric on glory and the commonweal of empire, Schlözer places the citizens in a condition of subjugation to the ruler.

Another vantage point on the relationship between ruler and citizen is exhibited by two Russian writers of the late eighteenth century, V. Bestuzhev and I. Pnin. Instead of tools, they conceive of conscious and active citizens; everyone in his or her proper station possesses specific virtues. Their spotlight focuses on education. Both strongly distinguish between the member of civil society (*chelovek grazhdanstvennyi*) and natural man, and envisage the path to the construction of civil society (*zdanie grazhdanstvennoe*) through character-building, the nurturing of a virtuous person. In public educational institutions, civic lessons should be taught by moral overseers, stressing sacrifice for the public good and allegiance to civil society. The status of "citizen," in the eyes of both authors, is accorded a high level of prestige. "Once a man becomes citizen, citizen could not turn back into man," argues Pnin.[12]

Two other outstanding authors of the late eighteenth century, the conservative Shcherbatov and the radical Radishchev, focused the discourse of citizenship on civic virtue by vehemently attacking corruption in Russia. The former criticized the attitude of dignitaries toward the public, while the latter attacked the system of serfdom depriving the bulk of the population of citizenship.[13]

During the first quarter of the nineteenth century, both the vocabulary of citizenship and its political range of meaning became intelligible to broader circles of the educated public. A new verb, *grazhdanstvovat'*, was created by the poet Aleksandr Pushkin in 1825. The neologism did not become embedded in Russian. The many usages which Pushkin had in mind with this word can be inferred from the story of the word's invention.[14] It encompassed a wide range of problems expressed by the idea of citizenship, but characteristically referred to the notion of civic virtue (*grazhdanskoe muzhestvo*). It called for citizen defense of the public good and exposure of bias and arbitrariness in an autocratic regime.

The exemplar of such civic virtue in Russia of that time was the renowned statesman Admiral N. S. Mordvinov. His independent standing on imperial decisions, his struggle for the rule of law, and his compassion for human suffering earned him an outstanding reputation among educated Russians. Many poets dedicated odes to him.[15] In the eyes of his contemporaries, Mordvinov personified the ideal of republican citizenship.

Besides the literary neologism of Pushkin and the visual model of Mordvinov, the period made a breakthrough in both the substantive and semantic proliferation of the idea of citizenship. This proliferation should be credited to Nikolai Turgenev, a Russian political thinker. In 1819 he extended the meaning of the word *grazhdanstvennost'* to include an alternative social order to the existing autocratic regime in Russia, related it to western European categories of citizenship, and suggested by it the mechanisms of citizens' participation in governance.[16] Planning to establish a journal on contemporary political thought, Turgenev explicitly strove to turn the concept into an instrument of civic education. Turgenev's plan was not realized, he himself spent most of his life as an expatriate, and his works became known to Russians decades later. Still, one should not underrate his innovation. He gave shape to what was in the air and popular with Russian adherents of republican citizenship.[17]

In contrast to the first quarter of the nineteenth century, which put citizenship on the political agenda of the empire, the three decades of the reign of Nicholas I used republican citizenship in a pronounced conservative, even archaic, manner. The new *Zeitgeist* found expression in conflating the positions of state official and citizen, both being seen as overseers of lower orders.[18] At this time the peculiar German idiom *Staatsbürger* became the quintessential definition of the official Russian understanding of *grazhdanin*. It is no wonder that in such a setting the state appropriated for itself the right to teach citizenship and nurture the citizens.

From this perspective, citizenship-building was a long-range, controlled educational experiment, with a focus on the processes of selection, refining, and cohesion. Fears of the gradual amalgamation of existing ranks, nobles and masses, into a civil society, a society of citizens, emerged vividly in 1832 in a treatise by a Russian law professor, Fedor Moroshkin.[19] Moroshkin viewed pessimistically the mutual fusion of various social strata into a civil order of citizens. Particularly frightening to him was the absence of legal skills among the population. He focused on ordinary legal relationships to be constructed and learned by all members of civil society. The gulf in juridical-social perceptions dividing lower, middle, and upper classes was vast. Hence the process of enlarging their particularistic perspectives into a public one, pursuing the public good, would take, in his judgment, enormous time and effort.

This defeatist position notwithstanding, the government of Nicholas I undertook a number of practical steps toward public education in citizenship. Among them was the establishment of the Imperial School of Jurisprudence in St. Petersburg. Beginning with the introductory course on law, the students had to learn the six pillars of the Russian imperial citizenship catechism: obeying the government and following the laws, refraining from injuring citizens' welfare, pursuing the state's glory and commonweal, actively participating in the moral and intellectual advance of society, respecting the church, and being ready to sacrifice one's life for the state.[20] Upon graduating from the school, future legal officials and judges were to commit themselves to the observance of justice in society and the rights of state citizens. The school's ethos turned the graduates into living examples and role models to be emulated.[21] The moral power radiated by these "monuments of virtue"[22] was expected to contribute to the regeneration of Russia (another standard theme in the discourse on republican citizenship).

The first decade of the reign of Alexander II produced a major change in the official Russian approach to citizenship. The previous paternalistic approach, based on ideas of living models and guidance, was abandoned. Instead, a new pedagogy emerged, which proclaimed that citizenship should emerge from the people's participation in new public institutions, such as local self-government and the reformed court. Many ideas, borrowed from western European experience, that had been censored and silenced for decades reappeared and became prominent in public debates in the period between 1856 and 1867. The very term *grazhdanstvennost'* symbolized the new civil order in its many connotations. Toward the mid-1860s, many visions of republican citizenship, notably the civic ideal and civil society as well as more traditional representations of citizens' duties and public good, became firmly entrenched in Russian political thinking.

III

The brief survey of Russian ideas of citizenship during the period between 1767 and 1867 serves as the background for a discussion of how the idea of citizenship was applied to imperial eastern borderlands. This story covers the same period of time with basically the same division into four stages. However, in contrast to the Russian capitals, where the principal theme was the relationship between governance and citizenship, borderlands debates centered more upon governance and law formation.

The origins of the Russian imperial perspective on citizenship go back to the eighteenth century and Catherine II's interest in empire, specifically her dream of giving laws to various tribes on the eastern frontier. Her approach was certainly a blend of ancient examples and the contemporary teaching of great legal theorists whom Catherine admired and from whom she diligently borrowed for her great legislative projects. The aim of this approach was formulated in a typically Enlightenment style. In the words of a Moscow law professor lecturing on Montesquieu in French in 1782:

> On croit enfin qu'il est plus beau de civiliser, de policer, de cultiver et de peupler une province, que d'exterminer les paisibles habitants d'un empire et de les détruire par le fer et le feu.[23]
>
> [We believe it better to spread civilization, public order, and culture, and to settle a province, than to exterminate the peaceful inhabitants of an empire and to destroy them by fire and sword.]

Derzhavin's metaphor of Empress Catherine as a Kirgiz-Kaisak princess duly glorifies Catherine's involvement in the governance of the eastern borderlands. For three decades, by exchanging views with her proconsuls, reading reports, and meeting with native delegations, Catherine acquired an impressive command of matters relating to the governance of nomadic peoples. She firmly supported Orenburg governor O. I. Igel'strom (1784–92) in his pioneering effort to create special district courts and to build mosques for the Kirgiz and thus to prepare them to become loyal, obedient imperial subjects. But to pursue this goal was less difficult than to change the attitudes of Russian frontier commanders and the population toward the nomads. Here Igel'strom and Catherine touched what in the citizenship vocabulary of the eighteenth century was called despotism—vested interests of frontier Russians who lived by plundering the nomads. These people preferred their everyday practices to the newly proclaimed humanitarian approach. Catherine and her governors felt optimistic over the long-range prospects of incorporating the nomads into the empire, but saw the major handicap for this strategy in the contemporary frontier conflict among Russians themselves.[24] Thus the ideal and the problems of establishing a new humanitarian governance were passed to new generations of imperial administrators.

Early in the next century, the protostrategy of citizenship for imperial eastern borderlands was established. Two Russian statesman can be credited with this breakthrough—M. Speranskii and V. F. Timkovskii. It is important for our discussion to note that the goal of Speranskii's service as governor-general of Siberia was to solve the problem of corruption in local government.[25] As mentioned above, the vocabulary of the time defined corruption as a lack of citizenship. The pursuit of public good for all Siberian residents, including the native residents, was the leitmotif of Speranskii's reforming activity in this borderland.

Timkovskii is less well known.[26] He was the director of the Orenburg Border Commission (the Ministry of Foreign Affairs' administrative body for relations with eastern borderland tribes) from 1819 through 1821. His family and educational background, literary and public pursuits, and administrative expertise in dealing with nomadic peoples made him one of the most educated and capable officials in imperial Russia during the first quarter of the nineteenth century.[27] A salient fact for our discussion was his position as special assistant to Admiral Mordvinov in the latter's capacity as chairman of the Department of State Economy in the imperial State Council. His work under the guidance of the man turned into an icon of civic virtue by his contemporaries made a deep mark on Timkovskii. He was well prepared to propose explicitly the idea of a citizenship strategy for the Kirgiz.

Speranskii and Timkovskii assaulted the traditional principle of governance that they judged prevalent in the borderlands, namely, the policy of repression and bureaucratic controls. The most flagrant result of such a strategy, according to Timkovskii, was the failure of Russians after ninety years to integrate the Kirgiz Steppe into the empire. Instead of this approach, both statesmen hoped to strengthen civic well-being through lawgiving, thus strengthening the cohesion of the empire. In this they were close to and at the same time distant from Catherine the Great. The eighteenth-century idea of universal lawgiving was specified by Speranskii and Timkovskii in two proposals. Aware of the chasm between imperial (seen as universal) and nomadic (seen as particularistic) juridical mindsets, Speranskii aspired to bridge this gulf in the long term, ordering the study and codification of native customary law. Timkovskii intended to bring the Kirgiz directly under Russian imperial law, made intelligible to them by translation into their vernacular.[28] Timkovskii's proposal was never realized, and Speranskii's was abandoned after two decades of inquiry and debate.[29]

Still, the assessment of the efforts of both awaits research. Speranskii and Timkovskii dealt with the problem of reception by nomadic peoples of law from a foreign lawgiver—one of the central topics in the discourse on citizenship. Timkovskii was traditional. Speranskii went a step further, paying attention to native customary law and thus opening a long, fruitful, yet painful Russian debate on the subject. What is most important for this chapter, however, is that the ideas of Speranskii and Timkovskii, refuted by many of their contemporaries[30] and relegated by historians to the archival dustbin, nevertheless contributed to new ways of knowing about governance in eastern borderlands.

This study was part of a legal discipline called Encyclopedia of Law, intended to be the general compendium of information about law and society. While in western Europe the courses and textbooks of the Encyclopedia of Law were known from late medieval times, they entered Russian educational institutions only at the end of the eighteenth century and bore a strong resemblance to those being taught in Germany at the time. The first Russian textbook for the discipline was written by Professor Nevolin.[31] It was published in 1839, becoming the standard textbook for students for sixty years.[32] The fundamentals of law as explained by Nevolin were considered a kind of legal canon in Russia.[33]

The theory of social evolution in this legal canon postulated that various forms of law formation corresponded to four stages of social evolution: family, kinship, civil society, state. The scheme was firmly entrenched within Aristotelian philosophy, medieval and Renaissance treatises, and Enlightenment doctrine. Nevolin's debt to this tradition appears in his reference to sources: "All existing treatises under various titles in which the history of gradual building of societies in humankind is elucidated." He specifically credited Hegel's *Grundlinien der Philosophie des Rechts*.[34] The most salient element in this theory was the strong dividing line between the states of family/kinship and civil society. They were placed in rather different historical planes, with family and kinship considered as belonging to the historical past and civil society to the historical present.

The central place in this theory was occupied by the concept of civil society, or community of citizens, based on contractual relationships, institution of property, and associations of citizens. Civil society related to the state. Sometimes the terms were used interchangeably, but the state symbolized elaborate governmental power, whereas the civil society was not in need of it. Civil society came to be seen as the defender of the public good from the interference of wicked private interests. Society was composed of a variety of territorial, hierarchical, and moral/religious associations. The membership in associations (collective persons) in this vision does not interfere with the membership in greater society—civil society— but rather they complement one another in pursuit of the public good. Within the general process of growing sociability (obshchezhitie), civil (or political) society turns into the articulator of public values. Civil society was viewed as a dynamic organization, with quickly developing relations. In a word, it was a progressive society, distinguished from earlier stages of family and kinship where prevalent customs slowed their evolution. Civil society was the ideal human order, with a hierarchical network of social status and deeply internalized attitudes toward obligations and duties. Participation in civil society brought with it emancipation from dependency upon earlier societal forms and therefore from the burden of custom and corruption.

The most crisis-ridden, problematic, and disruptive site on the ladder of social forms was considered the transition from the nomadic stage (kinship) to civil society. For Nevolin, the transition from stateless forms to state structure was aggravated by a blatant lack in the lower stages of the "genuine concept of honor," the rule of arbitrariness, and the lack of firm precepts of behavior. Therefore, those involved in planning the transition had to be acutely aware of the constraints on tribes' ability to civilize. To shed the skin given by nature, one should proceed either slowly or quickly, depending on the specific situation, but one must never forget that those resisting might meet an unpleasant end. Every lower social stage has in it seeds of higher formation, but the way to the top of the hill is long and stressful. Therefore, even limited participation in progressive societies enables those belonging to lower forms to climb the slope more quickly and thus to advance into the civil society.

This social theory formulated explicitly the task of "higher" societies to impose their authority upon lower forms. It broke the ground for social change legitimized by reference to laws of social evolution. It identified the imperial "other"—the borderland native peoples belonging to societies which should be changed in accordance with the theory of social evolution.

The principal ideas of this theory became popular among the reformers of the 1860s. When speaking of the Great Reforms, historians traditionally mean the emancipation of the peasantry, the promulgation of local self-government, and the introduction of a reformed judicial system. This list should be complemented by another central but still overlooked reform, namely, the introduction of the citizenship strategy on the eastern border-lands.

As is often the case with reforms, the introduction of citizenship in eastern borderland policy was a corollary of certain other processes. Along with the serfs in pre-reform Russia, a deprived social stratum was the military estate, in particular military settlers and irregular military forces (Cossack hosts). With the latter served many nomadic tribes, the most visible among them the Bashkirs. Notorious in Russian imperial history for their savage resistance to Russian conquest, the Bashkirs succeeded in negotiating for themselves the status of a distinct military force, known from 1798 as the Bashkir Host. In 1832, Speranskii placed them (in the ninth volume of the Digest of Laws) in the category of rural citizens, but this remained so only on paper.

After the Crimean War, the reform of the imperial army brought the proposal to abolish all irregular forces. The Bashkirs were named as the first candidates for transition to the status of free rural citizens. This change in the Bashkir social position was reflected in some Russian official documents. The Bashkir Statute of 1865 spelled out the integration of the Bashkirs into the regular civil order, with detailed presentation of Bashkir duties and obligations, and rural self-government very much akin to that of the Russian peasantry. (Later the 1865 statute was incorporated as a chapter into a Legislative Collection on Rural Citizenship.)[35] However, the most startling document crowning the Bashkir reform was issued on 2 April 1867. This was imperial decree number 44424a, prepared by the War Ministry, entitled "On the prohibition to grant military awards and ranks to Bashkirs, the Kirgiz, Kalmyks, and other *inorodtsy* tribes."[36] The decree stated that granting military awards and ranks to Asians of a low degree of citizenship (grazhdanstvennost') reinforced their warlike inclinations. This practice was injurious to the empire and to these peoples, since the government must strive to accustom these peoples to peaceful life and civil development. Therefore it was decided to abandon the practice of rewarding Asians with military medallions and ranks (except those serving in the army).[37]

The man who stood behind this salient document was the war minister himself, D. A. Miliutin. Miliutin was a veteran of Caucasian colonial wars and showed a deep interest in the strategy of imperial conquest and colonization. He belonged to the group of outstanding personalities in the Great Reforms. Furthermore—and this is of central importance—Miliutin, in a general statement made in the mid-1860s, explicitly endorsed the policy that to achieve the cohesion of various parts of the empire and the equality of its members, the government must strip the borderland elites of their privileges.[38]

That the wording of decree number 44424a has a bizarre flavor is no wonder. Russian legal experts serving in various ministries during the 1860s were recruited from former law students who had studied the Encyclopedia of Law. The scheme of social evolution from Nevolin's textbook was a catechism for them, and the editing of the decree suggests that its writers shared this worldview. The decree technically and symbolically denied governmental support to kinship aristocracy (who had previously served as a Russian ally in the borderlands) and invited those in the imperial periphery into the construction of new social structures and citizenship. This was a public rewriting of previous imperial texts and a formal sanction for a new policy in the borderlands.

IV

Tsarist plans for putting the theory of citizenship into practice among eastern subjects aimed at creating new institutions exercising a sort of paternalistic guidance. Once the despotic clanship elite lost influence, the institutions of new self-government would protect the masses, the weak, and the oppressed, and the reformed courts would be the guardian of the new order. This new kind of paternalism was radically different from the paternalism of Speranskii's Siberian Statute of 1822. Then, the natives were to be protected by officials; after the 1860s they were protected by institutions. During his study trip to the Kirgiz Steppe, Colonel A. K. Geins, later a close aide to Turkestan's first governor-general, K. von Kaufman, explicitly dismissed in a diary entry in 1865 Speranskii's attitude toward the natives. The note of imperial guardianship sounded in Speranskii's reforms was too loud for Geins.[39]

During the period 1868–1917, the policy of citizenship took shape sporadically on all five eastern borderlands of the empire: the Steppe krai, the Turkestan krai, Siberia, the Caucasus, and the protectorates of Bukhara and Khiva. The earliest and longest experiment began in the Kirgiz Steppe with the Temporary Statute of 1868; the second great experiment was embarked upon in 1897 in Transbaikal oblast', where imperial authorities launched sweeping land and administrative reforms for Buriats.[40] In 1910, the Ministry of Interior announced plans to extend similar policies in citizenship to other eastern borderlands.[41]

When put into practice, however, the strategy of citizenship turned into a negotiation for power with the natives' leaders. The natives succeeded in incorporating the Russian policy into their traditional political routines. Through power negotiations the natives demonstrated that they were able to create a revised political balance on the local level and in many cases to redefine Russian proposals to their benefit. The Russian planners of citizenship policy hoped that their innovations would lead to support for the imperial endeavor. Instead they were faced many times with popular mobilization for local aims. Thus the implementation of the citizenship policy turned into a sequence of ongoing Russian-native contests for legitimation. I would like to discuss here three cases of this power negotiation: the existence of a political machine, mobilization of financial resources for political aims, and coalition-building, as they became evident in Kirgiz and Buriat administrative reforms promoting citizenship.

The Temporary Statute of 1868 established territorial divisions in the Kirgiz Steppe in *volosti* whose borders overlapped individual kinship groups. Once every three years the populace of volosti had to elect native officeholders, in particular volost' elders. The Russians hoped that the new election system would promote citizenship by undermining traditional kinship elders and promoting new leaders. But all Russian observers of the Kirgiz Steppe from 1868 through 1917 accused the electoral system of fomenting continuous "party strife." They argued that local elections, beyond the control of clan elders, produced graft, bribes, and kickbacks. Supporters of competing candidates bought votes and extorted support, at times by threats and terror. Tsarist officials searched hard for a remedy. They located the source of vice, in accordance with prevailing economic views of the time, in the Kirgiz moneyed class. The "haves" and their henchmen, according to this argument, dominated elections and oppressed the populace. In 1910, the chairman of the Council of Ministers (and minister of the interior), P. A. Stolypin, proposed to deprive the volost' elder of economic influence by stripping him of his right to collect taxes. Stolypin wanted to leave him as administrative officer and to pass economic power and responsibilities for tax collection to the village community (*aul*).[42] Thus the public good would finally overrule self-interest.

But this widespread Russian view was challenged by another, more convincing political interpretation. It came from the ethnographer Divaev, an expert on Kirgiz everyday life. According to Divaev, the linchpin of the Kirgiz political system created after the 1868 reforms were the *atkamnary* (literally, "horsemen"), whom Divaev defined as "influential and respected Kirgiz, electoral activists for a candidate for native office." The atkamnary performed four roles in Kirgiz political life. They were electoral activists in elections of native officeholders; brokers between the officeholder and the constituency particularly active in providing means to reimburse election expenses of the officeholder; tax collectors; and agents who could arrange the dismissal of undesirable officeholders.[43]

The most accurate modern political term with which to label the networks of atkamnary in the Kirgiz Steppe is "political machine." Actually, these networks, organized among low- and middle-level officeholders, were the basic force behind the election machinations. They selected candidates, enlisted support in exchange for money, and performed risky orders. After the elections this machine worked for the officeholder, but if he did not satisfy the atkamnary for any reason, they were able to topple him.

What we observe here is actually the byproduct of the Russian citizenship program. Hoping to reinforce their power in the steppe, Russians created an electoral system which was redefined and rebuilt by Kirgiz political actors. Inventive native accommodation to the Russian proposals broke Russian attempts to intervene in local affairs and protected Kirgiz-Russian political negotiations and the sharing of power in the steppe. The Russians acquiesced in this balance until 1917.

While the Kirgiz used a sort of party machine in dealings with the Russians, the Buriat tactic was to disable the Russian citizenship drive by a system of "invisible taxes" (*temnye sbory*), or unauthorized mobilization of financial resources for what they saw as the public good. This was the traditional practice of Buriat kinship leaders in their dealings with Russian overlords. They raised money from tribesmen for bribing Russian officials, covered expenses of Buriat delegates in imperial and provincial capitals, and rewarded envoys for efforts on behalf of the public. We do know about conflicts which the Buriat delegates won by this tactic. In the 1880s they succeeded in annulling the Russian proposal for military conscription of their young men; in those years they also received a certificate from the tsar confirming their possession of certain agricultural lands.[44] In their visits to St. Petersburg, Buriat delegates benefited from support extended to them by their compatriot P. A. Badmaev, who was a graduate of St. Petersburg University, for a time an official at the Russian Ministry of Foreign Affairs, and a popular practitioner of Tibetan medicine. Badmaev had access to the tsar's family and considered himself the patron of the Buriats.

The Buriats again used their method of secret taxes and delegates to cope with Russian interference in their affairs during the fateful period 1897–1907. The tsarist administration prepared and enacted in those years new land and administrative statutes for the Buriats which degraded the status of the kinship's elite and introduced a new administrative-territorial framework. The Russians pursued this legislative work on changes for Transbaikal oblast' without consulting the Buriats.[45] State Secretary A. N. Kulomzin, director of the legislative task force, thought this procedure normal. The Buriats thought otherwise. They challenged the Russians by sending a delegation to St. Petersburg to watch the activities of Kulomzin's staff, and published a book on their problems which they passed to the tsar.[46] One group of Buriat delegates transmitted a supplication to the tsar at Livadiia Palace in Crimea in October 1902, and another group of ten delegates met Nicholas II in Livadiia in November of 1902.[47] These attempts by the Buriats to negotiate power with their tsarist rulers infuriated

Russian officials, who saw themselves as champions of citizenship for ignorant and ungrateful clients. They responded with a vehement verbal onslaught against the corrupt Buriat practice of secret taxes. Russian protests and Buriat bribes persisted until 1917.

In this power contest both Russians and natives were in need of and built coalitions that were sometimes unusual. In one case, M. Krol', a populist revolutionary exiled to Siberia, turned into an enthusiastic ethnographer of the Buriats and a collaborator in tsarist intervention in Buriat affairs. This democratic ethnographer took part actively in local reforms. State Secretary Kulomzin personally invited Krol' to work as part of his staff. The views held by Krol' on the disarray of kinship and the transformation of landholding patterns served as a basis for the later imperial attack on land and administrative traditions of Buriats. His conclusions were received angrily by educated Buriats.[48]

But no less bizarre coalitions emerged on the other side as well. Trying to preserve the old administrative order, the kinship leaders cooperated with Prince E. Ukhtomskii, who was sympathetic to the Buriats as well as a proponent of Russian expansion. In addition, they used in their defense the theory extolling the nomadic way of life developed by another exiled populist revolutionary, Dimitri Klements.[49]

The imperial bureaucrats believed that they could strengthen the empire on its eastern borderlands through citizenship policies. Instead they had to share power with networks of native leaders and contend with pervasive resistance. This was a disturbing experience for the Russians. The citizenship policy, the goal of which was to ensure tsarist hegemony, turned into a trial of strength, producing compromise and an occasional defeat. This precarious balance between the very unequal sides permits us to evaluate the disparaging Russian references to lower civic awareness (grazhdanstvennost') among the natives. They appear rather a coded acknowledgment of tsarist agreement, often under pressure and always reluctantly, to negotiate with the natives. As a result of this negotiation there emerged a certain institutional syncretism between Russian and native elites. The lofty dream of citizenship was absorbed into party machines and secret taxes.

V

This chapter on citizenship in the eastern borderlands would be incomplete without presenting the changes which took place within the very concept of citizenship in the first decade of the twentieth century. The citizenship policy was formed in the 1860s by state officials when the ideals of state and civil society in Russia were still unseparated in the public mind. By the end of the century, when Russia was undergoing social restructuring and economic development, there emerged a new concept of civil society as divorced from the state (referred to as *obsh-chestvennost'*).[50] Those who spoke for civil society defended for the first time in modern Russian history the right to articulate what was the public good of Russia. This pretension became obvious following the 1905 Russian revolution with the establishment of the State Duma and of political parties stating national priorities for Russia in their programs and public activity. Specifically it related to ways in which citizenship would be created in the Russian countryside.

While the members of this civil society supported the vision of citizenship proclaimed in the 1860s (institutions of self-government and courts will teach the people how to become citizens), the state bureaucracy inclined in the early twentieth century to another view. It denied the right of civil society to articulate the vision of Russian public good, claiming that power for itself. This approach was termed by Russian nationalist politicians the statist attitude (*gosudarstvennost'*).[51]

This statist attitude was an important factor in transforming the ideal of republican citizenship in late imperial Russia. As expressed by P. A. Stolypin in 1909, it was summed up in a catchword: "First citizen and then citizenship."[52] Stolypin indicated that the agrarian reform promoted by the government would in the end establish a vigorous stratum of farmers who would be the citizens of the empire loyal to the state, and only then would new civil institutions and arrangements work efficiently in Russia.

The emphasis on the citizen-citizenship relationship had serious repercussions for citizenship-building in the eastern borderlands. First, it led to the state's pronounced disregard of natives' civic activities, which grew spectacularly during 1904–1906. Secondly, the state insisted on its exclusive privilege to define policies in the borderlands without consulting the native leaders, whose representation was drastically cut in the State Duma. Promoting the idea of agrarian reform, the state bureaucracy firmly supported resettlement by European peasants in the eastern borderlands and promoted the settler as a prospective model citizen among the natives.[53] The state supported the idea of local self-government in the borderlands, but pursued this policy cautiously. The statist vision of citizenship was halted by World War I and then was suspended entirely by the revolutions of 1917.

Two chapters in this volume, Austin Jersild's and my own, address independently the definitions and practices of citizenship in Russian imperial borderlands. Comparison of these two chapters highlights both the differences in our respective ways of looking at the concept's definitions, and our complementary ideas about its practices. The discrepancy generated by the two chapters is epistemological in origin. While I have tried in my research to pinpoint the basic semantic and institutional fields in the formation of the specifically Russian notion of grazhdanstvennost', and thus followed its historical transformations and shifting meanings, Jersild worked with the prevalent explanation offered by the lexicographer Dal', which itself turned out to be only one—albeit influential—step in the concept's evolution. Moreover, I sharpened my focus on the very idiosyncratic Russian application of ideas of republican citizenship to the imperial milieu, which seems obviously confusing and is seldom encountered. But this allowed me to draw a distinction between such basic elements of the concept as its underlying social evolutionary scheme and the heavy stress on the idea of the public good.[54]

In contrast to my view, Jersild holds to a more customary, modern liberal vision of citizenship. This is revealed particularly in his ascription to Russian imperial officials and educated society of the hope for "a society without estates." In my opinion, this could be considered another liberal bias. As I perceive the basic contours of Russian bureaucratic political discourse on citizenship, it was inclined, in the late imperial period, to borrow from the liberal vocabulary, and particularly with regard to civil rights.

Concerning imperial practices of citizenship, we both delineate three basic dimensions of the grazhdanstvennost' program in the borderlands: identity-building, construction of public space, and the gospel of empire. Elaborating on the imperial vocabulary of virtue, duty, obligation, taxes, service, and so forth, we both have noted its crucial meaning: creation, dissemination, and inculcation of the identity of the loyal imperial citizen without sovereignty; the citizen excelling in the performance of his obligations toward the empire and autocracy. This is why the words "citizen" and "subject" may still appear in our texts interchangeably.

Describing the process of embedding citizenship in the imperial borderlands, we both stress that the authorities directed most of their efforts to the construction of cultural/social artifacts: theaters, courts, alphabets, religious books, self-government, schools, and so forth. These were novelties in the borderlands. Following Habermas, this newly established sphere may be called "the imperial public sphere," and it may be considered one of the greatest achievements of the Russian imperial grazhdanstvennost' project. This "universal" public space was depicted as radically contrasting with "particularistic" native society, and the transition from the latter to the former was conceived as a great social ascent.

Finally, as the third common theme, both chapters mention the concept of grazhdanstvennost' as the gospel of the empire, as its promise, as an ideological project, and as an imperial idea. It was represented as a noble goal and served as a prescription for proper social and cultural behavior for imperial citizens-subjects.

This inquiry into citizenship invites some general remarks on Russian imperial history. Michael Khodarkovsky's chapter, "Ignoble Savages and Unfaithful Subjects: Constructing Non-Christian Identities in Early Modern Russia," demonstrates the pattern of imperial identity-building grounded in ethnolinguistic, economic, and religious criteria. My research brings to the fore a radically different ideal of identity-building in imperial Russia, one founded on an abstract social evolutionary scheme. Seen in historical perspective, the patterns complement one another and form a new and interesting perspective on the connections in Russian building of empire and identity. In addition, the research opens an intriguing insight into parallels between constructing citizenship for nomadic populations of the empire and Russian peasantry. Previously, the research on these two social agglomerates of empire was done separately. The citizenship theme points for the first time to comparative history of the two, both chronologically and thematically.

NOTES

I would like to thank Dan Brower for his comments on an earlier draft of this chapter, and particularly for his proposal to change the title of the chapter to "Empire and Citizenship." The insightful suggestions of two anonymous readers helped greatly in the final revision. The continuous *Auseinandersetzung* with Austin Jersild's chapter in this volume substantially contributed to the formulation of my own ideas on citizenship, and for that I want to express my gratitude.

1. A. N. Kuropatkin, *Zadachi Russkoi armii,* vol. 2 (St. Petersburg, 1910), p. 124.

2. Ronald G. Suny, "Images of Armenians in the Russian Empire," in Richard G. Hovannisian, ed., *The Armenian Image in History and Literature* (Malibu, Calif., 1981), pp. 105–137.

3. For general background on the concept of citizenship, I am indebted to the following works: Paul Barry Clarke, *Citizenship: A Reader* (London, 1994); Peter Riesenberg, *Citizenship in the Western Tradition* (Chapel Hill, 1992); and Derek Heather, *Citizenship: The Civic Ideal in World History, Politics, and Education* (London, 1990).

4. Geoff Andrews, ed., *Citizenship* (London, 1991); Ursula Vogel and Michael Moran, eds., *The Frontiers of Citizenship* (New York, 1991); Bart van Steenbergen, ed., *The Condition of Citizenship* (London, 1994); Ralf Dahrendorf, *The Modern Social Conflict* (Berkeley, 1990), pp. 29–35.

5. J. G. A. Pocock, *The Machiavellian Moment* (Princeton, 1975). Pocock's book and Isaac Kramnick's article "Republican Revisionism Revisited," *The American Historical Review* 87, no. 3 (1982): 629–664, were crucial in forming my approach toward the notion of citizenship in imperial Russia.

6. This is a paraphrase of a sentence from the preface to Olga Crisp and Linda Edmondson, eds., *Civil Rights in Imperial Russia* (Oxford, 1989), p. vi.

7. Jacob Walkin, *The Rise of Democracy in Pre-revolutionary Russia* (London, 1963); Crisp and Edmondson, *Civil Rights in Imperial Russia*; Thomas S. Pearson, *Russian Officialdom in Crisis: Autocracy and Local Self-Government, 1861–1900* (Cambridge, Mass., 1989); Francis William Wcislo, *Reforming Rural Russia* (Princeton, 1990); Edith W. Clowes, Samuel D. Kassow, and James L. West, eds., *Between Tsar and People* (Princeton, 1991); Robert Philippot, *Société civile et état bureaucratique dans la Russie Tsarist: Les Zemstvos* (Paris, 1991); and G. M. Hamburg, *Boris Chicherin and Early Russian Liberalism, 1826–1866* (Stanford, 1992).

8. John Keane, "Despotism and Democracy: The Origins and Development of

the Distinction between Civil Society and the State, 1750–1850," in John Keane, ed., *Civil Society and the State* (London, 1988; reprint, 1993), pp. 35–69.

9. David M. Griffiths, "Catherine II: The Republican Empress," *Jahrbücher für Geschichte Osteuropas* 21 (1973): 323–344.

10. Marinus A. Wes, *Classics in Russia, 1700–1855* (Leiden, 1992).

11. August Ludwig Schlözer's introduction to the second edition of *Neuverändertes Russland* (Riga, 1769).

12. *Russkie prosvetiteli (ot Radishcheva do dekabristov)* (Moscow, 1966), vol. 1, p. 185.

13. M. M. Shcherbatov, "Pis'mo k vel'mozham, praviteliam gosudarstva," *Russkaia starina* 5 (1872): 3–15; A. N. Radishchev, "Puteshestvie iz Peterburga v Moskvu," in *Polnoe sobranie sochinenii* (Moscow, 1938), vol. 1, p. 315.

14. Introduction by A. G. Tseitlin to K. F. Ryleev, *Polnoe sobranie sochinenii* (Moscow, 1934), p. 53.

15. I know of at least four eulogies dedicated to Mordvinov, written by K. Ryleev, P. Pletnev, V. Petrov, and A. Pushkin. The title of Ryleev's was "Civic Virtue," the title of Pletnev's, "Citizen's Duty."

16. *Arkhiv brat'ev Turgenevykh* (Petrograd, 1921), vol. 5, p. 375. On the importance of Turgenev's ideas for the Great Reforms of the 1860s, see V. I. Semevskii, "Nikolai Ivanovich Turgenev," in S. A. Vengerov, ed., *Glavnye deiateli osvobozhdeniia krest'ian* (St. Petersburg, 1903), pp. 39–43.

17. Let us not forget that the radical Decembrist ideologue Colonel P. I. Pestel', by a stroke of a pen, transformed millions of voiceless imperial subjects into full-fledged citizens of free Russia in his constitutional project "Russkaia Pravda." Cf. *Izbrannye sotsial'no-politicheskie i filosofskie proizvedeniia dekabristov* (Moscow, 1957), vol. 2, pp. 131–133.

18. Thus argued P. Guliaev in the book *Rights and Duties of City and Land Police, As Well As of All Inhabitants of the Russian State in Accordance to Their Statuses.* Quoted in a review article by I. Tarasov, "Police Law," *Sbornik gosudarstvennykh znanii* 8 (1880): 13.

19. Fedor Moroshkin, *O postepennom obrazovanii zakonodatel'stv rassuzhdeniia* (Moscow, 1832).

20. P. A. Stöckhardt, *Iuridicheskii propovednik* (St. Petersburg, 1843), chap. 1, sections 7 and 19.

21. On the ethos of students of the Imperial School of Jurisprudence, see Richard S. Wortman, *The Development of Russian Legal Consciousness* (Chicago, 1976).

22. This term was coined by Professor P. A. Stöckhardt in 1836 when he called upon the students of the St. Petersburg Imperial School of Jurisprudence to serve as examples of citizenship. See Stöckhardt, *Iuridicheskii propovednik*, vol. 3.

23. I. Schneider, *Discours sur l'esprit des loix de M. de Montesquieu* (Moscow, 1782), p. 1 verso.

24. Dov B. Yaroshevski, "Attitudes toward the Nomads of the Russian Empire under Catherine the Great," in A. G. Cross and G. S. Smith, eds., *Literature, Lives, and Legality in Catherine's Russia* (Nottingham, 1994), p. 23.

25. On Speranskii's war against corruption in Siberia, see specifically W. Bruce Lincoln, *The Conquest of a Continent: Siberia and the Russians* (New York, 1994), pp. 156–161, based on Marc Raeff's *Siberia and the Reforms of 1822* (Seattle, 1956).

26. On him, see L. A. Sheiman, "Vasilii Timkovskii, dekabristy, Pushkin," *Voprosy prepodavaniia russkogo iazyka v kirgizskoi shkole* 2 (1969): 126–194.

27. On the five brothers Timkovskii, their upbringing and careers, cf. *Russkii biograficheskii slovar'*, vol. 20, pp. 520–529.

28. Timkovskii to the Ministry of Foreign Affairs, October 1820 (Russkii gosudarstvennyi istoricheskii arkhiv, abbrev. RGIA, f. 1291, op. 81, d. 73, l. 89).

29. Minutes of the Siberian Committee, 29 March and 10 April 1837, RGIA, f. 1251, op. 1, d. 171, ll. 12–14; Memorandum of Baron Korf, 20 June 1848, RGIA, f. 1149, op. 3 (1847), d. 68, ll. 2–24.

30. Director of the Asian Department, Ministry of Foreign Affairs, to the Orenburg Governor-General, 29 March 1831, RGIA, f. 1291, op. 81 (1830), d. 134, ll. 1–2.

31. On K. A. Nevolin (1806–1855), see *Russkii biograficheskii slovar'*, vol. 11, pp. 179–180.

32. This is told in N. K. Rennenkampf, *Iuridicheskaia entsiklopediia*, 2nd ed. (Kiev, 1898), p. 16.

33. The basic compendiums on Encyclopedia of Law in imperial Russia were as follows: L. Tsvetaev, *Nachertanie teorii zakonov* (Moscow, 1816); K. A. Nevolin, "Entsiklopediia zakonovedeniia" (1839), in idem, *Polnoe sobranie sochinenii* (St. Petersburg, 1857), vol. 1; Stöckhardt, *Iuridicheskii propovednik*; M. Speranskii, *Rukovodstvo k poznaniiu zakonov* (St. Petersburg, 1845); N. Rozhdestvenskii, *Entsiklopediia zakonovedeniia* (St. Petersburg, 1863); M. Kapustin, *Teoriia prava* (Moscow, 1868); N. Rennenkampf, *Ocherki iuridicheskoi entsiklopedii* (Kiev, 1868); P. Karasevich, *Programma lektsii po predmetu entsiklopedii prava* (1874); N. Korkunov, *Entsiklopediia* (1878); E. Trubetskoi, *Lektsii po entsiklopedii prava* (Moscow, 1917).

34. Nevolin, "Entsiklopediia zakonovedeniia," p. 53.

35. *PSZ*, Second Series, vol. 38 (1869), no. 39662; *PSZ*, Second Series, vol. 40 (1865), no. 42282; Robert F. Bauman, "Subject Nationalities in the Military Service of Imperial Russia: The Case of the Bashkirs," *Slavic Review* 46, nos. 3–4 (1987): 489–502; and Robert H. McNeil, *Tsar and Cossack, 1855–1914* (London, 1987), pp. 26–33.

36. Military ranks were normally granted by imperial authorities to produce a conspicuous tribal aristocracy. Cf. the hierarchy built in the Kirgiz Steppe: senior sultans; then tribal elders with officers' ranks; then officials without officers' ranks.

37. Cf. the Russian translation of Henry Thomas Buckle's *History of Civilization in England* (St. Petersburg, 1863), vol. 1, pp. 221–222.

38. P. A. Zaionchkovskii, "Biograficheskii ocherk," in *Dnevnik D. A. Miliutina*, vol. 1 (Moscow, 1947), p. 32; and W. Bruce Lincoln, "D. A. Miliutin's Views on Russia and Reform," in D. A. Miliutin, *Vospominaniia* (Tomsk, 1919; reprint, Newtonville, Mass., 1979), pp. 1–14.

39. A. K. Geins, *Sobranie literaturnykh trudov* (St. Petersburg, 1897), vol. 1, p. 209.

40. Cf. survey in N. P. Egunov, *Kolonial'naia politika tsarizma i pervyi etap natsional'nogo dvizheniia v Buriatii v epokhu imperializma* (Ulan Ude, 1963).

41. The borderlands should have received self-government and judicial institutions similar to those in the central provinces of the empire. *Okrainy Rossii* 22 (29 May 1919).

42. Minister of Interior to the governor of Turgai oblast', 17 February 1910, in M. G. Masevich, ed., *Materialy po istorii politicheskogo stroia Kazakhstana* (Alma-Ata, 1960), pp. 414–416.

43. Divaev, "Atkamnary," in *Sbornik materialov dlia statistiki Syr-Dar'inskoi oblasti,* vol. 3 (Tashkent, 1894), pp. 3–17.

44. M. Grulev, *Zapiski generala-evreia* (Paris, 1930), p. 190; I. D. Kuznetsov, *Natsional'nye dvizheniia v period pervoi russkoi revoliutsii v Rossii* (Cheboksary, 1935), p. 87.

45. A. N. Kulomzin to I. L. Goremykin, 26 March 1899, RGIA, f. 1274, op. 1, d. 3a, l. 303.

46. *Khori-Buriaty. Po povodu predpolagaemykh preobrazovanii* (St. Petersburg, 1899). The book, which I have consulted at the Library of Congress, bears the emblem of the tsar's library at the Winter Palace in St. Petersburg.

47. Orientalists' Archive, St. Petersburg Branch of the Institute of Orientology of the Russian Academy of Sciences, op. 1, d. 82, l. II; *Pravo,* no. 48 (24 November 1902): 2364.

48. *Zhizn' v vostochnoi okraine* (Chita), no. 83 (11 May 1897).

49. D. Klements, "Zametki o kochevom byte," first published in the newspaper *Sankt-Peterburgskie vedomosti* in 1903 and then reprinted in the journal *Sibirskie voprosy* 4, no. 49–52 (1907).

50. See the introduction to W. Clowes, Samuel D. Kassow, and James L. West, eds., *Between Tsar and People* (Princeton, 1991).

51. Cf. the definition of gosudarstvennost' in Wcislo, *Reforming Rural Russia,* p. 311.

52. Quoted in A. Ia. Avrekh, *P. A. Stolypin i sud'by reform v Rossii* (Moscow, 1991), p. 135.

53. V. Voshchinin, *Ocherki novogo Turkestana. Svet i teni russkoi kolonizatsii* (St. Petersburg, 1914), p. 77.

54. Cf. an American anthropologist writing on the idea of a public: "The idea of a public actually helps to constitute the powerful ruling group in society by silently excluding many categories of people and activities. . . . In eighteenth-century France, England, and the United States, for instance, it was women, blacks, and men without property who were categorized as necessarily particular-istic, partisan, and self-interested; their political actions would never have been seen as disinterested and so legitimately directed at the general, the 'common' weal, the 'public' good." Susan Gal, "Language and the 'Arts of Resistance,'" *Cultural Anthropology* 10, no. 3 (1995): 418.

·4·

SUSAN LAYTON

Nineteenth-Century Russian Mythologies
of Caucasian Savagery

Although imperial themes have a long lineage in Russian literature, the writers' impulse to construct well-articulated identities for borderland peoples dates only from the early romantic era. We may recall, for example, Gavrila Derzhavin's ode to Catherine II, "The Image of Felitsa" (1789). The poet concocted some distant, hairy "wild people" (*dikie liudi*) dressed in foliage and bark but overjoyed at their inclusion in the empress's realm of law.[1] A playful exaggeration of Catherine's views, this foray into exotica conveyed no special curiosity about the empire's non-Russian subjects. As of the 1820s, however, Russian *littérateurs* were trying to imagine Asian borderlands in abundant ethnographic and geographic detail. The mountainous territories of the southern frontier (Circassia, Kabarda, Chechnia, and Dagestan) stimulated the richest literary output, beginning with Pushkin's "Prisoner of the Caucasus" (1822). But Georgia, Armenia, Crimea, Siberia, and Central Asia, as well as western regions such as Ukraine and Finland, also aroused the imagination of Russian writers in the romantic era.[2] By the mid-1830s, the Russian readership thus had a large gallery of literary exhibits of peoples on the empire's periphery.

This lively engagement with other cultures revealed the writers' need to define their own nationhood. The basic tendency was already evident in the stirrings of Russian national consciousness in the eighteenth century: as Hans Rogger observed, the occidentalized Russian elite developed national awareness "on contact with the other, the foreign, the non-national."[3] Rogger explored two major cases in point—the Russian nobles' ambivalent interaction with western Europe, and their anxious efforts to understand the Russian peasantry as the repository of national virtues uncorrupted by outside influences. Nineteenth-century Russian treatment of the Asian borderlands would extend this practice of searching for the national self via encounters with some "other," non-Westernized sphere. Genuine perplexity about just what constituted distinctively Russian national character meant that two unknowns were operating at once. The elite was surely more familiar with its rural compatriots than with Caucasian mountaineers, Kazakh nomads, or other borderland peoples. But all the same, Russia's countryside intrigued the nobles as terrain still insufficiently known and yet paramount for understanding themselves as part of a nation. Aleksandr Griboedov strikingly articulated this outlook in 1826 when he characterized rural Russia as the home of a "different tribe," "wild," "incomprehensible," and "strange" in the eyes of his own "injured class of semi-Europeans."[4] Estrangement itself was the "injury": "Through some black magic we have become aliens among our own people" (*mezhdu svoimi*). To break the injurious spell of occidentalization, the elite obviously had to learn much more about the peasantry. Griboedov was describing an old condition, but his metaphor of tribal difference bespoke his era's growing interest in establishing taxonomies of all the empire's peoples, in the heartland as well as on the edges.[5]

The literary engagement with Asian borderlands is an intriguing aspect of the evolution of Russian national and imperial consciousness. But how are we to relate literary texts to the processes of empire-building? Mikhail Bakhtin's work urges us to read literature in its own time. Bakhtin emphasizes that the effort at "receptive understanding" of the past "usually requires introducing an immense amount of material" (concerning historical context, authorial intentions, and reader response).[6] The dialogue between "now" and "then" must be extensive if commentators are to avoid imprisoning the literary work in some intellectual fashion of their own era.[7] At a theoretical extreme from Bakhtin stand the cultural materialists, who find dealing with history much easier. What we essentially need to do, they argue, is "to observe the causes for which [an author] gets appropriated."[8] In between Bakhtin and the materialists (but veering closer to the latter) is Edward Said, the contemporary theorist most frequently cited in studies of Russian conceptions of Asia. With a debt to Michel Foucault, Said in his book *Orientalism* defines "orientalist" discourse as a textual system comprising rhetoric, specific concepts, and a whole style of thought pitting "us" (the Western observers) against "them" (the Muslim objects of interest).[9] Unlike wholehearted disciples of Foucault, Said takes great interest in individual *littérateurs* and repeatedly denies that literature is an institutionally determined, passive outgrowth of the power structure. The reader may easily lose sight of these theoretical convictions, however, because *Orientalism* so often concludes that writing is the self-perpetuating "enabler" of the power structure that made it possible in the first place.[10] Interestingly enough, the closest nineteenth-century Russian approximation of Said's model was the imposition of indolent Asian, and even quasi-Muslim, identity on Georgia, an ancient bastion of Christian civilization that participated in Russia's war against the Caucasian mountain tribes.[11]

For the most part, though, Said's paradigm of division between East and West is ill suited for inquiry into the role of Asian borderlands in Russian national and imperial consciousness. In looking across a border, observers from the more powerful domain always construct "others" to serve their own needs and may never gain insight into the foreigners' culture, nor recognize their right to sovereignty.[12] But in Russian experience, the cognitive boundary between "us" and the oriental "others" often grew blurry because Asia interpenetrated Russia so extensively in geographical, historical, and cultural terms. We should thus be wary of Said's tendency to construe "otherness" as something inevitably inferior and alien in the eyes of the perceiver. This is particularly true in the case of Russia's noble Caucasian savages. No historical investigation of these romantic personages can proceed from the a priori assumptions that Russians considered the mountaineers "alien" and wrote about them in order to "control" them.[13] Literary critics, of course, may sidestep this whole issue of the meanings that Russian authors and readers attributed to inventions of Asia in the era of empire-building. Peter Scotto, for example, has analyzed Lermontov's Caucasian tale "Bela" as a "modern reader" unconcerned with authorial intentions and responses of historical audiences.[14] Such an approach to a text's cross-cultural dynamics provides postcolonial insight, without presuming to illuminate nineteenth-century Russian mentalities.

If we listen to the full range of Russian voices from young Pushkin's era, we hear not one but two discursive tendencies in utterances about Caucasian mountain peoples. Persistent throughout the nineteenth century, these two tendencies shared some diction ("wild") and concepts (mountaineers are martial by nature), but diverged in their value judgments of the uncivilized foreigners. Many Russian officials and military commanders insisted on Asian alterity by characterizing the Caucasian tribes as ignoble brutes. Furthermore, mean tribesmen prospered in Russian pulp of the 1830s: they committed crimes at home (mainly against women), aided the Ottoman slave trade, and waged jihad (holy war) against Holy Russia. But the image of the ignoble mountaineer faced stiff competition from the noble mountaineers first invented in Pushkin's "Prisoner of the Caucasus." Throughout the nineteenth century, in fact, the bad savage was fighting a losing battle to displace romanticism's heroic tribes in the minds of Russian readers.

The steady coexistence of Russia's mythologies of noble and ignoble

Noble Savage
"Cherkess" (1859 poster, courtesy of the Russian
State Library print collection)

Caucasian savagery manifested a cultural tension of attraction toward and disaffection from the empire's ideological center. This historical aspect of the literary Caucasus is not acknowledged by recent researchers who claim that noble savagery was little or nothing more than entertainment to disguise the atrocity of imperialist war.[15] Romantic literature's colorful mountaineers undoubtedly provided enjoyment, although not of a consistently mindless sort. Moreover, no Russian author ever uttered a protest sufficiently powerful to prevent the conquest of the Caucasus.[16] But all the same, the romantics' captivatingly artful invention of rebellious mountain tribes evinced some strong disaffections from the state's imperialist agenda.

A poetics of flight from the center took shape in Pushkin's "Prisoner of the Caucasus." Its principal narrative depicted the Circassians as a free frontier people with strong resemblances to the Cossacks of folklore.[17] The notorious finale of "The Prisoner of the Caucasus" veered back toward the metropole's ideal of the imperialist Russian monarchy. However, Pushkin's first readership displayed a conspicuous refusal to identify with the empire's interests. Focused instead on the poet's vision of liberty in the Caucasian highlands, this romantic mentality exemplified a general Russian cultural tendency to flee the state as an alien institution, fundamentally hostile to the national community.[18] Throughout the war against the mountaineers, variations on the Pushkinian poetics of flight would recur in Russian writing and even exert an impact on readers' behavior. The prolonged romance of the wild Caucasian frontier thus exercised a seductive power that the state ultimately had to combat by declaring the conquest a Russian national triumph in the postwar period. As we shall see, this official "winners' epic" about the war would never have made sense without the ignoble savage.[19]

To begin analyzing how "The Prisoner of the Caucasus" encouraged readers to align themselves with Circassia instead of with the Russian state, let us immediately note the author's underplaying of religious difference—a traditional criterion for classifying the empire's inhabitants. Pushkin's tribe belongs to Islam, as indicated by references to Bairam and the *kalym* (brideprice). But the dominant ethos of alpine wilderness largely eclipses the "oriental" details. One might protest that Pushkin was aiming for verisimilitude: after all, Circassia never became a stronghold of the Muslim resistance movement, which was centered in Chechnia and Dagestan, the two regions targeted by General Aleksei Ermolov's "pacification" program.[20] However, although "The Prisoner of the Caucasus" did incorporate some reliable ethnographic detail, neither Pushkin nor the majority of his contemporaries had well-defined mental maps of the mountaineers' geographical distribution. For example, the poem's so-called "Circassian Song" virtually dissolves the tribal *aul* into a Terek Cossack *stanitsa*.[21]

Indicative of Pushkin's more general confusion about where to draw boundaries, this mélange produced an imaginative ethnography which proved immensely resistant to facts. Even in the young poet's time, knowledgeable Russian authors began trying to teach their compatriots that "Circassians," for instance, called themselves the "Adyge" and lived in the northwest Caucasus. Data about various mountain peoples proliferated from the 1820s onward. But thanks to Pushkin and subsequent romantics, "Circassian" lodged itself in the Russian imagination as a generic term for "mountain rebel" (or on the feminine side, a beautiful "mountain maid"). Indeed, as late as 1848, many educated Russians still conceived the Caucasus as one huge fortress manned by ubiquitous "Circassians," or simply "mountaineers."[22]

A matter of artistic emphasis, the alpine rather than Muslim ethos of Pushkin's Circassia dictated the poetics of escape into wilderness. A cult of sublime landscape had first penetrated Russian letters in the late eighteenth century, as exemplified by Nikolai Karamzin's treatment of the Swiss Alps in *Letters of a Russian Traveler*. Derzhavin's ode to Count Valerian Zubov (1804) and Vasilii Zhukovskii's address "To Voeikov" (1814) extended the aesthetics of dread and splendor to the Caucasian range, as well. However, it was Byron's *Childe Harold's Pilgrimage* which supplied Pushkin with a vision of rugged mountains as a refuge from the "torturing hum of human cities," a metaphor including the malicious *beau monde*. Widely read as an account of the poet's own wanderings, *Childe Harold* predicated creativity on flight from an inimical social realm and featured the Alps as an inspirational site.

With much less authorial self-dramatization, "The Prisoner of the Caucasus" poeticizes Russia's borderland in this Byronic alpine mode. Pushkin metamorphoses his exile into an inspiring trip, as seen in the dedication's negative evocation of St. Petersburg. Rather paradoxically, the fictional captive, too, participates in the romantic construct of restorative flight from the metropole. A "renegade" from Europeanized Russia, he was drawn to the Caucasus by the "apparition of freedom" (Pushkin 92). As the phrase implies, the quest proves largely futile: the hero makes no life for himself outside his own repressive society and simply recrosses the border after escaping the aul. And yet during captivity, the Russian "friend of nature" relishes his contact with the mountains and achieves a Byronic sense of release from a repellent homeland. As we shall see later on, this impermanent but apparently thrilling touristic experience gripped the Russian readership's imagination with extraordinary force.

While adopting Byron's romantic construct of restorative flight into mountains, Pushkin added a distinctive accent by naming the Caucasus his "new Parnassus." The classical allusion reminded readers that the territory had impressive mythic ties to Prometheus, Medea, and Jason. Pushkin's tale contains no direct allusions to legends of antiquity. But those compelling stories of adventure and heroic rebellion already surrounded the Caucasus, thanks in part to eighteenth-century Russian poetry. As Nikolai Grech's review of "The Prisoner of the Caucasus" put it, Pushkin transported readers to the "poetic land which saw Prometheus's suffering and the sojourn of the Greek Argonauts."[23] A part of every educated Russian's cultural baggage, these traditions gave the Caucasus an unmatchable aura of monumental heroism.

More particularly, the story of Prometheus's rebellion sustained a Russian conviction about mountains as the cradle of freedom. Grounded in Montesquieu's *théorie des climats*, the conception of mountain liberty had a pastoral and a savage variant. Karamzin's *Letters of a Russian Traveler*, for example, had perceived a captivating attachment to freedom in Swiss shepherds. On the wilder side, Byron's *Childe Harold* celebrated the Albanian highlanders' fierce hostility to the imperial designs of oriental despots, the Ottoman Turks. Eighteenth-century Russian explorers of the Caucasus had attributed martial ferocity to the local mountaineers, but withheld Byronic approval: on the contrary, these men in service to Catherine II pegged the Caucasian peoples as pillagers and warriors always prone to prey on their neighbors.[24] Although modulated by attention to many peaceable aspects of tribal culture, a belief in the mountaineers' bellicose, predatory ways endured in the major contribution to ethnography and natural science in Pushkin's era—Semen Bronevskii's *A New Geography and History of the Caucasus* (1823).[25]

The imagined tribal milieu of "The Prisoner of the Caucasus" has a complex relation to these traditions. Pushkin's story of a waylaid Russian twice calls the Circassian a "predator," ready to pounce on foreigners. The poet also features the mountaineers as men "born for war," as illustrated by their martial games and the decapitation of slaves on Bairam. On another occasion, a Circassian fatally assaults a Cossack border guard. These events constitute savagery's menace, while twice showing men from Russia as the victims.

Yet while dramatizing risks on the wild frontier, Pushkin celebrates the aul itself as a sphere of freedom and pleasing simplicity. Featured as the "enclosure of Circassian liberty," the village is a patriarchal community which arouses the "European" captive's admiration. He takes interest in the mountaineers' "religion, *moeurs* and manner of rearing children" (Pushkin 99). Rooted in contemporary Russian ethnography, Pushkin's central sketch of Circassian life also includes a scene of ritual hospitality: with meager fare but a generous spirit, a tribesman at home with his family gives food and shelter to a passing stranger on a cold night. Elsewhere in the poem the Russian captive tries to store in his "impatient memory" the native and Georgian songs that the Circassian heroine sings to him (Pushkin 97).

In the most significant deviation from Russian traditions of thought about "Asians" in general and rugged mountaineers in particular, Pushkin depicts the Circassians as tillers of the soil.[26] On his first full day of captivity, the shackled Russian remains alone in the village, while the residents work the fields. The mountaineers reappear at sundown and settle into their snug houses: "S polei narod idet v aul, / Sverkaia svetlymi kosami. / Prishli; v domakh zazhglis' ogni" (Pushkin 94). Russian dictionaries of the time defined *narod* as "a people" or "nation" (*gens*).[27] But in one of the first appearances of the word in Pushkin's verse, "The Prisoner of the Caucasus" employs *narod* to signify "the people"—the villagers as an agrarian aggregate, apparently comprising men as well as women. The poet knew that the Circassians were farmers: while traveling under the protection of several dozen Cossacks in the Kuban River basin, he had passed their lands (as noted in a letter to his brother in September 1820). But the actuality of the agricultural activity is not so significant as Pushkin's choice to register it and thus bring Circassia closer to Russia. To appreciate the decision, one need only recall Zhukovskii's "To Voeikov," where vaguely "eastern" Caucasian tribesmen spend their brutish existence in perpetual oscillation between pillage and sullen indolence.[28]

If intimations of agrarian simplicity color the entire Pushkinian aul, they are most heavily concentrated in the "mountain maid." The Circassian's affair with the callous "European" captive intermeshes exoticism with Russian rusticity. Viewed from the "wild" angle, the plot narrates a type of encounter recurrent in Western literature inspired by colonialism.[29] The heroine is drawn to the Russian before they even exchange a word. She nurses him and declares her love, while averring a lack of erotic interest in the local men. Ultimately heartbroken by the hero's jaded outlook, the tribeswoman sets him free and then drowns herself. While true to exotic type (especially Chateaubriand's Native American women), the Circassian in watery death declares her Russian origins, too: with its culmination in suicide by drowning, Pushkin's plot recycles "Poor Liza" (1792), Karamzin's sentimental tale of a Russian peasant traumatized by her affair with a Muscovite aristocrat.[30]

After taking the imaginative flight to a frontier community of noble savages, "The Prisoner of the Caucasus" fixes a jingoistic gaze on Circassia in the epilogue (Pushkin 117). Added about two months after Pushkin finished the captivity tale, this odic finale foresees Russian military victory over the mountain peoples. The monarchy directs "our" conquest, as symbolized by the Romanovs' heraldic sign:

> The glorious hour I will sing
> When o'er the Caucasus, grown wrathful,
> Our double-headed eagle winged,
> Anticipating bloody battle.

Ermolov and other commanders win mention, as in the following lines:

> Oh Kotliarevskii, scourge of war!
> I'll sing your heroism in action.
> Across the Caucasus you tore,
> Leaving a trail of black contagion
> To deal a death blow to the tribes.

After envisioning the "Russian sword" triumphant, Pushkin closes with the image of a traveler fearlessly riding alone in the Caucasus mountains. The wild frontier has been relegated to the past.

But to the ears of Pushkin's first readers, the captivity tale's song of noble savagery drowned out the epilogue's anthem of imperial conquest. Whatever the author's intentions might have been, Russians of the time behaved as if they had two texts before them: an engaging story of free Circassia, and an odic addendum which they preferred to ignore. Only one reviewer even noted the existence of Pushkin's chauvinistic coda (Zelinskii 87–88). Memoirs pertinent to the reception of "The Prisoner of the Caucasus" are likewise mute about this part of the poem. Lest we jump to the conclusion that silence meant consent, it is worth recalling what Petr

Viazemskii said about the epilogue in a letter to Aleksandr Turgenev. A veteran of the Battle of Borodino, Viazemskii raised both aesthetic and ethical objections to the unheroic spectacle that Pushkin had presented. Pushkin's old-fashioned odic mode of celebrating empire offended Viazemskii's romantic sensibility. But his biggest complaint stemmed from the poet's flat endorsement of carnage:

> What kind of a hero is Kotliarevskii or Ermolov? Just what is so good about his "leaving a trail of black contagion to deal a death blow to the tribes"? That sort of notoriety makes your blood run cold and your hair stand on end. If we were bringing enlightenment to the tribes, there would be something to sing about. Poetry should never be the ally of butchers.[31]

As the rest of Viazemskii's letter made clear, he knew that the censors would have disallowed any effort to explore the disjunction between "enlightenment" and "butchery." His review of "The Prisoner of the Caucasus" thus steered clear of the epilogue. Viazemskii's choice suggests that other commentators, too, might have exercised self-censorship: unable to say anything good about the "double-headed eagle" in bloody action, they circumvented the subject.

While the readers' mental flight to the wild frontier surely was fun, some of them apparently were also wondering how Rousseau's notions about the civilizing process might apply to the mountaineers. As recollected by the orientalist (in every sense) Il'ia Berezin, a habit of "philosophizing" about the Caucasus became endemic among Russian readers enthralled by Pushkin's mountain liberty.[32] One finds an indication of this speculative activity in the first reviewers' response to the erotic encounter in "The Prisoner of the Caucasus." Why had the "European" captive treated the Circassian tribeswoman so badly? In the most extended discussion of the question, Mikhail Pogodin approved the prisoner for having taken the opportunity to observe the mountaineers' way of life and learn rudiments of a foreign language (Zelinskii 110). Unfortunately, though, the Russian had "inexcusably" failed to "master his passions," to the detriment of an "innocent" woman wholly unlike a "high-society *belle*" (Zelinskii 111). Of serf origins, Pogodin was forging cultural links between the Caucasian mountaineers and Russia's own rural "tribe" (as Griboedov would term the narod).[33] Although largely eclipsed by official nationalism and Slavophilism during the reign of Nicholas I, Rousseauist convictions about *moral* similarities between the best of the "simple" folk both at home and in the Caucasus would endure in Lermontov's long poems "Mtsyri" (1840) and "Izmail-Bey" (1843).[34]

But if Caucasian noble savagery and Russian *narodnost'* were sometimes constructed as functions of one another, Pushkin's vision of valiant liberty exerted the most powerful hold on the readership's imagination.

Despite the poem's exhibits of violence, readers of the 1820s proclaimed the mountaineers heroic warriors, rather than dangerous predators alien to Christendom. Aesthetics were clearly overriding any real or imagined issue of national security along the border: Pogodin and Petr Pletnev, for example, read the assault on the Cossack as an example of stunningly innovative narrative poetry (Zelinskii 91–92, 114–115). As these remarks suggest, romantic temperament took the mountaineers as symbols of aesthetic freedom. Pletnev made this explicit when he described the Circassian tribesmen as "courageously venturesome" (*otvazhnyi*), just like Pushkin's romantic style. Viazemskii's review of "The Prisoner of the Caucasus" elaborated the aesthetics of freedom most extensively, while permitting "Circassian liberty" to take on connotations about essential Russianness. A major contribution to the Russian romantics' attack on the standards of French classicism, Viazemskii's article employed a martial idiom (perhaps in parodic dialogue with Pushkin's bellicose epilogue). On one side of the battlefield stood Russia's "old Parnassian dynasty"—the defenders of classical order who judged romantic art "wild," "predatory," and "lawless" (Zelinskii 101). But to Viazemskii's mind, the defiantly "wild" side held the key to the future. With an appeal to "national pride," the critic urged the romantics to rally and repel French influence from the literary domain once and for all. The cause was urgent because a traditional dependence on "foreigners" had enfeebled Russia: Viazemskii saw isolated achievements on the home front, but no extensive, nationally distinctive body of belles-lettres—no "worthy expression of a mighty, virile people" (102). In perfect harmony with Viazemskii's romantic agenda, this assessment of Russian national spirit mirrored his thumbnail characterization of the Circassians as an "unrefined but bold, martial, handsome people" (102).

The Caucasian mountaineers were, of course, just one set of literary personages who bespoke a yearning for freedom particularly acute among Russian liberals during the prodromes of the Decembrist revolt. Russian literature of the period favored various forms of rebellion (ancient Roman struggle against tyranny, medieval Novgorod's independence from the Muscovite state, the current Greek resistance to Turkish domination).[35] But a combination of spatial and temporal immediacy distinguished the wild Caucasian frontier: the place was contiguous, and the time was "now." One might assume that any good fight would appeal to romantic imagination. However, a comparative glance at Western literature stimulated by empire-building indicates that violent resistance to colonial domination typically brings a people vilification (as seen in British denigrations of Indians after the Sepoy Mutiny of 1857), whereas ready capitulators to "civilization" generally receive magnanimous treatment in winners' epics (British presentations of Burmese, for example).[36]

The unusual Russian impulse to celebrate the officially designated enemies in an ongoing imperialist war points to an imaginative inter-change between Pushkin's free Circassians and legendary Cossacks, a group with no exact parallel outside Russia. In a study moving from seventeenth-century folklore into twentieth-century literature, Judith Deutsch Kornblatt has persuasively argued that Russians achieved a mythic resolution of "historical oppression and metaphysical liberation" by identifying with Cossacks: to the extent that they could merge spiritu-ally with the semicivilized frontiersmen, Russians of the heartland could tell themselves that they too possessed a free essence, just temporarily shackled by repressive institutions.[37] Kornblatt underlines the Cossacks' participation in Orthodoxy and their links to Kiev, the mother of Russian cities. But she overstates the case when she asserts that nineteenth-century Russians perceived Asian borderland peoples as strictly "alien" foreign-ers, located across an "unbridgeable gap." The admiring readers of "The Prisoner of the Caucasus" spoke no such idiom. They articulated instead a sense of self-identification with Pushkin's free frontier community of handsome martial men with an agricultural base, simple *moeurs* and charming folklore (intimated by the "Circassian Song," an invention which enjoyed tremendous popularity in Russia). As constructed by Pushkin prior to the heroic Cossack's emergence in Russian literature, the Circassians thus tapped into the readership's spiritual hunger for liberty associated with the frontier.

Indeed, in contemplating the Caucasus, Russian imagination allowed the mountaineers to displace the Cossacks as the frontier's quintes-sentially free men, ever ready to fight for their independence. Tolstoi's Terek Cossacks are famous examples of noble savages, reliably likened in many respects to their Chechen neighbors and sharply distinguished from Westernized Russia. But unlike Tolstoi's novel (published in 1863), earlier contributions to the literary Caucasus tended to reduce the Cossack to a servant of the Russian state, none too adroit in executing his duties. Border guards of "The Prisoner of the Caucasus" exemplify this domestication of legend's wild Cossack. Akin to the "tired" Terek sentry who "has dozed off, leaning on his spear" (in the poem's "Circassian Song"), Pushkin's principal Cossack protagonist is a daydreamer "leaning on his spear." The poet supposes that the man is mulling over "former battles" but also longing for home. An attachment to civilian life then dominates the apos-trophe to the doomed guard: "Farewell to the free *stanitsy*, the ancestral house, the quiet Don, war and the pretty girls!" (Pushkin 101). Lost in his "treacherous dream," Pushkin's Cossack proves no match for a Circassian archer. With a new relish for lurid detail, Lermontov would imagine the same inequality in martial prowess: his poem "Izmail-Bey" cheers Cir-cassians as they slaughter Cossacks in battle.

Literary motifs of the Cossack's inadequacy for combat in the Caucasus harmonized with a perception in the actual theater of war. In 1832, when the jihad had dispelled the Russian high command's illusions about quickly subjugating the mountaineers, General Aleksei Vel'iaminov ruefully assessed his Cossack soldiers. He complained that they were basically farmers whose martial arts and horsemanship were far inferior to those of the tribesmen.[38] Especially under the conditions of combat in mountain terrain, there was surely much truth in this comparison. But Vel'iaminov seems to have taken Stenka Razin and his ilk as measures of Cossack machismo. When real Cossacks failed to live up to the legends, they shrank in negative proportion in the general's eyes, to become a motley peasant crew more adept with hoes than with weapons. Vel'iaminov likewise could find no chinks whatsoever in the armor of the (grantedly formidable) mountaineers, who stalked his mind as absolute martial ideals—the enviable *opposite* of the debased Cossacks.

In the Caucasian context, then, the tribesmen stole much of the Cossacks' legendary thunder in Russian imagination. A Cossack conceptualized strictly as a guard of Russia's borders lost the allure of a fully "free man": he was geographically on the edge but politically serving the center. The romantic poetics of flight thus craved an expansion and ran past Cossack outposts—across the frontier and into the aul. The military exiles Bestuzhev-Marlinskii and Lermontov kept cultivating the Pushkinian poetics of Caucasian escape throughout the romantic era. The most popular author of the 1830s, Bestuzhev-Marlinskii won renown with his dashing Dagestani rebels and effusive renderings of alpine *paysage*. In very different romantic registers, where parody assumed a big role, Lermontov, too, encouraged Russian daydreams about the Caucasus's pristine terrain and valiant tribesmen (especially Izmail-Bey). Both writers indulged fantasies of erotic adventure with mountain maids. But the two exiles also promoted visions of the Caucasus as a refuge from the *beau monde* and the oppressive Russian state. Undoubtedly the most famous of these elaborations of the poetics of escape is Lermontov's acidic lyric "Farewell, unwashed Russia." Most likely written in 1841, just before the author's second departure for the Chechen front, this verse tries to imagine a haven "beyond the Caucasus" (over the mountain crest) where the Russian police state and its slavish population will not intrude.

As illustrated by "Farewell, unwashed Russia," the trope of flight to Caucasian highlands did not remain on the printed page: it was part of Russian experience, both voluntary and involuntary. Unlike the forced "travels" of exiles, touristic trips to the Caucasian borderland became increasingly fashionable in Russia from the mid-1820s onward. With heads full of romantic literature, armchair travelers bestirred themselves to flock to the Piatigorsk spas in order to see the mountains for themselves and visit tribal villages allied to the Russian state. One of them noted in 1857 that there were still no actual guidebooks for the region.[39] But writings such as Pushkin's "The Prisoner of the Caucasus," Bestuzhev-Marlinskii's

Caucasian essays, and Lermontov's *A Hero of Our Time* served as substitutes.

Besides taking trips to the Piatigorsk area, ordinary Russians had culturally interesting fantasies about outright flight to the aul. As reported by Bestuzhev-Marlinskii in 1830, some of his compatriots believed that the first Caucasian imam, Gazi-Muhammed, was the grandson of a Russian fugitive.[40] After Bestuzhev-Marlinskii's own death a few years later, certain of his devoted readers thought that he had faked injury on the battlefield and then fled to make a heroic new life with the tribes.[41] At a later phase of the conquest, Russian civilians imagined that men were deserting the imperial army by the thousands—to join ranks with the mountaineers, convert to Islam, marry local women, and father untold numbers of children.[42]

Like most rumors, such scenarios had points of reference in actuality. Military desertion was the most important. Although desertions occurred throughout the war, they took on major proportions in the 1840s, when a greater number of Poles and Ukrainians were being drafted into the Caucasian army.[43] If never so numerous as Russian civilians imagined, the turncoats did sometimes abandon Christian "civilization" entirely, by converting to Islam and establishing families on Shamil's side. The Russian high command expressed special concern about the peasantry's enacting this version of the poetics of flight en masse: it was learned that Shamil was promising freedom and land to all deserters.[44]

In addition to military desertion, the conquest saw one spectacular case of fleeing Russia in the name of love: Anna Ulykhanova's marriage to Shamil. An Armenian abducted from Mozdok during her teenage years in the early 1840s, Ulykhanova became Shamil's captive in Dagestan but gave no encouragement to her brothers' efforts to ransom her.[45] She converted to Islam, took the name "Shuanet," and became Shamil's favorite wife ever after. The most famous prisoner of the Caucasus who decided to stay, Shuanet held great fascination for Russians, as indicated by the attention she received in postwar memoirs, and by the extensive quotes attributed to her in the enormously popular account of two Georgian princesses held captive in Shamil's household during several months in 1854 and 1855.[46]

Besides tourism and full flight to the aul (both real and imagined), the poetics of escape operated as well in enlistment in the Caucasian army. As recounted in memoirs, romantic writings prompted men to sign up, not in order to defend *la patrie* or "civilization," but in order to get out of Russia, see the alpine terrain, and encounter heroic tribesmen (some of whom fought in the imperial ranks). Pervasive bureaucracy and Arakcheev's style of regimentation provided sufficient reasons for wanting to serve far from the imperial center. But literature made the Caucasus the primary magnet for men hungry for stimulating travel. According to Lermontov, who attended the St. Petersburg military academy from 1832 to 1834, young cadets "were fired with passion" for the alpine borderland after reading "The Prisoner of the Caucasus," which they often hid in their manuals to be savored surreptitiously during lectures.[47] Although Pushkin's Circassia remained an active point of reference, Bestuzhev-Marlinskii was the major stimulus to militarized wanderlust in Lermontov's time. As recollected by Arnold Zisserman and other war veterans, Bestuzhev-Marlinskii's awesome *paysage* and valiant tribesmen inflamed the imagination of gullible young Russians and made them sign up for service in the Caucasus.[48] This paradoxical behavior was one of the most fascinating aspects of nineteenth-century Russia's entrancement with the alpine borderland: many men who extolled the territory and its vigorous, free mountaineers ended up fighting the war (including Pushkin's brother, Lev). And yet the desire to flee the dull, oppressive homeland and encounter an invigorating frontier realm seems to have been their primary motivation for going into the army. In young Tolstoi's phrase, Russians enlisted for service in the Caucasus in search of a "promised land," where their souls might be healed.[49]

Reality was naturally ready to puncture all aspects of the collective daydream of military escape. Zisserman and other enlistees complained that even in the Caucasus, army life was frequently dull and left them insufficient time to admire nature as they had planned. Moreover, military men made the dispiriting discovery that the tentacles of imperial bureaucracy had stretched beyond the legendary mountain crests: like the Russian heartland, the Caucasus was divided into *gubernii*.[50] But the cruelest disillusionments came from baptisms of blood. Russians enlisted with heads full of fantasies of camaraderie and heroic contest with the likes of Bestuzhev-Marlinskii's Ammalat-Bek. However, some of them found that Russia's war was "bestial" and "unjust," as young Tolstoi and Zisserman named it.[51] The Decembrist exile Nikolai Lorer also recalled service in the Caucasus in these terms.[52] Never able to convince himself that military carnage was the right way to advance the cause of European enlightenment, Bestuzhev-Marlinskii came to associate the conquest with the story of Richard III; Lermontov's poetry featured Russia's assault on the mountaineers as the action of a "predatory beast" ("Izmail-Bey") or just a plain, bloodthirsty "beast" ("Valerik").[53] In a transposition of a Lermontovian theme of bestiality, Tolstoi's old Cossack, Eroshka, would typify the imperial Russian raider as a smasher of tribal babies' skulls (*The Cossacks*). Such disclosures of Russian atrocity were quantitatively few but carried much *qualitative* weight as denials of the state's professed aim of bringing enlightenment to Asia.

Perhaps doubts about the war's glory helped make so many Russians loath to relinquish noble Caucasian savagery once the military victory was won. The old "apparition" of mountain freedom took on tangible form in the person of vanquished Shamil (accompanied, of course, by Shuanet). As demonstrated in Thomas Barrett's article on Shamil's captivity, the Russian state's magnanimous manipulation of the imam sought to rally national pride around the empire. In this atmosphere, Shamil became a source of exotic entertainment for Russians into the early 1860s. And yet in one observer's estimation, many ordinary Russians of the period took a dim view of their country's military victory because now all the Caucasus's "poetry was dead."[54]

This testimony suggests that Shamil's defeat inflicted a spiritual, emotional loss on those people—a loss unassuaged by whatever enjoyment he provided as an honored captive: by crushing the mountaineers at last, the empire had deprived Russians of a real, contiguous place to embellish with an ideal of unbounded liberty. An extraordinary need to hold on to that cognitive refuge seems evident in the impassioned words that Russians shouted to Shamil as he left Petersburg under official escort to go take up residence in Kaluga: "Goodbye Shamil! Stay with us! . . . Tell him that we love him very much! Tell him that we wish him the very best!"[55] Were those people not voicing their irrational preference for the dream of freedom, rather than the undeniable fact of Russia's advance in the "Orient"? And might some of those Petersburgers not already have been asking themselves the question that one of their compatriots would pose in *Russkoe slovo* in April 1861: What had the conquest really achieved except the exportation of gambling, vodka, and venereal disease?[56]

Such a big question demonstrated that the powerful concept of noble savagery could still induce cultural and political alienation at a time when the Russian state had just begun a systematic constitution of the conquest as a civilizing mission. The official treatment of Shamil showed a desire to let the "good" mountaineer shine as a symbol of Russian power and magnanimity. But to instill Russian national pride in a war whose tangible achievements were so dubious, the metropole needed a contribution from the noble savage's bad brother—the bestial aggressor against Christian civilization. The savage duo mounted the stage in Rostislav Fadeev's *Sixty Years of War in the Caucasus* (1860), an effort at public education underwritten by the Russian military.[57] Focused on campaigns in Dagestan, Fadeev's book starred the tribesman as a "carnivorous beast" which Russia had been forced to "exterminate." But beneath the extant mountaineer's surface "depravity," Fadeev revealed a "child" in need of proper training. Colonel Dmitrii Romanovskii's series of public lectures in the Passazh hall in St. Petersburg in 1860 narrated the same story of Christian Russia's triumph over Muslim villains whose redeemable relatives were now under colonial control.[58]

In later periods, the mean tribesman sometimes made solo appearances, no doubt favored by fervent Russian nationalism during war with Turkey in 1877–78 and the subsequent Pan-Slav crusade in the Balkans. A

"Cherkess Returning from a Raid" (Niva, *no. 29 [1878]: 517–518)*

definitive picture appeared in 1878 in *Niva* (1870–1917), the popular maga-
zine which started breaking all circulation records in Russian periodical
publishing soon after its debut.[59] Entitled "Cherkess Returning from a
Raid," the illustration shows a band of tribesmen crossing a river with
captives, rustled horses, and cattle.[60] Near the center rides a swarthy
mountaineer with a blonde woman on his horse. She is naked to the waist,
with some cloth loosely draped about her legs. Another woman with an
infant is visible on a raft in the foreground. This iconography gave even
illiterate Russians access to the postwar mythology of national victory
over Asian fiends. There were also special efforts to reach newly literate
Russians—the emancipated serfs and lower-class townspeople who were
swelling the size of the reading public. A pedagogical manual of 1887, for
example, extracted from Lermontov's "Izmail-Bey" the Russian raid on a
Circassian village but contextualized it with commentary about the irredeemable "savagery" that had necessitated the imperial army's atrocities
against children, old people, and women.[61] To try to demonstrate what he
meant, the compiler also reproduced a catalogue of Circassian weaponry
from Pushkin's "The Prisoner of the Caucasus."

By the end of the century, the noble and ignoble savages were still
fighting it out to gain top billing in imperial Russia's drama about the
conquest of the Caucasus. In late-nineteenth-century literature the mean
tribesman would once again yield the limelight to a carefully groomed
version of his better half. A prime instance was Vasilii Nemirovich-Danchenko's *The Forgotten Fort* (1897), a novel which manipulated Shamil in
the same way the Russian state had begun to do in 1859.[62] Partly in

response to such expressions of blind patriotism, Tolstoi's *Hadji Murat* (written between 1896 and 1904) would dismantle the winners' epic about the Caucasian war: with a striking throwback to the romantic motif of bonds between uncorrupted mountaineers and the pre-Emancipation *narod*, this book told a story of imperialist aggression perpetrated by the occidentalized Russian elite led by Nicholas I.

Hadji Murat was attacking a mythology of national triumph in the Caucasus which the Russian state itself had inaugurated in the immediate postwar period. Although writings by Pushkin, Bestuzhev-Marlinskii, and Lermontov got appropriated for the extended construction of the winners' epic in the second half of the nineteenth century, they themselves had specialized in the poetics of flight which spun away from imperialism's *raison d'être*. Even the epilogue of "The Prisoner of the Caucasus" posed a problem because all it did was boast about an imperial Russian killing field in Asia ("The Orient will raise a howl!"). But infinitely more troublesome than Pushkin's text were the depictions or intimations of Russian bloodlust in writings produced during the conquest by Bestuzhev-Marlinskii and Lermontov, as well as young Tolstoi (*The Cossacks* was begun in the early 1850s). Such material signaled a real imperial bestiality which postwar Russian officialdom had to attempt to legitimize by propagating the fiction of defensive warfare against Asian barbarism.

NOTES

I wish to thank Marc Raeff and the participants in the borderlands conference for stimulating comments on an earlier draft of this chapter.

1. G. R. Derzhavin, *Stikhotvoreniia,* 2nd ed. (Leningrad, 1957), p. 135.

2. For an extensive bibliography, consult R. F. Iusufov, *Russkii romantizm nachala XIX veka i natsional'nye kul'tury* (Moscow, 1970). See also the survey of Russian curiosity about outlying areas of the empire in Paul M. Austin, "The Exotic Prisoner in Russian Romanticism," *Russian Literature,* nos. 16–18 (October 1984): 217–229. Austin remarks that Russian romanticism was "surprisingly unnationalistic," p. 218.

3. Hans Rogger, *National Consciousness in Eighteenth-Century Russia* (Cambridge, Mass., 1960), p. 6.

4. A. S. Griboedov, *Sochineniia* (Moscow, 1953), p. 389.

5. The intellectual antecedents are explored in Yuri Slezkine, "Naturalists versus Nations: Eighteenth-Century Russian Scholars Confront Ethnic Diversity," in this volume.

6. M. M. Bakhtin, *Speech Genres and Other Late Essays,* ed. Caryl Emerson and Michael Holquist, trans. Vern W. McGee (Austin, 1986), pp. 1–9, 126–127, and 139–146. See also my own large-scale effort at historical investigation in *Russian Literature and Empire: Conquest of the Caucasus from Pushkin to Tolstoy* (Cambridge, 1994).

7. See the warning applied to feminism in Caryl Emerson, "Bakhtin and Women: A Nontopic with Immense Implications," in *Fruits of Her Plume: Essays on Contemporary Russian Woman's Culture,* ed. Helena Goscilo (Armonk, N.Y., 1993), pp. 15–17.

8. Alan Sinfield, "Untune That String," *Times Literary Supplement* (22 April 1994), p. 4. Consult also Jonathan Dollimore and Alan Sinfield, *Political Shakespeare: New Essays in Cultural Materialism* (Manchester, 1985).

9. Edward W. Said, *Orientalism* (New York, 1979), pp. 1–24.

10. Compare similar remarks on Said in Yuri Slezkine, *Arctic Mirrors: Russia and the Small Peoples of the North* (Ithaca, N.Y., 1994), pp. 392–393. Elsewhere, Said underlines that it is impossible to say whether literary texts merely "accompany" imperialism or act as "preparations" for it, or else are its "results." See his *Culture and Imperialism* (London, 1993), pp. 61–62.

11. Susan Layton, "Eros and Empire in Russian Literature about Georgia," *Slavic Review* 51 (Summer 1992): 195–213.

12. Hayden White, "The Noble Savage Theme as Fetish," in *Tropics of Discourse: Essays in Cultural Criticism* (Baltimore, 1978), pp. 183–196; and "The Forms of Wildness: Archeology of an Idea," ibid., pp. 150–182. See also Said, *Culture and Imperialism*, pp. 158–159.

13. These assumptions govern Katya Hokanson, "Literary Imperialism, *Narodnost'* and Pushkin's Invention of the Caucasus," *Russian Review* 53 (July 1994): 336–352, especially pp. 337 and 349.

14. Peter Scotto, "Prisoners of the Caucasus: Ideologies of Imperialism in Lermontov's 'Bela,'" *PMLA* 107 (March 1992): 246–260. Consult also the feminist reading of "The Prisoner of the Caucasus" in Stephanie Sandler, *Distant Pleasures: Alexander Pushkin and the Writing of Exile* (Stanford, 1989), pp. 145–165.

15. In addition to the previously cited studies by Sandler, Scotto, and Hokanson, consult Thomas M. Barrett, "The Remaking of the Lion of Dagestan: Shamil in Captivity," *Russian Review* 53 (July 1994): 360–365.

16. European literature's failure to "prevent or inhibit" the advance of empire is a major theme in Said, *Culture and Imperialism,* as illustrated on pp. 96–98.

17. My use of "poetics" obviously takes inspiration from Iurii Lotman's work, such as "The Decembrist in Daily Life (Everyday Behavior as a Historical-Psychological Category)," trans. Andrea Bessing, in *The Semiotics of Russian Culture*, ed. Alexander D. Nakhimovsky and Alice Stone Nakhimovsky (Ithaca, N.Y., 1985), pp. 95–149.

18. See the general tendency defined in Rogger, *National Consciousness*, pp. 277–278. Consult also the suggestive discussion of tensions between nationalism and imperialism in Benedict Anderson, *Imagined Communities*, rev. ed. (London, 1991), pp. 83–111; and Marlon B. Ross, "Romancing the Nation-State: The Poetics of Romantic Nationalism," in *Macropolitics of Nineteenth-Century Literature: Nationalism, Exoticism, Imperialism*, ed. Jonathan Arac and Harriet Ritvo (Philadelphia, 1991), pp. 56–85.

19. The quoted term comes from a book not about noble savagery: David Quint, *Epic and Empire: Politics and Generic Form from Virgil to Milton* (Princeton, 1993), p. 16.

20. Ermolov was chief administrator of the Caucasus from 1816 to 1827. On the military history, consult John F. Baddeley, *The Russian Conquest of the Caucasus* (London, 1908), and Moshe Gammer, *Muslim Resistance to the Tsar: Shamil and the Conquest of Chechnia and Daghestan* (London, 1994).

21. Focused on a Cossack border guard, the song has a refrain about a Chechen raider from "across the river." See A. S. Pushkin, *Sobranie sochinenii v desiati tomakh*, vol. 3 (Moscow, 1959–62), p. 110 (cited hereafter parenthetically in the text).

98

EMPIRE AND ORIENT

22. A. L. Zisserman, *Dvadtsat' piat' let na Kavkaze (1842–1867),* 2 vols. (Moscow, 1897), vol. 1, pp. 328–329.

23. V. A. Zelinskii, ed., *Russkaia kriticheskaia literatura o proizvedeniiakh A.S. Pushkina. Khronologicheskii sbornik kritiko-bibliograficheskikh statei,* 7 vols. (reprint, Ann Arbor, 1967), vol. 1, p. 87 (cited hereafter parenthetically in the text).

24. Iusofov, *Russkii romantizm,* pp. 138–144; and M. A. Polievtkov, *Evropeiskie puteshestvenniki XVI–XVIII vv. po Kavkazu* (Tiflis, 1935), pp. 116–118, 122–126, and 155–156.

25. Semen Bronevskii, *Noveishie geograficheskie i istoricheskie izvestiia o Kavkaze,* 2 vols., 2nd ed. (Moscow, 1823), vol. 1, pp. 36–37.

26. On the traditional bias, see Marc Raeff, "In the Imperial Manner," in *Catherine the Great: A Profile,* ed. M. Raeff (New York, 1972), p. 215; Seymour Becker, "The Muslim East in Nineteenth-Century Russian Popular Historiography," *Central Asian Survey* 5 (1986): 34–38; and Peter Weisensel, "Russian Self-Identification and Travelers' Descriptions of the Ottoman Empire in the First Half of the Nineteenth Century," *Central Asian Survey* 10 (1991): 74.

27. An example is A. Kunitsyn, *Pravo estestvennoe,* 2 vols. (St. Petersburg, 1818, 1820), vol. 2, appendix 6. Hokanson's "Literary Imperialism" addresses the coinage of *narodnost'* but contends that the literati came to equate the concept with the power of the Russian language to represent (and thus "colonize") foreigners. Even her main case in point—Orest Somov—resists this argument: *moeurs* and *mestnost'* (local color, sense of place) remained uppermost in his discussions of narodnost'. Similar criteria appear in Pushkin's own "O narodnosti v literature," in *Sobranie sochinenii,* vol. 6, pp. 267–268. Belinskii adhered to the same tendency. Whatever else he thought about "The Prisoner of the Caucasus," he asserted that it was not nationally distinctive ("any European poet might have written [it]"), but that only a *Russian* could have produced *Eugene Onegin* and *Boris Godunov.* See Belinskii, *Polnoe sobranie sochinenii,* 13 vols. (Moscow, 1953–59), vol. 1, p. 94.

28. Austin pinpoints the type but neglects Pushkin's deviations from it. See "Exotic Prisoner," p. 233.

29. See discussion of Western traditions in Peter Hulme, *Colonial Encounters: Europe and the Native Caribbean, 1492–1797* (London, 1992), pp. 141 and 249–254.

30. M. Kagan, "O pushkinskikh poemakh," in *V mire Pushkina. Sbornik statei,* ed. S. Mashinskii (Moscow, 1974), pp. 102–103.

31. P. A. Viazemskii, *Sobranie sochinenii v dvukh tomakh,* 2 vols. (Moscow, 1982), vol. 2, pp. 313.

32. I. N. Berezin, *Puteshestvie po Dagestani i Zakavkaz'iu,* 2 vols., 2nd ed. (Kazan, 1959), vol. 2, pp. 51–52.

33. On Pogodin's subsequent career as a spokesman for official nationalism, see Nicholas Riasanovsky, *Nicholas I and Official Nationality in Russia, 1825–1855* (Berkeley, 1959), pp. 54 and 159–161.

34. Iu. M. Lotman, "Istoki 'Tolstovskogo napravleniia' v russkoi literature 1830-kh godov," *Trudy po russkoi i slavianskoi filologii* 5, vyp. 119 (1962): 35–46.

35. G. A. Gukovskii, *Pushkin i russkie romantiki* (Moscow, 1965), pp. 236–241.

36. Patrick Brantlinger, *Rule of Darkness: British Literature and Imperialism, 1830–1914* (Ithaca, N.Y., 1988), pp. 68 and 199–224.

37. Judith Deutsch Kornblatt, *The Cossack Hero in Russian Literature: A Study in Cultural Mythology* (Madison, Wis., 1992), pp. 14–17.

38. A. A. Vel'iaminov, "Zamechaniia na pis'mo glavnokomanduiushchago

deistvuiushcheiu armeiu k voennomu ministru ot 27 iulia 1832 goda," *Kavkazskii sbornik* 7 (1883): 82–83.

39. E. A. Verderevskii, *Ot Zaural'ia do Zakavkaz'ia. Iumoristicheskie, sentimental'nye i prakticheskie pis'ma s dorogi* (Moscow, 1857), p. 1.

40. A. A. Bestuzhev-Marlinskii, "Pis'ma iz Dagestana," in *Sochineniia v dvukh tomakh*, 2 vols. (Moscow, 1958), vol. 2, p. 6.

41. A. L. Zisserman, *Dvadtsat' piat' let*, vol. 1, p. 329.

42. George Leighton Ditson, *Circassia, or A Tour to the Caucasus*, rev. ed. (New York, 1850), p. 365.

43. Baddeley, *Russian Conquest*, p. 311; *Dvizhenie gortsev severo-vostochnogo Kavkaza v 20-kh gg. XIX veka. Sbornik dokumentov*, comp. V. G. Gadzhiev and Kh. Kh. Ramazanov (Makhachkala, 1959), pp. 471–486 and 730; and Gammer, *Muslim Resistance*, pp. 252–254.

44. *Dvizhenie gortsev*, pp. 329–330.

45. For further details, consult my *Russian Literature and Empire*, pp. 135, 147, and 153–155.

46. E. A. Verderevskii, *Plen u Shamilia* (St. Petersburg, 1856).

47. M. Iu. Lermontov, "Kavkazets," in *Sobranie sochinenii v chetyrekh tomakh*, 4 vols. (Moscow, 1983–84), vol. 4, p. 143.

48. Zisserman, *Dvadtsat' piat' let*, vol. 2, p. 3, and vol. 1, pp. 1–5 and 204–205. See also I. von der Hoven, "Moe znakomvstvo s dekabristami," *Drevniaia i novaia Rossiia* 2 (1877): 221; K. P. Belevich, *Stikhi i razskazy* (St. Petersburg, 1895), p. 171; and V. L. Markov, "Vospominaniia ulanskago korneta," *Nabliudatel'* 10 (1895): 165–166.

49. L. N. Tolstoi, "Rubka les," in *Sobranie sochinenii v dvenadtsati tomakh*, 12 vols. (Moscow, 1972–76), vol. 2, p. 64.

50. Ibid.

51. L. N. Tolstoi, diary of January 1853, in *Polnoe sobranie sochinenii*, 90 vols. (Moscow, 1928–58), vol. 46, p. 155; and Zisserman, *Dvadtsat' piat' let*, vol. 1, p. 58.

52. N. I. Lorer, *Zapiski dekabrista* (Moscow, 1931), pp. 248–249.

53. See analysis in my *Russian Literature and Empire*, chaps. 10 and 12.

54. A. V., "Pokorenie Kavkaza," *Russkii vestnik* 27 (June 1860): 348.

55. Quoted in Barrett, "Remaking of the Lion," p. 354.

56. F. V. Iukhotnikov, "Pis'ma s Kavkaza," *Russkoe slovo* (April 1861), otd. 3, pp. 9–13.

57. R. A. Fadeev, *Shest'desiat let Kavkazskoi voiny* (Tiflis, 1860), pp. 17–23.

58. D. I. Romanovskii, *Kavkaz i kavkazskaia voina. Publichnyia lektsii, chitannyia v zale Passazha v 1860 godu* (St. Petersburg, 1860), pp. 210–228.

59. Niva is discussed in Jeffrey Brooks, *When Russia Learned to Read: Literacy and Popular Literature, 1861–1917* (Princeton, 1985), pp. 111–114.

60. F. Gorshel't, "Vozrashchenie cherkesov s nabega," *Niva*, no. 29 (1878): 516–517.

61. E. Voskresenskii, comp., *Kavkaz po sochineniiam Pushkina i Lermontova* (Moscow, 1887), pp. 19 and 35–39.

62. V. I. Nemirovich-Danchenko, *Zabytaia krepost'* (L'vov, 1897). For a reading of this novel alongside Tolstoi's *Hadji Murat*, see my "Primitive Despot and Noble Savage: The Two Faces of Shamil in Russian Literature," *Central Asian Survey* 10, no. 4 (1991): 31–45.

Crimea and Caucasia

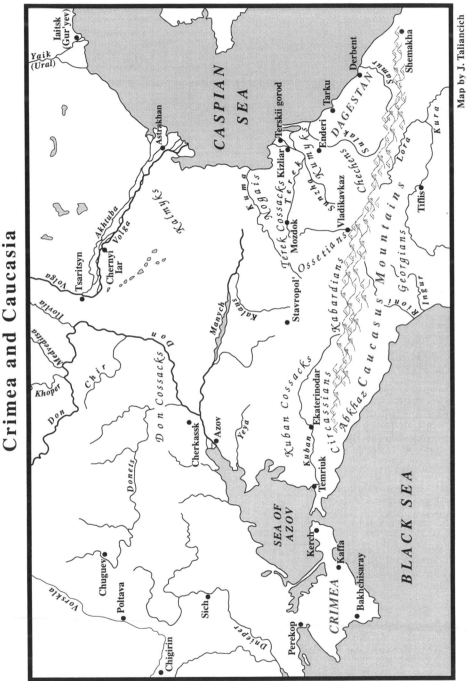

Map by J. Taliancich

·5·

AUSTIN LEE JERSILD

From Savagery to Citizenship: Caucasian Mountaineers and Muslims in the Russian Empire

> Rossini, Mozart, and Bellini can force a mountaineer
> to stop dead in his tracks for an entire hour.
>
> —A. VISKOVATOV, 1860[1]

In the mid-nineteenth century, influential imperial officials began to search for new solutions to rule in the empire's turbulent Caucasian borderland. Their plans drew on ideas, common in the reform years, to end the oppressive division of the population by social orders (*sosloviia*). Instead, reformers promoted the concept of a uniform "citizenship" (*grazhdanstvennost'*), which extended comparable responsibilities and status of imperial subject to all ranks of society. The contemporary understanding of the term included high standards of personal morality and of honesty and propriety toward one's superiors, and "a level of education necessary for membership in civil society [*grazhdanskoe obshchestvo*]."[2] As Dov Yaroshevski explains in this volume, legal authorities and imperial administrators judged this "republican citizenship" a progressive method of integrating non-Russian peoples into the imperial political order. While many officials and educated Russians remained committed to the old authoritarian notion of imperial society, subjugation of borderlands peoples, and the status of citizen as inferior subject, the new usage opened the possibility for a different foundation for Russian rule in the borderlands.

Earlier in the century, officials of the expanding Russian Empire paid little or no attention to the cultural differences and ethnic peculiarities of their new subjects. Their interest lay in integrating the upper classes, or nobility, of the borderlands into the imperial order.[3] They attempted these measures in the first half of the century in the Caucasus, rewarding Georgian nobles, beks and khans from Azerbaijan and Dagestan, and ruling families such as the Dadeshkilians from Svanetiia with the recognition of historic privileges, positions in Russian service, and money.[4] Respect for the privileges built into the estate structure had a powerful hold on Russian officials throughout the nineteenth century. Thus when it finally came time to find a place in Russian society for Abduragim, Shamil's son-in-law, Ministry of War officials referred to the 1859 military statute that offered rank in the Russian service to those mountaineers who could prove that they "genuinely" were the "sons of respected elders" in mountaineer society.[5] Abduragim had the right to exercise the privileges accorded to his social standing.

Yet the reason this son-in-law of Shamil was of such interest to Russian officials in Kaluga in the first place stemmed from a different sort of criterion. The Russian police official assigned to the family was attracted by Abduragim's youth and interest in Russian society, his lack of interest in religious scholarship, and his absence of "fanaticism."[6] Ministry of War officials praised his general "inclination to the European way of life."[7] By the middle nineteenth century, Russian officials in the borderlands began to imagine their realm in a new way.

This new version of colonial rule was prompted by serious doubts about the historical tradition of conquest and exile that accompanied the expansion of the Russian state into the southern borderlands. Exile meant exclusion, expulsion from the body politic, and a recognition that some belonged in the empire while others did not. An extensive population movement took place as a result of the Russian annexation of Crimea in the eighteenth century, when as many as 300,000 Muslims left the lands of the former khanate for Ottoman Turkey.[8] Eighteenth-century leaders such as Catherine the Great and Potemkin felt little need to justify or explain the massive population transfers that accompanied the state's southern expansion.[9] Faith was an important part of imperial identity, and Muslim mountaineers might naturally seek refuge among those of similar faith in the lands of the Ottoman sultan, the spiritual head of Sunni Islam. Religion seemed to Russians to distinguish one imperial community from the other, in particular in a region that bordered the great empires of Islam. Russians also traditionally associated Muslim and mountaineer traditions with "savagery" (dikost'), which cast doubt on the possibility of inclusion in the imperial order in conformity with the notion of citizenship. While savagery in the romantic tradition suggested primitive nobility, free of the artifice acquired by civilized people, it was most commonly used by administrators and educated Russians to imply something less than human, fit for either exile or military destruction.

In the Caucasus, exile continued throughout the course of the early and middle nineteenth century. Muslims sometimes left by choice, in the form of the *makhadzhirstvo*, the voluntary flight from infidel rule, or they were forced by the Russian military onto Black Sea ships that carried them to Ottoman Turkey, as occurred during the massive exile of the Adyge tribes (the "Cherkess") from the west Caucasus in 1861–64. While voluntary migration in times of trouble has been a prominent theme in Muslim history, the primary source of the flight from the Russian Empire was the brutal assault of the Caucasian army, which destroyed the villages of the Adyge, expropriated their livestock, and left them hapless on the shores of the Black Sea.[10] Russian sources in the nineteenth century estimated the extent of the Adyge exile to be roughly 500,000 people, while certain Soviet and Turkish scholars of a more recent day put the number even higher.[11]

In the eastern Caucasus, the war ended in 1859 with the capture of Shamil. However, rebellions persisted throughout the 1860s and 1870s, culminating in the extensive rebellion of 1877 that coincided with the outbreak of another war between Turkey and Russia. In spite of the fact that the northeast Caucasus was far from the easy exit route provided by the Black Sea, many administrators still contemplated various forms of exile for the Ingush, Chechens, Dagestanis, and other mountaineers of this region. General Aleksandr Petrovich Kartsov informed Minister of War Dmitrii Miliutin in 1865 that north Caucasian mountaineers "continue to hate us, as unbelievers, and they will maintain this feeling as long as we remain in their eyes the infidel [*giaur'*]."[12] Others, such as Captain Zolotarev, understood exile of the non-Russian population and the building of Cossack settlements as a logical course of action, as a continuation of the "basic Russian historical system of state settlement of the borderlands [*okrainy*] with Cossacks."[13] Zolotarev worried that the protracted war and the cultural divide between the world of Russia and the mountaineers made progressive cultural change unlikely. The instability of the region was particularly troublesome in the light of the "inevitable war with the European powers," Zolotarev informed the Main Staff, making exile the only policy offering a "final resolution" of the problem.[14] The traditions of the past continued to resonate among such administrators. Muslims and mountaineers in their view were irredeemable, unfit for life in the Russian Empire, incapable of absorbing a notion such as citizenship.

Mikhail T. Loris-Melikov, who served as the commander of Terek oblast' from 1863 to 1875 in a career that would eventually see him more famous as minister of interior, was aware of the strength of Sufi Islam and the hostility of the Chechens to Russian rule.[15] His efforts to address what officials referred to as the Chechen question included cooperation with an enigmatic Ossetian named Mussa Kundukhov, promoted to the rank of major-general in the Russian service. Kundukhov convinced Loris-Melikov of his loyalty to Russian rule, and led with Loris-Melikov's support an emigration of almost five thousand families from Muslim villages in the north Caucasus to Turkey.

This was a remarkable drama of deception and betrayal, with many intriguing questions of motive and personal identity, played out in the context of imperial conflict and international exchange. Loris-Melikov himself was warned by General Kartsov of the ambiguous position of Kundukhov and of the possibility of his betrayal; the viceroy warned all those involved that he was especially concerned with the maintenance of domestic order during the exile across the Caucasus; and plans were slowed as a result of the Turkish government's initial intention to resettle the exiled Chechens on the Russian border.[16] Rebellion and disorder accompanied the process, more mountaineers than expected became interested in leaving, and rumors began to surface among mountaineers in Dagestan that the circumstances were appropriate for a migration.[17] The exile took place from May to September of 1865. Some 4,989 families, approximately 23,000 people, left the Russian Empire.[18] The suspicions of some Russians about Kundukhov were later confirmed. Like Shamil's son, Kazi-Magom, he turned against the Russians, became the commander of the Main Staff of Turkish troops in Asia Minor, and returned to the Caucasus to lead a mountaineer contingent against the Russians in the war of 1877–78.[19]

The ethnic complexity of the actors is striking: an Armenian and an Ossetian in the service of the tsar in effect reshaped the ethnic landscape of the empire he ruled. Armenian, raised in Tiflis (Georgia), fluent in Caucasian languages and in French, Loris-Melikov later became famous as the minister of interior and advisor to the Russian tsar.[20] His work as commander of Terek oblast' was highly commended by Grand Duke Mikhail, who promised to inform the tsar of his favorable impressions.[21] Loris-Melikov's plan to resolve the Chechen question reflected his judgment of the viability of the notion of grazhdanstvennost' among the different peoples of Terek oblast'. The Mussa Kundukhov affair was just one aspect of his plan. Loris-Melikov's resolution of the Chechen question was not massive exile, as took place in the west Caucasus, but a mix of voluntary exile, population movement from mountainous terrain to the plains, cooperation with select mountain peoples, and the further growth of the Cossack settlement system into the foothills of Chechnia. Some Ingush in the mountains were to leave, as "they are positively incapable of accepting any kind of citizenship," Loris-Melikov informed General Kartsov.[22] Other mountaineers, however, such as the Ossetians, Kabardians, and Kumyks, were to be resettled and made subject to tribute, and other Chechen groups

"Peoples of the Russian Empire: [from left] *A Georgian, Chechen, Armenian, Imeretinets, Kurd, and Lezgin" (1900 poster, courtesy of the Russian State Library print collection)*

were to be moved to available lands near the Sunzhen Cossacks, where they would be severed from contact with Dagestan. Without such a plan, Loris-Melikov worried, the regime could only wait in hope that the passage of time would gradually introduce the "idea of citizenship" among the Chechens, but this was unlikely.[23] The state had to intervene in order to create the necessary basis for a workable empire. The "decisive [solution]—that is, the resettlement of all the Chechens by force"—was opposed by not only Loris-Melikov, but also Dmitrii Miliutin and the tsar himself.[24] Enlightened monarchy as the propagator of citizenship was preferable to an imperial monolith founded upon coercion.

Several variations of the notion of citizenship were evident in the ideas and policies of tsarist administrators such as Loris-Melikov. "Civilian rule," or simply "civil rule" (*grazhdanskoe upravlenie*), was a common phrase among Russians in the Caucasus. In 1859 High Commander Aleksandr Bariatinskii wrote to A. O. Kruzenshtern of his new plans related to "civil matters" (*grazhdanskie dela*), by which he meant his efforts to found a missionary society, construct a railroad, build a new Tiflis city square, dispense aid to victims of another earthquake in Shemakh, and so on.[25] Civil administration was a state of normalcy, preferable to war, military rule, or the previous historical practices of the region. The Ministry of War intended civil administration to apply to everyone who was not a Cossack or a mountaineer in the north Caucasus.[26] Like the French in the Maghrib, who left mountaineer and nomadic regions under military administration in the *bureaux arabes*, the Caucasian administration designated for the mountaineers a special form of military rule (*voenno-narodnoe upravlenie*).[27]

Of greater significance to Loris-Melikov's project were two other aspects of citizenship. He clearly had a notion of the importance of the development of civil duties among the mountaineers of Terek oblast'. He also, however, directed attention to resettlement, agricultural productivity, and taxation. Administrators who emphasized the obligations of grazhdanstvennost' assumed that the communal responsibilities expected of the Russian peasant population might be extended to mountaineers and other non-Russians of the empire. Service was understood by Russians as a precondition for participation in the realm of the civil life of the empire. The administrative structure of the state itself, in this view, thus served as a means of achieving the goal of citizenship in the borderlands. General Iurkovskii, a successor to Loris-Melikov as commander of Terek oblast', complained in 1882 that his mountain subjects lived blissfully unaware of the expectations and demands of the Russian state. The mountaineers remained free, he said, from the requirements "obligatory of every citizen [*grazhdanin*] throughout the entire fatherland [*otechestvo*]."[28] By this he meant that the mountaineers enjoyed exemptions from taxes, construction and transport obligations, and military service. In addition, he complained, Russian troops built the roads, and the government paid for schooling and police and financed the large contingent of soldiers in Terek oblast' still necessary long after 1859.[29] Iurkovskii used the term *grazhdanin*, but thought of the people he ruled as subjects (*poddanye*).

Military conscription was one form of service that the mountaineers particularly feared. Michael Stanislawski has traced the remarkable impact of the demands of such service upon the Jewish community in the early nineteenth century.[30] In a different context, Eugen Weber has explored the culturally transformative and normalizing experience of military service in nineteenth-century France.[31] Russian administrators viewed imperial military service in much the same terms as their counterparts in the Third Republic. "Service in the army will undoubtedly widen the worldview of the native . . . and will be of enormous educative [*vospitatel'nyi*] significance," wrote General Mikheev, an early twentieth-century commander of Terek oblast'.[32] Though "peasants," however reluctantly, became "Frenchmen," to borrow from Weber's title, mountaineers and Muslims resisted their remaking as subjects of the Russian tsar. Service in the military was a particularly explosive issue for Muslims in an avowedly Christian country, of course, and such resistance extended far beyond the Caucasus. In the 1890s, Ministry of Interior officials estimated with alarm that 27 percent of the "Tatars" from the fourteen provinces of the interior, using tactics (such as self-inflicted wounds) "in particular practiced by the Jews," managed to get themselves rejected from service in the army.[33] North Caucasian mountaineers even suspected the educational programs of the Restoration Society (a missionary society) and the Geographic Society to be preparation for servitude in the tsar's army. In Chechnia and Dagestan, rebellions in the 1860s and 1870s were in part inspired by rumors of impending military service.[34] Still, Prince Bariatinskii's promise to the mountaineers of Terek and Dagestan oblasti that the claims of the Russian military would never extend to their villages remained in effect.[35] The mountaineers managed to remain free of this aspect of "civil life," in return for the payment of a modest tax.[36] At the onset of World War I, just a few years before its collapse, the regime remained unable to compel the mountaineers to serve in the army.[37]

Agricultural labor was another aspect of the ideal imperial order. During the 1865 debate on the Chechen question, Aleksandr Tumanov, an *okrug* commander in Terek oblast', wrote to Loris-Melikov that the primary goal of administration policy should be to attach the Chechens to the land, and "thus transform them into peaceful citizens." They must become convinced, Tumanov emphasized, of the "advantages of the honest labor of agriculture."[38] General Iurkovskii as well correlated the "beginnings of grazhdanstvennost'" with the "state of agriculture."[39] These officials spoke an administrative language of imperial responsibility and obligation. This was precisely what mountaineers feared most about the expansion of the Russian state.

The notion of citizenship offered Caucasian Muslims and mountaineers something beyond this world of civic obligation, however. In the Caucasus, ethnographers, educators, and linguists provided important support for the viability of an empire united by grazhdanstvennost'. Petr K. Uslar, who combined three occupations, emphasized that with Russian help, mountaineers were capable of cultural progress. Well aware of the work of Nikolai Il'minskii in Kazan, Uslar contended that schooling for the mountaineers was most effective in their native tongue. For Uslar, however, the health of the empire did not require the cohesion offered by the common profession of Orthodoxy.[40] His schools for the mountaineers were to counter the Arabic language and culture of the Muslim world with those of Russia. His special "Caucasian alphabet," which he composed with extensive help from many native mountaineers, was based on Cyrillic, and intended to expose mountaineers to the world of Russian language, literature, and culture. Mountaineers for Uslar were capable of responding favorably to the challenge of his secular learning and secular worldview.

Educated Russians in the Caucasus believed that Western cultural institutions were effective transmitters of citizenship. Like grazhdanstvennost', such institutions were understood by Russians to possess a self-evident appeal and to be accessible to all the peoples of the empire. The Italian opera was founded in the 1850s, noted historian A. L. Zisserman later in the nineteenth century, not only because it diverted the youth of Tiflis from "other less moral entertainments," but also because it served as a cohesive factor among the "diverse tribes" (*raznorodnye i raznoplemennye*) of the region.[41] The notion of citizenship reflected the optimism of the Enlightenment values that informed it. Grazhdanstvennost' was an idealized Russian image of proper social and cultural behavior that was derived from ideas about life in a more civilized West. The ideal was characterized by traditional nineteenth-century markers of cultural achievement. Literacy, education, and even attendance at the new Tiflis Theater were some of the ways in which the peoples of the Caucasus could affirm for Russians their willingness to participate in the civic life of the empire.

The Tiflis Theater was an important site where citizenship was on display. Georgians were in the best position to take advantage of what was offered by the theater. It embodied, as a Russian commentator in the newspaper *Kavkaz* put it, grazhdanstvennost' itself, for it offered exposure to the "delicate pulse of education and the noble aspirations of society."[42] The Tiflis Theater quickly became the model for theater construction and productions elsewhere in the Caucasus. In early 1850 a theater was built in Lenkoran, near the Persian border (Azerbaijan), and the event was celebrated in Tiflis as a great victory for "what the world of Russia had to offer."[43] In 1869 Loris-Melikov, still the commander of Terek oblast', was proud to announce that in the tradition of the Tiflis Theater, a new theater had been established in Vladikavkaz.[44] The promise of Russian rule extended beyond educated Georgians in Tiflis, and included even north Caucasian mountaineers.

Early Orthodox missionaries were not compelled to distinguish between their work and that of the theater. At midcentury the claims of the Orthodox faith were still easily compatible with the promotion of citizenship. Stanislawski has clarified this matter regarding the controversial issue of efforts to convert the Jews. S. S. Uvarov, the minister of national enlightenment, was in favor of conversion, Stanislawski notes, yet he did not view the purpose of education as a means of converting Jews. Rather, like most Russians in the Caucasus at this time, Uvarov assumed that education and knowledge inevitably led to interest in the Christian faith.[45] This is why the agenda of Orthodox missionary societies in the Caucasus was dominated by apparently secular activities. The Ossetian Spiritual

Commission was the predecessor of the more active and ambitious Society for the Restoration of Orthodoxy in the Caucasus (founded 1860). The latter worked with the Caucasian Department of the Geographic Society to transcribe alphabets for the mountain languages, translate church materials into the newly written languages, restore decrepit churches and religious monuments, train teachers and priests, and sponsor schools for mountain children.[46] There was no contradiction for Russians in the Caucasus between the claims of Orthodoxy and civility. To be Orthodox was to be civil, just as literacy and education by definition prompted one to understand the relationship between the Orthodox faith and civil life. As late as 1886, society educators still described their task as the "fostering of Christianity and Russian grazhdanstvennost' among the mountain tribes of the Caucasus."[47] While the circumstances and course of the Caucasian war had compelled Russian missionaries to focus their attention on groups such as the Ossetians, Svans, Tushins, Khevsurs, Pshav, and Abkhaz, the founders of the Restoration Society understood all of the north Caucasus, including the troublesome Chechens, the Adyge, and the mountaineers of Dagestan, to offer suitable ground for their educative work.[48] All were invited—to become literate, and to attend theaters, operas, and schools, irrespective of faith or cultural background.

To this version of citizenship the "native" of course responded, but in ways that would eventually prove disturbing to administrators of the regime. As anticipated by educators and orientalist scholars such as Adol'f P. Berzhe, Georgians, Armenians, and Azerbaijanis were the first to respond to their hopes and expectations.[49] Even from among the mountaineers, educated figures advocated a worldview that probably qualifies them for Isaiah Berlin's definition of an "intelligentsia," a group "devoted to the spreading of a specific attitude to life, something like a gospel."[50] Their gospel was cultural progress achieved with the help of Russian culture and the Russian Empire. Its advocates included figures such as N. G. Berzenov from Ossetia, Khan-Girei and Shory Nogmov from the Adyge, and Abdulla Omarov from Dagestan.[51] As in other colonial empires, however, the formation of a native intelligentsia was eventually to be a mixed blessing for the regime. Educated in colonial schools but then denied access to positions of authority and responsibility within the colonial state, educated natives questioned the benefits of colonial rule.[52]

One such figure whose life spanned the period of this study was Hasan Melikov-Zardobi. He attended Russian schools in Tiflis and Baku and university in Moscow, and eventually founded in 1877 the first Azerbaijani Turkish-language newspaper in the Russian Empire. After the regime closed *Äkinçi* (Sower) and exiled Zardobi to his native village of Zardob in response to the Caucasian revolts of 1877, he became a frequent contributor to the Baku newspaper *Kaspii*. Initially a perfect match for Zardobi, *Kaspii* attributed the rebellions of 1877 to the ignorance of the population, and frequently portrayed Muslim *maktabs* and *madrasas* as impediments to the moral and intellectual development of children. Contributors to *Kaspii* emphasized the cruelty and corruption of the Muslim clergy and the suspicion of the local Muslim population toward modern medicine and schooling; they also denounced the superstitions of Muslim village culture.[53] The Caucasus, the editors of *Kaspii* maintained in 1881, was a backward borderland of Russia, in need of Russian aid and guidance in order to facilitate the "development of grazhdanstvennost'."[54] Zardobi's initial estimation of the weaknesses of traditional Muslim culture and his vision of a future for the borderlands within the Russian Empire were similar to the *jadid* concerns of Ismail Bey Gasprinskii and the Central Asian writers discussed by Edward Lazzerini and Adeeb Khalid in this volume.

However, Zardobi's long stay in exile in the small Muslim fishing village of Zardob on the Kura River west of Baku compelled him to rethink his vision of progress through Russian colonial rule. He developed a greater appreciation for the ideas and practices that informed village culture, and in particular for the importance of Islam to the daily lives of his fellow villagers. He had the opportunity to observe misguided Russian colonial policies at the local level, and was impressed by the callousness and lack of understanding of village conditions by officials who barely passed through Zardob on their way from Tiflis to Baku. In his later essays Zardobi actively worked to create a public space or civil sphere independent of the regime. Citizenship was an ideal that he used to criticize the regime. In 1899 he suggested that Russia's educational policies would best contribute to "peaceful progress and grazhdanstvennost'" if they granted respect for the native languages and religions of the Caucasus.[55] This was the beginning of a more modern politics of rights and demands, articulated in opposition to the state. Subsequent critics of tsarist rule in the Caucasus, such as Joseph (Djugashvili) Stalin from Georgia, wrote in 1904 not of grazhdanstvennost', but of *grazhdanskie prava* (civil rights).[56] The notion of citizenship, initially prompted and fostered by the regime, eventually turned against that regime.

As used in the borderlands, the notion of grazhdanstvennost' represented profoundly colonial efforts to define the identity of the empire. Most Russian administrators in the Caucasus emphasized or understood grazhdanstvennost' to be primarily about obligation and responsibility, subservience and a commitment to labor, and the rendering of military service, taxes, and the other requirements of imperial life. They understood Russian forms of service and rural organization as the natural and ordained form of existence. It should be noted that they came to believe Islam to be compatible with this world of order and obligation. By the latter nineteenth century, administrators worried about how their actions would be viewed "in the eyes of the Muslims of Central Asia and India."[57] When officials constructed model (Russian) resettlement villages in Saratov province for mountaineers accused of participation in the 1877 rebellion, they placed mosques on their center squares.[58] St. Petersburg and Moscow, Russians hoped, might serve in their own way as a Mecca for those increasingly known as the "Russian Muslimś" of the empire. This version of citizenship was undoubtedly useful to the Russian state as it attempted to govern its colonial borderlands.

Even the understanding of grazhdanstvennost' as a set of ideas or worldview that was suggestive of a modern citizenry was accompanied by a heavy emphasis on order and obligation. The founding charter of mountaineer institutes in the north Caucasus declared that grazhdanstvennost' was to be achieved by introducing mountaineers to the "rules of honor, duty, love of labor, [and] order."[59] When General Mikheev linked the construction of roads, telegraphs, and telephones with not only the development of citizenship but also an improvement in "legality and order," Tsar Nicholas II penciled alongside this statement, "Of course."[60] This version of citizenship justified the empire in terms novel to the Russian past. But the new version of grazhdanstvennost' possessed the potential for nationalist resistance to empire beyond the control of the Russian state and Russian educated society.

NOTES

For their responses to previous versions of this chapter, my thanks to Daniel Brower, Edward J. Lazzerini, Yuri Slezkine, Dov Yaroshevski, and the participants of the Russian Orient Conference, held in Berkeley 23–24 September 1994. The Education Abroad Program of the University of California supported my research in Russia.

1. A. Viskovatov, "Obshchii kharakter prirodi i cheloveka na Kavkaze," *Russkii vestnik* (1860), in P. Nadezhdin, ed., *Priroda i liudi na Kavkaze i za Kavkazom* (St. Petersburg, 1869), p. 8.

2. Vladimir Dal', *Tolkovyi slovar' zhivogo velikorusskogo iazyka* (Moscow, 1978; based on 2nd ed., 1880–82), vol. 1, p. 390.

3. A. E. Nolde, *Ocherk po istorii kodifikatsii mestnykh grazhdanskikh zakonov pri grafe Speranskom*, vol. 1 (St. Petersburg, 1906), pp. 11–19. Also see Raymond Pearson, "Privileges, Rights, and Russification," in Olga Crisp and Linda Edmondson, eds., *Civil Rights in Imperial Russia* (Oxford, 1989), pp. 93–94.

4. For this approach applied to the Adyge, see Gosudarstvennyi voenno-istoricheskii arkhiv Rossiiskoi Federatsii (GVIARF, formerly TsGVIA), Moscow, f. 14719, op. 1, 1832, d. 153, ll. 1–2, List of Asians.

5. GVIARF, f. 400, op. 1, 1863–67, d. 3, Letter from Pavel Przhetsslavskii to Nikolai Ivanovich, 12 January 1864, l. 37.

6. Ibid., Letter from Przhetsslavskii to Nikolai Ivanovich, 12 June 1863, l. 1; Letter from Przhetsslavskii to Nikolai Ivanovich, 16 November 1863, ll. 14–15.

7. Ibid., Report, 7 January 1864, l. 34.

8. Peter J. Potichnyj, "The Struggle of the Crimean Tatars," *Canadian Slavonic Papers* 17, nos. 2–3 (1975): 302.

9. Sankt-Peterburgskii filial Arkhiva Rossiiskoi akademii nauk (PFA AN, for-

merly LO AAN), St. Petersburg, f. 100, op. 1, d. 100, Letter from Potemkin to Catherine, 24 April 1777, l. 8.

10. For a harrowing account, see N. Drozdov, "Posledniaia bor'ba s gortsami na zapadnom Kavkaze," *Kavkazskii sbornik* 2 (Tiflis, 1877): 387–457.

11. The most thorough work devoted to west Caucasian exile is G. A. Dzidzariia, *Makhadzhirstvo i problemy istorii Abkhazii XIX stoletiia* (Sukhumi, 1982). There are as many different estimations of the extent of the exile as there are interested scholars, who in addition generally neglect to cite the source of their information. A detailed Russian account left by the Ministry of War counts a total emigration of 332,000 in the fall and winter of 1863–64, and 418,000 total from 1861 to 1864. See GVIARF, f. 400, op. 1, 1864, d. 4736, ll. 77–78. My thanks to Larisa Isinovna Tsvizhba for directing me to this file.

12. G. A. Dzagurov, ed., *Pereselenie gortsev v Turtsiiu. Materialy po istorii gorskikh narodov* (Rostov-on-Don, 1925), Memorandum on the Chechen question, General A. P. Kartsov to Dmitrii Miliutin, 3 January 1865, p. 40.

13. Ibid., Memorandum on Terek oblast', Captain Zolotarev, 14 June 1863, p. 9.

14. Ibid., pp. 11–12.

15. Ibid., Letter from Loris-Melikov to Kartsov, 28 July 1863, pp. 13–14.

16. Ibid., Letter from Loris-Melikov to Kartsov, 16 February 1865, p. 49; Letter from Loris-Melikov to Aleksandr Georgievich, 8 March 1865, p. 56; Letter from Loris-Melikov to Aleksandr Georgievich, 12 March 1865, p. 58.

17. Ibid., Letter from Levan Ivanovich Melikov to Loris-Melikov, 20 April 1865, p. 65. L. I. Melikov, not to be confused with Loris-Melikov, was at this time the commander of Dagestan oblast'.

18. Ibid., Letter to Loris-Melikov from Captain Smekalov, 28 November 1865, p. 137. The continuation of this exile story into Turkey, which included the use of Turkish arms against the Karabulaki (Ingush), is in GVIARF, f. 400, op. 1, 1866–68, d. 49, ll. 4–26.

19. M. S. Totoev, "K voprosu o pereselenii Osetin v Turtsiiu (1859–1865)," *Izvestiia Severo-Osetinskogo nauchno-issledovatel'skogo instituta* 13, vyp. 1 (1948): 34–39.

20. Loris-Melikov thus surfaces as a main character in Tolstoy's novel *Khadzhi-Murat*, devoted to the Avar khan. On Loris-Melikov's efforts to reform the autocracy as minister of interior, see Petr A. Zaionchkovsky, *The Russian Autocracy in Crisis, 1878–1882*, ed. and trans. Gary M. Hamburg (Gulf Breeze, Fla., 1979). Zaionchkovsky describes Loris-Melikov as "intelligent, energetic, flexible as well as extraordinarily ambitious and insincere" (p. 98).

21. Rossiiskii gosudarstvennyi istoricheskii arkhiv (RGIA, formerly TsGIA), St. Petersburg, f. 866, op. 1, 1866, d. 37, Letter from Grand Duke Mikhail to Loris-Melikov, 21 March 1866, ll. 1–2. Mikhail Nikolaevich Romanov was the son of Nicholas I, and at this time the Caucasian viceroy.

22. Dzagurov, ed., Letter from Loris-Melikov to Kartsov, 21 February 1865, p. 54. The Karabulaki tribe was almost entirely exiled to Turkey in 1865.

23. Ibid., Notes on Terek oblast', Loris-Melikov, August 1864, p. 24.

24. Ibid., Report from Miliutin to Namestnik, 3 November 1864, p. 36.

25. Letter from A. I. Bariatinskii to A. O. Kruzenshtern, 16 June 1859, in A. L. Zisserman, *Fel'dmarshal Kniaz' Aleksandr Ivanovich Bariatinskii, 1815–1879*, vol. 3 (Moscow, 1891), pp. 37–39.

26. GVIARF, f. 400, op. 1, d. 68, l. 3, Memorandum by Dmitrii Miliutin, 17 May 1866.

27. Similar cases in North Africa include the Tunisian Service des Renseignements and the Moroccan Service des Affaires Indigènes. See Kenneth J. Perkins, *Qaids, Captains and Colons: French Military Administration in the Colonial Maghrib, 1844–1934* (New York, 1981). In spite of the fact that voenno-narodnoe upravlenie was intended to be temporary, the system lasted until 1917.

28. RGIA, f. 932, op. 1, 1882, d. 303, l. 2, Report by Commander of Terek oblast', 31 March 1882.

29. Ibid., ll. 1–14.

30. Michael Stanislawski, *Tsar Nicholas I and the Jews: The Transformation of Jewish Society in Russia, 1825–1855* (Philadelphia, 1983), pp. 13–42.

31. Eugen Weber, *Peasants into Frenchmen: The Modernization of Rural France, 1870–1914* (Stanford, 1976), pp. 292–302.

32. RGIA, Biblioteka, op. 1, 1909, d. 99, l. 45, Report by General Mikheev.

33. RGIA, f. 1149, op. 11, 1894–1895, d. 103, ll. 17–19.

34. GVIARF, f. 400, op. 1, 1872, d. 319, l. 1, Viceroy Mikhail to Tsar, 11 August 1872.

35. RGIA, f. 866, op. 1, 1866, d. 40, l. 13, Proclamation to the Chechen People, Bariatinskii, 1860; f. 932, op. 1, d. 316, l. 3.

36. In 1887 the Ministry of Finance declared that the mountaineers of Terek and Kuban oblasti, and in 1890 those of Abkhaziia, could pay a tax rather than serve in the army. See RGIA, f. 1149, op. 11, d. 1, ll. 2–3, 1891–1892.

37. Graf Vorontsov-Dashkov, *Vsepoddanneishii otchet za vosem' let upravleniia Kavkazom* (St. Petersburg, 1913), p. 12. On military service and the Bashkirs, see Robert F. Baumann, "Subject Nationalities in the Military Service of Imperial Russia: The Case of the Bashkirs," *Slavic Review* 46, no. 3 (1987): 489–502.

38. Dzagurov, ed., Letter from Aleksandr Tumanov to Loris-Melikov, 19 February 1865, p. 50.

39. RGIA, Biblioteka, op. 1, 1909, d. 99, l. 2, Report by General Iurkovskii, 1884. On the ideas of Russian administrators about the contrast between peasants and nomads, note Marc Raeff, "Patterns of Russian Imperial Policy toward the Nationalities," in Edward Allworth, ed., *Soviet Nationality Problems* (New York, 1971), p. 36.

40. P. Uslar, "O rasprostranenii gramotnosti mezhdu gortsami," *SSOKG*, vol. 3 (Tiflis, 1870), pp. 7 and 16.

41. Zisserman, *Fel'dmarshal Kniaz'*, p. 53.

42. N. P., "Tiflisskii Teatr," *Kavkaz* 80 (11 October 1859): 443.

43. "Smes'," *Kavkaz* 12 (11 February 1850): 45.

44. RGIA, f. 866, op. 1, 1869–1872, d. 48, l. 2, Report of Commander of Terek oblast', 20 May 1869.

45. Stanislawski, *Tsar Nicholas I*, p. 66. Stanislawski, it should be noted, remains virtually alone in this interpretation. By contrast, see Salo W. Baron, *The Russian Jews under Tsars and Soviets* (New York, 1964), p. 36, as well as scholars writing after the publication of Stanislawski's book, such as Stephen M. Berk, *Year of Crisis, Year of Hope: Russian Jewry and the Pogroms of 1881–1882* (Westport, Conn., 1985), p. 5.

46. The Restoration Society regularly published the *Otchet Obshchestva vozstanovleniia pravoslavnoi tserkvi na Kavkaze*.

47. *Otchet Obshchestva vozstanovleniia pravoslavnago khristianstva na Kavkaze za 1886 god*, 5. By this time, however, society educators were also concerned about the competing possibility of a secular education, as their occasional warnings about the influence of "Westernism" and the importance of the proper context for non-Russian education attest. See ibid., pp. 144–150. Orthodoxy as an aspect of imperial ideology changed in meaning from roughly 1850 to 1900, and missionary work among non-Russians in 1850 was a much different enterprise from missionary work in 1900. Writers such as Ladis K. D. Kristof, "The Russian Image of Russia," in Charles A. Fisher, ed., *Essays in Political Geography* (London, 1968), p. 350, and Pearson, "Privileges, Rights, and Russification," p. 95, do not make this distinction.

48. Memorandum by Bariatinskii, in Zisserman, *Fel'dmarshal Kniaz'*, p. 102.

49. Note the excitement of Berzhe at the appearance of literature and poetry from the pen of the "so-called Azerbaijani Tatar," in Sankt-Peterburgskii filial Instituta vostokovedeniia Rossiiskoi akademii nauk (SPbFIV RAN, formerly LO IVAN), St. Petersburg, f. 6, op. 1, d. 33b, ll. 9–12, Letter from Berzhe to P. I. Keppen, 25 August 1860. On the formation of non-Russian intelligentsias, see Ronald Grigor Suny, *The Making of the Georgian Nation* (Bloomington and Indianapolis, 1988), pp. 113–143; Ronald Grigor Suny, *Armenia in the Twentieth Century* (Chico, Calif., 1983), pp. 5–16; Tadeusz Swietochowski, *Russian Azerbaijan, 1905–1920* (Cambridge, 1985), pp. 23–36; Audrey L. Altstadt, *The Azerbaijani Turks: Power and Identity under Russian Rule* (Stanford, 1992), pp. 50–73.

50. From Stanislawski, *Tsar Nicholas I*, p. 109, who is discussing the maskilim. The original citation is Isaiah Berlin, "A Marvelous Decade," *Encounter* 4, no. 6, pt. 1 (1955): 29.

51. The works of Nogmov and Omarov have been reprinted in Soviet editions, as Sh. B. Nogmov, *Istoriia adygeiskogo naroda*, 5th ed. (Nal'chik, 1947), and Abdulla Omarov, *Dagestan: vremia i sud'by* (Makhachkala, 1990).

52. Benedict Anderson, *Imagined Communities*, rev. ed. (London, 1991), p. 140; also see Francis G. Hutchins, *The Illusion of Permanence: British Imperialism in India* (Princeton, 1967), p. 157.

53. "Ot redaktsii," *Kaspii*, no. 1 (1 January 1881): 1–2; "Mestnyia izvestiia," *Kaspii*, no. 41 (31 July 1881): 1; "Vnutrennee obozrenie," *Kaspii*, no. 46 (2 August 1881): 2–3; "Mestnyia izvestiia," *Kaspii*, no. 65 (25 September 1881): 2; "Sueverie musul'man," *Kaspii*, no. 84 (18 April 1886): 3.

54. "Baku, 4 iiulia 1881 g.," *Kaspii*, no. 30 (5 July 1881): 1.

55. "Nashi sel'skie shkoly," *Kaspii*, no. 176 (18 August 1899), in Z. Geiushov, ed., *Hasan-Bek Zardabi, Izbrannye stat'i i pis'ma* (Baku, 1962), p. 220.

56. I. V. Stalin, "Kak ponimaet sotsial-demokratiia natsional'nyi vopros," in *Sochineniia*, vol. 1 (Moscow, 1946), p. 36.

57. RGIA, f. 573, op. 12, 1901, d. 13390, l. 9, Journal.

58. For this exile story, see RGIA, f. 565, op. 5, d. 19814, 1877–1884; f. 385, op. 12, d. 7382, 1877–1880; f. 1286, op. 39, d. 363 and d. 345, 1878–1880; and f. 1282, op. 1, d. 970, 1880–1881.

59. RGIA, f. 1268, op. 10, d. 168, l. 10.

60. RGIA, Biblioteka, op. 1, 1909, d. 99, l. 56, Report by General Mikheev.

.6.

Daniel Brower

Islam and Ethnicity: Russian Colonial Policy in Turkestan

Ethnicity became an instrument of modern colonialism when European empires extended their dominion over peoples of Asia and Africa. Studies of the British and French expansion have told of the efforts by Western travelers and scientists to describe and classify these peoples according to the criteria of nineteenth-century ethnography. Benedict Anderson has stressed the importance attributed to ethnic naming of subject peoples by European colonial administrators, and to the impact of ethnic classification on the emergence of national identity among these peoples. Ethnicity in this perspective is a social invention with enormous cultural and political consequences.[1]

It became a tool of Russian rule in Turkestan after tsarist forces conquered the region in the 1860s and 1870s. The new administration, under the leadership of Governor-General Konstantin von Kaufman, confronted a population whose differences from, as well as its resemblances to, other borderlands peoples of the empire were cause for deep concern.[2] The Turkestan inhabitants were partly nomads, partly settled townspeople and farmers; they formed a compact society with a total population of more than three million ruled by, but isolated geographically and culturally from, the Russian core of the empire. By religion, these new subjects were almost entirely Muslim, as were the Caucasian mountaineers who had fought Russian troops for nearly a half-century under the leadership of a Muslim imam, Shamil. By language, they were predominantly Turkic, with linguistic ties to the Volga Tatars, who remained, despite two centuries of strenuous tsarist efforts, a largely unassimilated people. Governing Turkestan posed daunting social and political problems to its new rulers.

The religious bonds that linked Turkestan with the Ottoman Empire were an equally serious concern. The Ottoman sultan claimed the title of caliph of the Sunni Muslims and was beginning to champion Pan-Islamic (and soon Pan-Turkic) ties to distant Muslim communities, including the subjects of the Russian tsar. To suspicious tsarist officials, the very loyalty of Turkestan's peoples was open to question.

This was not the first time the tsarist regime had confronted difficult policy decisions created by the presence of non-Russian peoples on the edges of the empire. Frontier rule had occupied a distinct place in Russian government since Muscovite times. In this volume, the chapters by Michael Khodarkovsky and Dov Yaroshevski discuss the slow evolution of tsarist concepts of non-Russian peoples. These ideas inspired very different forms of imperial rule on the borderlands. One of the most influential was summed up in the time-honored formula of conquest, subjugation, administrative integration (*sliianie*), and conversion to Orthodox Christianity. It had set borderlands policy in the early eighteenth century among Bashkirs and Kalmyks. It reappeared in the Caucasian wars a century later.[3]

But such forcible methods of rule appeared inappropriate to Russian rulers and government officials drawn to Enlightenment theories of society. Writers such as Montesquieu and Voltaire found in human history an array of peoples whose human qualities appeared in national character, folkways, and custom. Religious practices belonged to social customs; all religions deserved to be recognized and tolerated, not persecuted. Primitive society was a stage of history, not a mark of the devil. All peoples would ultimately rise to the level of civilization if given the proper guidance. This conception of barbarism inspired a group of imperial administrators, supported by Catherine II, to formulate a new, progressive mission of enlightened rule over subject peoples. The chapter in this volume by Yuri Slezkine reveals how extensive (and confusing) was the ethnographic inquiry into the empire's peoples that the Enlightenment, and Catherine herself, promoted. The undertaking begun then of tolerance and recognition of ethnic differences did not supplant the policies aimed at administrative assimilation, but did become a meaningful part of tsarist frontier rule. It reemerged in the 1840s in Caucasia under the administration of Prince Mikhail Vorontsov.[4]

Subsequently, it formed the core of the Kaufman administration's policy toward Turkestan's subjects. One Western scholar recently concluded that ethnographic knowledge was "trivial" in the "grand process of imperial power" in Western empires.[5] If so, the importance Kaufman attached to the study of ethnicity in Turkestan is all the more remarkable. This chapter will explore the factors leading to the reemergence in Turkestan of the Catherinian frontier policy and will assess its influence on Russian rule during and after Kaufman's fifteen years (1867–81) as governor-general.

Turkestan's new ruler was personally familiar with the difficulties of governing Muslim peoples. Though he never wrote of the lessons that he drew from his years of service (1843–56) in the Caucasian wars, the experience helped prepare him for his Turkestan challenge.[6] The rebellion of the mountain tribes was already well under way when he arrived to serve as military engineer. It had been provoked in part by the Russian authorities' clumsy, brutal efforts to incorporate the peoples there into the Russian legal and administrative system, in disregard of Muslim law and local customs. The war itself dragged on until the early 1860s. Military heroism and romantic adventures aside, it proved, as Austin Jersild's chapter in this volume reveals, a sobering experience for tsarist officials. Victory had a bitter taste when several hundred thousand refugees, primarily tribes from the western Caucasus, fled at the close of the war to the Ottoman Empire to avoid rule by infidel Russians. At a time when Western leaders sought to win the loyalty of colonial peoples with the tools of modern civilization, the Caucasian war appeared a throwback to imperial rule in the style of Julius Caesar.

But Kaufman also had the opportunity to observe Catherinian policies at work during his Caucasian service. His supreme commander and viceroy of Caucasia between 1845 and 1856, Prince Mikhail Vorontsov, had encouraged his administrators to respect ethnic differences even while he, at Nicholas I's orders, pursued the bloody military campaigns against the mountain tribes. His principal innovation consisted of devising policies intended to implement what a recent biographer has termed "respectful tolerance" of his subjects. Their integration into the empire would come, he believed, when increasing numbers of the natives discovered "the benefits of Russian civilization."[7] Administrators who had closest contact with the Caucasian tribes had to win the respect of the peoples under their rule.

To that end, he encouraged subordinates in the region to acquire "knowledge of the customs of the people" inhabiting his vast territory. This daunting ethnographic project, despite its scholarly aura, had the practical objective of giving Russian officials the understanding and insight to govern justly their difficult subjects. The latter in turn were expected, by some miraculous turnabout, to acknowledge the cultural and political preeminence of their rulers.[8] In the midst of a destructive war, Vorontsov's policy promised a form of colonial rule that revived the Catherinian tradition and that was far less costly than enforced administrative integration.

Colonial rule on the empire's new Central Asian frontier provoked in the 1860s a new debate in which supporters of tolerance confronted defenders of state security. General N. A. Kryzhanovskii, the ambitious governor-general of the vast Orenburg territory, seized the opportunity presented by the conquest of Turkestan to warn of the dangers of toleration of the Muslim religion. He became in 1867 a member of the special committee appointed by the tsar to prepare the administrative guidelines for Turkestan rule. His personal views, contained in reports to the tsar, were forthright and troubling. The revolt of Muslim peoples under way in those years in western China appeared to him a portent of massive unrest among Russia's Muslims. He argued in 1867 that "holy war" brought on by the "fanatical barbarity" of an "aroused Islamism" was at the very "edges of our frontiers." Islam constituted a military threat to the empire. He claimed that its seditious influence was enhanced by the "protection" afforded the Muslim religious authorities by the tsarist policy of tolerance. He urged that measures be taken immediately to repress Muslim religious propaganda.[9] In effect, he proposed that the empire rely on military might and administrative controls to integrate Turkestan within the Russian state. His argument carried great weight, since it drew on fears of Muslim resistance to infidel rule and was buttressed by a tradition of frontier practices that was centuries old. Not incidentally, it also helped to promote his own candidacy to govern Russia's new colony.

But he faced the opposition of powerful officials committed to the policy of tolerance. Chief among these was the minister of war, Dimitrii Miliutin. He also had served in the Caucasus during the war against the mountaineers. He too had drawn the lesson that a policy of eradication or restraint of Islam was the worst approach to the establishment of effective imperial rule of Muslim peoples. He made his views absolutely clear from the moment of Russian expansion into Central Asia. In a letter in 1865 to General Cherniaev, commander of Russian forces there, he ordered his bellicose subordinate to do nothing that would arouse fears among the population of repression of their religion. Muslim laws and religious practices were to be respected, for to do otherwise would "strengthen the influence of the Muslim priesthood on the native population." Religious tolerance was for him a political necessity. He reminded Cherniaev that "our lengthy presence in Caucasia has already revealed that the influence of the Muslim clergy on the people is absolutely contrary to our interests, for they stir up fanaticism and hostility toward us."[10] He, like other Russian officials then and later, was by force of circumstances a supporter of the Catherinian heritage.

In these conditions, Miliutin must have found Kaufman a far preferable choice for Turkestan governor-general. In mid-1867, the tsar appointed Kaufman to this position at the same time as he approved the first, temporary administrative statute for Turkestan. Both measures revealed the special importance attached by the regime to the new colony, placed directly under the authority of the ministry of war. Kaufman received extraordinary powers in his vast territory comparable only to those, in the British Empire, of the viceroy of India. The statute granted the region was temporary precisely because its creators believed that Kaufman should have the time to formulate and introduce all revisions needed to govern effectively. We have only scattered clues to his approach, which emerge in early reports and in the overall pattern of policy making during his years of rule. In brief, the Catherinian legacy became the inspiration and defense of his grand colonial scheme.

But first he had to make clear his method of handling the Muslim "threat." In historical hindsight, the grounds for these fears appear to have been a mixture of apprehension of foreign political subversion and an abiding prejudice against Muslim religious piety ("fanaticism" was the preferred description). Still, they set the tone of policy making in the highest official circles. The tsarist government judged the solidarity of Islam, under the leadership of the Ottoman sultan, to be a menace to the unity and power of the empire, and Kaufman seems to have shared their concern. The first detailed enunciation of his approach is found in a lengthy memorandum on the handling of Muslim property and religious practices prepared as part of his revisions of the Steppe Commission's draft statute for the administration of Turkestan. In it he warned that Islam "cannot be at peace with any [alien] state." In the spirit of Kryzhanovskii's anti-Islamic statements, he denounced the solidarity of the international Muslim community. It, in his words, promoted "cosmopolitanism and religious fanaticism" and undermined "patriotism," by which he meant loyalty to non-Muslim rulers. In sum, formal agreement between the Russian Empire and Islam was impossible.

Having admitted the gravity of the problem, however, Kaufman claimed that he could make it disappear. The choice, which he presented in a dramatic (and often repeated) formula, was either "persecution or complete disregard" (*ignorirovanie*, from the French verb *ignorer*) of Islam. His rivals for the position of Turkestan governor-general (such as Kryzhanovskii) might prefer to employ the brutal methods of persecution, used with such disastrous results in the Caucasian wars. He chose the second, moderate option, which he described somewhat ambiguously as "the more tolerant and firm policy of the Russian state."[11] The spirit of Catherine the Great (and of Prince Vorontsov) was by his side. It is not surprising that in the reform years of the 1860s he became the tsar's chosen emissary to govern the new Turkestan colony.

"Disregard" summed up his modified Catherinian policy. It was based on the very problematical assumption that Islam existed in two separate spheres, one formed by public religious institutions and the other by Muslim religious practices. The former was the source of hostility to Western (and Russian) imperial rule, but the latter was a private affair of religious faith. Private was not political; hence these practices could and ought to be tolerated, or, in Kaufman's Gallicized Russian, "disregarded." In these terms, he could rightly claim that Catherine's legacy remained at the core of his policy.

In practice, this policy did call for firm measures against Muslim traditional institutions. The mild official language of Article 364 of his revisions to the statute for the new colony stated that "the Muslim faith in Turkestan will henceforth be tolerated but not protected."[12] It had a direct bearing on fundamental issues of law and religion. Kaufman's administration left unrestricted the scope of Muslim religious law (the Shari'a, known in Turkic as the "şeriat"), but his reforms did prevent its enforcement by Muslim authorities. His first measures in this direction included the abolition of the positions of Sheykh-ul-Islam (highest religious position) and of the chief Muslim judge (the qadi-kalan) in Tashkent, and a ban on the activity of special religious police (the reis) who had the power to punish Muslims for violations of the Shari'a. Leadership in his reformed Turkestan was to be secular, not religious.

His exclusion of Muslim organizations extended as well to the Muslim Spiritual Administration, created by Catherine II's reforms. It gave formal recognition to Islam on the southern and eastern borderlands, granting mullas the rights and responsibilities of Orthodox clergy. But the Turkestan governor-general's determination to weaken the public institutions and leaders of Islam broke precedent with this policy. He flatly rejected the request by the leader (mufti) of the Muslim Spiritual Administration in Ufa for authority over Turkestan's Muslims. He asserted in justification that the "native religious authorities" are "not as fanatically religious" and "are more readily reconciled with our rule" than the "fanatical fighters for Islam" among the "Tatar priesthood" in Orenburg.[13] "Disregard" guaranteed peace; presumably patriotism would soon follow.

But his confidence rested more on ideology than on observation of the Muslim community. It required a sort of act of faith to believe that his policies could so quickly weaken Muslim solidarity in Central Asia, one of the major centers of Islamic worship and study. From this point of view, his policy hid a grave paradox. How could one reconcile the threat posed by Islam with continued tolerance, even if supplemented by the dismissal of Muslim religious authorities in Turkestan? The dilemma, which would plague his successors in Tashkent, arose from his belief that he could maintain colonial policy on progressive, Catherinian foundations and at the same time break apart the solidarity of the Muslim community. At heart, Kaufman was a firm believer in the triumph of secularism. It is a fair guess that he had little regard in general for any religion, including Orthodox Christianity outside of its obligatory public functions. The established Orthodox Church formed a useful bulwark of Russia's political order; Tashkent's "Russian city" quickly got its Orthodox church. But it came without a bishop and, most important, without any Orthodox missionaries. The struggle for souls had no part in Kaufman's imperial project.

Christianity in Turkestan
Late-nineteenth-century Orthodox church, Vernyi (Almaty) (Courtesy of Daniel Brower, 1992)

His secular faith closely resembled, and probably drew upon, the views of the positivist school of nineteenth-century European social theory. These writers (such as Ernest Renan of France and Sir Henry Maine of England) asserted that religion in its public organization and traditions was part of social customs and not of essential acts of faith. In these terms, religion evolved along with the way of life of a particular people. Sir

Henry Maine was persuaded that "a belief system of a particular society is molded by communal needs." It was an easy step for colonial administrators to conclude that religious opposition to their rule was nurtured by a backward society. The British viceroy of India found this a reassuring argument to justify British imperial rule in the face of the antagonism to colonial domination revealed in the so-called "Sepoy mutiny" of 1857, provoked in part by British actions that appeared to defile Muslim religious laws.[14] It followed that if progressive colonial policies encouraged social development, animosity based on religious beliefs would lessen. Kaufman brought this European positivism to Turkestan.

These theories, which included a strong ethnographic ingredient, were his key to unraveling the present and future condition of Turkestan's Muslim peoples. His analysis drew a simple distinction between the conditions of nomads and of settled peoples. Echoing the judgment of other Russian officials and writers, he claimed to detect a basic difference in their observance of the Muslim faith. He was convinced that, though "the nomads officially adhere to Islam, in reality [they] shun it and have no specific religious faith." His explanation for their alleged laxity relied on his positivist theories, for he stressed that their "special way of life [was] based on natural and still primitive principles." "Primitive" might be close to barbarism, but from his imperial perspective it was a bulwark against Islam. The townspeople of Turkestan, on the contrary, were "fanatics" who had "absorbed the spirit of this [Muslim] faith, have organized their lives around the general type of Muslim life and observe the moral code of the Shariʿa." The secret to pervasive Muslim solidarity and opposition lay in social conditions.

Two conclusions appeared evident. For one, Turkestan nomads (identified usually as "Kirgiz") had to be isolated as much as possible from the townspeople. More important, the townspeople had to be the objects of particular tsarist attention. Their fervent piety was linked, or so it seemed, to the backwardness and isolation of Central Asia. Imperial social policies had to bring modernity in its Russian guise to the area. In doing so, the empire would strengthen secular practices and would eliminate undesirable manifestations of religious fanaticism. Kaufman did not have to share Catherine's benign opinion of official Islam to defend her policy of tolerance. His faith lay in the transformative powers of progressive colonial rule. "Disregard" plus progress equaled the disappearance of Muslim religious solidarity. In a wildly utopian prophecy, he foresaw the time rapidly approaching when "Islam, never existing independently, will not be in a condition to survive."[15]

The vital actors in this process, of course, had to be his colonial administrators. They were the agents of transformation, on condition that they possessed accurate scientific knowledge of the territory and its diverse peoples. Kaufman's years of Caucasian service had given him the opportunity to observe Vorontsov's progressive colonial policy at work. The Caucasian viceroy had shown him the importance of geographers, linguists, and ethnographers in unraveling the complex, poorly understood "customs of the people." By the 1860s, this faith in "scientific" knowledge had spread to sympathizers of reform in and out of government. One important facet of this belief was the assumption that a civilized empire such as Russia had the obligation to understand the ways of life and belief of its subjects.

Ethnography was the premier science in this project. When the first Russian Ethnographic Exposition opened in Moscow in 1867, its president justified its enormous array of exhibits devoted to the empire's peoples by pointing out that "the study of our native land" was "a necessity for every educated Russian."[16] The tsar himself attended the exhibition, granting his patronage to its sponsors and proclaiming in the process his support for this imperial ethnographic crusade. Kaufman, departing that year for Turkestan, made the exhibition's motto his own. In doing so, he brought Vorontsov's policy to life in Turkestan on a far greater scale than had occurred in Caucasia. Ethnicity was to become a servant of his colonial rule.

The investigation of ethnic groups was an integral part of his project to make the land and peoples of Turkestan the subjects of systematic study and display. To this end, Kaufman had the advantages of his exceptional authority as governor-general and the intellectual and political climate of the reform era. Using all his powers, he called upon the skills of a group of Russian officers with an advanced education, and the expertise of the Russian scholarly community working in the natural and social sciences. He appointed as head of chancellery Aleksandr Geins, a graduate of the General Staff Academy and experienced practitioner (perhaps self-taught) of geography and statistics. Another well-educated officer, Captain N. A. Maev, became the editor and publicist of his provincial newsletter (*Gubernskie vedomosti*).

He searched for his civilian specialists across the entire country. His artist-in-residence during his first years in Turkestan was Vasilii Vereshchagin, a former naval officer converted to art and trained in St. Petersburg and Paris in the skills of portraiture and orientalist art. Among the explorers whom he invited to conduct expeditions in Turkestan were Aleksei Fedchenko, a botanist, and his wife, by training a geologist. Fedchenko had graduated in the early 1860s from Moscow University. There he had become one of the disciples of Anatolii Bogdanov, a biologist and proponent of the new French school of physical anthropology. Kaufman obtained in the late 1870s the skills of an educator and Turkic linguist, Nikolai Ostroumov, a graduate of the Kazan Theological Academy, where Nikolai Il'minskii had a decade earlier begun arguing for the use of native languages in schools for eastern peoples. These and other military and civilian specialists in Turkestan had nothing in common with the much-maligned Turkestan provincial officer-administrator with the reputation in later years for drunkenness and corruption. Though their numbers were small, their work marked Kaufman's administration with a unique stamp of erudition.

The center of their activities, particularly in the first years, was the Tashkent branch of the Society for Amateurs of Natural Science, Anthropology, and Ethnography (OLEAE). It had first appeared in Moscow in 1863 under Bogdanov's leadership to promote the study of and popular interest in Darwinian science and anthropological investigation into the cultural and physical (especially craniological) characteristics of human races. Its leaders had been the organizers of the 1867 Ethnographic Exhibition. Kaufman himself sponsored the Tashkent section, calling on the handful of members at the opening meeting in December 1870 to conduct a "thorough study" of their "new and scarcely explored region." His zeal to make the area a known place included the public display of that knowledge among the Russian public. In the same speech he expressed the wish that Turkestan be well represented at the Polytechnical Exhibition, scheduled to open in 1872 in Moscow under the auspices of their society.[17] Other scholars and scientists joined in, sent by such organizations as the Imperial Russian Geographical Society. They all were pioneers and publicists for Russia's scientific exploration of Turkestan.

Considering the inaccessibility of the area and the difficulties of its study, the work proceeded remarkably swiftly. Expeditions set out to map the geology and geography of Turkestan, enlarged in 1875 with the annexation of the remnants of the Kokand khanate. Fedchenko conducted three separate trips between 1868 and 1872, gathering along the way a collection of skeletons and skulls that appeared (along with some 3,000 other artifacts from Turkestan) at the 1872 Moscow exhibition.[18] The Tashkent newspaper became the voice of these explorers as well as of the administration, appearing at times more like a scholarly journal than a weekly official newsletter. The line between science and the state was blurred, in part because the explorers were often themselves officers. As Maev noted in one of the first issues, "We see scientific expeditions ending in skirmishes and storming of fortified places." But the challenge was worthy of the risk, for "we found here an exotic way of life, thoughts, social order, and economy" that was "unimaginable from a European point of view."[19]

A potent new method of midcentury social analysis in Russia came from statistics, and Kaufman put that tool to work in his territory very soon after he arrived. He formed a statistical committee to gather information on Turkestan's population, urban and peasant, settled and nomads. The editor of the newspaper, Maev, had the responsibility to gather this material into a statistical yearbook, the first volume of which appeared in time to be shown at the 1872 Moscow exhibition.[20] The plan spelled out at

Islam and Ethnicity

Borderland as Frontier
Surprise Attack *(Vasilii Vereshchagin, 1871)*

the first meetings of the committee in 1871 and 1872 looked beyond the mere "collection of statistical data." It included as well the publication of information on the "geography and ethnography of localities," on the "past lives of the people and the description and study of their monuments," and on other economic and social peculiarities of Turkestan.[21] The outpouring of scholarly and popular articles and books on Turkestan reached within a few years the proportions of a small flood. To ensure that the mass of information remained accessible, Kaufman commissioned in 1869 a special ongoing private "scrapbook" of articles on Central Asia, which within ten years had in 300 issues catalogued more than 4,000 publications on the region.[22]

The array of intended readers for this "textual production" of the new Russian colony suggests that Turkestan officials believed their scientific knowledge to be useful in winning the support of Russians as well as in educating Turkestan officials. These audiences had widely differing interests. Between the colonial administrators confronted by a large and suspicious Muslim population and a curious Russian public attracted by the exotic qualities of the territory lay an enormous and in some respects unbridgeable cultural gulf. Yet Kaufman seems to have attempted to reach them all. Clearly the diffusion of new ethnographic, geographical, and scientific findings was as important to him as their collection and analysis. The Russian organizers of the Third International Congress of Orientalists in St. Petersburg in 1876 asked him (as well as other administrators of the empire's eastern regions) both for regional costumes and photographs and for "the presence of live representatives of the Asian peoples belonging to the Russian Empire."[23] Kaufman obliged, personally selecting artifacts, both dead and alive (three natives), to be sent to the congress.

He relied on texts and images to convey the proper human face of his

Ruined Empires
Tomb of Timur *(Vasilii Vereshchagin, 1869)*

Turkestan subjects. Images held a powerful attraction, which Kaufman turned to his own advantage. The public exhibits displaying the artistic work of his temporary artist-in-residence, Vasilii Vereshchagin, drew enthusiastic audiences at exhibits both in Russia and in Europe. The story of Vereshchagin's encounter with the Orient began with his break with the Academy of Arts and with its neoclassical artistic canons. His search for artistic inspiration took him (like poets before him) to Caucasia, and then to Paris to the art studio of one of the most famous French orientalist artists, Jean-Léon Jérôme. His interest in eastern "oriental" settings and his

Islam and Ethnicity

Artist as Ethnographer
Uzbek, Elder of Village of Khadzhikent *(Vasilii Vereshchagin, 1869)*

progressive artistic convictions suited perfectly the needs of Kaufman. He traveled to Turkestan "on special commission" *(po osobomu porucheniiu)* of the governor-general in 1868 and 1870. Kaufman gave him free rein to create his own images of the territory—its peoples, its monuments, and the conquest itself—and to present this visual picture to the Russian public.

His artistic work served Kaufman's project well. His "Turkestan Series" included more than 250 drawings and paintings. The largest number consisted of portraits of individuals given specific ethnic (but not individual) identity—*Uzbek Elder, A Kirgiz, A Sart Woman,* etc. Notably absent were works portraying the Muslim presence among the population; only two paintings confronted this aspect of Turkestan, and both cast an orientalist gaze at the exotic dress and behavior of Sufi religious elders. Vereshchagin presented these works in 1874 at very successful exhibits in St. Petersburg and Moscow.[24] Tens of thousands of visitors found there a visual display of Russia's new Muslim subjects.

The task of ethnographic classification of the various groups among the Turkestan population raised far more complex problems than those Vereshchagin faced. The difficulties originated on both the Russian and Central Asian sides. The claims of ethnography to scientific precision, in Russia and in the West, were in the mid-nineteenth century both problematic and controversial. The original linguistic, folkloric tradition in ethnography had practiced a very eclectic approach, using in addition to languages a great variety of social data subsumed, in the words of Yuri Slezkine (in this volume), under the categories of "sustenance, sex, and settlement." This methodology suited well the style of explorers and geographers, who compiled the principal ethnographic studies until the mid-nineteenth century. It also had the advantage of accommodating objective criteria (appearance, habits, language) and subjective naming practiced by the subjects themselves. It appealed to the public at large as well, primarily because it fit easily into a ranking of peoples on the basis of presumed civilized attainments.

On the other hand, it did create colossal confusion at times. Peoples often did not produce a neat set of ethnic features all distinct from other groups; frequently they used multiple and contradictory names to describe themselves (e.g., self-styled Bashkirs speaking the "Tatar" language). It had the added disadvantage of producing a mountainous pile of data which lent itself only partially to the rigorous systematic classification of populations that appeared to be the hallmark of the scientific method. An escape from this clutter and confusion emerged in France, where the naturalist Georges Cuvier had long proposed classifying peoples according to the strict methodology of physical anthropology. Sweeping away the debris of ethnographers, he had argued that the science of humanity had to begin with the study of the "permanent inherited physical differences which distinguish human groups." Cranial type promised the easiest measure, and craniology became key to the new science of physical anthropology. Popularized by Paul Broca in the 1850s and spreading quickly east and west, it competed with the folkloric school for dominance in Russia as well as in other Western countries.[25] It arrived in Turkestan in the baggage train of the members of the Society of Amateurs for Natural Science, Anthropology, and Ethnography.

From the perspective of the Russian ethnographers, the Central Asian scene presented particular complexities. The geographical label of Turkestan, generally used by surrounding peoples, conveyed no useful knowledge other than the vague suggestion of a common language (and even that failed to meet the test of rigor, since Tajik, widely spoken there, was not a Turkic tongue). The native peoples themselves had no difficulty using simultaneously several types of ethnic names (for both themselves and others). But these made little sense in a scientific world. Recorded conversations suggested that ethnic identity might derive both from ancestry and from social status. "'I'm a Kirgiz,' says a native [nomadic tribesman—DB] from the shores of Issyk-Kul', 'but I'm an Uzbek.'" The puzzled observer, a trained linguist and zealous ethnographic investigator, noted that "even Sarts affirm, 'We are Uzbeks.'"[26] Tribal origins linked them with "Uzbek," while their way of life was the grounds for identifying themselves as "Kirgiz" (nomads) or "Sart" (townspeople). To complicate the situation further, terms such as "Sart" changed meaning from one region to another, and town dwellers often called themselves by the name of their city.

Ethnographers, unlike Turkestan's dwellers, had to find grounds to differentiate Sarts (and Uzbek, Kirgiz, etc.) from everyone else. The apparent confusion surrounding the term "Sart" produced scientific debates that lasted throughout the tsarist period. The first investigator from the Imperial Russian Geographical Society declared flatly that "only Tajiks and Sarts" lived in settled areas of Russian Turkestan, but recognized that the latter spoke "the Chagatai dialect of the Turkic language."[27] Since the Chagatai and Uzbek tongues were very similar, some observers insisted that this "dialect" fell clearly into the general category of Uzbek, which they promoted to the category of a unique language. On these linguistic grounds, therefore, they could claim that the Sart people did not exist. Others claimed that the Sart tongue was sufficiently unique, when combined with other folkloric (and even craniological) evidence, to provide a "scientific" basis for recognizing its ethnic separateness. Anatolii Bogdanov became so deeply embroiled in the debate that he conjured up an entire array of craniological studies to prove that Uzbeks and Sarts constituted distinct peoples.[28]

While scholars pursued their endless debate, Turkestan administrators resolved the dilemma by letting their subjects name themselves and be named in the simplest possible fashion. They probably had an abiding inclination to distinguish above all between nomads and settled peoples, and among the latter between townspeople and peasants. After all, these basic social categories constituted a tangible reality that in many respects shaped their relations with their subjects. From their perspective, folkloric ethnographic criteria gave sufficient grounds to delimit the ethnic markers characterizing the hierarchy of peoples in the region: pastoral nomads were usually called "Kirgiz," townspeople usually "Sart" (or Tajik), and peasants either "Sart" or "Uzbek."

Certain essential social traits easily fit these labels. Russian observers noticed that the Sarts appeared to have abandoned tribal affiliation and were primarily traders, artisans, or farmers; hence by Western standards they occupied the highest social rank among the Turkestan natives. They were alternatively praised for industriousness and damned for religious fanaticism. The Uzbeks seemed to be at a transitional stage of semi-nomadic life with strong tribal loyalties, and the Turkmen and Kirgiz nomads (occasionally refined to distinguish between Kirgiz-Kaisak and Kara-Kirgiz) clearly occupied a lower rung on the ladder of human evolution. Beyond that, there was always a residual category of "Turk" for other Turkic-speaking natives, and "Tatar" for Turkic-speaking migrants from other parts of the empire. Ethnographers proved their usefulness through detailed descriptions of these groups; quarrels over naming did not concern the colonial administration.

The population was classified in this apparently straightforward manner in the first census of Tashkent, undertaken in the early 1870s; the 1897 census made a few refinements, but essentially adhered to these ethnic categories. The Turkestan administration produced multicolored ethnographic maps to place the various ethnic groups in their proper geographic locations.[29] These findings helped in delimiting official districts to avoid the undesirable mixing of peoples, especially of Sarts and Kirgiz. The latter's "virtues," Kaufman noted early in his rule, would only suffer if they were territorially integrated with the Sart population. The Sarts were a pernicious influence, for they harbored in their midst "bigoted, hypocritical, and corrupt Muslim holy men, mullas, judges, pilgrims, saints, and dervishes."[30] Ethnography in this context was specifically intended to help construct a barrier to Islam.

It also determined ways of life on the ladder of human evolution in Turkestan. Taxes paralleled human evolutionary stages, and administrative borders tried (unsuccessfully) to segregate peoples. The human sciences served imperial needs on a basic level. The Turkestan newspaper and scholarly journals presented an array of refinements and complications to this basic ethnic classification, but the real needs of Kaufman's ethnographic project were met. As for religion, the only census entry was "Muslim."

If one can judge from his passing remarks in later official reports concerning ethnicity and Islam in Turkestan, Kaufman believed that the problems of naming and ruling had in the main been resolved. He continued to express concern about the religious influence of Islamic zealots on the Kirgiz, but he hoped that the civilizing influence of effective administration and Russian schooling would attenuate Islam's social impact. In a preliminary report (never sent) to the tsar discussing his rule between 1867 and 1872, he claimed to possess a clear ethnographic picture of the population, and to have successfully achieved "strict conformity of [administrative] measures with the population's customs and laws which have been elaborated during their millennial existence."[31]

With respect to Islam, he argued in his 1881 report that his administration understood so well the outlook of the population that "no administrative undertakings in our Central Asian possessions will encounter serious obstacles from the religion that dominates the area, on condition that these measures be in accord with the needs of the economic and civil order of the region." The "restless preaching of fanatics" no longer stirred the people to revolt. "Bloody anarchy," he concluded, had given way to "well-being" in a "new order."[32] In that new order, ethnographic knowledge was an important guarantor of the solidity of Russian rule.

One can wonder at the optimism revealed in Kaufman's assessment, but his grounds for this conviction were clear. A progressive Western empire brought its backward peoples to respect and collaborate with their imperial rulers. He accorded the city of Tashkent the form of municipal government granted most of the empire's towns in the 1870 municipal reform statute. With propertied natives seated in the town council alongside Russians, he could claim to have brought *grazhdanstvennost'* (that is, "citizenship" in the imperial mode, as described in Dov Yaroshevski's chapter) to his capital city. Economic improvements (in the event, the increase of cotton production) went hand in hand with enlightened administration in the attempt to make the Turkestan colony a productive as well as a progressive undertaking. Kaufman launched the first efforts to increase cotton cultivation (principally by promoting improved strains of cotton). The official formula for colonial success was, in the words of an 1885 report, the "establishment of agriculture and citizenship [*vodvorenie sel'skokhoziaistva i grazhdanstvennosti*] in Turkestan."[33] As Austin Jersild points out in his chapter in this volume, similar aspirations shaped colonial policies in Caucasia in the same period.

Kaufman had put in place a policy that was the direct descendant of the Catherinian legacy of colonial rule. The militaristic style of administration resurfaced periodically in Turkestan in later decades. Still, Kaufman's project remained firmly embedded in local practices and imperial visions of the future. Paternalistic policies, backed by modern science, sought to combat the vestiges of backwardness and foster constructive cultural, economic, and political ideals and behavior. Ethnic differences constituted meaningful bases for imperial rule. When the governor of one of the steppe provinces north of Turkestan advised his officials "to learn all the facts about the [way of] life of nomads and the reasons for it," he was reiterating one essential ethnographic truth of Kaufman's policy. The most well-meaning administrator, he warned, could not "speed up the civilizing process."[34]

The imperial mission, promoted by an enlightened provincial administration and backed by state leaders and public opinion, had as its first task to overcome the resistance of Islam, and as its second duty to encourage civic and economic activity of the people. This message, repeated throughout Kaufman's rule, continued to be heard in St. Petersburg and Tashkent. Religious toleration was good; oppression was bad. Knowledge of the people and firm rule were beneficial to the state and to the subject peoples. Peace and prosperity were a certainty.

Never mind that most Russian officials remained in ignorance of the very language of their subjects. They constituted the most important public whom Kaufman sought to enlighten and to persuade. The provincial newspaper was directed most particularly toward them. So also were the museum and library that Kaufman organized. But these all bore in one way or another the stamp of Kaufman's cultural elitism. It seems doubtful that many Russians there became imbued with the new enlightened spirit. Most administrators did not learn the Sart language generally used in the towns, preferring to communicate through interpreters. One of Turkestan's most competent officials concluded that between them and their subjects "emerged a wall made of native administrators, traders, and translators," all seeking their own profit. Referring to the first decades of Russian rule, he concluded that "we looked through the eyes, heard with the ears, and thought with the cunning, grasping minds of this live wall."[35] Culture, not religion, emerged as the great barrier.

It is not surprising that at the end of the century the colonial administration was unprepared for armed resistance to Russian rule. A minor uprising led by a Sufi religious elder spread panic among Russian officials. Nor is it surprising that the governor-general, General Dukhovskoi, responded by warning of an upsurge in Turkestan of fanatical Islam, "hostile to Russia." In a direct reference to Kaufman's policy, he announced that "the further disregard of Islam is not only undesirable, it is impossible."[36]

Yet toleration in the spirit of Kaufman's policies still found influential defenders. When Dukhovskoi's frantic appeal for stern measures reached St. Petersburg, it encountered the unyielding opposition of Count Witte. His plans as minister of finances included prospects of a colonial pot of gold—in the form of cotton—in Turkestan. His vision of a unified empire mobilizing the labor and resources of the entire population made him a firm supporter of the Catherinian tradition. Dukhovskoi must have appeared to him a troublesome general who in the name of order would succeed only in stirring up the natives. He invoked in a special memo to the tsar the ghosts of Catherine and Kaufman, authors of the "time-honored policy of tolerance toward the Muslim religion." In words that echoed Kaufman's, he insisted that Russia's imperial vocation included "full equality of rights with other subjects, freedom in the conduct of their religious needs and nonintervention in their private lives." Ethnic divisions, not "religious-political unity," were the reality among "our native Muslims." These peoples, he was convinced (like Kaufman before him), were "reliable" subjects of the empire.[37] Railroads, not repression, remained the most effective means to ensure the loyalty of native peoples.

The program, from our late-century perspective, was only partially doomed. The period of war and revolutionary turmoil that began in 1914 revealed that hostility among Turkic peoples to Russian (and infidel) rule remained widespread. Soviet power came at the point of Red Army bayonets. But the ethnographic project thrived at the hands of Soviet officials, who proved far more zealous practitioners than Kaufman in claiming to "know" ethnic groups and in drawing ethno-territorial boundaries. Railroads did get their message across, but by the late twentieth century they operated among nation-states in Central Asia, not within an empire. The delimitation of a private space for religious practice and a public space for civil law (albeit originally presented in the form of imperial edict) remains to this day a promising solution to the presence of major religious communities within modern states.

NOTES

Research for this chapter was supported in part by a grant from the International Research & Exchanges Board, with funds provided by the National Endowment for the Humanities and the U.S. Department of State. None of these organizations is responsible for the views expressed.

1. See Manning Nash, *The Cauldron of Ethnicity in the Modern World* (Chicago, 1989), chap. 1; Talal Asad, ed., *Anthropology and the Colonial Encounter* (London, 1973); and Benedict Anderson, *Imagined Communities: Reflections on the Origin and Spread of Nationalism,* 2nd ed. (New York, 1991), esp. chap. 11.

2. A general discussion of Kaufman and Russian rule is Richard Pierce, *Russian Central Asia, 1867–1917: A Study of Colonial Rule* (Berkeley, 1960); see also David Mackenzie, "Kaufman of Turkestan: An Assessment of His Administration (1867–1881)," *Slavic Review* 26, no. 2 (June 1967): 265–285.

3. See Michael Khodarkovsky, *Where Two Worlds Met: The Russian State and the Kalmyk Nomads, 1600–1771* (Ithaca, N.Y., 1992); Alton Donnelly, *The Russian Conquest of Bashkiria* (New Haven, 1968).

4. See Dov Yaroshevski, "Imperial Strategy in the Kirghiz Steppe in the Eighteenth Century," *Jahrbücher für Geschichte Osteuropas* 39 (1991): 221–224; also L. Hamilton Rhinelander, "Russia's Imperial Policy: The Administration of the Caucasus in the First Half of the Nineteenth Century," *Canadian Slavonic Papers* 17, nos. 2–3 (1975): 218–234.

5. Talal Asad, "From the History of Colonial Anthropology to the Anthropology of Western Hegemony," in *Colonial Situations: Essays on the Contextualization of Ethnographic Knowledge,* ed. George Stocking (Madison, Wis., 1991), p. 315.

6. See A. Semenov, "Materialy dlia biograficheskago ocherka," in *Kaufmanskii sbornik* (Moscow, 1910), pp. v–viii.

7. Rhinelander, "Russia's Imperial Policy," pp. 232–233.

8. See Austin Jersild, "Authenticity and Exile: Ethnography, Islam and the Mountaineer in Russian Caucasia, 1845–1877" (Ph.D. diss., University of California–Davis, 1993), esp. pt. II ("Ethnography and Culturalism").

9. "Otchet," 31 January 1867, Russkii gosudarstvennyi istoricheskii arkhiv [henceforth RGIA], f. 821, op. 8, d. 594, l. 35.

10. Cited in A. G. Serebrennikov, ed., *Turkestanskii krai. Sbornik dokumentov dlia istorii ego zavoevaniia* (Tashkent, 1914), vol. 19, p. 90.

11. "O zemliakh vakufnykh," RGIA, f. 821, op. 8, d. 612, ll. 6–7.

12. "Vypiska iz proekta polozheniia ob upravlenii Turkestanskim kraem," ibid., l. 10.

13. "Perepiski s Turkestanskim general-gubernatorom . . . o zapreshchenii Orenburgskomu magometanskomu dukhovnomu sobraniiu vmeshivat'sia v dela Turkestanskago kraia," 10 December 1879, RGIA, f. 821, op. 8, d. 612, l. 22.

14. Roger Owen, "Imperial Policy and Theories of Social Change: Sir Alfred Lyall in India," in Asad, *Anthropology and the Colonial Encounter*, pp. 226–227.

15. "O zemliakh vakufnykh," RGIA, f. 821, op. 8, d. 612, l. 9.

16. *Vserossiiskaia etnograficheskaia vystavka* (Moscow, 1867), p. 40.

17. *Turkestanskie gubernskie vedomosti* [henceforth *TGV*], no. 1, 14 January 1871.

18. A. Fedchenko, *Puteshestvie v Turkestan* (Moscow, 1950), pp. 190–194 (the book first appeared in St. Petersburg in 1875).

19. "Nashe polozhenie v Srednei Azii," *TGV*, 14 June 1871.

20. *Ezhegodnik: Materialy dlia statistiki Turkestanskago kraia*, vol. 1 (St. Petersburg, 1872); five more volumes appeared during the 1870s.

21. Ibid., vol. 3 (1874), pp. 294 and 297.

22. V. I. Mezhov, "Turkestanskii sbornik. Sobranie statei o stranakh Srednei Azii voobshche i Turkestanskoi oblasti v osobennosti," 300 vols. The sole copy of this collection is located in the Navoi State Library in Tashkent. Mezhov subsequently compiled an index to the collection, published in St. Petersburg (*Turkestanskii sbornik. Sistematicheskii ukazatel'*, 3 vols. [St. Petersburg, 1878–88]).

23. *Trudy Tret'ego mezhdunarodnago kongressa orientalistov*, vol. 1 (St. Petersburg, 1875), pp. iv and xv.

24. See my essay "Images of the Orient: Vasilii Vereshchagin and Russian Turkestan," in *Working Papers of the Center for German and European Studies*, no. 3.5 (University of California–Berkeley, 1993).

25. See Nancy Stepan, *The Idea of Race in Science* (London, 1982), pp. 45–46; also George Stocking, ed., *Race, Culture and Evolution: Essays in the History of Anthropology* (Chicago, 1982), pp. 30–40.

26. A. Khoroshin, "Narody Srednei Azii," *TGV*, 22 March 1871.

27. A. I. Maksheev, "Geograficheskie, etnograficheskie i statisticheskie materialy o Turkestanskom krae," *Zapiski Imperatorskago russkago geograficheskago obshchestva* 2 (1871): 37–38 (henceforth IRGO).

28. A. Bogdanov, "Antropometricheskie zametki otnositel'no Turkestanskikh inorodtsev," *Izvestiia Imperatorskago obshchestva liubitelei estestvoznaniia, antropologii, i etnografii* 34 (1880): 85–87. From a late-twentieth-century perspective, his proclaimed search for "facts" and rejection of "subjective impressions and chance juxtapositions" in pursuit of ethnic reality puts him in the company of other exemplars of ethnographic self-delusion. See Stephen Jay Gould, *The Mismeasure of Man* (New York, 1981). The confusion returned in the 1920s to bedevil the Communists after they had decreed the Sarts out of existence, for their brand of objective ethnographic classification required that they extract the one "real" Uzbek language out of a number of distinct dialects (Ingeborg Baldauf, "'Kraevedenie' and Uzbek National Consciousness," *Papers on Inner Asia* 20, Subseries Central Asia, 1992, pp. 1–29).

29. The first census of Tashkent followed this pattern (*Ezhegodnik*, vol. 1, pp. 8–12); the 1897 census tried for greater ethnic clarity, though with only limited success (*Obshchii svod po imperii rezul'tatov razrabotki dannykh pervoi vseobshchei perepisi naseleniia* [St. Petersburg, 1905], vol. 2, pp. xxv–xxvii). The first official ethnographic map of Turkestan appeared at the end of the 1870s ("Etnogra-

ficheskii sostav narodonaseleniia Turkest. General-Gubernatorstva [po ofitsial'-nym materialam 1869–1879 godov]," Tsentral'nyi gosudarstvennyi arkhiv Respubliki Uzbekistana [TsGARU], f. 1008, op. 1, d. 152, l. 7).

30. "Vsepoddanneishii otchet Turkestanskago general-gubernatora po voenno-narodnomu upravleniiu za 1867–1869 gg.," TsGARU, f. 1008, op. 1 (1870), d. 1, l. 17.

31. "Vsepoddanneishii otchet za 1867–1872 gg.," TsGARU, f. 1008, op. 1, d. 4, ll. 19–20.

32. K. fon Kaufman, *Proekt vsepoddanneishego otcheta . . . po grazhdanskomu upravleniiu i ustroistvu v oblastiakh Turkestanskago general-gubernatorstva, 7 Noiabria 1867–25 Marta 1881* (St. Petersburg, 1885), p. 11.

33. "Ocherk khlopkopromyshlennosti v Srednei Azii," 1885, RGIA, f. 183, op. 1, d. 17, l. 2.

34. A. K. Geins, "Motirovanie vremennykh instruktsii uezdnym nachal'nikom," *Sobranie literaturnykh trudov* (St. Petersburg, 1898), vol. 2, pp. 546–547.

35. N. Nalivkin, *Tuzemtsy ran'she i teper'* (Tashkent, 1913), p. 71.

36. *Vsepoddanneishii doklad Turkestanskago general-gubernatora General ot infanterii Dukhovskago: Islam v Turkestane* (Tashkent, 1899), p. 13.

37. "Ministr finansov S. Iu. Vitte po proektu Vremennikh pravil," 25 October 1900, RGIA, f. 821, op. 150, d. 409, l. 5.

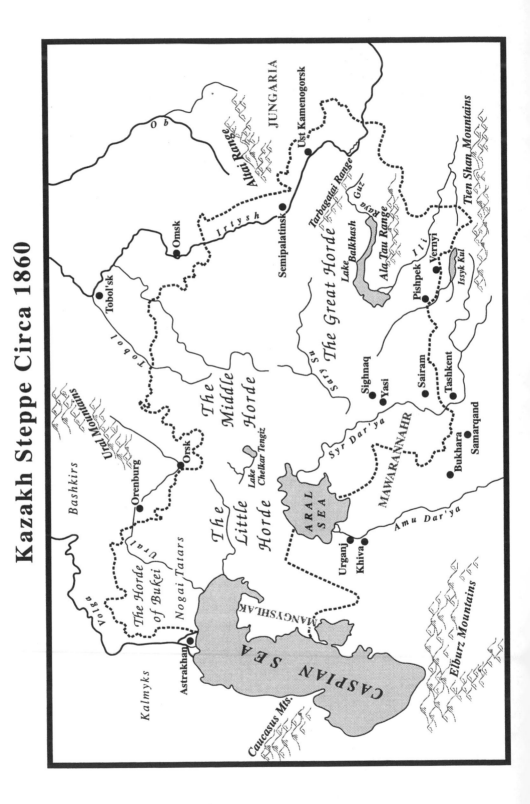

Kazakh Steppe Circa 1860

JUNGARIA

O b

Altai Range

Ust Kamenogorsk

Tarbagatai Range

I r t y s h

Omsk

Semipalatinsk

Guz

Raya

Lake Balkhash

Ala-Tau Range

I l i

Tien Shan Mountains

Pishpek

Vernyi

Issyk Kul

Tobol'sk

T o b o l

The Great Horde

S a r y   S u

The Middle Horde

Ural Mountains

Sighnaq

Yasi

Sairam

Tashkent

Bashkirs

Orsk

Samarqand

Orenburg

Lake Chelkar Tengiz

Syr Dar'ya

MAWARANNAHR

Bukhara

The Little Horde

ARAL SEA

Amu Dar'ya

U r a l

The Horde of Bukei

Nogai Tatars

Urganj

Khiva

Elburz Mountains

V o l g a

MANGYSHLAK

Kalmyks

Astrakhan

CASPIAN SEA

Caucasus Mts.

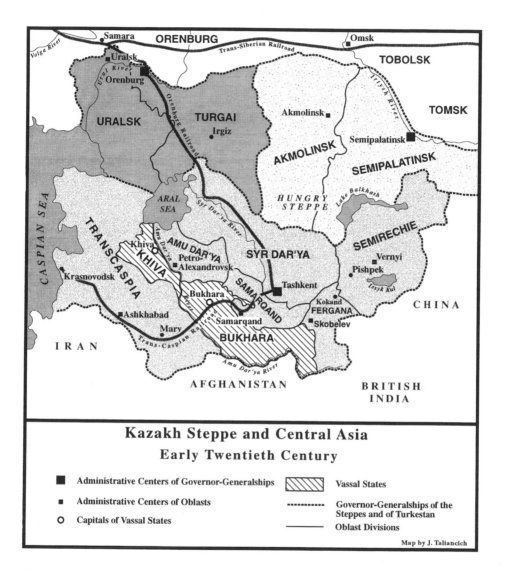

Kazakh Steppe and Central Asia
Early Twentieth Century

■ Administrative Centers of Governor-Generalships

■ Administrative Centers of Oblasts

O Capitals of Vassal States

▨ Vassal States

---------- Governor-Generalships of the Steppes and of Turkestan

——— Oblast Divisions

Map by J. Taliancich

·7·

Robert Geraci

Russian Orientalism at an Impasse: Tsarist Education Policy and the 1910 Conference on Islam

In relations with its eastern peoples, a mind-body problem plagued tsarist Russia. The empire's geography seemed to dictate a manifest destiny of cultural assimilation for the inhabitants of all its borderlands. Russians were hopeful and even confident that they would make their Muslim subjects, among others, a true and organic part of their country. As Seymour Becker has argued on the basis of popular nineteenth-century history books, "[Russia's] cultural superiority was so obvious that her Muslim subjects could not help but perceive it, given time, and voluntarily assimilate into the Russian nation."[1] Yet at least some of Russia's intellectual traditions, to a large extent inherited from western Europe, presented the situation otherwise. Russian culture had much invested in the permanence of the dichotomy made so popular by Kipling—or in Edward Said's words, "the absolute and systematic difference between the West, which is rational, developed, humane, superior, and the Orient, which is aberrant, undeveloped, inferior."[2]

Two factors allowed these contradictory attitudes to coexist with minimal tension. The first was time. As Becker notes, cultural assimilation in the East was considered much less urgent than in the western borderlands, where minority nationalism had challenged Russian control.[3] The second was Russians' belief in the transforming power of Christianity. Many thought that eventually Muslims would convert—with or without the efforts of missionaries—and the main source of their "otherness" would disappear, enabling them to become Russians in every sense.

Russian attempts to Christianize the Muslims, however, were largely a failure, for often subtle reasons that Agnès Kefeli treats elsewhere in this volume. Though hundreds of thousands of Tatars were converted following the conquest of Kazan in the sixteenth century and again in the first half of the eighteenth century, these gains later evaporated. Under the "enlightened" Catherine II, who instituted a policy of toleration and state administration of the Islamic religion, the Orthodox Church was forced to halt its missionary work. When conversion efforts resumed in the second quarter of the nineteenth century, the onset of mass defections of baptized Tatars (such defections would recur at least once a decade) made it clear to the church that its past methods had been unsound.[4] From then on, Russian missionary ambitions were mostly limited to converting peoples of traditional religions and retaining nominal or marginal Christians (many of them former Muslims) who were considered at risk of apostasy. The invention and spread of a methodology for such missionizing constituted the career of the famed Kazan orientalist Nikolai I. Il'minskii.[5] The church made no systematic efforts to recruit Muslims in the Volga region (and was barred entirely from missionizing in the new Central Asian possessions), for fear that the dissent it would provoke among the "fanatical" Tatar population would seriously challenge the state order. By the end of the century, many believed that Russian missionaries had "abandoned all efforts toward the conversion of Muslims to Christianity."[6] A wide cultural gulf between Muslim and Christian peoples in the empire was taken for granted, though in the Volga region, where Tatars had lived under Russian control for three centuries or more, this was hard for some Russians to accept.

In the final decades of the tsarist period, cultural changes among the empire's Muslim peoples made many Russians think that the time for assimilation had also run out. First came the jadid ("new method," or modernist) movement of Islamic cultural and educational reform. The movement is most often associated with the Crimean Tatar Ismail Bey Gasprinskii, who in 1883 began one of the first Turkic-language periodicals in Russia, and in 1884 founded a Muslim school based on a new method for learning Arabic.[7] It spread to all the Muslim peoples of the Russian Empire, and became especially powerful in the Volga-Ural region, where by the 1890s an older, conservative generation of Muslim clergy and teachers (mullas) was giving way to younger, more liberal personnel. Kazan and other cities in eastern Russia such as Orenburg and Ufa were increasingly considered centers of progressive Muslim culture worldwide. Since the movement increasingly treated vernacular languages such as Tatar as legitimate media for both Islamic thought and a growing secular literature, jadidism (modernism) was often interpreted as expressing Islamic or Tatar nationalism.

Another impetus for change was the religious toleration edict of 17 April 1905. The law concerned the right to convert freely from one Christian faith or denomination to another. With respect to Muslims, it represented no formal change in position. To convert from Christianity to Islam, a person had to prove that she or he had in fact always practiced Islam and had been Christian in name only. In other words, as had been the case before 1905, the state guaranteed the freedom to *be* a Muslim but not to *become* one. It was still illegal to convert without government permission, and Muslim proselytizing was still prohibited.[8] The law, however, sparked an explosion in unofficial conversions from Orthodoxy to Islam in the Russian Empire. Between the time of the edict and 1 January 1909, about 49,000 persons had converted legally; Kazan province alone reported nearly 39,000 of these.[9] Undoubtedly there were also many unofficial conversions.

The reforms of the Manifesto of 17 October 1905 also brought great changes to the Tatar and Muslim communities by admitting Muslims into areas of public life previously closed to them and creating new, more inclusive ones. The franchise gave Tatars great incentive to learn to communicate in Russian and to follow current events. Large numbers of Muslim deputies were elected to the First and Second Dumas, and most of these were aligned with the Kadets, a predominantly Russian party. Empire-wide congresses of Muslim leaders took place in 1905 and 1906. As a result of relaxed censorship, a vibrant Tatar periodical press emerged in 1906, in which debates on religious, cultural, and political issues between jadid reformers and their kadimist opponents (nativists, or conservatives; from *usûl-i kadim,* "old method") frequently took place. As a center of book publishing in Tatar and other Turkic languages, Kazan had become nearly as important as Istanbul. The new freedom of association was exercised within Muslim communities through the creation of libraries, charities, credit unions, and other organizations.

How exactly did these events influence Russian aspirations toward the cultural assimilation of Muslims? I will answer this question by examining one telling event in the history of tsarist policy toward Muslims after 1905, a "special interministry conference" on Islam in the Volga Region held in 1910. The way in which Muslims (particularly the Tatars) were represented at the conference illustrates the fundamental tension described at the beginning of this chapter.

The Special Conference on Islam

The meaning of all these changes in Muslim life was hotly debated in Kazan by Russians as well as Tatars. Though some saw the changes as potentially beneficial for relations between the two peoples,[10] most Russians interested in or officially concerned with the "Muslim question" harbored negative views. Even before the 1905 reforms, the Russo-Japa-

Russian Orientalism at an Impasse

*Suppression of the jadid movement by Russian and Islamic
authorities* (Mulla Nasreddin, *no. 17 [1908]*)

nese War had raised concerns about a general crisis in "the East" and about
the loyalty of all of the empire's "Asian" peoples. Because conversions to
Islam increased after the toleration edict, church leaders and missionaries
were sure that Muslims were using their newly acquired rights to step up
religious propaganda among baptized Tatars.[11] They feared that this influence might already be spreading to the smaller Turkic and Finnic *inorodtsy*
(non-Russians) of the region: the Chuvash, Cheremis (now known as the
Mari), Votiaks (now the Udmurts), and Mordva. This could occur, they
said, through the new Tatar social, economic, and educational organizations that had emerged in the region's urban centers. Tatars were also said
to dominate the cultural life of all the other Muslim peoples in the Russian
Empire by means of a missionizing clergy, a large network of schools, and
control of the Orenburg Spiritual Administration (muftiate). In the words
of one missionary, hope of making the Kazakhs into Christians declined
because "with each year [they] are more and more definitively leaning
toward the Muhammedan Tatars."[12]

The end result, many feared, would be a vast increase in Russia's

Muslim population. Since Muslims equated their religion with Tatar nationalism, it was thought, Russian power might eventually be outweighed by that of an emerging Tatardom. Finally, more cultural ties were developing between the Volga Tatars and Muslim communities in countries such as Turkey and Egypt, lending legitimacy to the idea that worldwide movements existed to unite all Turks (Pan-Turkism) or Muslims (Pan-Islam) for the purpose of creating new political entities. This, many Russian officials feared, could bring about the dismemberment of the Russian Empire.[13] Such fears were intensified by the 1908 revolution in the Ottoman Empire and the ascendancy of the Young Turks, who espoused Pan-Turkic views.

In 1908 and 1909, Prime Minister Petr A. Stolypin and Aleksei N. Kharuzin, director of the Ministry of the Interior's Department for the Religious Affairs of Foreign Confessions, were in correspondence with church and state officials in the Volga region, primarily Kazan, who were distressed about the growing religious and cultural influence of the Tatars. On the basis of this correspondence, Stolypin told the procurator of the Holy Synod in September 1909 that Muslim propaganda in the Volga region was evidence of a "struggle [bor'ba] between the Orthodox-Russian and the Muhammedan-Tatar principles." He characterized this as "not a religious struggle, but a political [gosudarstvennaia], cultural one." The movement among the Tatars, Stolypin said, was "a national revival that has taken on a religious tinge and has been expressed in the building of mosques even in the smallest villages, as well as the opening of schools and the publication of literary works." A few weeks later, Stolypin began planning a "special meeting" (osoboe soveshchanie) of church, educational, and administrative personnel knowledgeable about measures for "raising the cultural level of the local Orthodox population" in the Volga provinces.[14] Eventually the gathering became known as the "Special Meeting for Working Out Measures to Counteract the Tatar-Muslim Influence in the Volga Region." It convened in St. Petersburg from 10 to 18 January 1910.

Presiding over the meeting was Kharuzin; Stolypin himself was not even present. Other participants from the Ministry of the Interior were Governors Strizhevskii and Kamyshanskii of Kazan and Viatka provinces respectively, and two Petersburg officials. Church representatives were Kazan bishops Aleksii (rector of Kazan's Ecclesiastical Academy) and Andrei (the diocese's vicar for missions); Vladimir M. Skvortsov, the Synod's expert on missions; and Pavel N. Luppov, from the Synod School Council. The Ministry of Education sent the director of its Department of Public Education, S. I. Antsyferov; two members of its council, S. F. Speshkov and N. A. Bobrovnikov; and the curator of the St. Petersburg School District, A. A. Ostroumov.[15]

The group was strongly tied to the Kazan region, as well as being involved in missionary work, pedagogy, and ethnographic research among non-Russian peoples. Kharuzin himself had done ethnographic work on the Central Asian peoples. Speshkov had earlier been curator of the Kazan School District, Bobrovnikov director of the Kazan Teachers' Seminary, and Luppov had attended the missionary division of the Kazan Ecclesiastical Academy and published many articles on the Votiaks. Skvortsov was in the middle of preparations for a congress of missionaries to be held in Kazan in June 1910.[16]

After the meetings, Kharuzin prepared a report that wove the contributions of the various participants into one narrative about the rise of the Volga Tatars' cultural aspirations.[17] He used the terms "Pan-Turkism" and "Pan-Islam" copiously and attributed these movements principally to the Tatars' extensive contact with foreigners. Because of the nature of such movements and the central role played in them by the Tatars of Kazan, the document explained, the conference on the Volga region was just the first step toward a broad plan of action for keeping control over all of Russia's Muslim-populated regions.

The report offered three sets of recommendations for halting the spread of "anti-state" Pan-Islamic and Pan-Turkic ideas and the Tatar nationalism responsible for their dissemination. "Religious-educational measures" included improving the education of Orthodox inorodtsy by increasing state subsidies to Kazan missionary organizations and training programs for missionaries. The Ecclesiastical Academy's missionary division would get more faculty positions and provide better assistance to its graduates in finding work as missionaries. Religious seminaries in all dioceses with large inorodets populations, it was recommended, should require the study of the local languages. Also, missionary schools for inorodtsy should teach pupils how to engage Muslims in polemics, the Ecclesiastical Academy should publish a new journal on the subject, and the material conditions of Orthodox priests in communities with inorodtsy should be improved.[18]

On the administrative front, the report recommended the coordination of various state organs—church diocese, school district, and provincial governor's office—in areas with Muslim populations; a Ministry of the Interior periodical for reviewing the Muslim press in Russia and abroad; and the translation and publication of materials on Islamic law. In order to counteract the process of institutional Tatarization of Muslims, it prescribed a reform of the Orenburg muftiate's qualifying examinations for Muslim clergy (enabling them to be conducted in languages other than Tatar) and the division of the Orenburg muftiate into several bodies representing smaller geographical areas.[19]

The Confessional School Question

The most important topic of the meeting, however, was the schooling of Muslim peoples in the Volga region—particularly in confessional institutions. Traditionally, religious education had been extensive, if informal, among the Tatars. *Maktab*s, or primary schools, were attached to most mosques and run by the mullas. These schools for boys taught the Qur'an and its sacred language, Arabic. (Oftentimes the mulla's wife offered education to girls in her home.) *Madrasas*, or secondary schools, were for boys and young men (who sometimes stayed well into adulthood) preparing to become mullas. Still, the education consisted almost exclusively of language study and exegesis of theological texts.

Perhaps the Tatars' most important social institution, the schools found a prominent place in Russian critiques of Muslim culture. One Russian school inspector wrote in the 1870s that whatever the pupils of the maktabs were taught "remains for them dead material, since all this knowledge was acquired in the Arabic language, of which they didn't understand a single word." The centuries-old primers used for Arabic were of little help because they employed "names for the letters ... that give not the slightest idea of the sounds themselves."[20] "The schools have remained exactly as they have always been," he said, because the mullas who served as the schoolteachers, "only a few [of whom] receive an education, a modest one of course, and of a purely fanatical, religious sort," kept a tight hold on the schools and were "so accustomed to despotism and coarse prejudices from the past that they are prepared to see any kind of innovation as not only contrary to the Qur'an, but the work of the devil."[21] In sum, the schools were viewed as "one of the most powerful tools by which Tatar separateness and Muslim fanaticism are aroused, developed, and maintained,"[22] an obstacle to Russification and Christianization. Physical descriptions of the schools provided metaphors for this alienness. Il'minskii once described the madrasas as so "crowded, dirty, and stuffy" that "a well-bred person used to comfort and formality would feel impossibly sick to sit [in one] for just an hour."[23] Decades later, a school inspector reported that Tatar school buildings "fail to satisfy the most elementary sanitary as well as pedagogical requirements, and are seedbeds of infectious diseases not only among their pupils but also in the surrounding population."[24]

Despite the purely religious content of the curriculum, many Russians admitted that the maktabs and madrasas were quite effective at socializing children and adolescents into Islam, and even at providing native literacy.[25] For missionaries and other state agents, therefore, the schools were more dangerous than their provinciality made them appear. Tatar schools were often accused of having a hand in the proselytization and Islamization of inorodtsy, especially baptized Tatars. It was often said that they were opened in unnecessarily large numbers (along with mosques) in order to lure these Christians away from Russian schools.

In 1870, the Ministry of Education, recognizing the unlikelihood of assimilating Muslims into the Russian Empire through Christianization, devised a program for Russification and secularization of Muslims through schooling. Regulations promoted two new types of schools. First, a network of voluntarily attended "Russo-Tatar schools" (so called not because Russians would attend them but because they were established by the Russian government) would offer Russian language instruction, taught either by Tatar teachers or by Russians proficient in Tatar. Some school time would be taken by Muslim religious instruction provided by a teacher chosen and paid by the Tatar community. Second, community-financed "Russian classes" (teaching Russian language and arithmetic) would be opened in maktabs and madrasas; again, Tatars would be preferred as teachers.[26] In 1874, when the Ministry of Education took control of all Muslim schools in the empire, the opening of these classes and all pupils' attendance in them became mandatory for every confessional school. New laws also required all mullas to pass a Russian language examination.

To train Tatar teachers for both types of schools, the ministry opened teachers' seminaries in Simferopol', Ufa, and Kazan. These Tatar teachers' schools aimed to replace "fanatical" Tatar culture with a kinder, gentler (and more pro-Russian) variant by raising a generation of liberal clergy and teachers who could act as a counterweight to conservative mullas. The entire system created by the 1870 law, wrote the Kazan School District's inspector of Muslim schools, the German-born orientalist Vasilii V. Radlov, would be "a middle ground between our state education system and the Muslim population. [It] must show the Muslims that the government in no way desires to concern itself with their religious notions, but is trying only to raise the level of their development, for their own good."[27] Though Radlov was more liberal than most education officials, the 1870 law can be seen as representing the persistence of an optimistic, Catherinian view of Russia's Muslims within the state. The law implied that Islam and Tatar culture were somewhat flexible, that secular education, and particularly the learning of the Russian language, would make the Tatars resemble Russians in worldview and enable them to integrate more thoroughly into Russian life—without necessarily abandoning Islam.

In the Volga region, this project coincided to a large degree with the Kazan jadid movement. As early as the 1870s (even before Gasprinskii's activities), progressive-minded Kazan mullas such as Shihabeddin Merjani and Abdulkayyum Nasiri had promoted secularization by the use of the Tatar vernacular language as well as Russian in their schools, and applied Western methods in historical and ethnographic scholarship.[28] The Kazan Tatar Teachers' School employed some of that city's most progressive mullas, including Merjani, as well as Tatar laymen educated in Russian and foreign institutions. Its curriculum emphasized the teaching of Russian, Tatar, the natural sciences, and social studies such as history and geography (using Tatar translations of western European or Russian texts). In the traditional maktabs and madrasas, none of these subjects was considered permissible.

In the 1870s and 1880s, Muslims in Russia (especially the Volga Tatars) were generally unreceptive to these Russian schools and classes. They believed them to threaten their religion, often because of frequent rumors that the schools were a harbinger of Christianization. The opening of schools sometimes depended on the participation of police. Eventually, any change in the schools' regulations, whether liberalizing or constraining, might be accompanied by plummeting attendance, harassment or assault of teachers or inspectors, or even the destruction of schools—as well as more conversions of Christian Tatars back to Islam.[29] At the head of this popular unrest, oftentimes, were the mullas.[30]

As Tatar attitudes toward secular education grew more favorable, Ministry of Education schools experienced some increase in their numbers of Tatar pupils. Many Tatar publicists, beginning with Gasprinskii, recommended Russian schooling as a means of advancement. Still, relatively few of the ministry's schools survived in Muslim areas, especially compared with Tatar confessional schools. By 1904, only thirty-one Russo-Tatar schools existed in all of the Kazan school district, sixteen of them in Kazan province. By 1905, in all of the Russian Empire there were fewer than three hundred. One historian has counted in Kazan province for the entire prerevolutionary period only seven officially registered Russian classes in madrasas and no such classes at all in maktabs.[31] Most of the Ministry of Education's regulations for Muslim schools remained dead letters.

Tatar confessional schools, though increasingly receptive to the Russian language, the natural sciences, and other previously forbidden subjects, usually opted not to register this instruction as "Russian classes" under the 1870 regulations. As a result, the achievements of the jadid movement stayed, for the most part, independent of the state and outside its control, if not its knowledge. In 1906, the Third All-Russian Muslim Congress, meeting in Nizhnii Novgorod, adopted a resolution on confessional school reform that included use of the native languages for all instruction, and the obligatory teaching of secular sciences and the Russian language in the madrasas.[32] According to Azade-Ayşe Rorlich, by 1910 the reformers had decisively won out over the conservatives: 90 percent of Tatar schools in Kazan province had adopted a jadid curriculum; the madrasas offered remarkably little religious study and a great number of hours devoted to Russian.[33] Student strikes played a role in the pressure on schools to reform themselves, a difficult process since most Tatar teachers were not yet qualified to handle secular subjects, and teachers often had to be hired from foreign countries. The education of girls and the publication of Tatar textbooks also expanded during this period, but as a result of Tatar efforts, not Russian.

The report of the 1910 meeting charged that Muslim activists had turned the new-method maktabs and madrasas into institutions providing a general (*obshcheobrazovatel'nyi*) education:

Under the pretext that the rational study of [the Tatars'] religion—Islam—demands them, subjects having nothing to do with religion have been introduced: arithmetic, the history of Turkey and its geography. At the same time, Russian language, Russian history, and Russian geography have been completely ignored, and the artificially constructed Pan-Turkic language has been disseminated.

The conference's participants feared that these "modernized" Muslim schools, representing cultural autonomy for the Tatars, posed the danger that the pupils in them would develop a worldview more closely associated with Turkey than with Russia, and that the availability of a general education in them would keep Muslims from sending their children to Russian schools. Calling school organization "the whole essence of solving the formidable Muslim question," those attending the meeting decided to handle the threat of the new Muslim schools by making "a clear demarcation of the purely confessional sphere from the purely cultural-educational" and by prohibiting anything falling into the latter from being included in Muslim instruction.[34]

The principle behind the earlier laws on confessional schools (beginning in 1870), that Russian classes could help the schools be transformed into secular institutions over time, was declared invalid. All schools with any nonconfessional instruction would have to drop these subjects or be closed. On the other hand, all maktabs and madrasas now existing underground for failure to include such classes would automatically become legal. Later, in concert with representatives of the Muslim clergy, the Ministry of the Interior would draw up a uniform curriculum prescribed for the confessional schools.

The report declared that the Ministry of Education would cooperate with local organizations to open general schools for Muslims in order to compensate for the closing of many confessional schools. (Even those illegal maktabs and madrasas not wishing to resume a purely confessional character would be allowed to become private schools subject to certain regulations.) The Tatar teachers' schools would be preserved in order to train new Tatar educators for these schools until the time when Muslim communities would be willing to hire teachers from the regular teachers' seminaries. These seminaries normally trained only Russian teachers, but the report recommended that from now on Muslims interested in teaching careers be directed to them as well. The teaching of local non-Russian languages in these seminaries would be improved, and Muslim religious instruction would be made available.[35]

Taken at face value, the report's educational recommendations appeared sound and rational given the priorities of the tsarist system. The key issue may have been proper school administration. Of the two means devised in 1870 to Russify Muslims, the committee chose to discard the one that relied heavily on indigenous Muslim institutions because it had never been able to keep track of them. Instead, it decided, the education of all the empire's peoples should be in the hands of a state institution, the Ministry of Education. (Indeed, one would not expect the Russian state to tolerate schools with civic education directed more toward identification with a foreign power such as Turkey than with Russia, if this were really the case.) But simply to close all confessional schools would be seen as religious persecution at its worst. As an alternative, the state could try to lure children from them and, by exercising an absolute monopoly on all subjects—including the Russian language, but excepting religion—encourage their withering away slowly.[36]

Russian schooling for Muslims, as recommended by the committee, might have suited the needs of the Tatars. In 1907, Ministry of Education regulations allowed for all national minorities to receive instruction in their native languages, and for qualified teachers in state schools to offer non-Christian religious education.[37] And the allowance of at least three different options for the fate of maktabs and madrasas currently engaged in general education—to return to confessional status, to convert to private status under state regulations, or to close down—seems quite reasonable and realistic. Although extensive data on the exact educational preferences of Russia's Muslim population were lacking, some evidence of Muslims' improving attitudes toward Russian schools (as discussed earlier) in fact existed, which suggested that an attempt at mass education of these peoples in state schools would be much more successful than it had been a few decades earlier. More Tatar clergy than ever were willing to participate in such schools, and to see their communities' children receive a not entirely Islamic education. Zemstvos were becoming more attentive to this changing climate and were making plans for the education of Muslim constituents.[38]

The Power of Nostalgia

When one looks closer at the meeting—the discussions that took place, the personalities involved, and the political context—its approach to the education of Muslims takes on a different complexion. Kharuzin, it appears, intended to address the confessional schools' curriculum purely as a matter of prohibition, not as a strategy for strengthening any other schools. Early in the proceedings, he declared the central question of the entire proceedings to be: "Is it permissible to allow Tatar-Muslim schools to stray beyond the boundaries of the confessional school, and if not, then what measures must be taken to prevent their reorganization?" All members of the committee immediately agreed that such a state of affairs was intolerable, and that only state schools should be permitted to provide general education.[39]

Two days later, Kharuzin proposed the following formulation, which eventually appeared in very similar form in the report:

> 1. Confessional education, conducted in the mother tongue, must be separated from general education. Confessional schools should teach only subjects related to the study of religion; the study of other subjects is not permissible, and even the organization of Russian classes is undesirable.
> 2. A sharp distinction must be drawn between confessional and general education, and a curriculum for the purely confessional school worked out with the collaboration of the Muslims themselves.
> 3. Confessional education is the property of the population itself and must be wholly under the management of the clergy, with the state reserving the power of registration and oversight.[40]

A special cause of suspicion is the clause prohibiting Russian language classes in maktabs and madrasas. Even with the apparent gentleness of its wording, this absolute reversal of policy seems extreme, especially since nothing in the report indicated any negative consequences of Russian language study. (In fact, the document complained about the relative neglect of Russian in the schools.) Little discussion was given to the possibility of setting an acceptable nonreligious curriculum for the schools, or of barring only some secular subjects such as Turkish studies, or requiring Russian studies.

The consideration of what new schools would be needed to compensate for the closing of maktabs and madrasas and to enhance the likelihood that Muslims would get a well-rounded and sufficiently Russian education seems not to have been of great concern. Rather, it was first raised by Nikolai Bobrovnikov, who objected to the proposed crackdown on confessional schools. Such a strict policy, Bobrovnikov said, did not take into account the current limitations of the ministry schools and therefore would leave many children out of school and lead ultimately to Tatar unrest.[41]

Indeed, in 1910 the Ministry of Education had precious little to offer the Muslim population. The number of schools in Russia was insufficient even for the Russian population, and bills for universal education were being considered in the Duma. State-organized education for Muslims was little ahead of where it had been in 1870. And though the secularizing confessional schools were heavily enrolled, it was not clear that all these families would be willing to send their children to schools administered by the Russian state, no matter what kind of education the latter offered. Moreover, there is little reason to think that Stolypin was prepared to push the Ministry of Education to increase schooling for Muslims. The zemstvos were beginning to respond to Muslim educational demands, and in 1911 pursued negotiations with Muslim communities on this matter. In at least one school district, however, the Ministry of Education's representatives opposed such effort.[42] And shortly after the January 1910 meeting, one of its most influential participants, Bishop Andrei of Kazan, expressed opposition to zemstvo schooling of Muslim Tatars together with Russians and other inorodtsy.[43]

The Ministry of Education never acted to implement the prohibition against secular learning in Muslim confessional schools.[44] (Nor would it have been able to, because of likely mass protests by the Tatars.) Instead, the Ministry of the Interior chose to implement the prohibition on its own. Throughout the Volga-Ural region and Central Asia, it energetically pursued every opportunity to accuse Muslim intellectuals of Pan-Islamic or Pan-Turkic propaganda. Police raided Muslim schools, bookstores, newspapers, publishing houses, and community organizations; scores of teachers were barred from teaching.[45] Though this campaign had begun before 1910, it was given new vigor by the 1910 meeting. The most notorious raid, in 1911, resulted in the closing of the Bobi madrasa and the arrest of ten of its teachers for allegedly disseminating Pan-Turkic, Pan-Islamic, and anti-government ideas.[46] Through these systematic attacks on the Volga Tatar jadids, Stolypin, Kharuzin, and their associates made it clear that they were not especially concerned with fostering the kind of climate among the Muslims that would favor their enrollment in Russian schools.

At the same time, an alliance developed between the government and the conservative wing of the Muslim clergy, hinted at by the meeting's desire to strengthen the clergy's hold on the confessional schools. The kadims, to rid themselves of their opponents, were glad to provide the types of accusations the police sought against the jadids. The police, eager to please their superiors, were often appallingly uncritical of the logic behind such accusations.[47] As was documented by the historian Liutsian Klimovich, during the election campaigns for the Fourth Duma in 1912, Kharuzin and his department also attempted to put pressure on the governor of Kazan to manipulate local politics so as to ensure victory for kadim candidates over jadids.[48]

This alliance is remarkable since the jadids were much more likely than the kadims to look favorably on Russian influence in Muslim education. They had probably played an important role in the growing Tatar interest in education outside the confessional schools, while the kadims had usually opposed any Russian involvement whatsoever in Muslim education. It appears that men such as Kharuzin were more concerned with keeping Muslims *away from* secular and general education, and in their traditional position of isolation from Russian society. At the St. Petersburg meeting, perhaps on the basis of a twisted interpretation of the religious toleration law, Viatka governor Kamyshanskii had maintained that it was the government's duty to support the conservative Tatar clergy in their struggle for the religious purity of Islam and against the encroachments of the young, reformist clergy.[49] No matter how critical such statesmen-orientalists had been of the Muslim confessional schools in the past, they now realized how much they preferred Muslims to be parochial-minded and ignorant rather than worldly and enlightened. They became nostalgic for Muslims they could patronize rather than fear.

On 13 March 1912, Sadruddin Maksudi, a Kazan Tatar deputy with a Sorbonne education, spoke in the Russian Duma on the government's policies toward Muslims. Having noted the alliance with the kadims and the numerous attacks on Tatar cultural institutions that had occurred in the wake of the 1910 meeting, he proposed two explanations:

> Either the Russian government desires at any cost to destroy our progres-
> sive movement and cultural life because it doesn't want us to become
> cultured or to move forward, or [it] has made the mistake of imagining
> that some kind of anti-government movement or . . . organization exists
> among the Russian Muslims, which the state has to combat, to combat
> not by ordinary means . . . , but by means that are applied only in the
> event . . . of a military situation. It's as if all of our constitutional rights are
> being curtailed. In my opinion, both of these suppositions are correct.[50]

Maksudi was right, of course; moreover, the two motives he discerned were not independent but intimately linked.

Orientalist Déjà Vu

Though the concepts of Pan-Turkism and Pan-Islam were not invented by Russians,[51] their centrality in the government's discussions of the empire's Muslims undoubtedly exaggerated their importance greatly. In his own version of the report presented to the Council of Ministers, for example, Stolypin said, "The study of these phenomena [of Tatar cultural revival, publishing, school reform, and so on] shows that they are not coincidental, but emanate from the carefully organized program of the Pan-Islamists."[52] Tsarist police documents show, however, that attempts to ferret out Pan-Islam and Pan-Turkism usually ended in failure and an admission that these doctrines, though occasionally expressed in Tatar newspapers, had no specific program or organizational existence.[53]

In his book *Pan-Turkism and Islam in Russia,* Serge Zenkovsky identifies Pan-Turkism and Pan-Islam more as rhetorical devices than as credible political movements with mass support. By far the more popular of the two ideas in the Volga region, Pan-Turkism was undoubtedly present in the worldview and writings of at least a few Volga Tatar leaders. But particularly after the government's reactionary turn of 1907, Zenkovsky writes,

> Sympathy for Ottoman Turkey continued to be a salient trait of Tatar
> cultural and political orientation, but aside from the Crimea and Azer-

baijan, this was merely a platonic and sentimental attachment to a country of the same religion and a related tongue. Aside from some minor exceptions, it did not lead to activities directed against the political unity of the Russian Empire. Tatars, Bashkirs, and Kazakhs became more and more preoccupied with cultural, social, and economic problems of their own, as well as with those of Russia.[54]

In the words of Maxime Rodinson, the "obsession" of the European powers with the supposed threat of Pan-Islam around the turn of the century was "an essentially reactionary phenomenon" based on fears of "the real, but hardly inevitable, danger posed by a return in the East to an earlier theocratic state. . . . Adhering to this single archaic vision, [scholars concerned with Pan-Islam] not only devalued other active social forces present in the Middle East, but, by their contempt, encouraged these social forces to pursue a reactionary course."[55] Hence the orientalists' alliance with their former enemies, the conservative Muslim clergy.

Russian preoccupation with these elusive threats reflects the revision of an orientalist stereotype. In European tradition, Muslims were seen as theocratic, narrow-minded fanatics. When the secularization, self-criticism, and debate of the jadid movement challenged this stereotype, it was easier for Russians to reincarnate the old image than to discard it altogether. (Rodinson writes that European scholars frightened by the specter of Pan-Islam "were once again irresistibly drawn to a vision of the East that hearkened back to the Middle Ages: the struggle was still between two politically and ideologically opposed worlds.")[56] The Muslim with a purely scholastic outlook was a provincial-minded fanatic; now that he might be receiving a broader education, he was transformed into a political fanatic with global ambitions. Variants of this theme differed only as to whether Pan-Turkism or Pan-Islam was the more dangerous (though members of the committee could not even agree whether there was a difference between the two),[57] and whether they were "essentially" religious with political overtones or vice versa.

Some of Russia's foremost experts on Islam and policy makers on ethnic questions had been opposed to the allowance of secular education to Muslims in Russia under the 1870 school law. Konstantin P. Pobedonostsev, procurator of the Holy Synod, considered the Russian-Tatar schools a state subsidy to the Muslim religion and urged the minister of education to reconsider his support of them.[58] The St. Petersburg University Turkologist Vasilii D. Smirnov ridiculed the Russian classes for the notion that Muslim clergy could be effective agents of modern education and Russification.[59] Nor did he wish to support a lay Muslim intelligentsia; as the government's censor for Turkic-language publications, Smirnov for several decades frequently impeded the spread of secular books and periodicals in the Tatar language.[60]

The most determined opponent of the reform of Muslim education was Il'minskii. To him, the Russo-Tatar schools' failure was caused not by legitimate Tatar fears of Christianization, but by the "organic hostility of Islam to education" and its tendency to isolate Tatars from Russian culture.[61] If this was so, how did Il'minskii explain the increasing number of Tatars and other Muslims attending Russian and European schools (including universities) in the late nineteenth century? If education could not bring a Muslim true enlightenment (nor would a Muslim undertake it for this purpose), there must be an ulterior motive. Muslims, Il'minskii thought, wanted to acquire the trappings of European culture to be better armed to undermine the Christian world, to which they were inevitably hostile. It was therefore not only useless for Russians to offer secular education to Muslims, but dangerous as well.

When advising Pobedonostsev on choosing a new head of the Orenburg Spiritual Administration in 1883, Il'minskii wrote: "A fanatic without Russian education and language is better than a Russian-civilized Tatar; even worse is an aristocrat, and still worse is a man with a university education."[62] In 1881, the year in which Gasprinskii published his assimilationist book *Russkoe musul'manstvo* (The Russian Islamic World), Il'minskii warned of the "emerging national-political self-consciousness and unity of Tatars and Muslims throughout Russia," which he attributed primarily to "the European-Russian education of Tatars in the gymnasia and universities."[63] He also predicted that the new-method Muslim schools would be more dangerous than the old ones. Though he had few listeners before his death in 1891, by 1910 Il'minskii was being spoken of by many Russian statesmen as a visionary.[64]

Besides his efforts to persuade Petersburg officials to limit their support of the Russo-Tatar schools, Il'minskii frequently lobbied for other measures that would prevent the integration of the Muslim Tatars into Russian life and institutions. Bobrovnikov, Il'minskii's successor as head of the missionary schools, shared his view of Muslims and continued these various campaigns against Muslim integration. At the 1910 conference, Bobrovnikov invoked Il'minskii's opinion in arguing that European culture would not change the Tatars' worldview in any way, but would only "give a different tint to [*podkrasit'*] Islam."[65]

An Intellectual Impasse

In 1901 Nikolai P. Ostroumov, director of the Tashkent Teachers' Seminary and a graduate and former professor of the Kazan Ecclesiastical Academy's anti-Islam division, published a book entitled *Koran i progress* (The Qur'an and Progress). More or less reiterating the thesis of Ernest Renan's famous 1883 lecture "L'Islamisme et la science,"[66] Ostroumov argued that "the idea of progress as well as progress itself remains foreign to the Muslims. Their culture, retaining a purely local character, withers away quickly without any continuous development."[67] Even the alleged scientific achievements of medieval Islam, he agreed with Renan, belonged not to Muslims but to others whose efforts were tolerated only begrudgingly by the Muslims.

In the same book, however, Ostroumov invoked the authority of contemporary Russian orientalists whose views represented a less absolute view of Islam. The Moscow professor Agafangel Krymskii, in the 1899 *Musul'manstvo i ego budushchnost'* (Islam and Its Future), had argued (in Ostroumov's paraphrase) that "Islam, like any other religion, in and of itself should not be considered a hindrance to progress and civilization; everything depends on the spiritual capabilities of the race professing Islam, and on this race's attitude toward science."[68] Vladimir V. Bartol'd of St. Petersburg University had written in 1903 that a "renaissance" in Islamic culture—that is, Muslims' participation in world cultural progress, like that of the Japanese—was possible only by "adoption of the foundations of European culture, and not by the continuation of the work of Muslim scholars in past centuries."[69]

Ostroumov declared himself "in full agreement" with the views of both Bartol'd and Krymskii. He affirmed, "I have witnessed a beneficial change in the views of young Muslims who have received education in Russian schools, and know many Muslims who don't show any religious alienation in their relations with Russians."[70] To combat Muslim separatism and Pan-Islam, therefore, Ostroumov proposed the "introduction into the curriculum of existing madrasas of a Russian language course and modern scientific knowledge that would facilitate the dissipation of religious ideas rooted in the Muslims that do not accord with history."[71]

But in the book Ostroumov also sought to refute jadid leaders in the Russian Empire—Baiazitov, Mir-Ali, Agaev, and Gasprinskii—who argued for the compatibility of Islamic teaching with the idea of progress. These proponents of new interpretations of Islam maintained that the backwardness of Islamic societies compared with Europe resulted either from the influence of eccentrics who had "misread" the Qur'an, or from political and social factors external to religion altogether. Ostroumov opposed these views on the basis of what he claimed was the "literal and historical meaning" of the Qur'an's words,[72] and took for granted that Islamic life had been and always would be limited to the realization of those words, which were prohibitive of progress.

Ostroumov's reasoning reflected his background. At midcentury his alma mater and former employer, the Kazan Academy, had developed a polemical method for convincing Muslims of the superiority of Christianity over Islam by rational persuasion (*vrazumlenie*). The academy's most active polemicist, Evfimii A. Malov, applied the method both in numerous monographic publications and in frequent face-to-face meetings with Muslim scholars and lay people. Malov adhered to the assumption that religious beliefs were best described by philological research, without regard to historical or ethnographic factors. The final arbiter of the "meaning" of religious texts was he who had read the most—the Christian orientalist, of course. Malov's method of argumentation had two aspects working from opposite directions: to prove the Qurʾan as a source of false teaching on the basis of a sense of common morality,[73] and to prove Muslim practices or beliefs invalid *on the basis of* the Qurʾan (which for rhetorical purposes Malov assumed to be a true teaching). The first aspect attacked the content of Islam; the second, in a sense, attacked the very existence of Islam as a rival to Christianity, whatever its content.[74]

So what did it mean for Ostroumov to advocate the broadening of the confessional school curriculum? Evidently he was offended by the thought that the new subjects would be presented as compatible with Islam. What he would not admit was that he advocated the destruction of Islam—not its reform or adaptation—by means of secular education. Like the men at the 1910 conference, who recommended exactly the opposite regulatory measure, Ostroumov pretended to be adapting to a new development among the Muslims; the difference was that Ostroumov thought the coexistence of Islam and secular learning possible within a Muslim institution, while the committee judged that the juxtaposition of the two could occur only under strict Russian supervision. Neither party, it appears, really believed that the Tatar worldview had changed, nor had it renounced the older—quite obsolete—expectation that the Muslims could be integrated into Russian society by conversion. A similar dead-end position was reached by P. K. Zhuze, a Christian Arab on the faculty of the Kazan Ecclesiastical Academy. Zhuze answered the question "Can the followers of Muhammed ever achieve intellectual and moral perfection so as to be on the same level as Christian peoples?" with an optimistic yes, but then revealed that the means toward this would be education "based on Christian principles."[75] In other words: yes, the Muslims are capable of converting to Christianity. The appeal of such a solution in all these cases, perhaps, was the impossibility of its being realized.

That the participants in the meeting on Islam in the Volga region seem really to have believed that they were reacting to objective phenomena, not to subjective impressions and traditions, gives credence to Edward Said's description of orientalist thinking as "a system of truths . . . in Nietzsche's sense of the word,"[76] or as having become "a repeatedly produced copy of itself."[77] Every given observation made about the Tatars was accompanied by the exposure of its mysterious underside. (When it was remarked that the Volga Tatars had remained peaceful and loyal throughout the 1905 revolution, Kharuzin responded that the Tatars' loyalty was "a purely formal loyalty"; in fact, the Tatars were now unifying and preparing themselves for an all-out assault on Russian rule.)[78] The underside was never quite visible or identifiable, but the participants knew it was there. Its invisibility was even proof of its presence:

> It would be difficult to deny the existence of agitation in Kazan province directed toward converting to Islam those who are weak and unstable in the Orthodox faith, but the matter of recruitment is organized in such a skillful way that none of the investigations undertaken by the provincial administration has been successful, and no guilty parties in Muslim recruitment have been identified.[79]

Those few participants who saw Islamic reform and secularization as a positive phenomenon also saw it as insignificant. The majority, impressed and even intimidated by its success, denied its benefit, as if anything the Tatars would undertake on their own, that did not have to be imposed on them against their will, was ipso facto a cause for suspicion.

This situation bears a striking resemblance to what Said describes as the "intellectual crisis in Islamic Orientalism" in interwar Europe:

> The Islamic Orientalist expressed his ideas in such a way as to emphasize his, as well as putatively the Muslim's, *resistance* to change, to mutual comprehension between East and West. . . . Indeed, so fierce was this sense of resistance to change, and so universal were the powers ascribed to it, that in reading the Orientalists one understands that the apocalypse to be feared was not the destruction of Western civilization but rather the destruction of the barriers that kept East and West from each other.[80]

The main difference, however, was that in Russia there was little awareness of the contradiction; at least no one spoke of the situation as a crisis.

This is not to suggest that dissent from these "truths" about the East was impossible among Russians, or even among Russian observers of Islam. As noted earlier, the 1870 regulations (though they had ultimately proved unpopular and abortive) represented a more liberal way of thinking about Islam that was rooted in institutions and practices dating from the Catherinian era.[81] A similar exception was an article, "Musul'manskii vopros v Rossii" (The Muslim Question in Russia), published pseudonymously in the liberal journal *Russkaia mysl'* (Russian Thought) in 1909. While not denying that "Muslim culture in Russia . . . has stopped developing, [that] a strict dogmatism has taken hold of it, [that] stagnation has set in," the author refused to predict "whether the [contemporary Islamic] movement will lead to reform and rebirth, or to the decisive fall of the Muslim faith," "whether Muslim culture is an appropriate tool for the further development of the peoples who profess Islam," or even whether the outcome would be harmful or beneficial to Russia (though he clearly leaned toward the latter).[82]

The exception that perhaps proves the rule (in both senses) of a tauto-logical way of thinking about Islam in late tsarist Russia is the following: One of the publications on Islam established upon the recommendation of the 1910 meeting was the journal *Mir Islama* (The World of Islam), pub-lished by the Imperial Oriental Society and subsidized by the state. Bartol'd was appointed as its editor. At the outset, he set forth a list of "fundamental principles" governing the publication. In addition to assert-ing the journal's duty only to scholarship (not to politics) and its unwill-ingness to publish articles representing either missionary polemics against Islam or Muslims' defense of the religion, Bartol'd made the following theoretical statement:

> The journal views Muslim culture as a complex historical phenomenon, not to be explained exclusively by the influence of religious dogmas and instructions, and will attempt to elucidate all the cultural influences and political, economic, and other causes by which the actual life of Muslim peoples has been determined and is determined, irrespective of the ab-stract ideal constructed by the religion.[83]

After a year of sparring with the Oriental Society over the journal's content, Bartol'd was ousted; his approach was deemed too scholarly and too historical. He was replaced by a military specialist on Japan from the Oriental Society, who quickly "reorganized" *The World of Islam* and brought it into line with the government's expectations.[84]

NOTES

1. Seymour Becker, "The Muslim East in 19th-Century Russian Popular Histo-riography," *Central Asian Survey* 5 (1986): 25–47; here p. 44. For more on manifest destiny in Russian thought, see Mark Bassin, "Turner, Solov'ev, and the 'Frontier Hypothesis': The Nationalist Signification of Open Spaces," *Journal of Modern History* 65 (September 1993): 473–511.

2. Edward Said, *Orientalism* (New York, 1978), pp. 300–301.

3. Becker, "The Muslim East," pp. 26–27 and 44.

4. The best source on the history of the missions is A. A. Mozharovskii, *Izlozhenie khoda missionerskago dela po prosveshcheniiu kazanskikh inorodtsev s 1552 po 1867 goda* (Moscow, 1880). See also Chantal Lemercier-Quelquejay, "Les missions ortho-doxes en pays musulmans de moyenne- et basse-Volga, 1552–1865," *Cahiers du monde russe et soviétique* 8 (1967): 369–403.

5. See Isabelle T. Kreindler, "Educational Policies toward the Eastern Nationali-ties in Tsarist Russia: A Study of Il'minskii's System" (Ph.D. diss., Columbia University, 1969); and Robert P. Geraci, "Window on the East: Ethnography, Or-thodoxy and Russian Nationality in Kazan, 1870–1914" (Ph.D. diss., University of California, Berkeley, 1995), esp. chaps. 1 and 2.

6. A. Anastasiev, "O tatarskikh dukhovnykh shkolakh," *Russkaia shkola* 12 (1893): 129.

7. See Edward J. Lazzerini, "Ismail Bey Gasprinskii and Muslim Modernism in Russia, 1878–1914" (Ph.D. diss., University of Washington, 1973), esp. pp. 24–29, 150–152, 157–164; Serge Zenkovsky, *Pan-Turkism and Islam in Russia*, 2nd ed. (Cambridge, Mass., 1967), pp. 24–36; and Allan Fisher, *The Crimean Tatars* (Stanford, 1978), pp. 100–104.

8. RGIA, f. 821, op. 8, d. 795, ll. 102–103.

9. Ibid., d. 800, l. 64.

10. See, for example, N. V. Nikol'skii, "Mully i intelligentsiia u kazanskikh tatar," *Tserkovno-obshchestvennaia zhizn'* 1 (16 December 1905): cols. 22–25; and M. N. Pinegin in RGIA, f. 733, op. 173, d. 107, l. 79.

11. This interpretation was made despite the fact that according to the 1905 law, a petition for conversion would be satisfied if the person had de facto practiced Islam and not Orthodoxy before 17 April 1905. RGIA, f. 821, op. 8, d. 800, l. 64.

12. A. A. Voskresenskii, "Predislovie. Sistema N. I. Il'minskago v riadu drugikh meropriiatii k prosveshcheniiu inorodtsev," in N. I. Il'minskii, *O sisteme prosveshcheniia inorodtsev* (Kazan, 1913), p. xv.

13. RGIA, f. 821, op. 8, d. 800.

14. Ibid., ll. 51–51ob., 72–73.

15. Ibid., d. 801, l. 160.

16. On the conference, see Geraci, "Window on the East," pp. 395–400, 421–430; and Frank T. McCarthy, "The Kazan Missionary Congress," *Cahiers du monde russe et soviétique* 13 (1973): 308–322.

17. The report is published in an article, "Iz istorii natsional'noi politiki tsarizma," *Krasnyi arkhiv* 4 (1929): 107–127 and 5 (1929): 61–83. The article consists of an introduction by A. Arsharuni followed by the text, "Zhurnal osobogo soveshchaniia po vyrabotke mer dlia protivodeistviia tatarsko-musul'manskomu vliianiiu v Privolzhskom krae." I will refer to the report as "Zhurnal."

18. Ibid., pp. 120–127.

19. Ibid., pp. 74–79.

20. N. Domokhovskii, "Inorodcheskie shkoly v Rossii," *Narodnaia shkola* 1 (1878): 41–43.

21. Ibid., pp. 43–44.

22. Anastasiev, "O tatarskikh dukhovnykh shkolakh," p. 129.

23. N. I. Il'minskii, "Ex oriente lux," *Pravoslavnyi sobesednik* (1904), p. 48.

24. Anastasiev, "O tatarskikh dukhovnykh shkolakh," p. 131.

25. K. Fuks, *Kazanskie tatary v statisticheskom i etnograficheskom otnosheniiakh* (Kazan, 1991 [orig. 1844]), pp. 126–132.

26. "Postanovleniia Ministerstva narodnago prosveshcheniia," *ZhMNP* 148 (1870): 55–63.

27. TsGART, f. 92, op. 1, d. 10961, l. 2ob.

28. Azade-Ayşe Rorlich, *The Volga Tatars: A Profile in National Resilience* (Stanford, 1986), pp. 50–53 and 65–68.

29. See A. Kh. Makhmutova, *Stanovlenie svetskogo obrazovaniia u tatar* (Kazan, 1982); I. K. Zagidullin, "Tatarskie krest'iane kazanskoi gubernii vo 2-i polovine XIX v. (60-e–90-e gody)" (Cand. diss., Ibragimov Institute of Language, Literature, and History, Kazan, 1992); V. M. Gorokhov, *Reaktsionnaia shkol'naia politika tsarizma v otnoshenii tatar Povolzh'ia* (Kazan, 1941), pp. 175–176 and 226.

30. Ibid., pp. 157–159 and 221–228.

31. Makhmutova, *Stanovlenie*, pp. 25 and 28; N. P. Ostroumov, "K istorii musul'-manskago obrazovatel'nago dvizheniia v Rossii v XIX i XX stoletiiakh," *Mir Islama* 1, nos. 4–6 (1913): 322.

32. Rorlich, *The Volga Tatars*, p. 89; Zenkovsky, *Pan-Turkism and Islam in Russia*, pp. 46–49.

33. Rorlich, *The Volga Tatars*, pp. 89–96. Gorokhov's figures, however, are much lower. Gorokhov, *Reaktsionnaia shkol'naia politika*, pp. 194–195.

34. "Zhurnal," p. 119. Kharuzin exaggerated by neglecting the fact that the study of Russian in the madrasas had become extensive.

35. Other recommendations in the educational section of the report included the founding of local language institutes open to various state employees and anyone else wanting to learn the languages for practical reasons. It also envisioned the improvement of Eastern language programs at Petersburg and Kazan universities. Ibid., pp. 61–73.

36. RGIA, f. 821, op. 8, d. 801, l. 166.

37. The 1907 rules were the ultimate outcome of a 1905 conference on education which decided that Il'minskii's methodology could be applied to non-Orthodox peoples without any intention of converting them. An attempt to implement this resolution in Ministry of Education regulations of 31 March 1906 resulted in widespread Tatar opposition because it provided for the use of the Cyrillic alphabet in school texts. The 1907 rules that replaced them left this measure out. See A. S. Budilovich, ed., *Trudy osobago soveshchaniia po voprosam obrazovaniia vostochnykh inorodtsev* (St. Petersburg, 1905); and Gorokhov, *Reaktsionnaia shkol'naia politika*, pp. 177–185.

38. A particularly encouraging prognosis was offered in D. P., "K voprosu o prosveshchenii tatar," *Nachal'noe obuchenie* 8 (1910): 247–255, esp. 250–251.

39. RGIA, f. 821, op. 8, d. 801, ll. 169–170.

40. Ibid., l. 155–155ob.

41. Ibid., d. 800, l. 290–290ob.

42. Rorlich, *The Volga Tatars*, pp. 90–91; M. A. Miropiev, ed., *Zhurnaly zasedanii s"ezda direktorov i inspektorov narodnykh uchilishch orenburgskago uchebnago okruga v g. Ufe, 11–16 iiuniia 1912 goda* (Ufa, 1913), pp. 373–377.

43. Ieromonakh Serafim, *Pervyi v Rossii po vneshnei missii Kazanskii missionerskii s"ezd, 13–26 iiuniia 1910 goda*, vol. 1 (Nizhnii Novgorod, 1911), p. 42; "K voprosu ob inorodcheskoi shkole v Privolzhskom krae," *Okrainy Rossii* 13 (1911): 193–196 (here Andrei accuses the zemstvos of "liberalism" because of their involvement in the education of Muslims).

44. In 1914, another conference organized by the Ministry of the Interior lamented the transformation of the confessional schools and called for the same measure. While the 1910 report had argued against allowing such education on the basis that it was highly irregular ("all this general education is presented in the madrasas and maktabs in an insufficiently systematic way"; these schools "cannot be considered schools that can provide rational popular education"), in 1914 officials complained that the confessional schools had turned into a "systematic network [*planomernaia set'*] of institutions of general education" and that Muslims had even begun "the establishment of a special organ for the governance of

Muslim school affairs . . . a sort of special Ministry of Education for Muslims." "Zhurnal," p. 64; RGIA, f. 821, op. 10, d. 517, l. 69.

45. Speech by Sadri Maksudi, in *Gosudarstvennaia Duma. Stenograficheskie otchety. Tretii sozyv. Ch. III. Sessiia V. Zasedaniia 84–119 (5 March–28 April 1912)* (St. Petersburg, 1912), cols. 977–979 (hereafter referred to as Maksudi). In Kazan province, the law on freedom of the press was being violated with respect to Muslims almost from the time it was announced. In 1906, a Special Committee on Press Affairs was formed by the governor. Its chief activity was the preventive censorship of publications in Turkic languages; materials were even sent to the committee from other provinces. See A. G. Karimullin, *Tatarskaia kniga nachala XX veka* (Kazan, 1974).

46. The teachers were convicted in 1912. Rorlich, *The Volga Tatars*, pp. 97–99 and 231.

47. Maksudi, cols. 992–993; Rorlich, *The Volga Tatars*, pp. 97–98.

48. L. Klimovich, *Islam v tsarskoi Rossii* (Moscow, 1936), pp. 263–264.

49. RGIA, f. 821, op. 8, d. 801, ll. 169–170, 152.

50. Maksudi, col. 979.

51. Actually, Maksudi disingenuously called Pan-Islam "an invention of missionaries with political ambitions." He probably overestimated the influence of missionaries on Stolypin and the Soveshchanie as well. Ibid., cols. 982–987 and 996.

52. Quoted in Arsharuni, "Iz istorii," p. 108.

53. RGIA, f. 821, op. 8, d. 800, ll. 37–38, 64, 471–472.

54. Zenkovsky, *Pan-Turkism and Islam*, pp. 116–117.

55. Maxime Rodinson, *Europe and the Mystique of Islam*, trans. Roger Veinus (Seattle, 1991), pp. 67–68.

56. Ibid., p. 68.

57. RGIA, f. 821, op. 8, d. 801, l. 168–168ob.

58. ARAN (Spb), f. 177, op. 2, d. 11, ll. 9–11.

59. V. D. Smirnov, "Po voprosu o shkol'nom obrazovanii inorodtsev-musul'man," *ZhMNP* 222 (1882): 1–24.

60. See A. G. Karimullin, *Tatarskaia kniga poreformennoi Rossii* (Kazan, 1983), esp. pp. 99–144 and 179–233; and idem, *Tatarskaia kniga nachala XX veka*, pp. 186–235.

61. TsGART, f. 92, op. 1, d. 18324, ll. 16ob.–17.

62. *Pis'ma N. I. Il'minskago k K. P. Pobedonostsevu* (Kazan, 1895), p. 175.

63. GPB, f. 1004, d. 18, l. 1.

64. Klimovich, *Islam*, p. 222.

65. RGIA, f. 821, op. 8, d. 800, l. 371.

66. Albert Hourani, *Islam in European Thought* (Cambridge, 1991), pp. 29–30.

67. N. P. Ostroumov, *Koran i progress* (Tashkent, 1901), p. 230. Here Ostroumov was actually quoting and embracing the opinion of Vladimir Solov'ev, from the latter's *Magomet, ego zhizn' i uchenie* (St. Petersburg, 1896). Ostroumov did not agree with all of Solov'ev's views on Islam, especially the view that it could be a progressive force and a steppingstone to Christianity for polytheistic peoples.

68. Ostroumov, *Koran*, p. 243. See also Mark Batunsky, "Racism in Russian Islamology: Agafangel Krimsky," *Central Asian Survey* 4 (1992): 75–84.

69. Ostroumov, *Koran*, p. 243.

70. Ibid., p. 244.

71. Ibid., pp. 246–247.

72. Ibid., p. 232.

73. See, for example, BLKU, f. 7, d. 17, l. 2–2ob.

74. For more on Malov's polemical method, see Geraci, "Window on the East," pp. 89–100.

75. P. K. Zhuze, "Islam i prosveshchenie," *Pravoslavnyi sobesednik* 2 (1899): 529–539.

76. The Nietzsche reference is: "truths are illusions about which one has forgotten that this is what they are." Said, *Orientalism*, pp. 203–204.

77. Ibid., p. 197.

78. RGIA, f. 800, op. 8, d. 801, l. 67.

79. RGIA, f. 821, op. 8, d. 800, l. 64; see also ll. 319ob.–320.

80. Said, *Orientalism*, p. 263.

81. For a fuller discussion of this issue, see Geraci, "Window on the East," pp. 73–75.

82. G. Alisov, "Musul'manskii vopros v Rossii," *Russkaia mysl'* 7 (1909): 28–61; here pp. 60–61 and 36.

83. ARAN (Spb), f. 68, op. 1, d. 430, ll. 178–179.

84. See ARAN (Spb), f. 68, op. 1, d. 430, ll. 300–303; RGIA, f. 821, op. 133, d. 450.

PART TWO

Frontier Encounters

The eastern and southern frontiers of the Russian Empire were as diverse as the peoples inhabiting those territories and as disparate as the assorted images they held up of each other. It is no wonder that the encounters discussed in the chapters included in this section reveal an imperial borderland of great social and cultural richness and complexity. In chronological terms, the authors center their attention on the nineteenth century, though Thomas Barrett's chapter reminds us that Cossacks and Caucasian mountain tribes had a long previous history of border crossing as well as fighting. Geographically, the chapters encompass a territory stretching from Crimea to Sakhalin, from the middle Volga to Bukhara. The imperial metropole is at best a distant presence in their stories. Their gaze is focused on the encounter of peoples under tsarist dominion among those who lived the daily reality of colonial rule. They ask the reader to shift perspectives, to put aside the voices of those who viewed the borderlands from the imperial center and to heed those speaking from the frontiers. The story of the encounters, lived and pondered, between borderlands peoples and the emissaries of the state, settlers, travelers, and scholars brings to the history of the empire the immediacy of colonial life.

The colonial context is a central feature of all these stories. In the daily life of the borderlands, differences faded as peoples pursued their everyday affairs. Thomas Barrett's study of the Terek Cossacks brings to light the complex web of human relations that brought enemies to trade, to share a style of life, and to evolve a similar pattern of living. In this exchange, Cossacks learned much from mountain tribes. Tsarist policy and frontier wars dictated the creation of immutable borders to protect imperial subjects and to isolate rebellious natives. But the needs of daily life and the pursuit of familiar activities revealed that Cossacks and mountain tribes found common grounds for coexistence—until the next war or raiding party intervened.

Along the borderlands, the Russian presence was above all that of the successful conqueror. The conquest itself caused its own anguish and critical judgments of ingrained truths. Jo-Ann Gross provides us with a unique portrait of one Bukharan intellectual's struggle to reconcile his faith in the World of Islam with the tsarist conquest of Central Asia. But the rule by Russians posed a challenge so profound that some among the new generations of Muslim subjects accepted the necessity of a fundamental rethinking of their social and political ideals. Edward Lazzerini makes clear the remarkable daring of one Crimean activist, Gasprinskii, in accepting a vision of modernity drawn out of Russian practices and institutions. The jadids, whose activities in Turkestan Adeeb Khalid discusses, carried forward this new and exceedingly controversial agenda for reform of a Muslim community to which they were attached but whose feeble response to colonial rule they condemned.

The encounter of frontier peoples and imperial emissaries evolved in a context set only partly by the empire's institutions and policies. The power exercised by the empire was in theory autocratic and thorough. The realities of everyday life and local culture repeatedly altered and even subverted the plans laid in St. Petersburg. This capacity for resistance on the part of the non-Christian, non-Russian peoples of the eastern territories took as many forms as there were local encounters. Agnès Kefeli reveals the determination of Tatars of the Volga region (where Russian rule dated to the sixteenth century) to retain their traditional Muslim faith. Christian conversion appeared to have made major inroads among these Tatars. Yet Kefeli has discovered, through her study of one village, that Muslim practices remained strong and probably were undergoing a revival among the Tatars in the nineteenth century. What to the Russian Orthodox missionaries and provincial administrators constituted a grave case of apostasy—that is, abandonment of Christianity—meant to the villagers the return to their own faith within their own social and spiritual community.

A very different form of local resistance appeared among the steppe nomads, whose encounter with tsarist legal practices is discussed by Virginia Martin. Customary rules (*adat*) among the Kazakhs, as among other conquered peoples, came into conflict with the laws of the empire. What to Kazakhs was heroic defense of clan honor was in the imperial law code the crime of robbery. These laws disrupted the practices of customary law, at the same time as imperial administrative practices undermined the authority of traditional clan elders. This encounter brought about profound changes in Kazakh behavior. Martin's study reveals that Kazakhs continued to hold firmly to what they believed were customary standards of honor and justice. Ironically, though, the adjustments through which they reconciled their customs with their status as tsarist subjects produced new forms of heroic conduct far different from those that had earlier reigned among their clans.

The slow evolution of these borderlands peoples under imperial rule brought increasingly frequent encounters between Russians and even the remotest, least-known peoples. The new science of ethnography thrived on firsthand observation. Russians—even some who in fact were political exiles and enemies of the tsarist state—conducted their investigation of customs, material artifacts, languages, and physical types with all the zeal of scientists working in a vast laboratory of humanity. A primitive past appeared to come alive among tribes on the island of Sakhalin. But Bruce Grant shows to what extent their discoveries depended upon expectations they brought with them. The classification of "primitive" was the strongest marker of difference that these ethnographers possessed, but in their zeal to uncover authentic savagery they imagined far more than was there. Peoples of the borderlands escaped simple ethnographic identification, just as they evaded the legal and cultural guidelines by which the state's emissaries hoped to transform them into loyal subjects.

.8.

EDWARD J. LAZZERINI

Local Accommodation and Resistance to Colonialism in Nineteenth-Century Crimea

[When the] quest for distinction leads the dominated
to affirm what distinguishes them, is this resistance?
Conversely, if the dominated appropriate for the
purpose of dissolving what marks them,
is this submission?

—PIERRE BOURDIEU[1]

In 1884 the Russian Empire completed the process of territorial acquisition that its antecedent, Muscovy, had begun centuries before during the reign of Ivan IV (1545–1586). By a twist of fate, but also a certain logic, the final conquest bore similarity to the first: both were at the expense of Turkic peoples committed in substance to the cultural legacy of Islam, and both signaled the persistence (though not totality) of Russia's orientation eastward. Over the three centuries between the incorporation of Tatars settled largely along the Volga River and Turkmens wedged between the Caspian Sea and the once-powerful Amirate of Bukhara, the expanding Russian state gobbled up an exceptional array of peoples and cultures, in the process forming not only the largest country in the world but also one of the most ethnically and religiously diverse. At the turn of the twentieth century, that diversity would be revealed unmistakably in several ways:

by the census of 1897, which tracked 146 ethno-linguistic groups; by a burgeoning literature—scholarly, administrative, and popular—that gave central place to ethnicity and the assorted "questions" that concern for it evoked; and by a growing assertion of ethnic self-consciousness in one minority community after the other.

The Turkic subjects of the empire numbered approximately thirteen million, or about 10 percent of the total population counted as of 1 January 1897. Dispersed geographically from the Black Sea to the Pacific and engaged in nearly every type of economic activity possible for the time, including the full range of sedentary (urban and rural) and nomadic occupations, they were themselves a diverse lot. To be sure, language and the high culture centered on Islam provided points of common reference for most if not all Turks, but in the end an Azerbaijani was not a Kazakh, nor was a Dagestani an Uzbek. For that matter, none of these was a Crimean Tatar, whose community had made the Crimean Peninsula home since the fourteenth century. By 1897, these Tatars had been under Russian colonial rule for more than a century, during which time their numbers, thanks largely to successive waves of emigration to the Balkans and Anatolia, had fallen precipitously. Although we cannot determine an accurate population figure for the late eighteenth century prior to annexation, scholars have long believed that it was approximately 300,000, or twice as many as in 1897.

The decline in population was symptomatic of the colonial circumstances befalling Crimea. This was especially true following the consolidation of Russian authority when, despite some major social and cultural concessions to the local population (e.g., Tatars were never subject to serfdom or military conscription), economic conditions in rural areas, disputes over control of landed property, serious underdevelopment of education, and a near collapse of indigenous high culture made the Tatar experience increasingly grim and vulnerable to endless rumormongering. The latter fed the anxieties of many Tatars, thereby contributing significantly to the episodic, and sometimes frenzied, flight abroad. Among some Russian authorities it fueled suspicions about Tatar loyalty to the empire that raised administrative concerns and generated streams of police reports; among others, both Russian and Tatar, it offered opportunities to be seized literally, it turned out, in the form of land abandoned by those departing in haste. Reading police reports easily creates the impression that Tatar-Russian relations were inevitably and permanently hostile; that the authorities (central and provincial) would have liked nothing better than to see the peninsula emptied of its dominant native population; that provincial officials were fundamentally and typically indifferent to the needs of those for whom they were responsible; that chauvinism always deeply colored Russian attitudes, and that Russification, once embraced as official policy in the early 1880s, represented its logical extension; that the interests of Tatars were unprotected; and that local concerns were mostly subordinated to imperial dictates. Conversely, focusing on the exodus of Tatars from their homeland, on a superficial reading of the complexities of landholding, on the long decline of native education, and on the overall backwardness of Tatar society only strengthens our inclination to see Crimea as a colony and little more, where the indigenous cemeteries, for instance, attached to deserted Tatar villages were trampled and plowed over by others (whether Russian, Ukrainian, or German settlers), so that neither history nor the dead received any respect or protection.

I propose in the following pages a rethinking of colonialism in this one part of imperial Russia's oriental borderland over the course of the long nineteenth century. More specifically, I want to complicate our analysis of this borderland in two ways: first, by momentarily shifting attention from conflict across ethnic lines to the evidence of cooperation (accommodation, collaboration, though I intend to avoid the negative connotations of all of these terms) despite such divisions;[2] and second, by uncovering sources of resistance to Russian colonial rule that do not privilege forms most associated with revolutionary behavior and do not fit a requirement to affirm 1917. My purpose is not to diminish the importance of ethnic relations and their painful consequences in this or any other specific region, but to expand the context within which they are discussed so as better to understand the extent of their impact on events and lives, their greater complexity, and the circumstances in which they are less rather than more significant. Ethnicity surely counts, as Virginia Martin reveals in her chapter on *barïmta* later in this volume, but not always, simply, or inevitably. Likewise, I endeavor not to deny the significance of radical impulses and behavior that contributed to an evolving revolutionary situation by early twentieth-century Russia, but to show that these were not the only means by which to intervene in what some believed to be an oppressive sociopolitical *and* colonial situation. As Jean Comaroff has noted, "If we confine our historical scrutiny to revolutionary success, we discount the vast proportion of human social action which is played out on a humbler scale. We also evade, by teleological reasoning, the real questions that remain as to what *are* the transformative motors of history."[3]

I begin with several assumptions that will help shape my subsequent discussion: first, that we need to respect the synchronicity of colonial and modernist discourses more than we have, because together they encouraged as much accommodation as hostility between natives and outlanders, and not just among educated elites; second, that with some modification (specifically the interjection of the notion of "nesting subalterns"), we can fruitfully apply to members of ethnic minorities in the Russian Empire the theoretical construct, derived from South Asian studies, of subalternity as a social category; third, that dominant elites (rulers and their agents) were not a united force, but more typically redefined policies in response to local conditions and indigenous pressures; and fourth, that borderlands are not just arenas of civilizational struggles, of semiotic inequality, that produce and reflect relations of power where the colonizer seeks to define and program the borderland as "other" and "same" and, as Ashis Nandy argues, its inhabitants as an "intimate enemy,"[4] but are sites subject to peculiar social contradictions and interactions. These spawn, by a kind of local magic, the possibility of a new community and a subtle, not always conscious, but genuine resistance to colonial situations.

Crimea offers a marvelous case study for these and other issues. Situated on the southern periphery of the empire where it could enhance Russia's access to the Black Sea and the Mediterranean, blessed with good harbors, fruitful valleys, and a mostly temperate climate, possessing a long history of international commerce linked with the Silk Route through Kafa and Sudak, and very much an ethnic and cultural entrepôt, Crimea existed throughout the final century of the Russian ancien régime as a key segment along the extended imperial borderland. Once under direct Russian administration, the region became a well-known haven for travelers and sojourners, many of them wealthy, socially noble, and even royal. Romantic and dreamy along its southern shore, in "sleepy" Tatar towns, or in valleys such as that below Chufut-Kale, it produced, as has Guilin for Chinese, visions in poets (Pushkin most famously, but also Maksimilian Voloshin, who is more revered locally), in painters (I. K. Aivazovskii), and in academicians and bureaucrats (P. S. Pallas and P. Sumarokov, to name just two). Almost immediately following the absorption of its territory into the Russian Empire, and continuing with few interruptions until the Soviet period, plans for Crimea's future proliferated, first from outside the region (it was for Catherine II "the best pearl in the crown of Russia"),[5] but increasingly from within. And in the process, Crimea became for many a land of promise, a potential paradise that could be lost if left unattended.

In all likelihood one could find almost as many visions for Crimea as there were inhabitants, although most would fall within the range of a manageable typology. Some believed the territory to be nothing more than a logical, justifiable extension of Russia, an integral part of the European civilizational matrix seeking to fulfill its presumed historic mission to bring enlightenment to savages. One such commentator, celebrating Crimea's conquest a hundred years earlier, epitomized this viewpoint when he argued that if Crimea's acquisition was important for Russia, it was more so for Crimea. After all, here was a place, "once the flourishing and wealthy colony of Greece, Venice, and Genoa, the patron of the sciences and arts," that in time "fell to the Tatars, became a haven for robbers, and under the flag of the [half] moon [Islam] began persecuting Christians." Moreover, despite being rich in natural resources and blessed by its geographic location, "the peninsula grew poor, lost its significance, and became a threatening neighbor to the Christian kingdoms of Caucasia, to Poland, and especially to Russia." But Russia changed all of this:

Local Accommodation and Resistance to Colonialism

Crimea: Conquered yet Conquering

Top: *Panorama of the magnificent palace built by Prince M. S. Vorontsov between 1833 and 1852 at Alupka overlooking the Black Sea (Lithograph by V. Timm, 1855)*

Bottom: *Detail of grand entrance to Vorontsov's palace, with its dominating oriental motif (Photograph courtesy of Edward J. Lazzerini, 1994)*

In its forward movement to the south, to its natural borders, reclaiming the right to its ancient property, to the age-old Russian [Black] Sea, it [Russia] took possession of Crimea and restored to it the ancient time of enlightenment and peace. During the past one hundred years many cities in the European style were built, ports were opened, good roads were constructed, and, most important, numerous educational institutions were established that spread the light of science among a population that, until now, had dwelled in ignorance. In Crimea arrived the happiest of days![6]

The author of these words, unidentifiable except for his eminently distinctive Russian family name, Ivanov, could not have revealed himself more as an imperialist in the now classic mode than he did here. The arrogance of his language, redolent of the self-assurance that spills readily from the pens of victors, belies the critical value of his thought and reflects a basic Manichaean worldview untroubled by complications.

Bringing enlightenment to savages, however, could carry heavier religious overtones, as it did in a contemporaneous sermon by Germogen, Bishop of Tavrida and Simferopol'.[7] "O Crimea, Crimea, our beloved Crimea! How much of you is still not Russian, how much still not Orthodox!" he intoned. "Over the course of the last century have we done much to Russify the region and fix Orthodoxy's presence in it?" His answer was a resounding no. Instead, the Russian population of the region remained surrounded by a mass of *inorodtsy*, "especially Tatars." Worse than this is what one found happening in locales with mixed Russian and Tatar settlers: "It is not the Tatars who imitate the Russians in their customs, practices, and way of life, but rather the Russians who imitate the Tatars!" Here is where Germogen parts company with Ivanov, despite their shared cultural assumptions. Whereas the latter sees Crimea as a possession responding positively to an inexorable Russian presence, Germogen worries over the meaninglessness of that presence in Crimean lives. Whereas Ivanov can rejoice over accomplishments to date and wax optimistic about the future, Germogen laments the indifference of local Russians to the interests of church and state. Whereas Ivanov idealizes a world of his own creation, Germogen rails against a world that defies his reason and influence.

If we merely read Germogen and submit to his obvious text, we will find a cleric who believes in the righteousness of his faith and his obligation to proselytize among infidel "others." However, if we focus a more critical eye, we may discover a man whose certainty shows signs of withering before a reality in which the kinds of differences he holds dear make no difference whatsoever, apparently, to too many in his flock. The roles of master and guest, the latter term he applied to Tatars, have been reversed in "real" life, not inexplicably, but because of ideological indifference to difference. "Look for a minute at the Tatar. He is somehow withdrawn, immobile, rather incapable of progress and civilization, about which we worry so much, but he is by all accounts for the most part honest, good, and industrious; to the point of extreme he reads his Qur'an deeply as a regulator of his life; he never and nowhere forgets the hours of prayer dictated by that book." At least to Germogen, Tatars know the difference, and therein lies their success in avoiding assimilation. But even here, the good bishop refuses to recognize the real point: that people of varied ethnic backgrounds can live together peacefully, that they do find ways to be inclusive rather than exclusive of one another, that difference need not be primarily identifying, and above all, that colonialism, like power generally, may in practice be much less authoritative and defining than many like to believe.

I offer these observations as a kind of wedge to penetrate an ambiguous world of cooperation and resistance that needs attention and analysis. We have numerous studies, if not of imperial Russia then of other colonial settings, that have uncovered the manifold ways by which ordinary people defy and foil the expectations and demands of those who would claim authority over them.[8] What has largely prompted such research has been a concern to give voice to those whom mainstream historiography, wherever located, has typically ignored. Historians have increasingly championed marginal social elements of all kinds, whether rooted in ethnic, racial, or gender constructs, in order to produce a fuller history of communities than was possible by focusing always and merely on the politically, militarily, and intellectually powerful.

One example of this, exceptional for its organized commitment to theoretical and political engagement, has been the Subaltern Studies Group (SSG), whose research since the mid-1980s on South Asia has produced a series of volumes examining the experiences of non-elite, submerged groups and voices. This is not the place for an extended discussion of SSG's work, which in any event is too large and internally differentiated; rather, I want to suggest the potential usefulness of the subaltern concept for Russian imperial studies. In the preface to the first volume of *Selected Subaltern Studies,* Ranajit Guha proposed a simple, flexible, and relational definition of subaltern as persons "of inferior rank" possessing "the general attribute of subordination . . . whether this is expressed in terms of class, caste, age, gender and office or in any other way."[9] While not necessarily the best of definitions owing to its unmanageably expansive character, it does have the merit of allowing for the possibility that not everyone is subordinated in the same way and that no single axis (class, gender, race) serves as the measure of subalternity. Because Guha and his colleagues, however, are fundamentally interested in "the people," they make a clear distinction between dominant and subaltern groups, end up foreclosing some of the relational possibilities in their very concept, and implicitly reject the likelihood that subalterns can be found within elites. This is Gail Hershatter's complaint, in response to which she proposes the notion of "nesting subalterns" (also called "swing" groups): people who "at the local level acted in accordance with their own interests," who "may be elite with respect to some groups and situations, subaltern with respect to others."[10]

From this perspective, an important category of persons exists in any colonial context who "go to great pains to distinguish themselves from and speak for those 'below,' while allying themselves with and speaking to those 'above.'"[11] Many remain unidentifiable, largely because their speech was seldom public, although I suspect that local records, as in Crimea, will reveal some of them by virtue of their links to the region's administrative life or their involvement in important social activities.[12] Others were more prominent and have left us varying amounts of an examinable legacy. Through a close reading of their texts, analyzed from a comparative and cross-cultural life-history approach,[13] we may someday be able to reveal in a more nuanced fashion the forces that shaped accommodation in Crimea and how much was locally significant; who participated in it and who opposed it; what interests were served by it and whom it enriched; which institutions promoted and sustained it, and which strove to expose and condemn it; and what the cost of complicity was. When that happens we will have uncovered a Crimea that more fully reflects the complex imaginings of men from different ethnic backgrounds as they struggled to reconcile the burdens and promises of colonialism, the comforts of received traditions and the allure of the "modern," the centripetal voice of imperial authority and the pleasures of "talking back" on the basis of being where it (really?) counted: in Simferopol', Bakhchisarai, Yalta, Evpatoriia, Sevastopol', and any one of tens of Crimean places. Those who collaborated yet resisted, such as Seraia Shapshal and Il'ia Kazas (Karaims), Ismail Bey Gasprinskii and Mustafa Murza Davidovich (Tatars), as well as Mikhail Spiro (a Jew), to name just a few, are a fascinating and challenging lot. They were sometimes dismissed by their own as naive, foolish, politically incorrect, or, worse, toadying; and by others as villainous, dangerous subversives who stood, and thought, too close for comfort, especially *because* they were non-Russian. Coincidentally the defense of Crimean interests appears to have been an important note in much of their rhetoric—in fact, one of its common threads—so much so that being *krymchanin* (a Crimean) acquired increasing significance and resonated in their representations of the place, its people, and its future.

The results that will derive from more extensive examination of various Crimean lives are beyond the scope of this chapter. Here I can offer only glimpses into one life—Ismail Bey Gasprinskii's—and a framework within which to situate his and those of others to come; to suggest a nexus between accommodation and resistance to colonialism involving an emerging Crimean middle class, simultaneously insiders and outsiders, "nesting subalterns" whose demands for social change ultimately represented a form of resistance both to the organic traditional communities and to the colonial world within which they were reared.[14]

Crimean Tatar reformer, educator, and publicist Ismail Bey Gasprinskii (1851–1914) came to be regarded as the architect of modernism among Muslim Turkic subjects of the Russian Empire. Born in a small Crimean village to a family that had served in the Russian military for two generations, Ismail Bey was schooled first in a local *maktab* (Islamic primary school) and then in Russian military academies before spending nearly three years abroad, principally in France and the Ottoman Empire. Upon his return to Crimea he taught Russian briefly in the Zincirli madrasa (Islamic seminary) and served a four-year term as mayor of Bakhchisarai from 1878 to 1882. In that period he published a defining essay, *Russkoe musul'manstvo* (The Russian Islamic World), which challenged his community and its Russian leaders to awaken to a new age; he also received permission to produce a newspaper, *Perevodchik/Tercüman* (The Interpreter), that would appear in both Russian and Turkic. With the first issue, dated 10 April 1883, Gasprinskii launched one of the most important ethnic periodicals in Russian history and firmly committed himself to a life of public service dedicated to the modernization of Turkic society and the Islamic way, both in Russia and abroad.

For the next thirty years Gasprinskii endeavored to persuade his brethren to reassess their intellectual assumptions and sociocultural practices so as to overcome those conditions, derived largely from the overweening influence of a misdirected religious orthodoxy, that he believed condemned Muslims to cultural inferiority under modern Western technological, military, political, and intellectual hegemony. The declining fortunes of Muslims everywhere, along with his own cosmopolitan experiences, impelled Ismail Bey to advocate a message that change not only was possible and good, but also was absolutely necessary for cultural survival. He further argued that progress could be ensured only by educating children in modern schools teaching a modern curriculum by modern methods (*usûl-i jadid*), by encouraging social and economic cooperation, and by developing a willingness to borrow from other cultures (especially Europe's) whatever might prove useful and beneficial. *Perevodchik/Tercüman*, countless pamphlets, and (after 1905) other periodical publications (*Alem-i nisvan*, *Alem-i sibyan*, *al-Nahdah*, and *Kha! Kha! Kha!*) became the vehicles by which Gasprinskii spread his ideas and inspired the movement known as jadidism (modernism).

For Gasprinskii, creation of a new society able to compete effectively meant generating "new people." Education, of course, stood at the center of his project, for it was expected to reorient the way the younger generation thought and behaved. Islam would remain in the curriculum for moral guidance, but it would cease to dominate, diminished in that role by

Ismail Bey Gasprinskii is attacked by mullas brandishing the accusations "heresy" and "the new method is contrary to the Shariʿa." Grasprinskii holds a copy of Hoca-yi Sibyan, *his new-method primer, and* Perevodchik/Tercüman, *his dual-language newspaper.*
(Mulla Nasreddin, *no. 17 [1908])*

the sciences, mathematics, foreign languages, philosophy, and a range of practical subjects. The "new man" would be complemented by the "new woman," still expected to shoulder the major responsibility for nurturing society but given more autonomy and broader opportunities to participate in public affairs. Mobilization of the talents, resources, and energies of the largest possible number of people permeated Gasprinskii's writings, leading him to call for the development of a common Turkic literary language, the establishment of mutual-aid societies, and cooperation with the Russian government and people. By the second decade of the twentieth century, Gasprinskii's influence, intellectually moderate and consummately practical, was felt throughout Turkic Russia, as well as in Turkey, Egypt, and even Muslim India.

This sketch can barely do justice to the highlights of Gasprinskii's public life, let alone reveal any of the nuances of thought and relationships he may have developed, nurtured, or abandoned over nearly fifty years. Along with others, Gasprinskii belonged to that critical generation of native thinkers who armed themselves with the authority of two ideologies securely embedded in Russian thought and practice by the 1870s, that of a specific view of imperial order and that of modernism. As Dan Brower, Virginia Martin, and Adeeb Khalid point out elsewhere in this volume, a significant redefinition of the imperial mission occurred during the reign of Catherine II that was rooted in a commitment to toleration for the cultural "other" (ethnic and religious), with the aim of ensuring their active involvement in and accommodation to the life of the empire. European-wide intellectual trends linked principally to the Scientific Revolution and then the Enlightenment inspired the tempering of means for ordering society while not giving up any of the desire for order, stability, and growth. A kinder and gentler empire was to be the place wherein peoples of all sorts practicing a potentially infinite array of cultures could live harmoniously and cooperatively, working for the general good even as they preserved their separate cultural markers.[15]

For its part, the ideology of modernism, likewise a product of convergent European intellectual and social trends, reflected an epistemological turn away from custom, habit, the cumulative weight of the past, "tradition," and the conviction that time counts for little, to a belief in the calculability of the future and a split between fact and value that ultimately challenged cultures in their core meanings. A new mode of consciousness gradually emerged that fostered the disenchantment of the world and the increasing alienation of man from his surroundings. One of its consequences was the iconization of change and the possibility of becoming what one had not been. This was an epochal transformation whose promises have been alluring and whose accomplishments enormous. Modernism has also been, however, a historic wrecking ball, in the trail of whose destruction lie ruins both physical and spiritual.

For most of the nineteenth century, however, few worried about such consequences. In places such as Crimea, on the margins of the Russian Empire and inhabited by indigenous groups who expected little more than to be marginalized, the Catherinian compromise and modernism seemed especially enticing. They drew together liberal thinkers in both the Russian and native camps who could be together yet remain apart, who could crisscross boundaries at least intermittently, dissolve difference where it counted (as in the realm of the practical), while allowing difference where *it* counted (as in the world of the spiritual). The topos *sblizhenie* (accommodation, rapprochement) entered the public discourse, becoming popular precisely in those circles with which I am concerned. Gasprinskii offers a clear case in point.

In the summer of 1881, then in a series of articles subsequently reissued separately under the title *Russkoe musul'manstvo*, Gasprinskii endeavored to dissipate the fictive imaginings that he feared filled the Russian mind about his coreligionists. In doing so, he hoped that the two groups could achieve the sblizhenie from which both would benefit. He knew from personal experience, though he hated admitting as much publicly, what prejudices shaped the attitudes of Muslim and Russian toward one another, and the longer he labored, the more his worst fears were realized.

To his Russian critics, Gasprinskii was "that" *inorodets*, educated in Russian schools, conversant with the Russian language, privileged by the imperial context, yet setting out to apply his blessings inappropriately in pursuit of a cause ultimately detrimental to the empire and its presumed interests. Because he strove, as one critic charged, "to use all the advantages of Russian culture to defend [his] nationality," he could not be trusted; despite his partial assimilation, some believed, he continually evinced an anti-Russian bias.[16] Unlike Ibrahim Altynsarin, for example, a Kazakh protégé of the missionary/educator N. I. Il'minskii and a "good" native, Gasprinskii transgressed the rules of proper behavior by acting autonomously and presuming an interpretive privilege to which he had no right. As a Russianized Muslim, he was a partial insider who, it was feared, knew how to turn the dominant discourse of colonialism against itself. Foreign yet familiar, distant yet near, self yet other, to certain Russians Gasprinskii presented a threat all the more terrible for its ambiguity. He could move with ease across the cultural boundary separating two worlds, scattering within the heart of the dominant culture invisible seeds of subversion that would sprout poisonous shoots. The specter he evoked was too awful to contemplate.

Such strident views and negative stereotypes may have been atypical of most educated Russians, yet more subtle prejudices did act to obstruct Gasprinskii's plans. In response he consciously adopted the shrewd and effective tactic of appearing perfectly orthodox, of working within parameters set by authority, while proffering moderate criticism of the status quo and suggesting its reform. Unquestionably sincere in his quest for a Russian-Muslim rapprochement—he neither "ran away" nor encouraged others to do so, despite ample opportunity to emigrate—yet he was just as certainly clever in his use of this ideal to assuage Russian fears and make possible the realization of his many other goals. From early in his career he articulated a rhetoric of reason designed as much to mollify as to persuade.

However paradoxical its use might seem in view of subsequent Soviet policy, the term *sblizhenie* for Gasprinskii symbolized the fusion of creative energies likely to issue from close Russian-Muslim contacts. Its achievement—a cooperative, mutually encouraging, and egalitarian society—would provide substance to the otherwise romantic notion of a Russo-Islamic world sitting astride the Eurasian continent and separating the West from the greater Orient. In place of enmity between Russian and Islamic peoples would come respect, forging an unassailable compact able to defy external threats and overcome ill-considered prejudice; instead of discord would come harmony, opening up greater opportunities for pursuing joint interests bound to serve the modernist cause of progress, power, and prosperity. The promise of these two peoples working hand in hand, for all its utopian charm, was cradled in a web of argument redolent of the calm reason and logic that the modern West idealized.

One can sense throughout his writings Gasprinskii's urgency concerning the fate of Muslim peoples in a world dominated by power of a kind qualitatively different from any previously known. Membership in the "club of modernism" was now a precondition of survival, and time was vital. A context wherein one's nation was economically backward, educationally unsophisticated, technologically naive, and even uncomprehending of its plight required help from "friends."

Who, then, were the friends of the Islamic peoples? On the basis of historical and cultural relations, and considering the state of world politics, Gasprinskii believed them to be the Russians. To this theme he added an appeal to ethnic sensibility. If couched in moral terms, his quite blunt advocacy of a civilizing mission for Russia in the Islamic territories within and outside the empire also stroked—and not incidentally—Russian pride. The possibility for such a role was created at the beginning of the eighteenth century by the reforms of Peter the Great, which for Gasprinskii launched the empire into the modern age. Now, with well over a century of experience and development, Russia could provide leadership and guidance to those, like the Muslims, clinging to the past. In 1881 he lamented the failure of central Russian authorities to take up the task of leading the Muslims "to progress and civilization."[17] The government, he charged, was focusing too narrowly on administrative concerns so that "Russian power among the Muslims has not gone beyond the demands of the state treasury and the maintenance of social order and tranquility. . . . Is there nothing more to . . . the great civilizing mission of Russia in the East? . . . Do administrative changes really constitute all that that mission entails?"[18] Throughout the remainder of his life he criticized lost opportunities as well as shortsighted and inconsistent policies that limited the positive influence that Russia could have had on his brethren. Inevitably, he complained, both suffered immeasurably.

Mutual understanding, encouraged by Russian assistance and openness to Muslim secular needs, was the key, in Gasprinskii's judgment, to improving relations and awakening in Russian society a sense of the enormous value to be derived from fulfilling its responsibility: "Give them the possibility to acquire knowledge, improve their access to new ideas and principles; then you will see how quickly the Muslims come alive and lose their apathy."[19] Active, loyal, productive subjects were Gasprinskii's promise in return for enlightened, generous, and liberal Russian attitudes toward Muslims. Why not? "*Except for religion, everything else* draws [the two] together and binds them fast."[20] What needed cultivation on both sides was belief that the empire's peoples, for all their cultural differences, had common interests and aspirations that far outweighed all other considerations. Thus, Gasprinskii bristled at charges by certain Russians that the Tatars were guilty of separatist intentions because they strove to become modern and yet retain a separate cultural identity.[21] Hence the meaning of a remark he made in response to complaints about the publication of his newspaper *Perevodchik/Tercüman* in Turkic as well as Russian: "There are only Russian newspapers," he wrote, being published in the empire; the single difference is that they "appear in various languages."[22]

While acknowledging the legitimacy and appropriateness of Russia's civilizing mission, Gasprinskii was careful to distinguish it from imperial policy commonly identified with Russification. The latter he defined as total assimilation of all groups by the Russians for the sake of ethnic homogeneity and a presumed augmentation of control over the empire's entire population. Such a policy would serve the interests of bureaucrats and administrators concerned above all with power, but it bore within itself "the character of constraint, of limitation on the rights of a given nationality" in relationship to another. As such, Gasprinskii admonished, administrative Russification lacked justification (except for authority and "hot-headed patriots"), was historically counterproductive, and in the long run would be ineffective and harmful. Better to unify people and groups "on the basis of equality, freedom, science, and education," to Russify them "morally" by valorizing ethnoreligious differences and allowing cultural autonomy, and thus build bridges leading to sblizhenie.[23]

Among the natives, those who most bought into the two ideologies that the term *sblizhenie* ultimately captured were men and women who came from different social backgrounds—no peasants that I can discern, but certainly commercial types, professionals, and some holding noble rank (as did Gasprinskii) by virtue of state service—but who collectively formed a budding middle class, in the sense of being situated in several different and important ways: *between,* for example, the traditional Tatar nobility (those descended from the Giray and other great clans of the khanate) and the mass of peasants; *between* Russian colonial and Tatar colonized societies; and, along a continuum of resistance to colonial hegemony, *between* what Basil Davidson terms "primary resistance" (the physical struggle against outside intrusion) and "ideological resistance" (the effort to reconstitute a "shattered community, to save or restore the sense and fact of community against all the pressures of the colonial system").[24] Forging "lives in between," to borrow Leo Spitzer's phrase, this middle class struggled to redefine the world according to principles suitable to its own identity search, but not threatening to that segment of the colonial elite likewise committed to the ideologies of modernism and liberal imperialism. Those natives inclined to ponder the state of things inevitably generated adversaries—within their own community and among Russians—but they were able to fend off some of the worst attacks by laying claim to cultural terrain but not political. Concern for the schooling of children, language reform, the creation of new media forms for the voicing of public opinion, the emancipation of women, and economic development—the very heart, in fact, of the jadid project—all appealed to the Russian liberal/modernist mentality and allowed Russian "friends" to partake comfortably in the defense of the native cause against assault from its own troubled traditionalists (kadims) and from imperialists who feared the political ramifications of ethnic diversity.

Gasprinskii belonged to a prepolitical generation of cultural nationalists who were much more concerned with pointing out the limitations of their own community than they were with the consequences of imperialism. Interestingly, he could find fault with imperial authority, but usually elsewhere, in British, French, or German domains, and always in contradistinction to a more beneficent Russia. For him, the fate of Turkic (and Muslim) peoples inside and outside the Russian Empire would always be better served by association with a Russia that had had a longer and more intimate relationship with such peoples than any other power—except, perhaps, the Chinese; but they hardly counted. Though he sought improvement in the lives of his brethren and expected Russians, as the vanguard of the modern domestically, to show the way, the truth of the matter was that Gasprinskii was "comfortable" with the Russian Empire and much more annoyed with his own people for standing still, holding them responsible for their own condition, and finding the historic fault line not at the point of Russian conquest but earlier, during the long internal descent that followed the golden age of Islamic development in the ninth to eleventh centuries. From him and many like him, a general case against all imperial hegemony was never forthcoming; hence, the political menace was left unspoken, to be raised only by a subsequent generation.

By way of conclusion, let me offer a series of seeming trivia that cumulatively encapsulates, I believe, the nexus captured by the title of my project, reemphasizes the value of life history as a historical method, and shows something of the interaction across cultures at the local level as well as the significance of mediation in borderland contexts. In July 1880, the governor-general's office for Tavrida province, under whose supervision

Crimea resided, received a request from Il'ia Kazas, a local gymnasium teacher and holder of the official rank of *statskii sovetnik,* to publish a newspaper in Simferopol' on a twice-weekly basis with the title *Tavrida.* Mr. Kazas received the permission he sought on 27 August and produced his first issue in mid-October, wherein he announced editorially that the newspaper was dedicated to "the public discussion of the needs and interests of Crimean society." Several aspects of this simple story are not apparent, but deserve highlighting. Mr. Kazas, as I noted in passing earlier, was a Karaim, a member of a small but long-dwelling Crimean community of Turks who had adopted Judaism in the distant past. Its native language is similar to Crimean Tatar, with major differences located primarily in the lexicon. Kazas was the newspaper's editor, but not its owner. That person was a certain Mikhail Spiro, or as a police report described him, perhaps scurrilously, "the Jew Spiro, a man of questionable morals and political unreliability." One of the frequent writers for *Tavrida* during its brief existence (it was closed down in May 1882, apparently for printing "articles that discuss security measures taken by the state as regards the press") was a young Tatar Muslim who signed his contributions with various noms de plume ("Malen'kii Mulla," "Tatarin") and at times, with his real name, Ismail Bey Gasprinskii. As best as I have been able to discover, these pieces for *Tavrida* represent Gasprinskii's first published works. It was Russian authorities, of course, who both gave the newspaper life and then killed it.

But there is more. While all of this was going on, Gasprinskii found a patron in Mr. Spiro for the publication of his seminal *Russkoe musul'manstvo* in 1881 and was petitioning the authorities for permission to engage in his own publishing ventures, first being turned down in early 1880, trying again several times with the same result, but then achieving his goal and commencing the publication of his famous *Perevodchik/Tercüman* in April 1883. (The Crimean police were suspicious of Gasprinskii from beginning to end, but the governor's chancellery seems never to have cared about what the police thought they saw, heard, or knew, not just in the early 1880s but right up to Gasprinskii's death in 1914.) How this was accomplished is not entirely clear, but it seems reasonably certain to me that a critical factor for Gasprinskii was the support he received from Vasilii D. Smirnov, a prominent orientalist and long-time professor of Turko-Tatar studies at St. Petersburg University. Smirnov had an abiding interest in Crimea, especially its history under the khanate, had written a couple of important articles in 1877 and 1882 on educational problems among Crimean Tatars, and in succeeding years would follow closely the general phenomenon of "Muslim" publishing in the empire. By all accounts, he was a committed Russian patriot with decidedly conservative political views, and was especially wary of allowing minorities unrestricted opportunities for publishing. Since all provincial newspapers were subject to preliminary censorship down to the early twentieth century, and since Gasprinskii's *Perevodchik/Tercüman* appeared in both Russian and Tatar, potential censors were not easy to find. Smirnov was the initial choice, but by September 1884 he had been replaced by Il'ia Kazas, who would retain that duty until preliminary censorship was abolished in 1905. I should add that Smirnov's reputation in the popular and political lore of many Turkic minorities is not positive,[25] yet according to Gasprinskii family traditions, he and Ismail Bey became close friends, and Smirnov was a welcomed house guest when in Bakhchisarai.

One might ask, What's going on here? and recognize that the answers are instructive.

NOTES

1. Pierre Bourdieu, "The Uses of the 'People,'" in *In Other Words* (Stanford, 1990), p. 155.

2. The attention to ethnicity per se is not what concerns me here; what does concern me are its consequences. As a major driving force in history—especially since the nineteenth century, some would argue—we have had little choice but to address its impact. That ethnicity should have become a virtual icon among our social concerns and produced a growing body of theoretically novel and challenging viewpoints ought to surprise no one; nor should the politicization that logically attends resistance to colonialism or its analysis. Nevertheless, despite the ingenuity and imagination of scholars and activists, discussion of ethnic relations, particularly within the Russian context, too often still reflects a teleological impulse that expects resistance to take the form of separatism, exclusion, and ultimately revolution. For all the effort in recent years, we still need to be wary of arguments that objectively condemn yet subjectively perpetuate ideological categories, the evasion of context, and totalizing notions of colonial discourse.

3. Jean Comaroff, *Body of Power, Spirit of Resistance: The Culture and History of a South African People* (Chicago, 1985), p. 261.

4. Ashis Nandy, *The Intimate Enemy: Loss and Recovery of Self under Colonialism* (Delhi, 1983).

5. Cited in an editorial appearing in the Crimean newspaper *Tavrida*, no. 26 (4 April 1882), on the eve of the centennial anniversary of the region's incorporation into the empire.

6. A. Ivanov, *Stoletie prisoedineniia Kryma k Rossii* (n.p., 1883?), passim.

7. "Slovo po sluzhaiu prazdnovaniia stoletnei godovshchiny prisoedineniia Kryma k Rossii, proiznesennoe v Kafedral'nom sobor Ego Preosviashchenstvom, Preosviashchenneishim Germogenom, Episkopom Tavricheskim i Simferopol'skim," in Ivanov, *Stoletie prisoedineniia Kryma k Rossii*, pp. 5–8.

8. Worthy examples of this literature are Syed Hussein Alatas, *The Myth of the Lazy Native: A Study of the Image of the Malays, Filipinos, and Javanese from the Sixteenth to the Twentieth Century and Its Function in the Ideology of Colonial Capitalism* (London, 1977); and James Scott, *Weapons of the Weak: Everyday Forms of Peasant Resistance* (New Haven, 1985).

9. Ranajit Guha, "Preface," in *Selected Subaltern Studies*, ed. Ranajit Guha and Gayatri Chakravorty Spivak (New York, 1988), p. 35.

10. Gail Hershatter, "The Subaltern Talks Back: Reflections on Subaltern Theory and Chinese History," *Positions: East Asia Cultures Critique* 1, no. 1 (1993): 110.

11. Ibid., p. 111.

12. In a forthcoming article on Muslim pilgrimage to Mecca from Russia in the late imperial period, Dan Brower relates the activities of Said Gani Saidazimbaev, a Tashkent entrepreneur, who is precisely one of those natives who found ways to mediate the two worlds meeting in the borderlands. See Brower's "The Russian Road to Mecca: Muslim Pilgrimage and the Russian Empire," forthcoming in the *Slavic Review*. Similarly, elsewhere in this collection, though on a less personalized level, Thomas Barrett provides ample ground-level evidence of interaction and accommodation along a different stretch of the borderland.

13. A valuable example of this approach at work is Leo Spitzer's *Lives in Between: Assimilation and Marginality in Austria, Brazil, West Africa, 1780–1945* (Cambridge, 1989).

14. Historians are committed to generalization, yet we all know the limitations of the practice, despite the charm of quantitative and "objective" inquiry. Outside the market for popular literature, biography has fallen into disrepute of late, in part for good reason. However well done, much of it is wedded to narrative that seldom sees the forest for the trees, inadequately respects the interaction between the individual and his or her collective social and historical environments, or fails to generalize at all. On the other hand, generalization is inherently distorting, with much of it smacking of the sterility of the collective wherein no single human being can be identified. In a future study I hope to work through the lives of identifiable people to uncover multiple perspectives that, while unique at the individual level, reveal, as Leo Spitzer has argued (ibid., pp. 8–9), "similar patterns in their life-course and societal orientation . . . [and] evoke the shadow areas of historical motivation that we cannot know, but only sense empathetically."

15. As several contributors to this volume have made clear, this view of empire did not go unchallenged in the second half of the nineteenth century. Anyone who studies late imperial Russian history is aware of the influence that calls for Russification came to have in the colonial discourse and on policy making; yet we have seen a tendency in the historiography to exaggerate that influence to the point where the more tolerant alternative is assumed to have been vanquished completely. It was not. In fact, as Brower and especially Geraci show, the legacy of Catherine's idealism remained potent despite the arguments against its liberalism.

16. N. P. Ostroumov, as quoted in K. E. Bendrikov, *Ocherki po istorii obrazovaniia v Turkestane (1865–1924 gody)* (Moscow, 1960), p. 255. Ostroumov spelled out his critical views of Gasprinskii in a 1901 memorandum, prepared at the request of the Turkestan governor-general, entitled "Po voprosu o narozhdaiushchemsia v srede tatarskago naseleniia Rossii progressistskom dvizhenii," Tsentral'nyi gosudarstvennyi arkhiv respubliki Uzbekistana, f. 1, op. 31, d. 123, ll. 7–13.

17. I. Gasprinskii, *Russkoe musul'manstvo. Mysli, zametki i nabliudeniia musul'manina* (Bakhchisarai, 1881), p. 9.

18. Ibid., p. 5.

19. Ibid., p. 30.

20. I. Gasprinskii, *Russko-vostochnoe soglashenie. Mysli, zametki i pozhelaniia Ismaila Gasprinskago* (Bakhchisaray, 1896), p. 5.

21. This issue was a source of polemical jousting between Gasprinskii and writers for such periodicals as *Okraina, Vostochnoe obozrenie, Moskovskiia vedomosti, Novoe vremia, Russkaia zhizn'*, and *Novoe obozrenie*.

22. I. Gasprinskii, untitled article, *Perevodchik/Tercüman*, no. 13 (18 April 1893): 25, and "Po nevolie," *Perevodchik/Tercüman*, no. 6 (22 February 1891): 11.

23. Gasprinskii, *Russkoe musul'manstvo*, pp. 16–17 and 31. For a revealing interpretation of Russian imperial policy during the crucial reign of Alexander III (1881–94) by a liberal-minded bureaucrat, N. Kh. Bunge, see George E. Snow, "The Years 1881–1894 in Russia: A Memorandum Found in the papers of N. Kh. Bunge— Translation and Commentary," *Transactions of the American Philosophical Society* 71, no. 6 (1981): 22–46.

24. Basil Davidson, *Africa in Modern History: The Search for a New Society* (London, 1978), p. 155. Note the presumed continuity between primary and ideological resistance, and the absence of anything in between that might distort the teleology of Davidson's analysis.

25. For a different emphasis on Smirnov's role in Turkic affairs, see Robert Geraci's chapter earlier in this volume.

·9·

Adeeb Khalid

Representations of Russia in Central Asian Jadid Discourse

In the summer of 1914, Mahmud Khoja Behbudi, the doyen of Central Asian jadids, traveled to the Ottoman Empire. One day near Hebron, he happened upon a Russian Orthodox monastery. His description of what he saw is typical of much of Central Asian jadid discourse of the tsarist period:

> The knotted dome of a large church caught my eye from the distance. To whom did it belong? They said it was a monastery of the Russians. We went there. On one side of the road were the houses of poor Arabs. We passed them, and entered an elegant garden through a big gate. Trees spread out along paths on all sides. Around the garden were special houses for the monks, as well as large halls [open to] everyone; [also] a school, a hospital, and an extremely elegant church. . . . I said to my guide, "Did you see the religiosity and the effort of the Russians? They have created such a heavenly spot on such a [far-flung] mountain. . . ." When, leaving the monastery, one sees slovenly Muslims resembling nomads and their poverty-stricken houses opposite, it leaves a [sad] impression on one's heart.
>
> . . . There are numerous churches in and around Jerusalem. Their brilliant domes and the crosses on them catch the eye. As for Muslim religious buildings . . . the crescents on the domes of mosques are rusted and exist in a state of slovenliness. They present a melancholy contrast to the crosses. The loyalty of the Christians to their faith and the heedlessness of the Muslims to theirs become obvious from this contrast.[1]

Representations of Russia in Central Asian Jadid Discourse

Native Representation of Culture in Collapse
*"The Imam Zade Madrasa in Sheki" (*Mulla Nasreddin, *no. 3 [1907])*

As modernizing reformers, the jadids of Central Asia focused largely on exhorting their community to undertake the reforms they saw as desperately needed in order to survive in the modern world that had burst upon their region in the shape of Russian armies.[2] Unlike their counterparts in European Russia, Central Asian jadids rarely engaged in an overt struggle with the state in pursuit of external political goals.[3] Nevertheless, Russia and the Russians were integral to the reformist project of the jadids and to their creation of a sense of self. Not only was the reform necessitated by the Russian conquest, but it was articulated and executed in a social space created under the colonial regime. The Russians have a silent presence in Central Asian jadid literature of the period. They serve as counterpoints for the jadid criticism of Central Asian society and help to delineate group boundaries on which Central Asian identity came to be based.

This chapter is concerned with an analysis of these various representations: What do they tell us about the nature of jadid discourse and colonial society in Central Asia? How do we account for the variety of images? By asking such questions, this chapter seeks to place jadidism in the broader context of the colonial world. Too often it is seen as merely an expression of nationalism (or rather of Pan-Turkism and Pan-Islamism), a discourse unflinchingly directed against the colonial power by reformers upholding the interests of a colonized nation. A more nuanced reading of jadidism, by focusing on the terrain in which its ideas were articulated, points to ambiguities of modernist reform in the colonial world. In common with Edward Lazzerini (see his chapter in this volume), I hope to show that jadidism arose in a public space that had been created largely by empire; the interests that the jadids defended were articulated in that context and therefore could not be unaffected by it.

There are few major Russian characters in jadid literature, and little of Central Asian journalism expressly addresses the theme of relations with the Russians. Yet much of what the jadids wrote and thought, indeed the jadid project as a whole, was underlain by an acute awareness of Russia and Russians.

The only Russian character of note in prerevolutionary jadid literature appears in *Tales of an Indian Traveler* by the Bukharan jadid Abdurrauf Fitrat.[4] Written in Persian while Fitrat was studying in Istanbul, and published there, this fictional travelogue of an Indian Muslim who visits Bukhara during his *hajj* (pilgrimage) to Mecca represents a severe indictment of the present state of Bukhara, as well as the jadid prescription for the future. The Indian Muslim, Fitrat's mouthpiece, is appalled by what he sees: chaos and disorder in the streets, filthy, unhealthy water in the city, saint worship at tombs, widespread pederasty, venality and ignorance among the *ulama*, and lack of planning and foresight on the part of the Bukharan government. The traveler's account is a catalogue of the jadids' desiderata for reform.

In the middle of his trip, the traveler falls ill. His hosts call a Bukharan "doctor," a practitioner of traditional medicine, who prescribes a mixture for the illness but is unable to explain the nature of the illness, leading the traveler to refuse his ministrations (*RIP*, p. 44). "Until a doctor can explain to me my illness and how his medicine will work," the traveler tells the next physician to visit him, "I will not take anything" (*RIP*, p. 46). Disappointed again, he finally insists on being treated by a Russian doctor. The physician duly arrives and prescribes medication for the traveler. The traveler engages him in a conversation about the health situation in Bukhara that turns into a sustained critique of the "ignorance" of the people and the inaction of the government. The doctor was invited to Bukhara by the government to provide modern health care. He has had extreme difficulty in winning the trust of the people, who, out of ignorance and lack of education, treat him as an infidel and automatically assume that anything he prescribes must be against the tenets of Islam (*RIP*, p. 49). The doctor then launches into a lengthy harangue against the situation in Central Asia:

Representations of Russia in Central Asian Jadid Discourse

You have seen, of course, our [Russian] districts as well as several European cities. European governments spend money to maintain the health of their people. City streets are cleaner than are the insides of people's living rooms here. Nowhere in Europe do they slaughter sheep inside cities, nor do they bury the dead on their outskirts, or leave the innards of animals on the streets. In many of our cities special medical schools exist . . . that send out doctors to all parts of the country every year. . . . In our schools, children study hygiene and qualified professors write medical essays in newspapers every day, explaining the rules of hygiene to the people. Therefore, many inhabitants of European cities know the fundamentals of medicine as well as a doctor. . . . The inhabitants of Turkestan are the complete opposite. You have seen their streets; they still slaughter sheep inside the city, and leave the innards by the roadside; . . . on some streets they still throw animal and even human excrement. Their drinking water enters the ponds after passing through hundreds of latrines. (*RIP,* pp. 49–50)

The doctor and the traveler then proceed to discuss the steps that might be taken in Bukhara to improve the situation. The Russian doctor becomes Fitrat's mouthpiece. (He is the only person the traveler encounters during his visit with whom he fully agrees.)

Europe and Russia here function as models to be emulated. The connection between education and literacy on the one hand and hygiene and public health on the other, as well as the connection between order and organization (an organized system of medical education) and cleanliness, is forcefully made. For Fitrat, the reason behind the filth and disorder of Central Asian cities is simply ignorance: of modern medicine, but more fundamentally of Islam itself. Like most Muslim modernists of the period, Fitrat proceeds to argue (through the words of the Indian traveler) that modern medicine and matters of public health are in complete conformity with Islam and are indeed enjoined by the Qur'an (*RIP,* pp. 52–53). The traveler quotes from the Qur'an to prove his point, suggesting that Russians and Europeans come closer to fulfilling the commandments of Islam than do Muslims.[5]

Yet Russians represented more than just the successes of modern civilization to the jadids. They also represented a threat. The Russian prostitute Liza in Behbudi's play *Padarkush* is an example of the other side of the Russian presence in jadid literature.[6] The first locally written and locally produced piece of modern theater in Central Asia, *Padarkush* is concerned with showing the evil that results from the failure to acquire knowledge. The play opens in the house of an illiterate rich man who has steadfastly refused to send his son, Tashmurad, to school. The son, unable to distinguish right from wrong as a result of his ignorance, falls into bad company. The second scene of the play shows Tashmurad living it up with his friends at a tavern. The group decides to seek the company of Liza for the

The Power and Challenge of the Modern Newspaper
"In Bukhara" (Mulla Nasreddin, no. 15 [1907])

evening, but is unable to raise the fifteen rubles required for it. Tash-murad's friends, especially one Tangriqul, talk him into stealing the money from his father's safe. In the next scene, the rich man, awakened as Tashmurad and his friends break into the house, is killed as he challenges the burglars.

While the root cause of the tragedy is unquestionably ignorance, it is significant that the action of the play revolves around the temptation personified by Liza. (Liza herself makes only a brief appearance in the last scene of the play, when she joins the gang in the tavern just before the gathering is broken up by the police, who have come to arrest the malefactors.) Ignorance leads eventually to death and murder, but it also takes the form of alcohol and sexual misconduct.

Yet there is more ambiguity here than first meets the eye. Is Behbudi simply arguing that ignorance leads to the country's falling prey to the temptations wielded by Russians? The connection between Russians and sin and temptation is not simple. Elsewhere in the jadid repertoire, sin exists independently of Russians or of the Russian presence. Pederasty and addiction, for example, are common themes in jadid literature of the period, and indeed *Padarkush* is the only place where they are connected to the Russians. If anything, many jadids saw indulgence in such practices as the *cause* of Central Asia's subjugation to foreign rule.[7] To this extent, the jadids' vision of their condition was formed by the dominant paradigm of moral decrepitude leading to social and political decline that had shaped Central Asian views of history for centuries. For example, the following analysis of the decline of Central Asia written in 1906 by Munawwar Qari, the leading jadid figure in Tashkent, could easily have been written by a man of the old order such as ʿAbd al-ʿAziz Sami (discussed by Jo-Ann Gross in this volume):

> More than a hundred years ago, breaches began to appear on all sides in the walls of the nation [*millet*]. This was because our scholars [*ulama*] and rulers [*umara*] began to act only for their own benefit. Service to the nation was [now] limited to taking women, . . . and exiling [or] murdering uncorrupted men of religion. They [the rulers] knew or cared little about the nation or the law [*Shariʿa*]. Because of this, the breaches in the walls of the community widened. Forbidden acts such as drinking, gambling, pederasty, feasting, turning men into women and women into men [*erkekni khatun qilmaq wa khatunni erek qilmaq*], adultery, backbiting . . . became common among us. We now think of these acts as part of our ancestral traditions.
>
> Finally, because of these vile deeds, our lands were captured and we were reviled and demeaned [*khwar-u zalil bolduk*].[8]

Here, too, ignorance produces moral and sexual depravity and leads to social and political decline. The difference between Munawwar Qari and ʿAbd al-ʿAziz Sami lies more in the solutions the two prescribe for the ills of the present than in the nature of the problem.

Moreover, the evidence of *Padarkush* itself suggests that Behbudi viewed the connection between Russian ways and moral decline in a more ambivalent fashion. One of Behbudi's two protagonists in the play is the "enlightened" (*ziyali*) youth who makes an appearance in the first scene to exhort the rich man to educate his son, and who also makes the final exhortatory speech usual in jadid theater. There is no question that he is Behbudi's mouthpiece in the play, and that as such, he embodies all the virtues that Behbudi hopes for in Central Asia's future. Yet here is how he makes his first entry on stage:

> Enlightened Muslim enters; hangs his coat [*palto* in original] and walking stick on a peg. Rich Man looks at him with hesitation.
> Enlightened Man: *"As-salamu alaykum."*
> Rich Man (with disgust): *"Wa alaykum as-salam."* Calls the servant: "Khayrullah! Bring a chair. This fellow can't sit on the floor. . . ."
> The Enlightened Man sits down and takes out a cigarette. (*P*, p. 5)

The young man's Russian mannerisms are further accentuated when he uses a Russian word in the second sentence that he delivers (*Ah ha, qiziq wa interesnyi hadisa emish* [*P*, p. 5]). Nevertheless, it is obvious that Behbudi does not share the rich man's sarcasm about the ziyali's adoption of Russian manners and dress, which goes with the rich man's resistance to education. For Behbudi the young man's education is sufficient safeguard against moral corruption; sin and temptation can be overcome through it. Indeed, very soon after this sentence, the young man loses his affectations and begins to sound exactly like Behbudi! By associating criticism of Russian ways with the rich man, Behbudi is clearly suggesting that there is nothing intrinsically wrong with wearing a coat or carrying a walking stick; what matters is the ability, acquired through knowledge, to discern good from evil, something the rich man lacks.

The predominance of positive images of Russians can partly be explained by the need to bypass censorship. To be sure, the existence of overt forms of censorship in the Russian Empire—by no means limited to the borderlands—curtailed the jadids' freedom to choose topics and their ability to launch into criticisms of the colonial power. Overt criticism of the Russians would have brought upon the jadids the wrath of the censors and destroyed the social space in which their reform existed. Closely connected to this was the necessity for the jadids to allay suspicions of the Russians—belonging both to officialdom and to *obshchestvo*—about their loyalty to the empire.[9]

However, the positive portrayal of the Russians was based on much more than simply the fear of censorship and an impulse to political prudence. Many jadids had close personal relations with members of the local Russian population. Russian officials were guests of honor at the annual graduation ceremonies in jadid schools, and some of them attended theatrical performances (especially when held for the benefit of the Russian war effort). Several jadids lived in the Russian quarters of Central Asian cities. Behbudi's house, which also served as a bookstore and the editorial office for *Ayna*, was in Russian Samarkand. The Tashkent jadids, Abdullah Awlani and Munawwar Qari, lived in the Russian quarter as well.[10] The "Russian quarters" were, of course, not segregated, but the choice to live in the new, "well-ordered" settlements was nevertheless significant. Moreover, I would argue that there was a certain admiration for Russians among the jadids simply because of the imperial might that they represented. The imperial nation had attained power as just deserts for its cultivation of knowledge, and the jadids admired the bearers of this power.

Ultimately, however, the largely positive images of Russians were rooted in the jadids' esteem for those attributes of contemporary life that they saw as lacking in Central Asia (and in the Muslim world in general): modern knowledge, order, discipline, cleanliness, power—in a word, modernity. The jadids were motivated by an intense feeling of their country's backwardness, which they located in Central Asia's failure to cultivate modern knowledge and the order and discipline that came with

Representations of Russia in Central Asian Jadid Discourse

The Humor and Pain of Backwardness
"A Muslim railway system" (Mulla Nasreddin, no. 28 [1907])

it. They were acutely aware that knowledge brought power, and that the possession of knowledge, skills, and technologies underlay Europe's economic and military superiority over the rest of the world.

Jadid reform was premised on a cult of knowledge: "The developed [*taraqqi qilghan*] peoples of the world achieved progress through knowledge; the colonized and declining peoples [*asir wa zabun bolganlar*] are so because of their lack of knowledge" (*P*, p. 17). Ignorance bred all other evils; *Padarkush* was the classic statement of this sentiment, but hardly the only one in the jadid repertoire. The observations of the Indian traveler noted above provide a catalogue of the shortcomings discerned by the jadids in their society. Ignorance led to a lack of cooperation within society, and ultimately to the dissolution of social bonds and a weakening of religious zeal that would spell the demise of Central Asian Muslim society that Behbudi metaphorically presented in *Padarkush*.

The jadids, intensely aware that theirs was "a new and completely different age" (*P*, p. 6), saw the creation of modern institutions of discipline as desperately needed in their society. Similarly, they despised the traditional *maktab* because of its lack of organization, and sought to replace it with their new-method schools that would not only be marked by an ordered curriculum, but also be part of an organized network of schools.

As a jadid activist noted, the reason for France's greatness was that every boy and girl there went to school.[11]

The jadids' concern with hygiene and health was also entirely new to Central Asia. It was clearly articulated in Fitrat's works quoted above, but was also mirrored in jadid journalism. One of Behbudi's most interesting excursions during his travels of 1914 was a day spent visiting various spas in the Caucasus. He treated his readers to seven pages' worth of description of the various facilities available at these resorts, combining his admiration for the wealth of modern industrial society with his concerns about hygiene and personal health.[12]

If in jadid writings Russians serve to advocate admirable traits, however, they do so only generically. The jadids esteemed modernity, not necessarily the Russians. The Russians were the example closest at hand of the traits that the jadids admired in their world and sought to cultivate in their society. Many of the positive traits of Russians that appear in jadid literature are also shared by other Europeans. For example, the protagonist in Fitrat's renowned *Debate between a Bukharan Teacher and a European*, arguably the most influential jadid work of the period, was a European.[13] Fitrat portrays a dispute between a Bukharan *madrasa* teacher (*mudarris*) of the old school and a European in which the jadid viewpoint is taken up by the European, an Englishman so well versed in Islam that he out-argues the mudarris and quotes the Qur'an to him in Arabic (*M*, pp. 6, 11, 18ff.). It is remarkable, but seldom remarked upon, that the protagonist in the most renowned work of jadid literature should be a non-Muslim. The tract is important for several reasons, but here I shall note only that the Englishman represents a new approach to religion (he argues like a modernist Muslim), new methods of learning (which are much more efficient, for he can speak Arabic fluently, while the mudarris, for all his twenty-year education in the old style madrasa, cannot), and a new notion of knowledge itself. The Englishman can understand Islam better than the Bukharan mudarris because he has acquired modern knowledge through modern schooling. Here Fitrat is again suggesting that (modern) knowledge brings even Christians closer to Islam than Muslims with no education.

Finally, it is worth noting that the protagonist in *Bayanat* is an Indian Muslim who visits Bukhara during his hajj. While the Englishman in *Munazara* was a modern scholar of Islam, the Indian traveler is a modern (and modernist) Muslim himself. The purpose of the book was to criticize Bukhara (and Central Asia in general) through the eyes of a sympathetic external protagonist. Both protagonists share the basic jadid concerns for rationality, the cult of knowledge, and progress. Both criticize the existing order in Bukhara while expressing optimism about its future. What unites them with the Russian doctor discussed above, and makes them attractive to the jadids, is their embodiment of the ideas of modernity and rationality.

(Most jadid plays, of course, had no foreign characters; the role of the admonisher is typically played by an enlightened Central Asian, such as the ziyali in *Padarkush*.)

Russians, Europeans, and modern Muslims in jadid literature serve the fundamental rhetorical function of criticizing Central Asian society. Jadid literature was directed at the Muslim society of Central Asia, which it aimed to exhort to action, or as the favorite jadid metaphor put it, to wake it from its sleep of ignorance. All tropes and rhetorical devices used by jadid authors were subordinate to this basic consideration. Praise for others was invariably coupled with criticism of Central Asia. Behbudi's travelogue is a classic example of this. The description of the monastery in Hebron serves to criticize the slovenliness of mosques in the area; praise for the industry of Russian peasant women espied from a moving train gives way to the denigration of Kazakh women (the only ones among "us" who work in the fields), who "can do nothing but gossip";[14] and a description of avid pilgrims and tourists from all over Europe and North America in Palestine concludes with the observation that guidebooks to the sites do not exist in any Muslim language.[15]

The jadids had appropriated the literary device of *ibrat*—taking admonition from noteworthy example—which had deep roots in Islamic tradition but was now given a new form. Russians (and other outsiders) showed the audience what the jadids wanted them to show: the shortcomings of Central Asian society itself. As such, their portrayal had to be largely positive, with only the occasional intimation of danger (as in the case of Liza). The Muslim Indian traveler in *Bayanat* is a highly positive figure, who speaks Arabic fluently; he is not an Indian Muslim in any realistic sense, but rather a type. Few contemporary Europeans would have recognized the interlocutor of Fitrat's mudarris in *Munazara* as one of themselves, for he argues not like a European but like a jadid. His command of Muslim scriptures and of Arabic, as well as his innate sympathy for the modern Muslim cause, distances him from the current reality of European imperialism. The Russian doctor in *Bayanat* is also motivated by a concern for the well-being of Bukhara. Here again, the concern is that of the jadids, not that of any real Russians at the time (whose expressions of concern for the well-being of the natives of the empire took a rather different form). Fitrat takes no notice of the negative aspects of Muslim India, Europe, and Russia because that is not his purpose. Similarly, Behbudi in his travelogue, as in the rest of his journalism, focuses on the wealth, order, and cleanliness he sees in Russia and among Europeans abroad. A balanced critique of Russian life, including the squalor of the slums and the oppression in the factories in every Russian town, would have conflicted with his rhetorical purpose. When he travels by steamer from Odessa to Istanbul and finds all the Muslim passengers traveling third class, he sees it not as a sign of global economic inequities but as a sign of the degradation of Muslims as a result of their not heeding his call for education and the acquisition of modern knowledge.[16]

This was partly a reflection of the fact that Muslim cultural debate in Central Asia was open by this time to influences and criticism from outsiders. This had been the case for much longer elsewhere in the Muslim world and had given rise to a whole genre of modernist apologetics. Fitrat, who spent four formative years in Istanbul, was deeply affected by this phenomenon, and indeed mentions (through the words of the European!) the need for Bukharan ulama to produce anti-Christian polemics in defense of Islam (*M*, p. 41). Similarly, it was a sign of the times that Behbudi quotes an American tourist in Damascus to the effect that the glories of early Islamic architecture were a match for the highest achievements of Italian art.[17]

However, in talking about the Russians, the jadids were, in the end, talking about themselves. Jadid discourse was crucial to the elaboration of a new set of identities in Central Asia, and the representation of Russia and Russians played a central role in the process. The jadids' appropriation of the grand narrative of progress placed them in the ambit of a universal history inhabited by various communities, necessitating the definition of group boundaries. Again, representations of the Russians were important to jadid self-definition.

Exhortation to reform carried within it an implicit statement of the distinctiveness and autonomy of the Central Asian Muslim community. In presenting the Russians as worthy of emulation, the jadids asserted the distinctiveness of Central Asia from Russia, since the Russians were clearly the outsiders against whom the Central Asian "Us" was to be defined. As non-Turkic non-Muslims who had only recently conquered Central Asia, the Russians were rank outsiders who did not threaten Central Asia with physical assimilation. Thus Behbudi could even claim, echoing the words of Ismail Bey Gasprinskii from 1881,[18] that Muslims were better off under Russian than any other colonial rule without fear of collapsing the walls of the community.[19]

The depiction of Russians as a homogeneous group also enabled the construction of their opposite, a homogeneous Central Asian "Us." In defining themselves and their community against the Russians, the jadids came to valorize their own adherence to Islam as a major source of their self-definition. This Islam, however, was defined in largely desacralized terms, a source of communal identity rather than a normative moral force. The jadids came to see the excellence of a faith and of its adherents in the material progress that they attained. Hence, the splendor of the Selimiye mosque in Edirne or of the Umayyad mosque in Damascus was to Behbudi a symbol of the moral excellence of early Muslims; the grandeur of the Russian monastery in Palestine was a sign not of imperial pretention but of the Russians' adherence to their faith, which was possible through education. Mosques in ruin became a sign of moral decay as much as they were a sign of economic disarray; the two are intimately connected for Behbudi: "A people without knowledge and skill lose their wealth and possessions, just as they lose their morals and honor; even their faith is weakened" (*P*, p. 7). This connection between the material development of Muslims and the moral perfection of Islam is made even more forcefully by Fitrat in his *Munazara*. Although the text itself is cast as pure advocacy of modern means and skills, it is framed with a concern for the well-being of Islam and Muslims (*M*, pp. 2, 65–68, and passim). The epilogue is a heartfelt appeal to the amir to fulfill his duties as a Muslim sovereign and save Bukhara, through modernizing reform, from the enemies of Islam, specifically Christians, bent upon the destruction of Islam and Muslims.

The rhetoric of Muslimness did not automatically translate into a Pan-Islamic identity, however. Central Asian relations with Tatars and Azerbaijanis, also latterly arrived in the area, often in the service of empire, but with far more nebulous boundaries separating them from the local population, were always complex. The Tatars often combined a claim to the leadership of the Muslim community of the Russian Empire with a marked condescension toward most Central Asians. In Tashkent they lived in a distinct Tatar community that straddled the geographic and social space between the Central Asian and Russian populations. Central Asian jadids tended to be quite conscious of their distinction from the Tatars. Unfortunately, a full discussion of the rhetorical ploys used by the jadids to draw boundaries with other Muslim groups, both within and without the Russian Empire, remains beyond the scope of this chapter.[20]

As modernists, the jadids sought not to criticize the new cultural practices introduced by the Russians, but to appropriate them. Theirs was not a rejection of the world built by modern science and capital, but a hope of full participation in it. Accepting the basic premise that modern knowledge—and the skills and technologies it brought—was the only way through which their society could improve its position, they unhesitatingly subscribed to a unilinear vision of progress, and admired those who had achieved power and glory through modern education, organization, and discipline. For the jadids, Islam could best be served by acquiring modern education and using the possibilities allowed by the colonial state to help the community. The distinction between Islam as a faith and Muslims as a community seemed to disappear completely in their thinking.

Progress for the jadids was the triumphal march of knowledge in which there was nothing culturally specific; the achievements of the countries of Europe, including Russia, could be replicated by any group that acquired the necessary skills. The jadids routinely used expressions such as "developed" (*taraqqi qilgan, taraqqi etgan*) and "civilized" (*mutamaddan*), while presenting various aspects of modern civilization as worthy of imitation and adoption. Their press published snippets of acts of philanthropists in Russia and Europe; Behbudi routinely cited the numbers of libraries, theaters, books, and newspapers in various European countries as indicators of civilization; and as we have seen, when he traveled abroad in 1914, he found much in the ways of the Europeans with which to admonish his readers.

Since there was nothing culturally specific in what had made Europe (including Russia) so powerful, there was nothing to stop Muslims from emulating it. An aggressively modernist interpretation of Islam allowed the jadids, in common with other modernist Muslims of the day, to claim the complete compatibility of Islam and modern science. It was sheer ignorance on the part of obscurantists to claim that Islamic law prohibited the cultivation of modern knowledge, for, as a jadid publicist wrote, "the scholars of Islam find most of the sayings of the scholars of today to be in accordance with the verses of the Qur'an."[21] Indeed, the jadids argued, Islam *required* knowledge, and it was knowledge that allowed one to be a good Muslim.

In the imperial context, even the assertion of the universality of progress could be subversive. The jadids had internalized several categories of colonial knowledge, yet their very assertion of the universality of progress subverted these categories. It is perhaps foolhardy to expect an anti-orientalism (in the sense of a polished critique of imperialism and the epistemological structures it generates) in the writings of colonial intellectuals.[22] Rather, it is far more fruitful to focus on the manner in which colonial intellectuals appropriated the dominant discourses of the metropole for their own purposes.[23] Behbudi's assertion about the superiority of Russian colonial rule, for instance, tapped into notions of the universality of Russian culture current in Russian society and marshaled them for a cause that most Russians found suspicious.

To be sure, jadid discourse emerged in the context of empire, and the Russian presence in it was pervasive. Yet to see the jadids as mere imitators of Russian ways is to miss the complexity of the colonial encounter. The Russia of the jadids may have been just as imaginary as the Central Asia of Vereshchagin, but the uses of that Russia were their own.

NOTES

1. Mahmud Khoja [Behbudi], "Sayahat khatiralari—XXI," *Ayna*, 27 November 1914, p. 53.

2. Jadidism, the movement for modernist cultural reform that arose in Crimea in the 1880s and spread to all Muslim areas of the Russian Empire, has received far less scholarly attention than it deserves. The subject was taboo for much of the Soviet period, and therefore no satisfactory treatment exists in any language of the

Representations of Russia in Central Asian Jadid Discourse

former Soviet Union (but see Dzh. Validov, *Ocherk istorii obrazovannosti i literatury Tatar* [Moscow, 1923; reprint, Oxford, 1986]). Outside the former Soviet Union, the study of jadidism has been hampered by lack of access to the primary sources. For various aspects of the movement, see Serge A. Zenkovsky, *Pan-Turkism and Islam in Russia, 1905–1920* (Cambridge, Mass., 1960); Alexandre Bennigsen and Chantal Lemercier-Quelquejay, *La Presse et le mouvement national chez les Musulmans de Russie avant 1920* (Paris, 1964); Edward J. Lazzerini, "Ismail Bey Gasprinskii and Muslim Modernism in Russia, 1878–1914" (Ph.D. diss., University of Washington, 1973); Hélène Carrère d'Encausse, *Réforme et révolution chez les Musulmans de l'empire russe,* 2nd ed. (Paris, 1981); and Adeeb Khalid, "The Politics of Muslim Cultural Reform: Jadidism in Tsarist Central Asia" (Ph.D. diss., University of Wisconsin–Madison, 1993).

3. I am concerned in this chapter solely with the jadids of Central Asia. As I have argued elsewhere ("Politics," pp. 21–22 and 179–193), it is hazardous to speak of a single jadidism in different regions of the Russian Empire; the social and political context in which the movement existed varied enormously, and so did the primary concerns of the jadids.

4. Fitrat Bukharayi, *Bayanat-i sayyah-i hindi* (Istanbul, 1330/1911–12). Unfortunately, I have been unable to consult the Persian text of this tract. I have used instead a Russian translation by A. N. Kondrat'ev, a Samarkand orientalist: *Razskazy indiiskago puteshestvennika* (Samarkand, 1913), hereafter cited in the text as *RIP*; all translations are mine from the Russian. It might be noted that the title of the tract is often mistranslated (e.g., in Edward Allworth, *The Modern Uzbeks: A Cultural History* [Stanford, 1990]), p. 145), as *The Tales of the Hindu Traveler*; the *hindi* in the title is an adjective derived from Hind, India, and has nothing to do with Hinduism.

5. Elsewhere in *Bayanat*, Fitrat makes the point explicitly. The traveler visits the tomb of Bahauddin Naqshband, the founder of the Naqshbandi mystical order, on the outskirts of Bukhara and is astonished to see saint worship going on openly. He gets into an argument with his local friend in which he defends Christians against the charge of being *kafirs*, infidels, but suggests that saint worship is indeed idolatry (*RIP*, pp. 11–13).

6. Mahmud Khoja Behbudi, *Padarkush, yakhud oqumagan balaning hali* (Samarkand, 1913); hereafter cited in the text as *P*. For a translation into English, see Edward Allworth, "Murder as Metaphor in the First Central Asian Drama," *Ural-Altaische Jahrbücher* 58 (1986): 65–97. However, all the translations in this text are my own.

7. The prostitute is Russian at least partly because putting a Muslim woman on stage in the role of a prostitute would have scandalized an audience already suspicious of the "new" theater. On the controversy engendered by the jadids' advocacy of theater, see Khalid, "Politics," pp. 380–386.

8. Munawwar Qari ibn Abdurrashid Khan, untitled article, *Taraqqi—Orta Azyaning umr guzarlighi*, 7 March 1906.

9. For a nuanced discussion of this problem in the context of Crimean jadidism, see Edward J. Lazzerini, "Ismail Bey Gasprinskii (Gaspirali), the Discourse of Modernism, and the Russians," in Edward Allworth, ed., *Tatars of the Crimea: Their Struggle for Survival* (Durham, 1988), pp. 149–169.

10. TsGAUz, f. 461, op. 1, d. 57, ll. 607–607ob.

11. Mirmuhsin Shermuhammad oghli, "Ilm wa aning samarasi," *Sada-yi Farghana,* 21 May 1914.

12. Behbudi, "Sayahat khatiralari—III," *Ayna,* 5 July 1914, pp. 880–887.

13. Fitrat Bukharayi, *Munazara-yi mudarris-i bukharayi ba yak nafar-i farangi dar Hindustan dar bara-yi makatib-i jadida* (Istanbul, 1911); hereafter cited in the text as *M.*

14. Behbudi, "Sayahat khatiralari—IV," *Ayna,* 12 July 1914, p. 904.

15. Behbudi, "Sayahat khatiralari—XVI," *Ayna,* 4 October 1914, p. 1191.

16. Behbudi, "Sayahat khatiralari—V," *Ayna,* 19 July 1914, p. 928. For this reason, it is also not surprising that most Russians who appear in jadid literature are respectable or authoritative figures: doctors, policemen, pilgrims; other than poor Liza, there are no working-class Russians in jadid plays.

17. Behbudi, "Sayahat khatiralari—XII," *Ayna,* 6 September 1914, pp. 1099–1100. Similarly, Behbudi concludes his description of the excellence of the Selimiye mosque in Edirne thus: "This is not just my opinion, but the opinion of qualified European engineers and scholars" ("Sayahat khatiralari—VI," *Ayna,* 26 July 1914, pp. 960–961).

18. Ismail Bey Gasprinskii, *Russkoe musul'manstvo. Mysli, zametki i nabliudeniia musul'manina* (Simferopol', 1881; reprint Oxford, 1985).

19. "Ot redaktsii," *Samarqand,* 19 April 1913.

20. For a fuller discussion, see Khalid, "Politics," pp. 238–258.

21. Siddiqi, "Turkistanda maktab, jarida wa ulama," *Ayna,* 23 August 1914, p. 1055.

22. Juan R. I. Cole, "Invisible Occidentalism: Eighteenth-Century Indo-Persian Constructions of the West," *Iranian Studies* 25, nos. 3–4 (1992): 3–16; cf. Partha Chatterjee, *Nationalist Thought and the Colonial World: A Derivative Discourse* (London, 1986).

23. Xiaomei Chen, "Occidentalism as Counterdiscourse: 'He Shang' in Post-Mao China," *Critical Inquiry* 18 (1992): 686–712.

.10.

JO-ANN GROSS

Historical Memory, Cultural Identity, and Change: Mirza 'Abd al-'Aziz Sami's Representation of the Russian Conquest of Bukhara

In 1868, following his military defeat, Muzaffar al-Din (r. 1860–85), ruler of the Bukharan Amirate, concluded a treaty that effectively made his domain a protectorate of the Russian Empire. It left him and his successors with nominal sovereignty and a significant degree of control over internal affairs. For the Muslims of Central Asia, this event marked the beginning of a double-edged crisis involving colonial rule and modernity. Russian rule in Central Asia introduced cultural, social, political, and economic challenges that ruptured an entire system of thinking and ushered in a series of transformations that would result in the creation of new economic relationships, a new cultural elite, and in time, a new political order.[1] The few studies of native responses to the Russian conquest of Central Asia have focused on two types of reaction: religious and/or tribal-based opposition assuming the form of popular revolt, and progressive reform embodied in the jadid movement.[2] The purpose of this chapter is to augment this analysis by exploring an alternative response to crisis and change through an analysis of one significant but little-known historical source, the *Ta'rikh-i Salatin-i Manghitiya*, composed by 'Abd al-'Aziz Sami. The historiographical form of Sami's response conforms to tradi-

tional Perso-Islamic literary models; his perspective is rooted in a historical memory of a glorious past of political and cultural strength as epitomized by the Timurid period; and his value system is predicated upon
Islamic notions of justice and propriety (*adab*).[3]

The Author, His Time, and His Work

In a study of nineteenth-century Bukhara, Sukhareva divides the inhabitants of the region into three groups: warriors (*sipah*), scholars (*ʿulama*),
and subjects (*fuqara*).[4] Qualification for membership in the ulama was
based on one's educational background, specifically the acquisition of
knowledge through a *maktab* then *madrasa* (primary then higher religious)
education, during the process of which the student was exposed, through
oral transmission and memorization, to a variety of scriptural and literary
texts.[5] Moral character, knowledge of authoritative texts, ethical norms,
personal development, and spiritual cultivation (all aspects of the Islamic
ideal of adab) were acquired by individuals through the shared experience
of traditional Islamic education. In precolonial Central Asia, those individuals possessing such qualifications formed the bureaucratic elite and
the religious class. This shared experience or "habitus," to borrow Bourdieu's concept, reproduced a system of knowledge based on doctrinal
texts (the Qurʾan, *hadith*, and Shariʿa), a body of classical Perso-Islamic
literature, and a moral prescription of behavior.[6]

During the late nineteenth and the early twentieth centuries, the normative transmission of knowledge, the basis of moral as well as political
authority, and the use of traditional models of literary expression in Central Asia were challenged. The introduction of Russo-Native schools (although limited in their impact in Bukhara), the influence of new technology and modes of communication (e.g., the railroad and the printing
press), the exposure of the intelligentsia to imported printed books, and
the introduction by jadids (modernists) of new-method schools and benevolent societies (although they were relegated to an underground level
in Bukhara) all served to propagate new ideas and encourage hope for the
future. Within the Perso-Islamic tradition, historical narrative and poetry
had long served as the primary literary forms for social and political
commentary in the eastern Islamic world. Now, however, prose fiction
developed as a new vehicle of social reform. With the new-method schools
introduced by the jadids, moreover, modern knowledge became accessible not only to the traditional elite, but to anyone who chose to acquire
the skills of language, science, history, and an understanding of Islam. To
use Adeeb Khalid's phrase, a "desacralization of knowledge" was initiated.[7]

Throughout the conquest period, economic, religious, and political

Kalan mosque and minaret, Bukhara (Photograph by Nadar, ca. 1895;
courtesy Garnet Publishing Limited)

turmoil characterized the Bukharan Amirate. Tribal conflicts intensified, in large part as a result of the attempts by Amir Nasr Allah (r.1827–60) and his heirs, Muzaffar al-Din and ʿAbd al-Ahad (r. 1885–1920), to thwart the power of the Uzbek tribal aristocracy and establish a competing network of support.[8] The religious class voiced its opposition to any appearance of cooperation with the Russians and called for *jihad* (holy war). Economic upheaval led to widespread dissatisfaction among the peasants, who suffered most from the heavy taxes imposed on them; among the independent nomadic tribes; and among the Uzbek aristocracy, whose landed wealth and power were endangered by the amirs' attempts to redirect their patronage.[9] All this, combined with the loss of honor and prestige resulting from defeat at the hands of a Christian army, ensured a turbulent period for the Bukharan sovereign, the tribal leadership, and the population at large.

The inclusion of Central Asia in the European-dominated global economy resulted in the rise of a new merchant class as well as the influx of new ideas concerning education and administration.[10] In Bukhara, such economic conditions provided some of the impetus for the rise of a new cultural elite, the jadids, who were involved in the development of new-method schools and benevolent societies, and the publication of magazines and newspapers.[11] The jadids of turn-of-the-century Bukhara such as Sadriddin Ayni (1879–1954), Abdulwahid Munzim (1877–1934), and Abdurrauf Fitrat (1886–1937) were from traditional families "whose personal experiences had convinced them of the need to change the intellectual basis of the collective life of their community, but whose commitment to their cultural tradition remained strong."[12] Nevertheless, in Bukhara, fierce conservatism on the part of the rulers, who feared that change would undermine their authority, effectively forced the jadid movement into an underground, secretive existence.

Where does our author, ʿAbd al-ʿAziz Sami, fit into this complex picture? How can his life and writings help us to understand how educated Muslims responded to such turmoil and new ideas? Sami is, first and foremost, a liminal figure who complained bitterly about the state of affairs in Central Asia and bemoaned the loss of a more glorious historical past; but his worldview and personal experience, his habitus, seem to have prevented him from engaging in a discourse about the future. Born in the village of Bustan, Sami received his maktab/madrasa education in Bukhara some forty kilometers north, a long-established center of learning in the eastern Islamic world.[13] In his *tadhkira* (memoir dealing with poets), Mir Muhammad-Siddiq ibn Amir Muzaffar writes about Sami's love of knowledge and his captivation with history from a young age.[14] After the completion of his studies, Sami began to work as a secretary (*munshi*) under several different governors (*hakims*), and was then employed at the court under Muzaffar al-Din. During the Russian military campaigns he was employed as *waqayiʿ nigar* ("observer of events") in Muzaffar's army. He also accompanied the heir apparent, ʿAbd al-Ahad, to St. Petersburg for the coronation celebration of Alexander III in 1881.[15]

As Franz Rosenthal so eloquently demonstrates in his book *"Sweeter Than Hope": Complaint and Hope in Medieval Islam*, complaint was a constant and prominent theme for reflection in Islam throughout history.[16] Certainly in times of crisis the voices of complaint become louder, as was the case in turn-of-the-century Bukhara.[17] Among those voices was Sami's. After some ten years of service at court, his complaints apparently caused him misfortune: sometime around 1898–99 he was dismissed from his post by Amir ʿAbd al-Ahad for his strong oppositional attitudes. Indeed, in the few biographical notices of Sami, he is identified not only as a scholar and a writer but as a social rebel.[18] In his *Namuneʾi adabiyat-i Tajik*, for example, Ayni relates how Sami's dismissal left him with little means of support.[19] In his later years he lived in poverty, earning what he could as a copyist. He died destitute and blind. Ayni applauds Sami's outspokenness, declaring that while others were composing *qasidas* (panegyric poems) in praise of the amir and vazir, Sami spoke frankly.[20] In Ayni's words, "As the degree of corruption of the amir and the court increased, Sami's tongue of criticism and complaint stretched."[21]

The diversity and scope of Sami's literary repertoire, which includes historical works, prose, and poetry, reflect his broad interests as well as literary skills. In addition to his poetry, Sami wrote three historical works on the Manghit dynasty: the *Tuhfat-i shahi*, the *Dakhmah-i Shahan* (in verse), and the *Ta'rikh-i Salatin-i Manghitiya*, the subject of this chapter. Also included in his extant works is a guidebook for secretaries, the *Manzar al-insha'*, in which he cites samples of documents and letters, excerpts from Tajik literature, and the prerequisite qualities for the position of munshi, including knowledge of literature, poetry, and grammar. A collection of poetry entitled the *Mir'at al-haiyal* includes panegyric poems of the reign of Amir ʿAbd al-Ahad as well as reports of the amir's persecution of writers critical of the court.[22]

The *Ta'rikh-i Salatin-i Manghitiya*, a historical chronicle embellished with verse, was written in 1324 (1906/1907) following Sami's exile from court. The chronicle begins with the last Astrakhanid, Abuʾl Fayz Khan (1710–1747), and ends in 1906, thereby including the Russian Revolution of 1905. Until the research of L. M. Epifanova, who published the *Ta'rikh-i Salatin-i Manghitiya* with a Russian translation and Persian facsimile in 1962, this text was believed by many to be identical to another chronicle by Sami entitled *Tuhfat-i shahi*. Epifanova argued convincingly that these are different works written for different audiences, although both treat the history of the Bukharan Amirate.[23] The *Tuhfat-i shahi* was compiled earlier, between 1316 and 1320 (1898/99 and 1902/1903), and is more than three times as long, beginning thirty-one years earlier and ending with the rule of Amir ʿAbd al-Ahad. On the basis of differences between the two works, it appears that the *Tuhfat-i shahi* was written for official public consumption, while the *Ta'rikh-i Salatin-i Manghitiya*, in which Sami openly expresses his dissatisfaction with the amirate and includes his critical appraisals of individuals and events, was produced for a private audience that sympathized with these views.[24] Epifanova refers to the former as the *legal'nyi*, or "official," version, and the latter as the *illegal'nyi*, or "unofficial," version.

The *Ta'rikh-i Salatin-i Manghitiya* is an important text for its place in the literary and social history of late-nineteenth- and early-twentieth-century Central Asia. Sami wrote this work at a time when Tajik and Uzbek literature were moving away from prose fiction based mainly on traditional Perso-Islamic models, to prose influenced by Middle Eastern writers from Ottoman Turkey, Egypt, India, and Afghanistan.[25] In Central Asia, Uzbek, Tajik, and Tatar writers such as Sadriddin Ayni, Ahmed Danish, Abdurrauf Fitrat, Ismail Bey Gasprinskii, and others of the jadid movement called for reform in education, religion, society, and government.

Particularly after 1905, these intellectuals spoke against the corruption of the Bukharan administration, but worked mainly to institute reform. Sami wrote his works during the formative stages of the reformist movement, and was therefore exposed to the new dialogue among Uzbek, Tajik, and Tatar intellectuals.

Sami evidently participated in the literary circles at which intellectuals regularly gathered to discuss poetry and literature, a tradition long established in the eastern Islamic world.[26] In Bukhara the topics of discussion at such gatherings often extended beyond the customary literary themes to include vexing political and social issues, and such meetings were attended by prominent figures within the jadid movement as well as by figures at court. According to Ayni, however, attendance at such gatherings by court officials was quite dangerous because it raised suspicions regarding loyalty to the amir's policies.[27] Sami is known to have participated in such meetings at the home of Muhammad Sharif Jan Mahdum (1865–1931), one of Ayni's teachers, and a student of Ahmed Danish, an early jadid writer who had also served at the Bukharan court.

Jadids shared Sami's concern with the moral decay and social breakdown of Bukharan society, and likewise criticized the corruption and ignorance they found rampant. But as Adeeb Khalid notes in his study of jadidism, the earliest jadids

> were, by and large, men of the old order whose personal experiences had convinced them of the need to change the intellectual basis of the collective life of their community, but whose commitment to their cultural tradition remained strong. They were thus united by a commonly held critical attitude toward the present state of the Muslim community of Central Asia. This critical attitude differentiated them from the established cultural elite of ulama and literati that had survived the conquest.[28]

Unlike the modernist reformers to whom Khalid refers, Sami never identified himself in any of his writings, either directly or indirectly, as an advocate of reform.[29] He despised the corruption and backwardness of the Bukharan Amirate, but his concern was the predicament of the present situation, and how far it had strayed from the ideal of the former stable, strong, and more just society. His was not a search for a new, more enlightened state informed by Western as well as Muslim traditions. This attitude influenced Sami's perception of the Russian conquest and its later role in introducing economic, political, and cultural changes. For Sami, internal political and social weakness and conflict were the critical factors impeding establishment of a true and just Muslim Bukharan state. He perceived the Russian incursion, albeit a dramatic one, to be merely an accessory to the steady decline already in progress. Therefore, while Sami's critique in the *Ta'rikh-i Salatin-i Manghitiya* was not a solitary expression of discontent, his views concerning the remedy for decay and corruption were apparently little affected by the new ideas that were evolving in Central Asia in the early twentieth century. Rather, in his text Sami draws a dismal picture in which he reveals the decay of the Bukharan state as a process predetermined by God but nevertheless acted out by oppressive and unjust rulers, a fanatical and obstinate clerisy, rebellious and divisive tribal leaders, a weak Bukharan army, and, contrarily, a well-equipped, militarily superior tsarist Christian army.

The remainder of this chapter will analyze two primary themes that underscore Sami's perception of the complex series of events surrounding the Russian conquest of Bukhara: first, his characterization of the Bukharan amirs Muzaffar al-Din and ʿAbd al-Ahad; and second, his narrative representation of the rebel leader and resistance fighter (Muzaffar's son and heir apparent) ʿAbd al-Malik Tūra.

Images of Conquest in the *Taʿrikh-i Salatin-i Manghitiya*

As E. P. Thompson has pointed out, historical change is not merely a structural modification. The very social and cultural fabric of society is called into question, and the ideals and values of that society are argued through the actions and choices of individuals. Human action and experience, therefore, are critical aspects of the historical process.[30] The textualization of history through the narrative medium provides the reader not only with a temporal marking of events and actions, but with a record of how those historical processes were conceptualized by the author. The historical memory, or the way history is experienced, is also influenced by discourses and experiences in both the past and the present. In the case of the conquest of Bukhara, I would argue that the repetitive motifs of disempowerment, defeat, unrest, and decay are vehicles through which Sami self-consciously historicizes not only the conquest itself, but the undermining of moral responsibility and personal choice, both at the heart of the Islamic worldview. As Hayden White has stated, "The more historically self-conscious the writer of any form of historiography, the more the question of the social system and the law that sustains it, the authority of this law and its justification, and threats to the law occupy his attention."[31] Sami is an extremely self-conscious and concerned writer. He writes of a frayed social and moral system, and in doing so he textualizes the disorder he perceives, but also the bankruptcy of the morality, justice, and faith implicit in Islamic law, just rulership according to Islamic political theory, and political authority as invested by Central Asian rulers of the remembered past. In the following pages, we shall examine specific images of conquest in an attempt to explore the ways in which the Russian conquest was experienced and conceptualized by our author.

In his narrative, Sami introduces Amir Muzaffar as a ruler who, in succeeding his father to the throne, was just and generous, made his treasury rich, and extended his influence to include Hisar-i Shadman and the Qoqand state (TSM fol. 64b, pp. 55–56).[32] However, he soon became arrogant:

> For several years the treasury filled with gold, and in the state there remained not a single challenger to the throne, while the whole district of Hisar-i Shadman, until Darvaz, Kulab, and Baljawan, was included in his possession. And the Qoqand state, equal to the Bukharan state, was trampled with the hooves of Uzbek and the Manghit horses, and the banner was not unrolled [until the territory of the Khanate] was conquered as far as the Kashghar pass. And [then] the crow of arrogance and conceit built a nest in his head and bore an egg. . . . Gradually, he came to violate the Shariʿa. . . . Because of coercion and oppression the affairs of the people became disordered, and the groans of the miserable ones came to be embodied in revenge.[33]

Sami thus introduces the reader to the recurrent theme of the downfall of the Bukharan state, and here the human element always plays a prominent role, be it a routed army, a rebel movement, or even an appeal for mercy on behalf of a city's population. The failure of the Muslim armies to repel the Russians appears to be more significant than the Russian army's victory, a fact noticeably present in Sami's description of the conquest of Tashkent and Samarqand.

In Sami's narration of the Russian conquest, what is most striking is his representation of Amir Muzaffar's insensitive self-serving attitude, and the ineffectiveness of the Bukharan army. At the outset of the Russian attack, the inhabitants of Tashkent sent Amir Muzaffar a letter requesting help.[34] The ruler of Qoqand, Mulla ʿAlimkul, had responded with an army. Amir Muzaffar also set out with an army, but stopped in Khujand. When the Christian army began the siege, according to Sami, Amir Muzaffar did not order his troops into the field. In the face of the attack, Sami describes the Tashkentis and Christians as equally fearless, and the Christian and Qoqand armies fought a heavy battle. However, "at that time, deceitful fate again played a trick that caused the defeat of the Qoqand army and the victory of the Christian."[35] If Muzaffar's inaction was insufficient insult to the dignity of the Tashkent population, he marched off with his own force, taking advantage of the Qoqand army's preoccupation with Tashkent. In response, the Qoqand army withdrew to defend its own city, leaving Tashkent to fall to the Russians.

Amir Muzaffar is described as taking decisive military action against the Russians in response to an uprising in Bukhara at the Registan. Ishan Baqa-Khoja Sadr, the raʾis of Bukhara, called for jihad and gathered a large crowd of religious leaders, mullas, and students.[36] The crowd became row-

Historical Memory, Cultural Identity, and Change

*Amir Muzaffar al-Din Bahadur Khan (Photograph by Hardet, ca.
1880; courtesy of Garnet Publishing Limited)*

dy, and Muzaffar, unable to quiet them, decided to march to the vicinity of
Maydayulghun (located on the bank of the Saykhun River). Sami describes the response of the Bukharans upon meeting the Russians as one of
simple fear and flight:

> When the banner of the Christian army became visible to the warriors for
> the faith, they all paled from fear and started to think. The strong whistle
> of the guns' bullets barely had time to resound when [the Bukharans], at
> the sound of the Christians' cannon shots, awoke from their imagination

and began to think of escape. Faced with the barest Christian pressure, the whole army and the people who had started off on the jihad dropped all of their equipment and belongings, ran, and dispersed.[37]

Muzaffar set off to Jizak, abandoning his treasury, equipment, and artillery to the Christian army.

After his treatment of the Russian siege of Jizak, Sami creates the atmosphere for his narration of events in Samarqand with a description of what appears to be a meteor shower—a natural event that, Sami suggests, symbolizes impending doom. He describes the evening of Wednesday, the 6th of Rajab, the year of the snow leopard, 1283 (1866/67):

> The numerous murders and the terror of plunder showed the people with their own eyes the signs of the Last Judgment. In half a night, the situation of the world has changed. All the stars fell from the sky at once and began to pour upon the earth like star-rain, and having brought the earth to the point of despair, they disappeared. This stellar downpour continued until morning, and when morning came, it ceased. At that time, the face of the sky became clear of stars and not a single one remained in the heavens. The meaning became clear: when the stars are scattered.[38] The one writing these lines asked several people who had arrived from the steppe [about what had happened]. This event took place everywhere and was seen in all the provinces.[39]

In Sami's description of events surrounding the siege of Samarqand, he continues to depict Muzaffar as a self-serving ruler insensitive to the urgent requests of the people as well as to the oppression of the Samarqand population. The Samarqandis actually wrote a letter to Amir Muzaffar asking him to replace their oppressive hakim, Shir ʿAli Inaq, and offering to fight the Christians to their death if the request was granted.[40] Muzaffar's response was to order the punishment of those who made the request, and to send several of his influential amirs to support Shir ʿAli Inaq. Muzaffar left for Karmina.[41]

The unrest in Samarqand continued, and included a massacre of mullas at the madrasa. Unlike his strong and emotional comments about the internal political and military affairs of state with which he was intimately involved, Sami's descriptions of the religiously inspired resistance inside the cities of Samarqand and Bukhara show no inherent sympathy. In Samarqand, groups of mullas gathered in the madrasas inciting people to jihad, and the crowd quickly grew violent. According to Sami, the riots that ensued were a response partly to Muzaffar's release of a Russian envoy who had been held, and partly to the rout at Maydayulghun. Sami appears to question the religious motivations and emotionally charged calls for jihad. He accuses the Samarqand mullas of inciting riots and humiliating the people, and describes the riots—which were quelled only after the hakim called out his army and killed many people—as contributing to increased disorder and the weakening of the state, and as a sign to the Russians of internal strife. "In one word, an event has taken place such as has not occurred in the Muslim community since the appearance of Islam."[42]

Sami suggests that the news of this unrest prompted the Russians to advance on Samarqand. The people of the city, he records, sent a letter to General von Kaufman requesting that he take their city, which the general "treated as a heavenly and indisputable gift from God."[43] Sami's description of the resistance to the Russian conquest of Samarqand underscores the inability of Muzaffar's army to repulse the Russians: the soldiers were feeble, confused, ill-equipped, and outmaneuvered. In his narrative, the author focuses on an often neglected aspect of this period of conflict, namely, the significance of tribal support and the divided loyalties and attitudes among the various tribes. Sami clearly resents the influence of the *ghulams* (slave soldiers) and the thwarted influence of the traditional Uzbek tribal leaders, a theme repeated throughout his chronicle, and he describes the banner of Muzaffar in the following unflattering manner:

> From the moment this sovereign ascended the throne, [his] banner became support for the dregs of society, and he zealously granted favors to lowly people, thereby causing discontent among the tribes. At that time, when the thorns of revolt and the dust of unrest stuck to the lap of power, and from four sides the causes of ruin and revolution appeared in the state, instead of having the continuous change of events and troubles serve as an occasion for understanding and the elimination of strife, and with the help of right reason and thought and commendable actions, to find a way to unite and increase the number of friends, they, with their bad thoughts, behavior, and incorrect measures, turned their friends into enemies and made the enemies trusted people. And they did not do anything but take on airs, insisting on their own way and inflicting insults on people.[44]

Following this accusation, Sami describes a meeting of tribal leaders prior to the Samarqand battle, and here the reader is presented with a clear difference of opinion and influence between the Uzbek amirs and tribal chiefs, and the ghulams and their supporters, represented by Ya'qub-Qushbegi.[45] The Uzbek amirs were in favor of conciliation and negotiation with the Russians, arguing that the Uzbeks no longer had any means of defense. Their arms could not match the Christians', and they had already suffered heavy losses. Ya'qub-Qushbegi, "who still had the wind of arrogance and stubbornness which caused the weakening of the state," felt that negotiating was a cowardly choice, and he slandered those advocating such action.[46] And so, in the face of the Christian army at Samarqand, the Bukharan army "fell into confusion, and in disorder turned to flight."[47]

A large army, made up of more than 100,000 sipahs and supporters of the jihad, met the Russian army at the Zarafshan River, where another 4,000 *sarbazes* (infantrymen) of another detachment joined them, the latter consisting of Arabs and Uzbeks who, according to Sami, were famous for their bravery and courage. Sami's poetic verse describes the soldiers who participated in this battle, to which he was an eyewitness, and reflects an image of moral weakness and, in effect, the saddened condition of the Bukharan state:

> There were more troops than flowers in spring,
> and [all the warriors] rushed headfirst, like buds.
> One, with a spear in his hand, is ready to attack,
> But, like an artist, he carries the spear like a paintbrush.
>
> Another walks with a dagger tied to his belt,
> But shakes like a willow.
>
> One stretches a bow string and inserts an arrow,
> Another is an exact copy of an alef-madde.
> One, like a bud, raises his mace,
> But he, like a withered rose, loses his color.
>
> Another arrays himself in steel,
> But, like a reflection in a mirror, has neither soul nor heart.
>
> One in a black caftan is fast and dextrous,
> But his look is fearful like the eyes of a gazelle.
>
> Another is dressed in red, but from fear
> His visage becomes yellow in the face of the enemy.
> For everyone who unsheathes a sword out of vanity,
> His own nose would unsheathe a sword against his own face.[48]

And so Muzaffar, in his attempts to defeat the Russian army, succumbed to the human frailties of self-interest and power, to the divided loyalties of tribal leadership, and to the one factor beyond his control—the military power of the Russian army. In response to von Kaufman's address to the Samarqand population, in which he called for peace and forgiveness, the mufti of Samarqand responded that Muslims have only one word, that was sent to them by God, which is called the Qur'an.[49] However, he continued, "It is impossible that [in the future] we could commit unworthy or harmful deeds against the [Russian] state. Despite Islam's appeal for justice, what kinds of oppression did we not see from the Uzbek sovereigns? A just ruler will stay in power even being an infidel, while a cruel one will not be able to stay in power, even professing Islam."[50]

Muzaffar al-Din's heir and successor, ʿAbd al-Ahad, continues the ruinous process of decay described by Sami. This decay is defined by a progressively weakening central government and a strengthening of Russian influence, increased representation and influence of the commoners and ghulams (as opposed to the traditional tribal aristocracy), and a general

Royalty Dallies While Society Suffers
"The Amir of Bukhara ['Abd al-Ahad] in St. Petersburg" (Mulla
Nasreddin, *no. 12 [1910])*

malaise on the part of the rulers. Most abhorrent to Sami is the loss of
Bukhara as the true residence of the sovereign, perhaps signifying to the
author that power no longer resided solely in the hands of the sovereign
rulers. But first, Sami relates the seemingly idyllic lifestyle of 'Abd al-
Ahad:

> The same affection and friendship existed between the Russian state and
> noble Bukhara, and it even grew and increased from day to day. Agree-

ment and friendship were maintained. His Majesty ['Abd al-Ahad] even acquired an estate in Yalta that was subject to Russia—a healthy, fresh, merry, and pleasant locale. There he built beautiful buildings. . . . Every year, without fail and fear, he set out to that place with fifteen to twenty servants, and spent two months in a garden adorning heaven, enjoying life and happiness to his heart's content. Having spent a considerable sum from his treasury on everything his appetite demanded and his eyes desired, he returned. At that time, noble Bukhara lost the honor of the blessed presence [of the amir], and Karmina became the sovereign's residency.[51]

However, it is in Sami's description of the last rulers of Bukhara after the tsarist conquest that his nostalgia for past days of honor is most apparent. The glorious army of the Timurids, or the powerful army of the Uzbeks at their height of power, stands in sharp contrast to the Bukharan army described by Sami. Other details concerning the makeup of the army shed further light on Sami's perceptions of the affairs of state:

All the magnificence of the kingdom is made up [now] of three or four detachments of sarbazes, the majority of whom are thieves, gamblers, drunkards, some crazy and insane, others lame or blind, who never heard a gunshot. A new creation is the army of the Caucasus, which was named the personal escort of the sovereign. This detachment is made up of effeminate men, and whenever a youth gains the upper hand in a fight, he is drafted and attached to the Caucasian army. Numerous multicolored military uniforms are put on these sarbazes. Sitting on top of horses of various colors, they enliven the bazaar with the sounds of their kettle drums and trumpets. In every *wilayat* (district), whenever thieves or robbers are caught, instead of an execution they are given a gun and arms and are included in the number of sarbazes in the army mentioned. Such [men] are appointed military commanders of the sarbazes that it is a shame to even move a pen to tell about them.[52]

In Sami's representation of events, the external cause of the Bukharan state's downfall is obviously the arrival of the Russian army and its success in subordinating the rulers. However, it should be noted that for most of his text, especially in his narration of the events leading up to and including the conquest of Samarqand and Tashkent, Sami portrays the Russian army as a brave and strong force. It is not until the concluding chapters of his chronicle that he describes the Russians in blatantly negative terms, as infidels and oppressors. For instance, Sami describes the armies invading Tashkent, subjecting the inhabitants to "swords and daggers" and capturing the city, but he portrays them as no more brutal than the Bukharan army in its capture of Qoqand or Shahr-i Sabz. The Russians appear in Sami's text as well-intentioned despite his opposition to them; they negotiate and appear levelheaded. Following the Draft Treaty of

1867, Sami discusses the cooperation between the Russians and Muzaffar, and it is obvious that each side promotes its own political interests in doing so. For instance, Muzaffar called on the Russian army to help him rout the rebel ʿAbd al-Malik, to quell the revolt raised by the Keneges tribe in Shahr-i Sabz, and ultimately to recapture Shahr-i Sabz and Kitab (1873–74). Only later, in his comments about ʿAbd al-Ahad, in which Sami again returns to the causes for the decay of the Bukharan state, does he accuse the Russians of undercutting the power and influence of the amirs. Like other Asian intellectuals of this period, he openly praises the victory of Japan in the Russo-Japanese War of 1904–1905, implying that the war was Russia's punishment.[53] And finally, in his treatment of the internal situation in Russia after the war with Japan, he writes that the Russian people rose up against the tsar and the rich because of their suffering in the war.

ʿAbd al-Malik Türa: Heroic Rebel

In examining Sami's description of ʿAbd al-Malik Türa, Amir Muzaffar's heir and his eldest son, and hakim of Huzar, a parallel process of decline may be seen in which the heir apparent moves from being a strong supporter and representative of his father's rule, to a rebel representing the old tribal leadership, the religious class, and much of the populace, to a man exiled from his homeland. Sami's preoccupation with ʿAbd al-Malik's fate illustrates his view of the hopelessness of Bukharan society during this period.

Sami's first reference to ʿAbd al-Malik immediately follows his description of the situation in Samarqand at the time of the Russian conquest. As discussed above, the author reports that the Samarqand population suffered under Shir ʿAli Inaq's rule and wished for his overthrow, sending a letter to Amir Muzaffar requesting him to appoint another leader. The appeal to Amir Muzaffar and the response of the Bukharan army to the tsarist threat in Samarqand were both negative. Sami reported that the Bukharan army was disorganized and not prepared for combat. Muzaffar instead punished several people involved in the Samarqand appeal, left Shir ʿAli Inaq in Samarqand, put several influential amirs in the garrison, and safely left for Karmina. Shir ʿAli Inaq also punished those involved in this incident, and accused ʿAbd al-Malik Türa of inciting riots and revolts, banishing him from Samarqand and sending him to Huzar. According to Sami, "This served to humiliate Türa, break his heart, and in the end, because of the unfortunate accusation, force him to become a rebel. Along with these incorrect actions, a massacre of mullas took place, the commission of which completely upset the foundation of the kingdom, and the sun of the state began to set toward dusk."[54] The textual environment in which Sami presents ʿAbd al-Malik is one of oppression, revolt, and dissatisfaction. ʿAbd al-Malik's transformation into a rebel is not self-willed but fated. Sami's report of this change is sandwiched between the Samarqand population's appeal to Muzaffar and the revolt of the mullas in the same city. However, it is not until some sixteen folios later that Sami again returns to ʿAbd al-Malik, this time devoting a lengthy discussion to him.

Sami represents ʿAbd al-Malik as a heroic rebel who, despite terrible odds, fights a courageous battle to restore honor to the Muslim population. In this attempt he loses more than his effort to restore the dignity of the Muslim community by defeating the Russians. ʿAbd al-Malik loses his position as a ruler and as Muzaffar's heir. He opposes two powers, the Russian Christian army and the political authority of the amir. In his resistance, he represents the popular sentiment of the townspeople, the tribal leadership, and the religious class, all of whom find Muzaffar's actions either ineffective, unjust, or oppressive. This characterization of ʿAbd al-Malik is not only a mirror image of the plight of the Bukharan Amirate, but also a reflection of Sami's personal plight as a rebel in his own right. As is evident in this chronicle and from his other writings, Sami was dissatisfied with the weakness of Amir Muzaffar and the Bukharan army, and was opposed to Muzaffar's deference to the lower classes and ghulams, upon whom he and his successor, ʿAbd al-Ahad, had increasingly relied. ʿAbd al-Malik's exile and loss of political power is reminiscent of Sami's own exile from the Bukharan court. Although still in the city of Bukhara, Sami also became isolated from the official bureaucracy, of which he was a part for ten years. In his lengthy discussion of ʿAbd al-Malik's resistance, of the support and opposition to him, of his efforts to defeat the Russian army, and of his final exile, one cannot but suppose that Sami identified with and perhaps even emulated this rebel. For ʿAbd al-Malik not only represented strength and courage, he also provided Sami with a personality who symbolized the slow but progressive decay of the Bukharan Amirate.

Sami's description of ʿAbd al-Malik and his resistance movement may be divided into three stages: first, the organization, composition, and success of this resistance; second, Amir Muzaffar's attempt to crush the movement and capture ʿAbd al-Malik; and third, ʿAbd al-Malik's defeat and exile.

In his treatment of the first stage, Sami depicts ʿAbd al-Malik as a strong, courageous, and just fighter to whom many elements of the population were drawn. His descriptions of the rebels and their motivations in joining ʿAbd al-Malik provide insight into the sociopolitical history of the period, and support the notion that religious opposition was not the only basis for organized resistance.[55] Opposition to Muzaffar as well as to the Russian invasion was rampant, and among those mentioned by Sami as supporters of ʿAbd al-Malik were the Qungrats of Shirabad, the Uzbeks of Qarshi, the Turkmen tribes of the Ersari, the Qaraqalpaq, the Samarqand Tajiks, and the Khitay-Qipckaq.[56] Joining ʿAbd al-Malik in opposition to Muzaffar did not merely signify opposition to a Christian, Russian army; it signified resistance to Amir Muzaffar as well.

In his narrative, Sami describes the allegiance paid to ʿAbd al-Malik by the various tribes who arrived in Huzar, the revolts that spread to the provinces as a result of this movement, the support from the hakims of Huzar, Shirabad, Kulab, and Shahr-i Sabz, and the attempted seizure of Samarqand by ʿAbd al-Malik's army.

In the second stage, during which Muzaffar pursued ʿAbd al-Malik and attempted to crush the resistance, Sami reports that, with the advice of one of his begs, Muzaffar concluded peace with the Russians. This agreement was to have a great effect on the outcome of ʿAbd al-Malik's resistance. In fact, there were two turning points in the rebel's fate: first, his defeat at Samarqand, and second, the inclusion of the Russian army in Muzaffar's fight to crush him. According to Sami, ʿAbd al-Malik did not succeed in capturing Samarqand because Muzaffar sent a deceptive letter to the Shahr-i Sabz hakims, who were fighting with the rebel leader, in which he stated that he and General Abramov had concluded an agreement and that the Christian and Bukharan army were about to attack Shahr-i Sabz as punishment for the locals' support of ʿAbd al-Malik. Although ʿAbd al-Malik tried to convince the hakims of the letter's falsity, the hakims refused to defend their city, and ʿAbd al-Malik's attack failed. At the same time, according to Sami, with the advice of the amir, Shukrü Beg Inaq, Muzaffar actually did send a letter to the Russians seeking to establish peace. And so, as the reader is impressed with ʿAbd al-Malik's defiance of two oppressive powers, Muzaffar himself seeks peace with one of the opponents whom ʿAbd al-Malik and his supporters are fighting. As a result of the letter, ʿAbd al-Malik retreated and lost much of his army.

In this section of the narrative, Sami also illustrates the shifting loyalties of Muzaffar's begs, whom he sends to capture ʿAbd al-Malik. The Bukharan army set out to Qarshi to fight ʿAbd al-Malik and his army, and his begs were ordered to capture him. The armies clashed, and many were killed. ʿAbd al-Malik retreated, but when the army of Qarshi ultimately captured him, the begs decided with the local hakim that they would allow him to escape. Another incident reflects this same ambivalence on the part of Muzaffar's so-called supporters. Muzaffar asked the hakims of Shahr-i Sabz and Kitab to capture ʿAbd al-Malik, but the hakims refused and hoped Muzaffar would show mercy. Sami follows this description with Muzaffar's reaction. According to Sami, Muzaffar "soared from great anger and rage, like a burning hair. He jumped up from his seat and immediately ordered the army to start the battle. The brave warriors from both sides rushed onto the battlefield and began to fight."[57]

In the remainder of Sami's narrative about ʿAbd al-Malik, he reveals the rebel's hopeless situation, his gradual loss of support, and his final search for a place of exile. In describing these details, Sami's speech is markedly sentimental:

> After the Türa's flight from Qarshi and the victory of the Christians there, no opportunity remained for family and for people to flee, and having stayed in the Qarshi ark, they were all taken prisoner by His Majesty. No place remained for the Türa to find peace. He stopped counting on the nomad tribes and their help, tore Bukhara out of his heart, and decided to set out for distant lands . . . and having said good-bye to the country and to the love of homeland, the Türa put his foot into the stirrup of ill-fatedness and, having sunk his head into the bosom of hopelessness, set out from Tashqurghan for Shahr-i Sabz.[58]

ʿAbd al-Malik settled in Kashghar for ten years with the help of the local hakim, Yaʿqub-bacha, whose daughter he married. After this he went on pilgrimage, eventually settling in Peshawar, where the English government provided him with a salary. According to Sami, he "spent his life in prosperity, became addicted to opium, and lived there until 1316 (1898/99)."[59]

Why did Sami devote such a lengthy discussion to the circumstances surrounding the growth of ʿAbd al-Malik's resistance movement? At the conclusion of the discussion, the lines that define ʿAbd al-Malik as a rebel, or as a hero, are ambiguous. Sami refers to him as a rebel early in his narrative, and this is certainly so from Muzaffar's perspective. However, Sami presents an alternative view through his references to the various attitudes of the factions involved: the religious and tribal opposition, Muzaffar and his begs, the townspeople, and the Russian governors. Throughout the narrative, in fact, ʿAbd al-Malik gains legitimacy as a heroic figure, until his tragic end. It should be noted that Sami paid greater attention to this person than did any of his contemporaries recording this period. His preoccupation may be related to the strength of ʿAbd al-Malik's symbolic value and the connection between historical memory and identity. ʿAbd al-Malik the rebel/hero symbolized the antithetical identities that defined Bukhara, as well as Sami: Bukhara, the noble religious center of the past but also the city defeated by a Christian army; Sami, the scholar-munshi, but also the destitute exiled copyist.

As John Gillis has recently stated in a study of commemorations and nationalism, "We need to be reminded that memories and identities are not fixed things, but representations or constructions of reality, subjective rather than objective phenomena. . . . Memories help us make sense of the world we live in; and 'memory work' is, like any other kind of physical or mental labor, embedded in complex class, gender and power relations that determine what is remembered (or forgotten), by whom, and for what end."[60] An examination of the history of the Manghit dynasty, and particularly the period during which Bukhara became a Russian protectorate, reveals that Sami's perceptions are rooted in the social and moral order of a glorious past long gone. For Sami, unlike the jadids, technology, communications, and the reform of social institutions (particularly education) are not primary concerns, despite the glaring reality that the technological and organizational superiority of the Russian army is a critical factor in the Bukharan defeat.[61] Indeed, Sami was an eyewitness to many of the battles that led to the amirate's military defeat. The reference points of his cultural identity as a member of the intelligentsia were the markers of the literary, historical, and cultural legacy of the eastern Islamic world. They define his viewpoint as well as his approach to understanding the predicament of the Bukharan amirate in the late nineteenth and early twentieth centuries.

ʿAbd al-ʿAziz Sami's unofficial history represents a worldview firmly rooted in the memory of a shared historical past that reveals an often neglected perspective of the status of the Bukharan state in the late nineteenth century. Viewed in the context of the period's historiography, this text is a local source distinctive for its candor, emotionality, and pessimism. Although it conforms to a classical Perso-Islamic form, Sami wrote this "unofficial" version of his history not for his former patrons, but seemingly for fellow dissatisfied members of the literati. He provides no prescription for change; rather, the history itself is a form of complaint and perhaps a plea for a return to a more perfect past. Given the scholarly emphasis that has been placed on administrative policy, military history, Russo-Bukharan relations, and reformist movements in the study of the "Russian Orient," Sami's text provides a contrasting perspective rooted in the cultural history of Central Asia from which to view local sentiment regarding the conquest period and the changes that were to follow.

NOTES

I am grateful to the International Research and Exchanges Board for a Developmental Fellowship that made possible the initial research for this chapter.

1. For sources on the Russian conquest of Central Asia, see Hélène Carrère d'Encausse, "Systematic Conquest, 1865–1884," in *Central Asia: 130 Years of Russian Dominance—A Historical Overview,* ed. Edward Allworth (3rd ed., Durham, N.C., 1994), pp. 131–150; Seymour Becker, *Russia's Protectorates in Central Asia: Bukhara and Khiva, 1865–1924* (Cambridge, Mass., 1968); Dietrich Geyer, *Russian Imperialism: The Interaction of Domestic and Foreign Policy, 1860–1914,* trans. from the German by Bruce Little (New York, 1987); N. A. Khal'fin, *Prisoedineniia Srednei Azii k Rossii (60–90-e gody XIX v.)* (Moscow, 1965); Richard A. Pierce, *Russian Central Asia, 1867–1917: A Study in Colonial Rule* (Berkeley, 1960); Peter Morris, "The Russians in Central Asia, 1867–1887," *Slavonic and East European Review* 53 (1975): 521–538; Mehmet Saray, "The Russian Conquest of Central Asia," *Central Asian Survey* 1, nos. 2–3 (1982): 1–27; Geoffrey Wheeler, "Russian Conquest and Colonization in Central Asia," in *Russian Imperialism from Ivan the*

Great to the Revolution, ed. Taras Hunczak (New Brunswick, N.J., 1974), pp. 264–298.

2. For a review of the study of scholarship on jadidism, see Adeeb Khalid, "The Politics of Muslim Cultural Reform: Jadidism in Tsarist Central Asia" (Ph.D. diss., University of Wisconsin–Madison, 1993), pp. 7–28. See also Edward J. Lazzerini, "Beyond Renewal: The Jadid Response to Pressure for Change in the Modern Age," in *Muslims in Central Asia: Expressions of Identity and Change,* ed. Jo-Ann Gross (Durham, N.C., 1992), pp. 151–166.

3. On adab, see F. Gabrieli, "Adab," in *Encyclopaedia of Islam,* vol. 1, p. 175. For a study of the classical Muslim concept of adab, see Ira M. Lapidus, "Knowledge, Virtue, and Action: The Classical Muslim Conception of *Adab* and the Nature of Religious Fulfillment in Islam," in *Moral Conduct and Authority: The Place of Adab in South Asian Islam,* ed. Barbara Daly Metcalf (Berkeley, 1984), pp. 38–61.

4. See O. A. Sukhareva, *Bukhara: XIX–nachalo XX v. (Pozdnefeodal'nyi gorod i ego naselenie)* (Moscow, 1966), pp. 182–187.

5. On concepts of knowledge implicit in Muslim education, see Dale F. Eickelman, "The Art of Memory: Islamic Knowledge and Its Social Reproduction," *Comparative Studies in Society and History* 20 (1978): 485–516. See also Franz Rosenthal, *Knowledge Triumphant: The Concept of Knowledge in Medieval Islam* (Leiden, 1970). For sources on maktab education in Central Asia, see Jiří Bečka, "Traditional Schools in the Works of Sadriddin Ayni and Other Writers of Central Asia," *Archiv Orientální* 39 (1971): 284–321 and 40 (1972): 130–163; D. S. M. Williams, "The Traditional Muslim Schools of the Settled Regions of Central Asia during the Tsarist Period," *Central Asian Review* 13 (1965): 339–349; and R. R. Rakhimov, "Traditsionnoe nachal'noe shkol'noe obuchenie detei u narodov Srednei Azii (konets XIX–nachalo XX v.)," in *Pamiatniki traditsionno-bytovoi kul'tury narodov Srednei Azii, Kazakhstana i Kavkaza* (Leningrad, 1989). See also the report of O. Olufsen, *The Amir of Bokhara and His Country: Journey and Studies in Bokhara (with a Chapter on My Voyage on the Amu Darya to Khiva)* (London, 1911), pp. 386–388. The work of Sadriddin Ayni is particularly informative for his personal view of Islamic education. See especially *Bukhara (Vospominaniia),* trans. S. Borodin, in Ayni's *Sobranie sochinenii,* vol. 4, and *Yaddashtha,* ed. Saʾidi Sirjani (Tehran, 1984). The work of N. K. Khanykoff, a Russian orientalist who traveled extensively in the region of Bukhara, is informative on the madrasa system in Bukhara, and provides a detailed account of the curriculum. Khanykoff, *Bokhara: Its Amir and Its People,* trans. Baron Clement A. De Bode (London, 1845), pp. 278–294.

6. Bourdieu's notion of habitus, related to his "theory of practice" model, takes into consideration not only self and group interests and cultural expressions, but the way in which unconscious knowledge and experience are made conscious. Habitus refers to a set of schemes that produce representations and practices based upon an unconscious selectivity. The commonality of experience and the habitus engendered by this provides familiarity as well as an awareness of shared community. Pierre Bourdieu, *Outline of a Theory of Practice,* trans. N. Nice (Cambridge, 1977), p. 72.

7. Khalid, "The Politics of Muslim Cultural Reform," p. 438.

8. The tribes continued to be important throughout the conquest period, as shown by Amir Muzaffar and ʿAbd al-Ahad's increased reliance on and patronage of local begs and *ghulam*s (slave soldiers). See N. V. Khanykov, *Opisanie Bukhar-*

skago khanstva (St. Petersburg, 1843), p. 182; A. Semenov, *Ocherk ustroistva tsentral'nogo administrativnogo upravleniia bukharskogo khanstva pozdneishego vremeni* (Stalinabad, 1954); O. Sukhareva, *K istorii gorodov bukharskogo khanstva* (Tashkent, 1959). H. Carrère d'Encausse (*Islam and the Russian Empire: Reform and Revolution in Central Asia*, trans. Quintin Hoare [English edition, Berkeley, 1988], pp. 16–17) also discusses the issue of tribal rivalry between the two Uzbek tribes, the Manghits (the ruling elite) and the Keneges, in Shahr-i Sabz.

9. For administrative policy and internal conditions, see O. A. Sukhareva, *Bukhara: XIX–nachalo XX v. (Pozdnefeodal'nyi gorod i ego naselenie)* (Moscow, 1966). For a discussion of the centralization policies and their problems, see d'Encausse, *Islam and the Russian Empire*, pp. 27–30. Although the administration was largely controlled by Uzbeks, the office of *qushbegi* was one traditionally held by Persian ghulams.

10. For a study of tsarist educational policies in Turkestan, see H. Carrère d'Encausse, "Tsarist Educational Policy in Turkestan, 1867–1917," *Central Asian Review* 4 (1963): 374–394. Three excellent studies of nationalism and Russian imperial culture are Mark Bassin, "Russia between Europe and Asia: The Ideological Construction of Geography," *Slavic Review* 50 (1991): 1–17; Seymour Becker, "The Muslim East in Nineteenth-Century Russian Popular Historiography," *Central Asian Survey* 5, nos. 3–4 (1986): 25–47; and Jeffrey Brooks, *When Russia Learned to Read : Literacy and Popular Literature, 1861–1917* (Princeton, 1985).

11. Khalid, "The Politics of Muslim Cultural Reform," pp. 130–135.

12. Ibid., p. 147.

13. ʿAbd al-ʿAziz Sami, *Taʾrikh-i Salatin-i Manghitiya,* Persian facsimile and translation, preface, and introduction in Russian by L. M. Epifanova (Moscow, 1962). Epifanova (p. 13) notes that there is no mention in the sources of Sami's date of birth. Based upon Sami's report in the *Tuhfat-i shahi* that he served at the amir's court until the age of sixty, and the fact that the *Tuhfat-i shahi* was written in 1902–1903, she concludes that he was born in 1838 or 1839. He died in 1907 or 1908 at the age of seventy-two, according to Ayni.

14. Ibid., pp. 14–15.

15. Ibid., p. 15.

16. Franz Rosenthal, *"Sweeter Than Hope": Complaint and Hope in Medieval Islam* (Leiden, 1983).

17. The copious array of writings critical of the amirate are too numerous to list here. However, notable among the early jadid writers are Mahmud Khoja Behbudi, Abdurrauf Fitrat, Ahmed Danish, and Sadriddin Ayni. Edward Allworth quotes the following passage from Ahmed Danish's *Nawadir al-waqaʾiʿ* (Allworth cites from Muminov): "The Manghit [dynasty's] leaders have seized everything which their wickedness has inspired them to take. From the widow they have snatched away her hearth, from charitable institutions their resources. . . . Amongst the rulers and propertied classes reign drunkenness and games of chance, revelry, and debauchery, while the poor people are at their wit's end. Whether the poor wretched are from the country or the city, they cannot utter a single word nor escape the constant levies" (Allworth, *Central Asia,* pp. 173–174). It should be noted that, like Sami, Danish served at the Bukharan court, and in fact made three trips on behalf of the amir to St. Petersburg (Turaj Atabaki, "A Study in the History of Bukharan Modernism: The Journey of Ahmad Danish to St. Petersburg," *Bam-*

berger Zentralasienstudien Konferenzakten ESCAS IV Bamberg . . . 1991, ed. I. Baldauf and M. Friederich [Berlin, 1994], pp. 263–269). It was after returning to Bukhara from his last trip that Danish retired from court service after his appeals to Muzaffar for reform were ignored. For a discussion of themes of resistance in Central Asian literature, see Edward Allworth, "The Focus of Literature," in *Central Asia*, pp. 397–433.

18. For a discussion of biographical sources on ʿAbd al-ʿAziz Sami, see Epifanova edition of Sami (n. 13), pp. 14–23; for a list of Sami's works, see Sadriddin Ayni, *Namune-i Adabiyat-i Tajik* (Moscow, 1926), pp. 335–339. Ayni evidently made use of Sami's chronicles when writing his own history of the Bukharan Amirate.

19. See Epifanova edition of Sami (n. 13), pp. 23–25, for a discussion of the Russian interpretations of Sami's criticism and dismissal.

20. Ayni, *Namune-i Adabiyat-i Tajik*, p. 338.

21. Ibid.

22. Epifanova edition of Sami (n. 13), p. 19.

23. I rely on the comments of Epifanova concerning the differences and similarities between the two texts, since the unpublished manuscript copies of the *Tuhfat-i shahi* have not been available to me.

24. Epifanova edition of Sami (n. 13), p. 13. On pp. 8–12 she discusses three manuscripts at the Institut Vostokovedeniia, Tashkent, which she believes are copies of the "official" version, entitled *Tuhfat-i shahi* (#1458, 4330, and 7419). The "unofficial" version, entitled *Taʾrikh-i Salatin-i Manghitiya*, had been mistakenly named *Tuhfat-i shahi*, but in the one autograph copy in Dushanbe, the author names the work *Taʾrikh-i Salatin-i Manghitiya-i dar al-Saltana-i Bukhara-i Sharif*, and this is the manuscript copy translated by Epifanova (Dushanbe, Institut Vostoko-vedeniia #927/III, #1737). See Epifanova, pp. 1–13, for a discussion of the differences between the two works in Sami's treatment of a variety of events. Notable omissions from the "official" version include the Andijan revolt of 1898 and the meeting of amirs in Karmina after the fall of Samarqand.

25. See Eden Naby, "Transitional Central Asian Literature: Tajik and Uzbek Prose Fiction from 1909–1932" (Ph.D. diss., Columbia University, 1975).

26. For example, the cultural life of the court in early sixteenth-century Central Asia was largely based on Timurid tradition, including the infamous poetic circle of ʿAli Shir Navaʾi. See Maria Eva Subtelny, "Art and Politics in Early 16th Century Central Asia," *Central Asiatic Journal* 27 (1983): 121–148.

27. Ayni, *Yaddashtha*, ed. Saʾidi Sirjani (Tehran, 1984), p. 340.

28. Khalid, "The Politics of Muslim Cultural Reform," p. 147.

29. See Epifanova's comments concerning the Soviet interpretation of Sami's role. For example, Z. Radzhabov characterized Sami as a jadid, while I. S. Braginskii portrayed him as a "winged lion of the enlightenment" as well as a supporter of the Russian Revolution of 1905. Epifanova edition of Sami (n. 13), p. 24. Z. Radzhabov, *Razvitie obshchestvennoi mysli tazhikskogo naroda vo vtoroi polovine XIX v. i v nachale XX v* (Stalinabad, 1951), p. 3, and I. S. Braginskii, *Sadriddin Ayni* (Stalinabad, 1948; 2nd ed., 1954), p. 24.

30. E. P. Thompson, *The Poverty of Theory* (London, 1978).

31. Hayden White, *The Content of the Form: Narrative Discourse and Historical Representation* (Baltimore, 1987), p. 13.

32. All subsequent references to the *Taʾrikh-i Salatin-i Manghitiya* are to the

published text translated by Epifanova and including the Persian facsimile. References to the text will be as TSM, and will note the folio page number from the facsimile followed by the page number in Epifanova's Russian translation.

33. TSM, fol. 65a–65b, pp. 55–57.

34. TSM, fol. 66a, p. 58.

35. TSM, fol. 66b, p. 58. Bukhara and Qoqand had a long history of rivalry. See Becker, *Russia's Protectorates*, pp. 5–6.

36. TSM, fol. 68a–68b, pp. 60–62.

37. TSM, fol. 68b, p. 62.

38. This Qur^ɔanic verse is from Chapter (*Surah*) 82, "The Cleaving," which refers to the disorder that will take place when the Day of Judgment arrives. Implicit in Sami's reference to this verse is a basic tenet of the Islamic worldview: that it is incumbent upon each individual to exercise moral choice and responsibility, for which each individual will ultimately be judged. Those who commit such acts of murder and plunder, therefore, will be punished.

39. TSM, fol. 71b–72a, pp. 66–67.

40. TSM, fol. 72a, 72b; p. 67.

41. Karmina, originally named Karminiya according to V. V. Bartol'd, is a town within the district of Bukhara. Narshakhi, historian of the Samanid period and author of the *Ta'rikh-i Bukhara*, indicates that Karmina was located fourteen farsakhs from the city of Bukhara, while Yakut places the town eighteen farsakhs from Bukhara. Barthold, *Turkestan Down to the Mongol Invasion* (4th ed., Norfolk, Va., 1977), pp. 98–99 and 113.

42. TSM, fol. 73b, pp. 69–70.

43. TSM, fol. 74b, p. 70.

44. TSM, fol. 75b, pp. 71–72.

45. TSM, fol. 76b, p. 73.

46. Ibid.

47. TSM, fol. 77a, p. 74.

48. TSM, fol. 77b, p. 75. The alef-madde is the initial letter *a* in Persian. It is a straight horizontal line topped by a short, wavy line. Sami is using this figurative image to personify the cowardly army, wavering in its ability to resist.

49. TSM, fol. 80a, p. 78.

50. TSM, fol. 80a–80b, p. 79.

51. TSM, fol. 106b, pp. 115–116. See S. Becker's comments on 'Abd al-Ahad, who he says "bridges the two worlds," i.e., the sociopolitical and cultural worlds of Bukhara and of Russia. Becker's remarks emphasize 'Abd al-Ahad's apparent fondness for the European lifestyle, and the new role he began to play in Russian society. Becker, *Russia's Protectorates*, pp. 195–198.

52. TSM, fol. 109b, p. 119.

53. Epifanova edition of Sami (n. 13), pp. 26–27; TSM, fol. 118a. See Klaus Kreiser, "Der japanische Sieg über Russland (1905) und sein Echo unter den Muslimen," *Die Welt des Islams* 21 (1981): 209–239; and Milan Hauner, *What Is Asia to Us? Russia's Asian Heartland, Yesterday and Today* (Boston, 1990).

54. TSM, 72b, p. 68.

55. See Beatrice Forbes Manz's analysis of the Andijan revolt, in which she concludes that the rebellion must be understood not only as religiously inspired, but also as a way in which the displaced tribal leadership in Ferghana could aspire

to power and leadership. B. F. Manz, "Central Asian Uprisings in the Nineteenth Century: Ferghana under the Russians," *Russian Review* 46 (1987): 267–281.

56. TSM, fol. 84a–85b, pp. 84–85.

57. TSM, fol. 91a, p. 93.

58. TSM, fol. 97a–97b, pp. 102–103.

59. TSM, fol. 102a, p. 109. See also footnote 141, pp. 145–146.

60. John R. Gillis, "Memory and Identity: The History of a Relationship," in *Commemorations: The Politics of National Identity,* ed. John R. Gillis (Princeton, 1994), p. 3. On approaches to the sociopolitical aspects of memory and history, see Paul Connerton, *How Societies Remember* (Cambridge,1989); Thomas Butler, ed., *Memory: History, Culture and the Mind* (Oxford, 1989); Eric Hobsbawm and Terence Ranger, eds., *The Invention of Tradition* (Cambridge, Mass., 1993); and Jacques Le Goff, *History and Memory,* trans. Steven Rendall and Elizabeth Clamon (New York, 1992).

61. See S. A. M. Adshead, *Central Asia in World History* (New York, 1993), for an analysis of Central Asia as a factor in world history. In his analysis, Central Asia begins its political, economic, and military decline in the middle of the seventeenth century, becoming a "passive" rather than "active" participant in the world order. Recent studies that focus on local, interregional trade patterns challenge this viewpoint. See, for example, Stephen Dale, *Indian Merchants and Eurasian Trade, 1600–1750* (Cambridge, 1994).

.11.

Thomas M. Barrett

Crossing Boundaries: The Trading Frontiers of the Terek Cossacks

In the mid-nineteenth century, the Greben Cossacks (*Grebentsy*) of the north Caucasus told a story about the origin of Cossack-Chechen enmity two centuries earlier. According to this account, in the early days after the Grebentsy had resettled from the mountains south of the Terek River to the Russian side on the left bank, a specialization of economic functions developed between the Chechens of the mountains and the Cossacks, recently of the valley.[1] The Chechens continued to live off of plunder, attacking villages and travelers as they always had, but now they exchanged their booty with a rich Cossack, Batyrev, who then sold it at Astrakhan for a nice profit. In one plunder exchange Batyrev received an expensive gun, which he decided to keep for himself. When the original owner, a Chechen, spotted the gun and tried to buy it back, Batyrev refused to part with his keepsake; sometime later he and his brothers were attacked by the same Chechen and his comrades, the gun was stolen, and all the Batyrevs were killed. Thus began, so the story goes, the centuries of hatred, raiding, and killing between Chechen and Cossack across the Terek River, and from then on the Cossacks obtained their booty by attacking their erstwhile colleagues.[2]

It was a popular type of story in the north Caucasus—a successful bandit enterprise falling out over stolen goods, violence, and vendetta. As with most folk memories, there was a fair element of truth and also considerable distortion in this summation of Cossack-Chechen relations. The Cossacks of the north Caucasus did take part in the economy of plunder, but this by no means came to an end in the eighteenth century. The resettling of the Greben Cossacks to the Russian side in 1711–12 was an important turning point, but as much because of their new difficulties with the Russian state as because of any developing animosity toward their old neighbors to the south. And the trade relations between the Cossacks of the Terek and the peoples of the Caucasus mountains did not diminish, but were vital to the Cossack economy into the nineteenth century, even during the period of the most intense warfare of Russian against Chechen. Trade was as important a frontier encounter as was war, and at times war was indirectly dependent upon trade.

Like the Cossack folktale, the Western historiography of the north Caucasus has focused on the chasms between Russia and the native peoples, representing the frontier as a fault line of war, conflict, and religious division where Cossacks and *gortsy* (mountaineers) stand on opposite sides of the divide, glaring at each other with hostile intent.[3] The defining moment for the north Caucasus in this history is the systematic Russian military conquest of the nineteenth century and the Islamic resistance, centered in Chechnia and Dagestan, and culminating in the imamate of Shamil (1834–59). Earlier treatments of the conquest, such as Baddeley's *The Russian Conquest of the Caucasus* and Allen and Muratoff's *Caucasian Battlefields*, fixed on the Russian advance; the most recent works—Moshe Gammer's *Muslim Resistance to the Tsar: Shamil and the Conquest of Chechnia and Daghestan* and the collection of articles edited by Marie Bennigsen Broxup titled *The North Caucasus Barrier: The Russian Advance towards the Muslim World*—portray the mountain peoples' resistance.[4]

If we oppose the reduction of this frontier to a line of battles, it is not to lessen the importance of the military conquest or to accept the Soviet generalities of *druzhba narodov* (friendship of peoples) and *sblizhenie* (drawing together), but to add nuance to a history and a region of great complexity.[5] The Russian settlement of and building of new communities in the north Caucasus created powerful economic demands and opportunities; an examination of local trade reveals not just that there were many peddlers and merchants crisscrossing the border at all times, but that the goods flowing north from the mountains were essential to the Cossack communities and structured their material culture in many ways. And no matter how many barriers of customs control were erected, and how many disruptions of war, this trade had to continue, and it always did.

Such a history of society, economy, and transcultural contact in one borderland region of Russia helps to "ground" our understanding of the empire, an understanding that is all too often portrayed from the perspective of the center, and only in terms of policies, institutions, and cultural representations. What has been missing, and what is essential to an understanding of how the borderlands fit into the Russian Empire, is a history of those who moved there and lived at the edge of empire, how diverse people interacted there, their cultural exchanges, and the new landscapes, economies, and societies that they created. The following examination of frontier trade suggests that the Russian incorporation of the north Caucasus was a more uncertain and ambivalent process than the one usually depicted—colonization occurred, but so did nativization; military power came up against economic dependency. It also shows that the boundaries between colonist and native, between Cossack and "enemy," indeed between Russia and "the Orient," could be rather loose and at times nonexistent. And I hope it proves the need to reconceptualize the empire "from the outside in" and "the bottom up," since life at the edge was often quite different from what policy makers in St. Petersburg imagined or desired.

Seventeenth-Century Trading Frontiers

To understand Terek Cossack trade in the eighteenth and nineteenth centuries, we must first sketch out an earlier backdrop. The Russian forts and Cossack *stanitsy* (villages) that popped up along the Terek River in the sixteenth and seventeenth centuries were part of the frontier economy of the north Caucasus, an economy that existed in the interstices between three great states (Russia, Persia, and Turkey) and drew nourishment from each, in trade and in plunder. The history of the Terek Cossacks before the eighteenth century is sketchy, but it is clear that they, like most of the peoples of the north Caucasus, supplemented their existence in a less than bountiful mountain terrain through thieving and trading. The richest targets for the Cossacks were the Persian merchants sailing to and from Astrakhan, the traders traveling the Caspian coastal road, and the towns along the same. The Cossack pirates of the Caspian were the scourge of Persian merchants; they became so aggressive that Persian traders quit sailing the Caspian for a few years sometime before 1650 and again after 1668, when Stenka Razin and his gang—some of whom were Terek Cossacks—began their Caspian raids.[6] As late as 1737, the Persian consul in St. Petersburg complained of the Russian pirates on the Caspian, operating with some seventy boats from an island base near Baku.[7]

Booty is of limited value without a market—Cossacks or Chechens could use only so much Persian silk or so many rugs. They had to sell it or trade it for something else, and thus the Russian fort town of Terskii gorod and Astrakhan became important outlets for plundered goods.[8] Petitions from Persian diplomats in the seventeenth century accused the *voevody* (administrators) of Terskii gorod and Astrakhan of regularly receiving illicit goods. The Dutch traveler Jan Struys traveled to Terskii gorod in

1670, where he heard of a prince on the other side of the Terek who habitually gathered an army of 15,000 that went on plundering sprees and then sold the goods at the twice-weekly Terskii gorod bazaar. The plunder-market nexus was so well established that Astrakhan merchants could put in orders for stolen foreign goods with Terek Cossacks via Russian servitors at Terskii gorod; they then resold them at relatively low prices at Astrakhan, undercutting the trade of Indian, Bukharan, and Persian merchants there.[9]

It would be wrong, though, to see seventeenth- and early-eighteenth-century trade along the Terek as simply a by-product of banditry. The Terek Cossacks made wine and sold it at Terskii gorod.[10] Even more important, they collected roots of wild madder and sold it to Persian merchants who used it to dye silk and other textiles. According to an Astrakhan tradesman in 1650, Persian ships came by the hundreds to buy madder from Terek Cossacks, and "without this grass there would be no dyeing at all in Persia." In the same year, Aleksei Silin of Kazan reported to Tsar Aleksei Mikhailovich that people along the Terek were receiving "large profits" from madder: they sent many boats filled with large bales of the root to Persia, and traders from Persia, Gilian, and Bukhara came to the Terek and exchanged their wares for madder. Cossack traders also traveled to Astrakhan to purchase goods such as sackcloth and lead for resale at Terskii gorod and across the Terek.[11] Pirates, highwaymen, and marauders, but also traders, wine merchants, and wild plant hunters, the Terek Cossacks of the seventeenth century carved out their niche on a violent but potentially lucrative frontier, far from the center of Russian power.

Whereas their remoteness from the center permitted the Cossacks and Terskii gorod servitors ample opportunity to enjoy the profit of plunder, it also meant that they often had a difficult time receiving food and supplies from the homeland. Grain provisions were sent down the Volga, through Astrakhan, and across the Caspian, but this supply line was long and tenuous, and if the food did arrive, it was far from sufficient to feed the local population. There was also little progress in establishing a peasant agricultural base until the early nineteenth century.

So the settlers often had to trade for grain with the local population, especially if something disrupted the grain shipment from Russia. The voevody of Terskii gorod referred to the "Circassian" lands as their granary, and if there were harvest failures to the south, the Terek settlers often suffered.[12] During the Time of Troubles in the early seventeenth century, provisions from Russia were cut off, and residents of Terskii gorod bought grain from Kabardians, Kumyks, and the towns of Derbent and Gilian; when there was a bad harvest in the Kumyk and "Circassian" lands a few years later in 1614, the Russian settlers had a difficult time of it until the convoy from the north resumed. In 1672 the supply of Kabardian and Kumyk grain to Terskii gorod was curtailed because of a campaign by the

Crimean khan in those lands, and only a few were able to go to the Terek to sell their millet, barley, and vegetables. According to the report of a Terek musketeer, prices for barley and millet skyrocketed, and "now Russian people on the Terek suffer great hunger," expending everything on food, including their guns. Many left for what they hoped would be greener pastures.[13]

Settlers and the State: The Limits of Control

As long as there was a Russian fort on the Terek, some degree of customs regulation and tariff collection was maintained, but trade was loosely controlled and, outside the palisade walls, totally free. With the founding of Kizliar in 1735 and the Kizliar customshouse in 1755 and the enticement of the Cossacks into Russian service, the state moved a little closer, and the customs policies of the center began to have an effect on the frontier trade of the north Caucasus. The rhythms of trade and customs control along the Terek were quite regular for the next century: the government would impose tariffs or try to channel trade through state trading posts, hoping to garner more income for the treasury. Then the Russian settlements—dependent as they were on a free flow of goods from the south—would suffer, as would the native traders, and customs policy would be relaxed for a decade or two until the next round of control began. The local commanders, realizing the dire straits the forts and settlements could be put in with a cessation of trade, sided with the native traders and the Russian subjects, all of whom petitioned for a free flow of necessary goods. Even the Kabardian delegation that went to St. Petersburg in 1764 to request the destruction of the new Russian fort of Mozdok asked at the same time for reduced trade tariffs at Kizliar.[14]

The food needs of hungry settlers immediately challenged the new tariff regime. The commander of Kizliar, A. A. Stupishin, reported to the College of Foreign Affairs in 1761 how the residents of Kizliar were always complaining to him about the trade tariffs "because of a lack of crops in Kizliar," and that the duties on the Kumyks' flour, millet, rice, honey, and walnuts "are bringing them to extreme ruin and grief." Central officials feared that reduced tariffs would lead to an outflow of Russian grain to the mountain dwellers, whom they assumed to be destitute and hungry. In order to persuade them otherwise, the next commander of Kizliar, N. A. Potapov, in his 1764 project for gortsy trade privileges, stated emphatically that grain and fruit should be freely traded "because more will be brought here than taken away." In 1765 the government gave in and allowed duty-free trade by Kumyks and Kabardians of food and other necessities, but only in Kizliar. This was an important decision—one official reported that up to the establishment of the quarantine in Kizliar in the early nineteenth century, the bulk of its grain came from the Kumyks.[15]

The appearance of the plague in the north Caucasus at the beginning of the nineteenth century made the Russian government much more concerned about regulating the flow of goods and people across the line of forts and stanitsy called the Caucasus Military Line that separated the gortsy from the settlers. After it first appeared in a village near Georgievsk in April 1804, the plague spread back and forth across the Terek to Russian forts and Kabardian villages; by the time it had made its way to the Tatar suburbs of Astrakhan in December 1806, the disease had killed at least 802 people in the Caucasus province and many times more in the uncontrolled areas across the Terek. In 1807–1809 quarantine posts and cordons were created along all of the borders of the Caucasus province, and fishing along the Terek was prohibited.[16] The subsequent "Statutes on Trade with the Gortsy" issued by the Committee of Ministers in 1810 inaugurated a new level of trade regulation in the north Caucasus.

By the new rules, six trading posts and four salt magazines were established along the military line, through which gortsy goods were supposed to pass, after a "cleansing" period that could last a few or up to forty days. At the trading posts, gortsy goods were free of tariffs, and they could be exchanged there at fixed prices for state salt and, theoretically, grain. There were bona fide health reasons for quarantining imported goods, but an equally powerful motive behind the new trade cordon was to make the people of the mountains dependent upon Russia for salt, which was almost the only Russian good stocked in the bins of trading posts until they were reorganized and their numbers increased in 1846.[17] This was no small matter, since salt—essential for livestock and preserving food—was scarce in the mountains, and the Ingush, Ossetians, and Kabardians had nowhere else to turn.[18]

Of course, Russian trade policy with the gortsy was directly connected to attempts to conquer the region through winning over, subduing, killing, or exiling the native inhabitants. Creating a salt dependency was one such tool. Forts or the central government also issued periodic bans on selling weapons or materials used for making weapons such as iron and steel. There was also a fair amount of scheming about how to draw the gortsy into the Russian orbit peacefully, through an expansion of trade. This resembled Catherine II's project for enlightened rule of the empire's natives, which included plans for whetting the appetite of her steppe peoples for Russian goods, thereby increasing trade and inculcating among the natives "new modes of behavior" appropriate for imperial subjects.[19]

Plans for the Caucasian tribes ranged from the narrow and practical to the visionary. Colonel M. Chaikovskii proposed to get the belligerents to trade in their weapons and metal for grain and salt (as naive as all weapons trade-in programs); the statesman Platon Zubov held out the visionary hope that trade would create new gortsy demands for European goods, and that gradually "their needs could be increased and luxury goods made a necessity," and they would lay down their arms and become good, civilized Europeans. "Luxury," wrote Zubov, "is the first step toward the education of the wild tribes." Most were more restrained in their dreaming and argued, as did the viceroy of the Caucasus, M. S. Vorontsov, that "trade is one of the most important and effective means toward our sblizhenie with the gortsy," and sought to use trade to win trust, change tastes, and make the "wild tribes" dependent upon Russia.[20] But ties of dependency are never clear-cut on distant frontiers, situated as they are at the edge of national economy and state power. The sblizhenie that policy makers dreamed of never came to be; instead the opposite happened, and trade drew the Cossacks into the world of the mountain people, nativized their material culture, and occasionally led them to subvert state policy.

The Cossacks needed frontier trade as much as the gortsy did and were threatened by every attempt to curtail or cut off trans-Terek exchange. Cossacks traded salt, melons, pumpkins, garden vegetables, sackcloth, cast-iron pots, fish, and fish products mostly to Kumyks, Chechens, and Kabardians, for a wide variety of essential goods—livestock, grain, firewood, lumber, and domestically produced wares such as clothes, carts, and weapons. With the tightening of customs control beginning in the eighteenth century, the Cossacks did what they could to continue their free trade across the Terek. As residents of all of the fort towns of the North Caucasus, they suffered just like everyone else from the price increases and periodic shortages caused by tariff policies. The situation in the stanitsy along the Terek was somewhat different because of their proximity to the gortsy and their distance from Kizliar officials. At first it seems that they simply ignored the rules—the Kizliar customshouse reported in 1765 that Cossacks did not collect tariffs in their stanitsy and that an unregulated free trade continued there, with the collusion of their commanding officers.[21] They also tried to get the tariff policy overturned—one of the *nakazy* (petitions) of the Greben Cossacks for Catherine II's Legislative Commission of 1767–68 requested that the *voisko* be allowed its previous tariff-free trade of salted fish to the gortsy for oxcart wheels, clothes, and other domestic wares, and of Kalmyk horses and cattle for Kabardian and other mountain horses.[22]

As open resistance became less possible, Cossacks diverted more of their trade through well-established underground channels. The history of smuggling is difficult to snoop out since the practice was—by definition—largely invisible. And since Cossacks along the line were the ones responsible for interdiction, a conflict of interest was created and many sentries undoubtedly looked the other way as their stanitsa-mates tried to keep the goods flowing. Smuggling was known to be common. S. M. Bronevskii, who served many years in the Caucasus, called it a normal

*A Greben Cossack in a watchtower scanning the
distance for enemy mountaineers, cattle and sheep
rustlers, kidnappers, and smugglers (Drawing
from an album by P. I. Chelishchev)*

practice and estimated that the value of contraband trade was more than
twice that of the official trade with the gortsy. Horses were one oft-
smuggled good. Before the establishment of the Kizliar customshouse,
Cossacks usually bought Kalmyk horses for a low price and then traded
them for much-sought-after Kabardian horses, which were more suitable
for the mountain terrain. In the face of the new customs, instead of paying
the tariffs Cossacks raided Nogais in the steppe, stole their horses, and
then drove them to the other side of the Terek, where they bartered for
Kabardian breeds. Cossacks also slipped their dugout canoes across the
Terek to trade (and steal) during health quarantines.[23]

Since the government salt monopoly went to the heart of Cossack
frontier exchange, it was natural that salt would be a favorite smuggled

commodity. Gortsy would cross the line, buy or trade freely for salt, and then sneak back to the mountains, avoiding the customs posts, or Cossacks took it across the river themselves. The inspector of one trading post reported that the sale of salt had nearly stopped at seven posts after new Cossack-manned forts were established farther into the interior of Kabardia in the 1820s—Cossacks would simply bring salt from other towns and trade or sell it to gortsy at these non-quarantine settlements. Another inspector recommended in 1839 the cessation of all "impermissible relations" between Cossacks and gortsy, particularly the trade in salt. Again in 1851, a trading post inspector, reporting on the fall of the state salt trade, wrote that the Cossacks of the Gortsy and Volga regiments "supply the Kabardians with it [salt] in quantities of no small importance through sale and trade, and they, being provided abundant supplies of this necessity by the Cossacks, have no great need for state salt." He went on, "I have no power to cut off this abuse."[24]

The Cossacks also continued to receive gortsy goods through the services of Armenian middlemen. These traders had begun settling in the north Caucasus in the eighteenth century, encouraged by the Russian authorities to move from Persia and the Islamic khanates on the Caspian to their own lands. The Armenians traveled to the mountain villages, bought or traded for the full range of goods, and then carted their stock back across the line to sell to Cossacks and other settlers. The Armenians of the north Caucasus—living in Kizliar, Mozdok, Cossack stanitsy, and their own villages—were especially well suited for this role and came to dominate the region's trade. They were exempted from service and had special tax-free status until 1836, they spoke mountain languages, and they often shared a common culture with the mountain communities from which some had only recently emigrated.[25] Armenian traders sold or traded their imports at a dearer price than the going rate across the military line, and this caused resentment with local officials, who upbraided them for their "self-interested motives" and periodically cooked up proposals to ban Armenians from mountain trading. But their enterprising spirit was unrivaled, and their profits were legendary as they hauled north everything from Circassian honey to Chechen oxcarts.[26]

The most important Cossack sources for gortsy goods in the nineteenth century were the trade fairs and bazaars in the fort towns and stanitsy, where Armenians traded their stock, and which mountaineers frequented to offer their livestock, grain, and homemade wares. The growing market trade along the Caucasus Military Line was the major reason for the failure of the trading posts—despite the distance, quarantines, and the tariffs and entry fees, the gortsy preferred to engage in the free-flowing commerce of the market square, where the prices were unregulated and the goods and customers more plentiful. Travelers to the north Caucasus were often

Terek Cossacks photographed at the beginning of the 1860s with papakhas, cherkeskas, *and arms probably obtained from mountain people. Notice the* kinzhals *attached to their belts and the* shashkas *held by the sitting Cossacks. (From* Im Kaukasus *[Berlin, 1862])*

surprised to see the throngs of gortsy in the towns and villages, swamping the local population during market days. Iu. Shidlovskii captured the diversity and vitality of the Kizliar bazaar in 1843:

> You see Ossetians selling cheese and felt cloaks, Circassians with green honeycombs of wild bees, Lezgins with copper vessels, Kists and Chechens with muskets and sabers, Karanogais with sheep and goats, Kalmyk sheepskin coats, coltskin coats, and lambskins, Terek Cossacks with weapons and fish. The Kumyks of Kostek bring firewood and stakes for grapevines, those from Aksai spread out leather and sheep's wool, Armenians and Georgians offer you apples, vegetables, and fruits. And there, closer to the Terek, ruddy Cossacks from Dubovskaia, Chervlennaia, Naurskaia, and other stanitsy of the Terek sit on oxcarts loaded with watermelons, melons, cucumbers, beets, cabbage, etc. . . . . Camels, rocking Turkmen on their two-humped, well-loaded backs, tower above the crowds.[27]

Gortsy sold and traded their goods at four types of market venues on the Russian side of the Terek: *iarmarki* (trade fairs held for several days or up to two weeks once or twice a year), bazaars (usually open two or three times a week), permanent shops, and informal markets that developed at new forts. By 1849 there were forty-nine iarmarki in the Stavropol' (previously Caucasus) province and along the Caucasus Military Line, at Cossack stanitsy, fort towns, and state peasant villages. The most popular iarmarka, in the town of Georgievsk, drew around 25,000 people at its peak in the 1850s; the most popular Cossack iarmarka, in the stanitsa of Naur, drew some 6,500. All of the towns and many of the stanitsy and peasant villages also had bazaars and shops. There were 302 permanent shops in the 113 stanitsy along the military line in 1849.[28]

Despite the potential for violence at these multiethnic gatherings, where there were plenty of weapons and people who were used to killing each other, markets and bazaars were remarkably peaceful, a tribute more to the importance that they held for all sides than to the ability of the Russian guards to keep control. Self-restraint was the order of the day. At the iarmarka of Naur stanitsa, it was said that not a single Chechen had ever been observed to rob or swindle; if they committed some other offense, they were not whacked with the whip or the birch rod as were the Russians and Armenians, but simply sat it out in a pit for a day or two. Of the 78,000 gortsy who came to Kizliar between 1848 and 1852 to work or trade, only 14 were arrested, jailed, or deported.[29]

Life across the line was not so peaceful. The Russian campaign begun in the 1820s for conquest of the mountain tribes included the construction of Russian forts south of the Caucasus Military Line. The spread of these forts caused a massive upheaval in Chechen and Kumyk villages: advancing troops destroyed villages, clear-cut forests, burned fields and gardens, killed resisters, and pushed many people farther south and farther into the mountains. In areas of the northeast Caucasus, local trade was destroyed or disrupted. When General Ermolov built Groznyi in 1817 and the other first forts of the Sunzha Military Line along the Sunzha and Argun rivers, he wrecked the local grain trade as Kumyks and Chechens fled to the mountains to escape punitive expeditions. But every historical force creates counterforces, and the thrust of the army produced eddies of trade in its wake. Once a new fort was constructed, Cossacks were settled, and troops were billeted, spontaneous barter took place, which often evolved into informal bazaars called *satovki* (from the Turkish word *satma*, meaning "sale"). The fort Vozdvizhenskaia was built in 1844 as part of the Sunzha Line on the spot of the former Chechen village of Chakhkeri. At first the small remaining neighboring population was none too eager to have relations with the fort. After a few years, though, the fort population of up to 6,000 (depending on troop movements), demanding food and supplies, was an irresistible lure, and Chechens and Kumyks filed through the gates in large numbers bearing food, cattle, clothes, and weapons; dozens of families began to resettle there. The same occurred near other Sunzha Line forts, most of which had small garrisons and modest bazaars, except when a detachment of troops moved through, and then, wrote S. Ivanov, "crowds of people buying and selling swarm about as in Moscow's *gostinyi dvor* [main market]." According to one general, from 1834 to 1840 some 40,000 gortsy came to the Sunzha Line annually to trade and sell.[30]

Mountain Economies/Cossack Dependencies

The centuries of trade between mountaineer and Cossack shaped Cossack material culture and domestic economy. Although the Cossacks always blamed the time-consuming service requirements for their agricultural and artisanal failures, there were also economic, ecological, and practical reasons why gortsy goods were so popular. Gortsy traded a wide variety of produce, grain, animals and animal products, handicrafts, and raw materials such as furs and wood; we are concerned here with only a few commodities that help illustrate the importance of this trade to the frontier life of the Terek Cossacks.

As has already been indicated, before the mass settlement of state peasants and the development of a broad agricultural base in the north Caucasus in the mid-nineteenth century, Cossacks frequently traded with gortsy for grain. The ecology of the lower Terek made the Cossacks residing there especially dependent upon purchased grain—they could produce a fair grain harvest in some spots (with a five-to-one yield), but only after they cut irrigation canals from the Terek, an extremely labor-consuming task. Elsewhere the land was too wet, salty, or sandy for productive agriculture. Unlike the gortsy, who practiced sophisticated fertilization methods, the lower Terek Cossacks did not manure, and this also reduced their harvests. By the mid-eighteenth century, state grain deliveries were dependable, but still insufficient to meet their needs. And the task of conveying their grain salary from the Caspian Sea to their stanitsy was an arduous undertaking for the Cossacks; they often had to hire Nogais to help, paying them half of the load, which in turn fueled the need to purchase more grain. So they turned to Chechens, Kumyks, Kabardians, and other Cossacks for supplemental wheat, millet, and rice. The Cossacks of the central Terek (Mozdok, Mountain, and Volga regiments) were, on the other hand, largely self-sufficient with respect to grain.[31]

All of the Cossacks raised sheep and cattle in sufficient quantities for their own use, and the Mozdok regiment raised a surplus, which they traded at local fairs. Horse breeding—much more demanding than cattle or sheep husbandry—was a different matter. Some regiments did not raise horses at all, or raised them only in small quantities, and had to trade for or purchase mostly Kabardian horses; others had herds large enough for their own use. But for all of the Tertsy, Kabardian horses (renowned for their gentle temperament, lightness, agility, strength, endurance, quick gallop, strong hoofs, and simple diet) were the most desired. So, as P. Kishenskii observed in 1856, "a good Cossack buys his horse in Kabarda."[32]

The Terek Cossacks also traded for and wore the clothes of the gortsy, especially the *papakha* (tall sheepskin hat), *burka* (felt cloak), and *cherkeska* (long, narrow, collarless coat). In fact, they looked so much like the gortsy that local peasants and travelers in the Caucasus often mistook approaching Cossacks for hostile Chechens or Circassians. In 1828 the head of the Caucasus oblast', A. A. Vel'iaminov, took the drastic step of ordering Cossacks not to come closer than one-half verst to peasants working in fields since "the Cossacks of the Line wear clothes identical to those of the gortsy, [and] peasants are not able to distinguish enemies from the Cossacks."[33]

Clothes production was one of the oldest and best-established branches of the mountain domestic economy, so there was always an ample supply of these garments, which were well-suited for local conditions. The burka protected riders from rain, snow, cold, heat, and wind, and could serve as a ground cover when resting or sleeping, or be propped up as a small tent. With a burka on his shoulders, a rider hid his weapons from sight and protected them from the elements, especially important for flintlocks, which were useless when wet. Cherkeski protected the legs of riders without hindering movement and mounted sixteen to twenty cartridges on the chest, a handy spot for quick loading. When the Kizliar commander recommended a tariff-free trade of burki and similar handicrafts in 1765, he made sure to mention their military utility.[34]

Wood was another gortsy commodity of great importance to the Cossacks. The Terek River region of settlement, at the edge of the steppe and the foot of the mountains, had only a thin belt of accessible forest. Although settlers rarely built wooden houses in the early days of Kizliar and Mozdok (reeds, clay, and straw were the materials used), wooden construction became more popular and in places the norm by the late eighteenth century. With the growth in the number of forts, stanitsy, and peasant villages, settlers quickly consumed the forests, and there came to be an insatiable demand for not just lumber but also firewood, vineyard stakes, and various wooden tools and other products. This developed into probably the largest-volume trade with the gortsy; each year Kumyks, Chechens, and Kabardians floated hundreds of rafts down the Terek and led thousands of oxcarts full of wood and wood products to Cossack stanitsy and fort towns.[35]

Deforestation was one reason why Cossacks also quickly adopted the native oxcart (*arba*). It was light and durable and, with only two large wheels widely spaced apart, could negotiate a variety of terrains. Cossacks hitched up arby not only for domestic work but also for state service, since they were responsible for much of the carting work in the north

Caucasus. Cossack dependency on the gortsy for arby became a matter of state concern when the imposition of tariffs on cross-Terek trade created such a shortage of arby and arba wheels in 1771 that Cossacks were no longer able to cart supplies for the army between Kizliar and Mozdok. They explained that their source had been cut off when the tariff walls went up, and that they did not have the time or the forest to produce arby themselves. The affair went to the State Senate, which ordered local commanders to force the Cossacks to trade for arby and pay the required tariffs. Arba trade continued to be big business for gortsy through the mid-nineteenth century, and they also cornered the market on spare parts, such as wheels.[36]

One of the greatest ironies of the Russian conquest of the north Caucasus is that Cossacks were armed by gortsy silversmiths and metalworkers. The Cossack weaponry—the *shashka* (sword), the *kinzhal* (dagger), and, until the mid-nineteenth century, the mountain musket—was manufactured mostly in native villages and obtained through trade. Weapons production was an ancient craft in the north Caucasus, where the secrets of master craftsmen were highly guarded and passed down from father to son; by the nineteenth century, some villages had advanced to the point of dividing up the production process with gun "assembly lines." The Russian esteem for gortsy weaponry had an equally long lineage: already in the seventeenth century, Russian forts were trading for "Circassian" weapons, coats of mail, and headpieces, and the central government was trying to attract north Caucasus armorers to Astrakhan and Moscow to train apprentices.[37] Through the nineteenth century, the majority of the silversmiths, smithies, and metalworkers in the fort towns of the north Caucasus were gortsy; Kabardian masters were even in Cherkassk making guns and swords for the Don Cossacks. This skewed the development of handicraft production north of the military line—Russians and Cossacks did not engage in metal handicrafts, preferring to obtain weapons from gortsy and other metal goods from the north.[38]

The mountain economy that was able to flood Cossack markets with so many highly valued goods, in the context of often minimal natural resources and the repeated disruptions of war and conquest, was one of great productivity and sophistication. All families produced handicrafts, and the women—the main producers of textiles and clothes—seemed to be continually working. More than one observer noticed how mountain women were always seen with work in their hands, sewing cherkeski or working a spindle even when walking between villages or trading at Cossack fairs. Gortsy engaged in wool, leather, metal, wooden, and silk handicrafts; according to a late-nineteenth-century survey, they were involved in a total of thirty-two different domestic industries (compared to the north Caucasus Russians' seventeen).[39]

People living in the alpine region (7,200 feet to 10,800 feet above sea level) were limited mostly to working with wool, and they lived so far from the major markets that they could not afford to cart their wares there. But their products made it to the Russian side also, with the help of Armenian traders and a system of mountain exchange whereby grain, salt, and other necessities moved up from the plains and wool handicrafts worked their way down from the mountains, sometimes through several exchanges. Some peoples or villages specialized in one or two types of products for trade; for example, several Dagestan and Chechen villages specialized in kinzhaly, shashki, or guns, and the mountain Jews were known for their dressed goatskins and the skins of young lambs (used to make papakhi). But gortsy also responded to the Russian market and broadened their product mix. In the first quarter of the nineteenth century, some forty different gortsy items were registered in trading post lists; by the 1840s the list had more than doubled.[40]

The plunder-market nexus that had been so strong in the seventeenth century continued to exist, although it is difficult to calculate how important it was to the local economy. The large herds of cattle and sheep—sometimes thousands of animals—that Terek Cossacks periodically rustled during punitive raids across the Terek must have, in part, made their way to market.[41] On the gortsy side, the Cossacks were convinced that a good amount of the money that Chechens received for ransoming captives was spent at Russian iarmarki. When N. Samarin visited the stanitsa of Naur, Cossacks told him that Shamil's men, after releasing the captive Georgian princesses Chavchavadze and Orbeliani in 1854, spent all of the 40,000-ruble ransom money at the Nikolaevskaia stanitsa fair, and that 20,000 rubles was pocketed by one Armenian alone. While this story smacks of typical frontier boasting, it is true that the ransom money that gortsy collected had to find an outlet, and that the markets along the Russian line were the most likely destination. Sometimes the captors skipped a step and simply made a desired commodity, such as tea, part of the ransom.[42]

Mountain captives were also a venerable commodity of exchange along the north Caucasus frontier. Gortsy sold slaves and prisoners to Russian subjects at the chattel market of the Kumyk village of Enderi and at Kizliar itself, until this practice was outlawed in the early nineteenth century. The commander of the Kizliar fortress reported in 1804 that the residents of Enderi became "well enriched" from this business. Armenians worked as middlemen in this trade too, until they were prohibited by a law of 1804 from "dragging them [slaves] in chains and selling them in Kizliar and at other places." Up to the emancipation of the serfs, Cossacks and other Russian subjects of the north Caucasus were also allowed to ransom captives from enemy gortsy, who then became indentured servants if they could not reimburse the purchase price. Published sources do not reveal the extent of Cossack participation in this trade, but we know that it did occur. Because of the lack of peasants and serfs, there was a severe labor shortage in the north Caucasus (and one of the most important branches of the Cossack economy—viticulture—was extremely labor-intensive), so captive purchase was a good way of picking up an extra hand or two and gave those Cossacks who could afford it a vested interest in gortsy kidnapping. Some Cossacks also went bounty hunting for "Circassians," hunting them "like game," killing them and trading the bodies to their relatives for money or for Russian captives.[43]

The trading frontiers of the Terek Cossacks also faced north: Tertsy traded with Nogais and Kalmyks for livestock and with Russians and local Armenians for manufactured goods. There is no space here to detail this or the fate of the Cossack trade in the fort towns. Suffice it to say that the Cossack's wine trade—their most important trade in the eighteenth century—was in the nineteenth century still a source of profit for Cossacks of the lower Terek, but in decline as a result of state alcohol farming, low prices, and Armenian competition. It was unfortunate that they fixed on a commodity of limited use to their Islamic trading partners. Cossacks still collected madder roots, but after 1757 they had to sell them to Russian merchants or their middlemen. Other Cossacks sold some honey, beeswax, or animal skins, and the Greben and Volga Cossacks also made a good living as truck farmers. Trade with the gortsy did not remain static either. With the destructive push of Russian forces into the Kumyk and Chechen plains in the 1840s and the establishment of a vibrant agrarian economy in the Kuban region and the North Caucasus steppe, the center of economic gravity in the north Caucasus moved north and west, and the lights of Stavropol', Ekaterinodar, and Vladikavkaz brightened, while those of Kizliar and the lower Terek stanitsy grew dimmer.[44]

Most contemporaries also agreed that by the mid-nineteenth century, Cossack artisanal activity barely existed. A statistical survey of the Caucasus oblast' prepared by the Ministry of Internal Affairs in 1830 stated: "The Cossacks settled here, continually on service, do not have time to devote themselves exclusively to any type of handicraft, and the Cossacks who are retired because of old age or infirmity are incapable of it; therefore the women of the regiments engage in handicrafts only as much as is needed to satisfy their domestic demands." The commander of the Semeinoe-Kizliarskoe regiment reported in 1839 that his Cossacks "do not engage in handicrafts" and wear "Asian" clothes, "which the majority of them buy." Again, in 1856, P. Kishenskii was surprised to observe that industry (promyshlennost') did not exist among the Cossacks and that they purchased all of their needs—burki, guns, Kabardian horses, cloth for cherkeski, leather for boots. It would be good, he advised, for Cossacks to develop some industries such as leatherworks, textiles, viticulture, or agriculture, because then the Stavropol' commissary could buy from them, as could the gortsy, who would in time become dependent on Cossack wares. It was an old dream.[45]

Thus, the great divide between the Cossack servants of Russia and the enemy mountaineers blurs upon close inspection of life on the north Caucasus frontier. There was a continual flow of goods between the two sides, through legal market relations and underground channels. Even the mountain banditry and kidnapping that so many Petersburg writers represented as a mortal threat to settlers and an affront to Russian morals stimulated local trade and provided occasional riches for the Cossack markets.

The economy of the mountains was not as backward as many writers and policy makers had imagined; we must conclude that one reason why gortsy never became dependent on Russian manufactured goods was that their economy was more advanced than that of their trans-Terek neighbors, or at least more capable of producing commodities for local trade. And the Cossack hunger for mountain products was not just a result of their remoteness from the center or of service requirements that gave them little time to devote to manufacture and trade. It was also a product of the limitations of their landscape of settlement (hence the grain trade) and the transformation of that landscape by settlers and the army. Every new village that popped up in the tree-hungry steppe and foothills and every stand of trees that was chopped down to create a military road boosted the demand for an item that the gortsy could best provide. It is also ironic how gortsy-Cossack trade was facilitated by the religiously charged policy of the Russian administration of encouraging Armenian migration to their lands. Instead of producing religious division, the resettlement created a social force in the north Caucasus that greatly expanded trade with the Islamic people of the mountains, making it nearly impossible to control by the Russian state. Frontier exchange had a dynamic of its own that often worked against the policies of the center.

The ambiguity of cross-Terek trade is only one aspect of the complex frontier society of the Terek Cossacks. A frontier history of settlers such as the Cossacks helps to uncover themes that usually go unnoticed in the well-known metahistory of Russian colonial conquest—the story of a group of independent settlers (the Terek Cossacks) that is transformed into a service estate with severely proscribed liberties and the pacification of the rebellious native peoples. Between these broad strokes are other, equally significant details—stateless villages; nativized frontier cultures, societies, and economies; and an ecology that conditioned colonization.

By the mid-ninteenth century, Russia had incorporated the north Caucasus into the empire. But the Russian state and the Russian economy were not powerful enough to assimilate the region; officials had no choice but to overlook, for example, the widespread smuggling and yield to a degree of economic dependency. But in the end, perhaps we should see this as a strength and not a weakness of Russian imperialism. One of the reasons why the Russian Empire grew relentlessly, incorporating so many different cultures, languages, religions, and economies, was that it tolerated a degree of diversity and spontaneity that would have been unthinkable in other empires. That, after all, is one of the important themes of Cossack history; Cossacks occupied a space in the empire somewhere between subservience and freedom, between loyalty and independence, between the chain of command and the needs of their communities, and in the north Caucasus, between Russia and "the East."

NOTES

Some of the research for this chapter was conducted under the auspices of a Fulbright grant at the Helsinki University Slavonic Library.

1. The Greben Cossacks—the first group of what was to become the Terek Cossack *voisko*—originally settled in the north Caucasus mountains in the mid-sixteenth century. They resettled to the left bank of the Terek and entered into Russian service in 1711–12. Some Cossacks also lived in the lower Terek region in the sixteenth century; they served in the Russian forts there and also became a part of the Terek voisko. (A voisko was the largest Cossack military/administrative unit and comprised *polki* [regiments], which were themselves subdivided into *stanitsy* [villages].)

2. T. M., "Korrespondentsiia 'Illiustrirovannoi gazety' s Kavkaza," *Illiustrirovannaia gazeta,* 5 January 1867, p. 11.

3. Russians used the term *gortsy* to mean the mountain- and foothill-dwelling people of the north Caucasus; the term could include everyone from the Adyge in the west to the peoples of Dagestan in the east. This chapter will be concerned with the mountaineers who had the most contact with the Terek Cossacks—for the most part Kabardians, Ossetians, Chechens, and Kumyks. "Gortsy" will be used to mean these people of the north-central and northeast Caucasus, and when the original source does not allow a more precise ethnic designation.

4. John F. Baddeley, *The Russian Conquest of the Caucasus* (London, 1908); W. E. D. Allen and Paul Muratoff, *Caucasian Battlefields* (Cambridge, 1953); Moshe Gammer, *Muslim Resistance to the Tsar: Shamil and the Conquest of Chechnia and Daghestan* (London, 1994); and Marie Bennigsen Broxup, ed., *The North Caucasus Barrier: The Russian Advance towards the Muslim World* (New York, 1992). For a more complete review of the historiography of the north Caucasus, see Thomas M. Barrett, "Lines of Uncertainty: The Frontiers of the north Caucasus," *Slavic Review* 54, no. 3 (1995): 578–601.

5. The best general Soviet histories of the north Caucasus are B. B. Piotrovskii, ed., *Istoriia narodov Severnogo Kavkaza s drevneishikh vremen do kontsa XVIII v.* (Moscow, 1988), and A. L. Narochnitskii, ed., *Istoriia narodov Severnogo Kavkaza (konets XVIII v.–1917 g.)* (Moscow, 1988). These still portray the conquest as tsarist "colonial politics" that was counteracted by the friendship of Russian settlers with

the native peoples. Three excellent bibliographies on the history of the north Caucasus are M. M. Miansarov, *Bibliographia Caucasica et Transcaucasica* (St. Petersburg, 1874–76); Narochnitskii, *Istoriia narodov Severnogo Kavkaza*, pp. 614–653; and Moshe Gammer, "Shamil and the Murid Movement, 1830–1859: An Attempt at a Comprehensive Bibliography," *Central Asian Survey* 10, nos. 1/2 (1991): 189–247.

6. "Otryvok nakaza Astrakhanskim voevodam, boiarinu kniazu Mikhailu Pronskomu, okol'nichemu Timofeiu Buturlinu i Il'e Bezobrazovu," *AI* 4 (1842): 129–144; I. Popko, *Terskie kazaki s starodavnikh vremen. Istoricheskii ocherk* (St. Petersburg, 1880), pp. 73–74; *Krest'ianskaia voina pod predvoditel'stvom Stepana Razina. Sbornik dokumentov*, vol. 1 (Moscow, 1954), pp. 120, 140, and 141.

7. P. G. Butkov, *Materialy dlia novoi istorii Kavkaza s 1722 po 1803 god*, vol. 1 (St. Petersburg, 1869), p. 168.

8. Terskii gorod was founded on the lower Terek in 1588.

9. Popko, *Terskie kazaki*, pp. 73–74; Ia. Ia. Streis [J. J. Struys], *Tri puteshestviia* (Moscow, 1935), pp. 212–214; V. A. Potto, *Dva veka Terskago kazachestva (1577–1801)*, vol. 2 (Vladikavkaz, 1912), p. 65.

10. "Tsarskaia gramota Astrakhanskim voevodam kniaz'iam Pronskomu i Volkonskomu, i otpiska ikh Terskim voevodam Volynskomu i Shapilovu, o vydelke vina, dlia opyta, iz rastushchago po Tereku vinograda," *AI* 4 (1842): 177–179.

11. "Otryvok nakaza," pp. 129–144; N. B. Golikova, *Ocherki po istorii gorodov Rossii kontsa XVII–nachala XVIII v.* (Moscow, 1982), p. 71.

12. "Circassian" (Cherkess) was often used to mean gortsy in general, and not specifically the peoples of the northwest Caucasus.

13. Piotrovskii, *Istoriia narodov Severnogo Kavkaza*, p. 356; E. N. Kusheva, *Narody Severnogo Kavkaza i ikh sviazi s Rossiei. Vtoraia polovina XVI–30-e gody XVII veka* (Moscow, 1963), pp. 107–108, 299; T. Kh. Kumykov and E. N. Kusheva, eds., *Kabardino-russkie otnosheniia v XVI–XVIII vv. Dokumenty i materialy*, 2 vols. (Moscow, 1957), vol. 1, p. 333 (henceforth *KRO*).

14. *Akty sobrannye Kavkazskoiu Arkheograficheskoiu komissieiu*, 12 vols. (Tiflis, 1866–1905), vol. 1, p. 81 (henceforth *AKAK*).

15. N. P. Gritsenko, *Goroda severo-vostochnogo Kavkaza i proizvoditel'nye sily kraia V–seredina XIX veka* (Rostov-on-Don, 1984), p. 109; *KRO*, vol. 2, pp. 215–218, 229–230, and 244–250; A. V. Fadeev, *Rossiia i Kavkaz pervoi treti XIX v.* (Moscow, 1960), pp. 63–65; *AKAK*, vol. 4 (Tiflis, 1870), p. 37.

16. V. S. Shamrai, "Kratkii ocherk menovykh (torgovykh) snoshenii po Chernomorskoi kordonnoi i beregovoi linii s zakubanskimi gorskimi narodami," *Kubanskii sbornik*, no. 8 (1902): 363 and 383; N. Varadinov, *Istoriia ministerstva vnutrennikh del*, vol. 1 (St. Petersburg, 1858), pp. 133–134 and 171. In May 1818, Ermolov reported that the plague had killed nearly one-fourth of the population of Kabardia. See "Iz proshlago Dagestanskoi oblasti (po mestnym arkhivnym dannym)," *Dagestanskii sbornik*, no. 2 (1904): 200–202.

17. T. Kh. Kumykov, *Vovlechenie Severnogo Kavkaza vo vserossiiskii rynok v XIX v.* (Nal'chik, 1962), pp. 25–28; Narochnitskii, *Istoriia narodov Severnogo Kavkaza* (Moscow, 1988), pp. 79–80.

18. Chechens, Kumyks, and the peoples of Dagestan were able to get salt from the *shamkhal* of Tarkovskii and the salt lakes along the Caspian Sea south of the Terek. See S. Sh. Gadzhieva, *Kumyki: Istoriko-etnograficheskoe issledovanie* (Moscow,

1961), p. 73; P. P. Nadezhdin, *Kavkazskii krai. Priroda i liudi*, 3rd ed. (Tula, 1901), pp. 56 and 59; Kumykov, *Vovlechenie Severnogo Kavkaza*, p. 111.

19. See Dov Yaroshevski, "Imperial Strategy in the Kirghiz Steppe in the Eighteenth Century," *Jahrbücher für Geschichte Osteuropas* 39 (1991): 221–224.

20. K. V. Sivkov, "O proektakh okonchaniia Kavkazskoi voiny v seredine XIX v.," *Istoriia SSSR*, no. 3 (May–June 1958): 192–196; Platon Zubov, *Kartina Kavkazskago kraia, prinadlezhashchego Rossii, i sopredel'nykh onomu zemel'* (St. Petersburg, 1834), pp. 71–82; *AKAK*, vol. 4, pp. 835–836; *AKAK*, vol. 10 (Tiflis, 1885), pp. 570–572; N. S. Mordvinov, "Mnenie admirala Mordvinova o sposobakh, koimi Rossii udobnee mozhno priviazat' k sebe postepenno Kavkazskikh zhitelei," *Chteniia v Imperatorskom obshchestve istorii i drevnosti rossiiskikh pri Moskovskom universitete* 4 (1858): section 5, pp. 109–112.

21. *KRO*, vol. 2, pp. 229–230, 237, and 239–244; Gritsenko, *Goroda Severovostochnogo Kavkaza*, pp. 109–111; Popko, *Terskie kazaki*, pp. 183–184.

22. "Materialy Ekaterinskoi zakonodatel'noi komissii," *Sbornik Imperatorskago Russkago istoricheskago obshchestva* 114 (1903): 490, 492.

23. S. M. Bronevskii, *Noveishie geograficheskie i istoricheskie izvestiia o Kavkaze* (Moscow, 1823), section 2, pp. 142–145; Potto, *Dva veka*, vol. 2, pp. 72–73; Popko, *Terskie kazaki*, pp. 177–180. According to Shamil's brother-in-law, even Shamil's men managed to smuggle lead, iron, and steel out of Groznyi and other border forts. See Georgii Paradov, "Rasskaz ochevidtsa o Shamile i ego sovremennikakh," *Sbornik materialov dlia opisaniia mestnostei i plemen Kavkaza* 32 (1903): section 1, p. 17.

24. Kumykov, *Vovlechenie severnogo Kavkaza*, pp. 29–35 and 110–111; A. V. Fadeev, ed., *Ocherki istorii Balkarskogo naroda (s drevneishikh vremen do 1917 goda)* (Nal'chik, 1961), p. 56.

25. Iu. Shidlovskii, "Zapiski o Kizliare," *Zhurnal Ministerstva vnutrennikh del* 4 (1843): 194–195 (henceforth *ZMVD*); N. G. Volkova, "O rasselenii Armian na Severnom Kavkaze do nachala XX veka," *Istoriko-filologicheskii zhurnal* 3 (1966): 259–261.

26. Shamrai, "Kratkii ocherk," pp. 363, 383, and 389; Iosif Debu, *O Kavkazskoi linii i prisoedinennom k nei Chernomorskom voiske* (St. Petersburg, 1829), pp. 80–81; *AKAK*, vol. 4, pp. 334–335; *AKAK*, vol. 10, pp. 570–571; Kumykov, *Vovlechenie Severnogo Kavkaza*, pp. 37–39 and 55–56.

27. Shidlovskii, "Zapiski o Kizliare," pp. 174–175.

28. Narochnitskii, *Istoriia narodov Severnogo Kavkaza*, p. 83; *Izvestiia Kavkazskago otdela Imperatorskago Russkago geograficheskago obshchestva* 5, no. 4 (1878): supplement, pp. 60–61 and 346–347; "Iarmarki na Kavkaze," *Kavkaz*, 16 February 1852, p. 50; A. V. Fadeev, *Ocherki ekonomicheskogo razvitiia stepnogo Predkavkaz'ia v doreformennyi period* (Moscow, 1957), pp. 197 and 205–210.

29. N. Samarin, "Dorozhnyia zametki," *Severnaia pchela*, 20 May 1862, p. 534; M, "Tatarskoe plemia na Kavkaze," *Kavkaz*, 19 November 1859, pp. 509–510.

30. V. A. Potto, *Kavkazskaia voina v otdel'nykh ocherkakh, epizodakh, legendakh i biografiiakh*, vol. 2 (St. Petersburg, 1885), pp. 90–91 and 97–98; K. Samoilov, "Zametki o Chechne," *Panteon* 23, no. 10 (October 1855): section 3, pp. 45–46; Fadeev, *Ocherki ekonomicheskogo razvitiia*, pp. 211, 215, and 220–221; S. Ivanov, "O sblizhenii gortsev s russkimi na Kavkaze," *Voennyi sbornik* 7 (1859): 541–547.

31. Potto, *Dva veka*, pp. 64–66; I. V. Rovinskii, *Khoziaistvennoe opisanie Astrakhanskoi i Kavkazskoi gubernii* (St. Petersburg, 1804), pp. 54–55; B. A. Kaloev, "Iz istorii russko-chechenskikh ekonomicheskikh i kul'turnykh sviazei," *Sovet-*

skaia etnografiia 1 (1961): 44; "Statisticheskiia svedeniia o Kavkazskoi oblasti i zemlei voiska Chernomorskago," *ZMVD* 3, no. 4 (1830): 123–130; Fadeev, *Ocherki ekonomicheskogo razvitiia*, pp. 156 and 160; Gadzhieva, *Kumyki*, pp. 101–103; Gritsenko, *Goroda Severo-vostochnogo Kavkaza*, p. 94; *KRO*, vol. 2, pp. 215–216; *Polnoe sobranie zakonov Rossiiskoi imperii* (St. Petersburg, 1830), vol. 19, pp. 517–518 (henceforth *PSZ*).

32. Rovinskii, *Khoziaistvennoe opisanie*, pp. 52–56; "Statisticheskiia svedeniia," pp. 131–140; A. V-v, "Kratkii ocherk Stavropol'skoi gubernii v promyshlennom i torgovom otnosheniiakh," *Kavkaz* 22 (1848): 84; P. K. [P. Kishenskii], "Vospominaniia o Grebenskikh kazakakh i Kavkazskoi linii," *Moskovskiia vedomosti*, 13 September 1856, pp. 463–465.

33. G. N. Prozritelev, comp., "Iz proshlogo severnogo Kavkaza. Materialy dlia istorii g. Stavropolia i Stavropol'skoi gub.," *Trudy Stavropol'skoi uchenoi arkhivnoi komissii* 2 (1910): section 4, pp. 19–23.

34. E. N. Studentskaia, *Odezhda narodov severnogo Kavkaza XVIII–XX vv.* (Moscow, 1989), pp. 82–87; *KRO*, vol. 2, pp. 245–248. For a few of the many statistics on this trade, see Kumykov, *Vovlechenie severnogo Kavkaza*, pp. 62–64 and 85–88. Burki also became fashionable with Russian officers serving in the Caucasus—there are well-known portraits of Ermolov, Lermontov, and Bestuzhev-Marlinskii wearing a burka cunningly draped across one shoulder.

35. Fadeev, *Ocherki ekonomicheskogo razvitiia*, p. 232; Rovinskii, *Khoziaistvennoe opisanie*, pp. 52–53; A. P. Berzhe, *Chechnia i Chechentsy* (Tiflis, 1859), pp. 87–89; A. I. Akhverdov, "Opisanie Dagestana. 1804 g.," in *Istoriia, geografiia i etnografiia Dagestana XVIII–XIX vv.* (Moscow, 1958), pp. 213–215; A. M. Pavlov, *Kratkoe obozrenie Kavkazskoi gubernii uezdnago goroda Kizliara* (Moscow, 1822), p. 7; M. Kriukov, "Putevyia zametki," *Kavkaz*, 8 October 1852, pp. 248–250; Narochnitskii, *Istoriia narodov severnogo Kavkaza*, p. 82. A total of more than 41,000 oxcarts of lumber passed through four central Terek quarantine posts in 1846, 1847, 1849, and 1852. See Kumykov, *Vovlechenie severnago Kavkaza*, pp. 65–66 and 93–96.

36. *PSZ*, vol. 19, pp. 267–268; Kumykov, *Vovlechenie severnogo Kavkaza*, p. 86.

37. Piotrovskii, *Istoriia narodov severnogo Kavkaza*, p. 356; *KRO*, vol. 1, pp. 322–327; G. N. Prozritelev, "Kavkazskoe oruzhie," *Trudy Stavropol'skoi uchenoi arkhivnoi komissii* 7 (1915): section 10, pp. 1–5; Samarin, "Dorozhnyia zametki," pp. 533–534.

38. O. V. Marggraf, *Ocherk kustarnykh promyslov severnogo Kavkaza s opisaniem tekhniki proizvodstva* (Moscow, 1882), pp. xiv–xl; *AKAK*, vol. 4, pp. 334–335; "Statisticheskiia izvestiia o Kavkazskoi oblasti i zemle voiska Chernomorskago," *ZMVD* 3, no. 5 (1830): 124–127.

39. Fadeev, *Ocherki istorii Balkarskogo naroda*, p. 54; Samarin, "Dorozhnyia zametki," pp. 533–534; Marggraf, *Ocherk kustarnykh promyslov*, pp. xiv–xl.

40. Berzhe, *Chechnia i Chechentsy*, pp. 87–89; Piotrovskii, *Istoriia narodov severnogo Kavkaza*, pp. 280–282; Samarin, "Dorozhnyia zametki," p. 533; Narochnitskii, *Istoriia narodov severnogo Kavkaza*, p. 80.

41. For three particularly lucrative raids, see V. P. Lystsov, *Persidskii pokhod Petra I* (Moscow, 1951), p. 98; "Materialy dlia statistiki Kizliarskago polka Terskago kazach'iago voiska," *Voennyi sbornik* 12 (1869): 213; and F. I. Soimonov, *Opisanie Kaspiiskago moria* (St. Petersburg, 1763), p. 102.

42. Samarin, "Dorozhnyia zametki," p. 534; Alexandre Dumas, *Adventures in Caucasia*, trans. A. E. Murch (Philadelphia, 1962), p. 67.

43. Shidlovskii, "Zapiski o Kizliare," pp. 179–181; Akhverdov, "Opisanie

Dagestana," pp. 213–229; *PSZ*, vol. 28, p. 245; V. S. Shamrai, "Istoricheskaia spravka k voprosu o iasyriakh na Severnom Kavkaze i v Kubanskoi oblasti i dokumenty otnosiashchietsia k etomu voprosu," *Kubanskii sbornik*, no. 12 (1907): 169–173; Popko, *Terskie kazaki*, pp. 299–302 and 426–428; Z...v, "Puteshestviia. Poezdka iz Moskvy za-Kavkaz," *Tiflisskiia vedomosti*, 10 July 1830, pp. 3–4.

44. "Statisticheskiia izvestiia," pp. 111–117; Popko, *Terskie kazaki*, pp. 175–177, 309–311, and 443–445; *PSZ*, vol. 14, pp. 793–794; Gritsenko, *Goroda severovostochnogo Kavkaza*, p. 96; Zubov, *Kartina Kavkazskago kraia*, pp. 126–128 and 130–132; I. S. Efimovyi, "O sovremennom sostoianii torgovli v gorode Stavropole," *Kavkaz*, 16 August 1852, pp. 196–197.

45. "Statisticheskiia izvestiia," pp. 124–127; F. Ponomarev, "Materialy dlia istorii Terskago kazach'iago voiska s 1559 po 1880 god," *Voennyi sbornik*, no. 12 (1880): 348–349; P. K., "Vospominaniia o grebenskikh kazakakh," pp. 463–465.

.12.

VIRGINIA MARTIN

Barïmta: Nomadic Custom, Imperial Crime

In 1822, the Russian government promulgated the *Ustav o Sibirskikh Kirgizakh* (Regulations on the Siberian Kirgiz),[1] which for the first time erected an administrative framework for colonial control over the Kazakh nomads of the Middle Horde. Although the tsarist regime had endeavored to use laws to control its steppe frontier since Kazakh clans first began submitting to Russian rule in 1731, the 1822 Regulations represent Russia's first systematic effort to enforce its imperial goals.[2] These goals included bringing and preserving order in the remote frontier region; introducing the Middle Horde nomads to the Russian, settled way of life; protecting the Russian population; and promoting trade.[3] The Regulations also involved the introduction of Russian legal norms to the native inhabitants of the steppe, with a recognition of the need to respect the distinct culture of the Kazakh nomads. This philosophy, introduced by Empress Catherine the Great through her policies promoting Islamic religion and education among the nomads, was further nurtured by Siberia's governor-general, Mikhail Speranskii, as he drafted laws for administrative incorporation of all of Siberia into the empire in 1822.[4] Speranskii's laws allowed the natives to judge internal affairs according to their own customs, as long as these did not infringe upon the goals of the imperial regime and the rights of the Russian population. Thus, according to the 1822 Regulations, Kazakhs could try all civil and criminal cases according to customary law (*adat*), with the exception of particularly harsh crimes, which were prosecuted within Russian legal jurisdictions. Aside from murder and treason, the most important new Kazakh "crime" was *barïmta*.

The 1822 Regulations defined barïmta as robbery or plunder (*grabezh*),[5] an act which the Russian government believed to be destabilizing, making it hard to administer and control the steppe, and making trade through the region problematic. It was viewed as an uncivilized act, and its perpetrators were barbarous criminals. By criminalizing barïmta, the Russian administration hoped to bring about its eventual disappearance. But to the nomads, barïmta was not a crime; rather, it was a legitimate judicial custom embedded in the Kazakh cultural understanding of wrongdoing, honor, and revenge. Although usually undertaken as the driving away of another nomad's livestock, barïmta was not simply stealing, for the livestock was eventually returned. It was considered an act of self-reprisal, which forced the review of a case that had not been justly settled, or had not been settled at all, and when it was practiced properly, it was viewed as an honorable, even heroic, deed. To the Russians, the cultural significance of barïmta held no legal weight; to the Kazakhs, the legal implication of barïmta as crime had no meaning. For the Russian government, the successful colonization of the steppe could not proceed while the natives acted like criminals. Terms of deviant behavior had been defined: Kazakhs who committed barïmta were criminals. At the same time, Kazakhs continued to practice barïmta as custom. Over the course of the nineteenth century, this apparent standoff of Kazakh and Russian legal and cultural understandings forced the redefinition of barïmta: while barïmta survived to mean both criminal threat to the Russians and heroic restitution to the Kazakhs, in practice it became nothing more than theft of livestock, with legal sanction by neither Russian nor Kazakh.

This chapter will trace the changes in meaning of the word *barïmta* as it was used in mostly Russian-language court records, in ethnographic reports, and in the national and provincial press, and then will argue that in practice barïmta survived as a Kazakh custom, unpunishable and heroicized, within the historical context of legal syncretism in the steppe territory in the nineteenth century. The colonial framework served paradoxically to elevate barïmta to a new level of permissibility in popular nomadic culture. Barïmta became permissible as theft in the context of a breakdown of the authority of the traditional nomadic judge, the *biy*; the inaccessibility of justice within the Russian system; and the Kazakhs' cultural propensity to demonstrate heroism and honor through acts of revenge. An examination of the Kazakh nomadic custom of barïmta demonstrates that the encounter of Russian and Kazakh on the steppe brought significant structural changes to nomadic life, but did not necessarily change the cultural values that shaped understandings of justice and wrongdoing on either side. Rather than leading to the legal assimilation (Russification) of the steppe in the nineteenth century, colonization presented the Kazakhs a new context within which to renegotiate their cultural identity and allow it to survive.

In this analysis of barïmta, semantics plays a key role. When we ask, "What was barïmta?" we must know who was defining it, Russian or Kazakh, tsarist official, ethnographer, or nomadic judge. When we ask, "Why did barïmta survive?" we must be clear as to what it was that survived: the crime, the custom, both? Multiple layers of meaning become blurred, as the historian is forced to confront the complexities of constructing a history of the colonized using texts prepared by the colonizers. An analysis of the semantics of barïmta will help us to grasp the realities of the frontier encounter. By teasing the changing meanings of barïmta out of the mostly Russian-language documents, we can begin to understand the subtle ways that Russia wielded power as colonizer, and the ways that the nomads struggled for existence in spite of colonial impositions.

In order better to understand the threat that Russia perceived in barïmta, we must first examine it from the native point of view, as a custom practiced by nomads. Etymologically, the Kazakh word *barïmta* (usually referred to in Russian as *baranta*) means "that which is due to me."[6] As such, we can preliminarily define barïmta as one method of resolving disputes, which was undertaken as self-reprisal when other solutions were deemed untenable, with the ultimate aim of avenging insult and upholding personal and clan honor.

As a method of dispute resolution, barïmta was the driving away of another nomad's livestock by an offended party, usually accompanied by members of his clan or *aul*, in order to force a fair settlement of a conflict. The livestock was kept by the offended side until agreement was reached, at which time it was either returned in full or kept as the just amount of the claim against the offense. Although almost always practiced in this way, barïmta could also be carried out by abducting a woman or confiscating property from an aul, for in general, it signified a claim to justice using property as ransom for what was owed. It was undertaken for a variety of reasons. Often it was considered legitimate to commit barïmta if a debt was left unpaid[7] or if *qalïm* (brideprice) had not been delivered in a timely manner.[8] Sometimes, when two sides could not come to an agreement about a land dispute, one would resort to barïmta.[9] If someone felt that he was unjustly judged by a biy and could not get his side of the case properly heard,[10] or if the biy violated established customs,[11] the plaintiff would gather his clansmen and undertake barïmta. A Russian ethnographer tells the story of barïmta committed by one clan in response to the murder of a fellow clansman: if normally a clan made payment in kind (*qun*, in sheep, horses, or camels, varying in amount by region and persons involved) to another clan as redemption for a murder, here the clansmen felt it was necessary to "wash the blood of the murdered" by committing barïmta.[12] The Tatar ethnographer and official in the colonial administration in Turkestan I. I. Ibragimov described a case of barïmta committed in response to the breakdown of *tamyrstvo* [*tamïrlïq*], a strong bond of friend-ship symbolically consecrated by the exchange of gifts (from the Kazakh word *tamïr*, meaning friend or soul brother, as well as root). In this case, one tamïr neglected to visit the other and bring the appropriate gift, so barïmta was carried out to demonstrate that offense had been taken.[13] Finally, one could commit barïmta by confiscating in revenge livestock from the person or aul that had stolen livestock from one's own aul in the first instance.

In a sense, barïmta could be seen as simply revenge for wrongdoing, and yet it was a legitimate recourse for justice only under certain condi-tions. It had to be done with the prior knowledge of a biy and one's own aul, and with a declaration of the reason why justice was being sought;[14] it had to be done during the day, not at night; and the confiscated animals or property had to be returned in full (or just compensation had to be made to the winning side) once the case had been settled satisfactorily for both parties.[15] One could not undertake barïmta for personal gain, as evidenced in the folk saying "Barymtoi imushchestva ne umnozhish'" (You cannot increase property through barïmta).[16] Barïmta was not done against Rus-sians or against other non-nomads. It was done only within the Kazakh cultural community; outside that context it was not legally valid. Thus it represented an act of self-reprisal which forced the nomadic judge and the Kazakh community as a whole to review the case and decide whether it was a legitimate claim to "what is due to me." If barïmta was undertaken legitimately, it could not be punished as an act of wrongdoing: custom sanctioned it as a way to seek justice.

Barïmta was a powerful recourse in a culture where the well-being of one's herds of sheep, goats, horses, and camels could determine the well-being of the entire community. Daily life in the nomadic community was structured around the securement of ample food and water for the nomad's herds. Seasonal migrations, undertaken on previously deter-mined routes and to designated pastures, were essential for the maximum exploitation of scarce natural resources in the steppe. Almost all human food supplies and many of the materials used for shelter were derived from animals. Thus, securing the well-being of one's herd was as crucial as life and death. In this sense, we can understand that when a nomad con-fiscated someone else's sheep in barïmta, his action prompted immediate response, with a demand that his fellow clansmen hear his case. He was using the community's wealth (its animals) as security that his claims would be addressed, not simply in his own name but in the name of his clan or tribe.

More than occasionally, however, barïmta got out of hand: sometimes murder would occur during the act (but even then the committal of barïmta was not punished; only the murder was).[17] At other times, the first act would not force satisfactory settlement of a case, and the offended party would commit reciprocal barïmta. In response, barïmta would be committed again, and more and more clan members from each side would become involved. This escalation went beyond the confines of legitimacy, for after two acts, it was considered punishable with a fine.[18] It was the reciprocal, lengthy exchange of barïmta, and the tendency for the legally sanctioned act to devolve into clan feud, that Levshin referred to when he wrote that "all Kirgiz law consists of arbitrary and unregulated baranta."[19] While this was a typical response from a tsarist official to barïmta gone out of control, even to the impartial observer barïmta appears to represent the breakdown of customary law as a system of justice. F. I. Leontovich, a tsarist official who published his observations on the legal culture of the Caucasian mountaineers, argued that the community had an unwritten agreement to live in harmony, which was called *maslagat*; when maslagat lost its power, self-justice in the form of barïmta took over.[20] Similarly, one could argue that by committing barïmta, the individual (or clan) was stating that he could not find justice within the system; in some cases he was directly questioning the authority of an individual biy, and taking justice into his own hands.

I would argue that barïmta as self-justice was in fact an integral part of the system, not representative of its breakdown. The key elements that anchored barïmta within the set of legitimate alternatives for dispute resolution were (1) the need to uphold personal and clan honor, and (2) the obligation to seek revenge. In the patriarchal nomadic culture, a man's personal image reflected the standing of the larger community—his aul, clan, and tribe. Respect and authority were granted to the man (and his clan) who either had proved his strength and daring in battle, or had demonstrated to fellow clansmen his capacity for wisdom and fairness and his knowlege of custom. An individual recognized for these qualities simultaneously elevated the image of his clan. Thus, personal actions were not taken lightly, because the clan's honor and integrity were at stake. When barïmta was committed, it inevitably represented the questioning of a person's (and his clan's) honor: his ability to repay a debt, his desire for personal gain, his understanding of customs, his willingness to uphold an agreement. If the act of barïmta succeeded in revealing wrongdoing, it would restore and preserve the prestige of the clan whose honor had been put in doubt.

On another level, barïmta was an integral part of the Kazakh system of justice because custom obliged an offended party to seek revenge. The first article of the *Jeti Jarghï* (Seven Statutes), the earliest known "code" of Kazakh laws, promulgated by Khan Tauke (1680–1718), proclaims the right to just retribution.[21] Not only did custom allow retribution, but it expected the offended party to avenge wrongdoing.[22] This sanctioning of self-justice fit within a legal culture that recognized an act as criminal only when a plaintiff arose to make a complaint.[23] That is, the system did not force an investigation based on some overarching sense of law and justice; rather, it was the individual's place to recognize an act as offensive, unjust, or wrong, to himself and his clan. Barïmta represented, first, an individual's declaration that an act of wrongdoing had occurred; second, his attempt to avenge that act; and third, his commitment to protect the honor and prestige of the larger community of which he was a part.

Barïmta operated in this way as one alternative within a larger system of judicial practices that formed what we call "customary law." Kazakh customary law (adat) was a set of rules, norms, and morals that guided proper behavior and prescribed just punishment for improper behavior. "Adat was not a universal set of laws, written down as guidelines for all adherents, but a particularistic set of principles that were applied within a cultural context that changed as the socio-economic and political conditions of nomadic life on the steppe changed."[24] Adat was orally transmitted from generation to generation by respected elders, called biys, who had the knowledge and wisdom to convey customs and make just judgments. Just as the principles of adat were prone to internal and external forces of change, so too was barïmta open to reinterpretation and reapplication. As one option for dispute resolution within adat, it necessarily adjusted to new social contexts as they formed. With the erection of a Russian legal system for the steppe in the 1820s and the folding of adat loosely into the Russian framework, barïmta became a less practicable judicial custom. However, being motivated by honor and revenge, barïmta did not lose its place in the Kazakh cultural matrix.

The Russian legal system in the Kazakh steppe was an entity administratively (and therefore judicially) separate from the existing judiciary in Russia proper. Construction of a separate judiciary for the steppe frontier began in the eighteenth century under Catherine the Great, who wished both to "soften the morals"[25] of the nomads by exposing them to Russian legal culture, and to maintain peace and avoid resistance to Russian rule in the region by allowing the nomads to practice their own legal customs.[26] This vision of at least partial accommodation of cultural differences guided Mikhail Speranskii when he wrote the 1822 Regulations for the Middle Horde Kazakhs.

Article 68 of the Regulations on the Administration of Indigenous Natives (inorodtsy) (1822)—the umbrella law under which fell the Regulations on the Siberian Kirgiz—ordered that laws and customs of all nomads be collected by local officials and examined by special committees with the goal of discarding "wild and savage" elements which contradicted imperial efforts to bring order to the region.[27] By 1824, the laws and customs of the Middle Horde Kazakhs had been gathered,[28] examined by a "Provisional Committee" in Omsk, and declared to be the adat of these nomads. This version of adat, prepared in Kazakh and translated into Russian for the purpose of adapting it to existing Russian laws, was never published as a code of laws, and was never made available to local Russian officials to help them understand Kazakh judicial customs.[29] Knowing adat well would have served the needs of local officials, because steppe law allowed Kazakhs dissatisfied with the decisions of biys to appeal to the appropriate Russian official in the regional administration (*okruzhnyi prikaz*) as a judge of the second instance. He would have to revisit the case and make a ruling for or against the biy's decision, based on his own understanding of Kazakh customs.[30] Only in cases involving crimes prosecutable under imperial laws were Kazakhs ever directly subject to Russian legal codes. In both civil and criminal cases, Chokan Valikhanov, Kazakh ethnographer and imperial official, argued that the number of appeals to Russian courts was insignificant, and that little change at all could be seen in the functioning of customary law in the forty years since it had come under Russian rule.[31]

By all reports, the judicial system as established by the 1822 Regulations did not fulfill the goals of bringing sufficient order, peace, and control to the steppe. In the wake of the Great Reforms and the military conquest of Turkestan, it was decided to develop an administrative framework that could more closely oversee the natives. The 1865 Steppe Commission, which was sent out into the steppe to study "the way of life of the Kirgiz" and to draft "a new statute for their administration," declared that while it was not yet feasible to impose imperial judicial reforms on the nomads because they were not sufficiently developed to comprehend Russian law, eventually Russian law would supplant customary law there. If only the nomads could see the benefits of Russian justice, they would learn to live by it.[32]

In this spirit of passively stimulating a Russian legal consciousness by gradually imposing Russian institutions, the Provisional Statute on Administration in Ural'sk, Turgai, Akmolinsk, and Semipalatinsk oblasti[33] (hereafter called the 1868 Steppe Statute) was drafted, signed into law on 21 October 1868, and enacted on 1 January 1869.[34] This statute served to bring a larger measure of judicial and administrative control over steppe inhabitants by more strictly defining official positions, jurisdictions, and procedures, while still allowing Kazakhs to be ruled by their own customs, as interpreted within the confines of the Russian judicial system as a whole. On paper, it allowed Kazakh nomads a number of new alternatives for seeking justice, resolving disputes, and guaranteeing just punishment.

The basic judicial organ for hearing legal cases among Kazakhs was the people's court (*narodnyi sud*), within which a biy, elected to a three-year term, would decide most civil and criminal cases according to customary law (except barïmta, murder, treason, et al., which remained under the jurisdiction of imperial laws; and land disputes, which were decided in the first instance by special electors chosen from among every ten or fifteen yurt owners). According to Article 137 of the 1868 Steppe Statute, "a biy can be chosen from among those who have the respect and trust of the people, have not been discredited by the court, are not under investigation, and are not less than twenty-five years old."[35] An entire judicial apparatus was established, with the biy as judge in the first instance for cases in value up to three hundred rubles, followed by a *volost'* assembly of biys for cases up to five hundred rubles, and an "extraordinary" assembly of biys for cases over five hundred rubles. The volost' assembly also acted as the court of appeals for the biy court, while the extraordinary assembly served the same function for its volost' counterpart. In all of these judicial instances, decisions were made according to popular custom. However, if both sides agreed, Kazakhs could appeal a biy's decision to the Russian court, specifically to the *uezd* judge, who was obligated to handle the case according to "good conscience, local custom, and general civil laws."[36] This decision could be appealed to the oblast' administration, where a final judgment would be based on imperial laws, both civil and criminal.[37]

In addition to this judicial hierarchy, representing a combination of Kazakh customary law and Russian judicial-administrative procedure, there were a few other alternatives. Disputes could be appealed directly to a Russian court of the first instance (uezd judge, who acted as justice of the peace [*mirovoi sud'ia*] on the basis of 1864 regulations) if both sides agreed. In this case, rulings would be based entirely on Russian imperial laws. Kazakhs also had the option to settle a dispute "peacefully" in a "court of arbitration" (*treteiskii sud*), a Russian euphemism for choosing to turn to a respected elder in one's aul or clan who was not recognized as a judicial official by the colonial regime, but who could serve to mediate a dispute. Finally, a Kazakh could turn to a mulla or *kadi* for guidance on behavior prescribed by Islamic law, particularly in cases involving marriage, divorce, or inheritance.[38] In an effort to direct Kazakhs away from Islamic law in these cases, the 1868 Steppe Statute allowed Kazakhs dissatisfied with a biy's decision of the first instance to appeal directly to the uezd *nachal'nik*, who would decide the case as he saw appropriate.[39]

In 1891, the "Provisional Statute" of 1868, which was originally intended to be reviewed and revised after only two years, and which had been criticized for years by local administrators, was finally replaced by a new body of regulations, the "Statute on Administration of Akmolinsk, Semipalatinsk, Semirech'e, Ural'sk, and Turgai oblasti."[40] Written in the wake of all-Russian legislation in 1889 that sought more centralized control of local conditions through the institution of the peasant land captain (*zemskii nachal'nik*) as well as through the promotion of state-controlled peasant colonization of the steppe, this Steppe Statute served to augment the power of the Russian administration over native administration[41] by increasing the disciplinary discretion of the uezd nachal'nik, and tightening police control over migrating nomads. Few changes were made in the functioning of the narodnyi sud system, however. Still in 1898, when a new statute finally brought in full the legal provisions of the 1864 judicial reforms to the steppe,[42] the narodnyi sud remained the main judicial organ for settling disputes among Kazakhs. As we shall see below, the effectiveness of the biy courts in bringing justice had significantly deteriorated by 1898.

Opportunities for resolving disputes legally among Kazakhs broadened considerably beginning in 1868, and throughout the century an atmosphere of legal syncretism reigned: customary, Russian, and Islamic laws intertwined and operated side by side. One keen Russian observer even speculated that a "new adat" was created out of this amalgam of legal alternatives, reflecting the growing influence of both the Russian and the Islamic presence among the nomads on the steppe.[43] What did the existence of multiple legal alternatives mean for the daily practice of justice and dispute resolution among Middle Horde Kazakhs in the second half of the nineteenth century? And how did changes brought about by new legal sensibilities affect the cultural meaning of barïmta? As was stated in the beginning, barïmta evolved in practice into theft or confiscation of livestock without the legal sanction of a Kazakh biy. The following is an attempt to provide an explanation of that change, first by examining the Russian-language usage of the term *barïmta,* and then by demonstrating that the context within which barïmta was practiced in the second half of the nineteenth century made seeking justice as a whole extremely difficult for the Kazakh nomad.

Where is the logic behind concluding that the custom of barïmta evolved in practice to be the stealing of livestock? To answer this question, we must look carefully at the use of the term *barïmta,* as well as at Russian-language terminology for theft, plunder, and raiding as crimes on the steppe.

First, a whole vocabulary arose around the word *barïmta* (*baranta*), which served as a way to represent Kazakh nomads as uncivilized and savage. Barïmta was committed by *barantachi* who sought to *barantovat'* in order to reap the *otbarantovannoe* as reward for their exploits, and later the *barantuiushchie* divided the spoils among themselves. Such vocabulary, when used by literati and local officials instead of other terms for robbery or plunder, served to demonize the act. Chokan Valikhanov, writing of the cultural prejudices displayed in the Russian approach to barïmta, stated: "It is criminal not in fact, but in the ominous sound of this word."[44] For instance, one case record described "barïmta" accompanied by murder, effectively creating in the text an image of a more brutal crime.[45]

Furthermore, we must note in a variety of Russian-language sources a tendency for the term *barïmta* to be conflated with other terms. The Central

State Archive of Kazakhstan in Almaty and the State Archive of Omsk oblast' in the city of Omsk contain hundreds of judicial cases from Akmolinsk and Semipalatinsk oblasti alone that include *barïmta* in the file title but describe nothing more than theft of livestock. No particular language is used in the documents themselves that would point to barïmta as meaning a biy-sanctioned Kazakh custom.[46] Evidence outside of court records also demonstrates a lack of understanding on the part of Russian observers of barïmta as nomadic custom. The 1822 Regulations defined it as grabezh; Levshin used it to mean "the holding of criminals or their relatives" and "the stealing of cattle."[47] An article in *Sibirskaia gazeta* in 1886 used the term *barïmta* to describe repeated incidents of horse theft by Kazakhs.[48] The steppe governor-general, in his 1898 annual report, discussed barïmta as "cattle theft."[49] The Akmolinsk military governor, in his 1872 annual report, showed that he had some sense of the basis of barïmta in custom, but not a full understanding of cultural distinctions among similar acts, when he described barïmta, together with robbery (*vorovstvo*) and horse theft (*konokradstvo*), as daring acts, not crimes.[50] Often, barïmta and *nabeg* (raid) were used interchangeably. And in a telling condemnation, tsarist official Grigor'ev in the 1870s accused Russians of having used the term *barïmta* for more than a century without knowing what it meant.[51]

In spite of this seemingly indiscriminatory usage of the term, there were clear distinctions in Russian definitions of the terms. Using Dal',[52] we find two clearly distinguishable types of theft. Vorovstvo and *krazha* are defined interchangeably as theft without violence, undertaken secretly, stealthily. On the other hand, grabezh, *razboi*, and nabeg are defined as theft accompanied by violence or force, often as an attack, but undertaken openly. Within this schema, barïmta is a type of grabezh or nabeg which is motivated by personal revenge (*samoupravnaia mest'*).[53]

These definitions are played out in Russian legal usage. In the language of laws throughout the century, barïmta was distinguished from other "crimes." In the 1822 Regulations, barïmta and grabezh were outlawed. In the 1854 "Statute on the Introduction to the Siberian Kirgiz of General Laws of the Russian Empire," barïmta and razboi were crimes, subject to trial and punishment by imperial laws.[54] All other cases, including krazha from individuals, vorovstvo-krazha, konokradstvo, and *skotokradstvo*, were considered civil cases, and therefore came under the jurisdiction of the biy court. Under the 1868 Steppe Statute, the following acts were considered crimes: razboi, grabezh, barïmta, *napadenie* on trade caravans, and nabeg in foreign territories. Finally, in the Steppe Statute of 1891 (and the accompanying 1886 statute for the Turkestan region, whose section on the narodnyi sud was adopted for the steppe region), razboi and grabezh were defined as crimes, but none of the other previously identified theft crimes were mentioned, including barïmta. Interestingly, the word *barïmta* seems to have been dropped from legal usage, as if the act disappeared from the consciousness of legislators. Still, horse theft and other acts of robbery signifying absence of the use of violence were prosecuted by the biy court according to customary law.

Unfortunately, Russian legal usage does not necessarily help us identify what barïmta was in practice. For instance, by the late nineteenth century, observers were declaring both a decrease and an increase in the incidence of the act. First, a number of sources point to a decline in the overall incidence of barïmta as a result of the 1868 Steppe Statute, and a rise in theft of livestock, particularly of horses. Some observers attribute barïmta's decline to the alternative opportunity to seek justice in the Russian court.[55] Others saw Russia's presence in the steppe as the cause of a decline in barïmta as part of clan feuding, and the increase in barïmta between individuals.[56] On the other hand, late-nineteenth-century observers also noted a rise in the incidence of barïmta. The governor-general of the steppe reported in 1898 that barïmta had increased, "taking on the character of open and armed attacks."[57] Makovetskii claimed that hundreds and thousands of new cases were being prosecuted each year. Barïmta was now being practiced "as a trade" with a *batïr* (warrior-hero) leading his band of barantachi.[58]

Given this lack of consistency from Russian observers, we need to ask, What was barïmta in the last quarter of the nineteenth century? Important clues can be found in evidence of a change in the perceived punishability of barïmta, according to Kazakh voices audible within Russian texts. By noting the change in Kazakh perceptions of appropriate punishment for barïmta—particularly as it was opposed to theft—we can begin to build a larger picture of active nomadic responses to the colonial context.

Before colonial times, barïmta was not punished when it was legitimately undertaken, but theft was. In the late-seventeenth-century Jeti Jarghï legal code, which was recorded in Russian by Levshin, theft (in Russian: grabezh and krazha) undertaken without just cause was considered a crime punishable by death, while barïmta was considered neither criminal nor punishable.[59] Unfortunately, we do not have even fragments of the Jeti Jarghï in any Turkic language, for this would help clarify the Kazakh understanding of the differences between these acts. The Soviet scholar Kul'teleev asserts that crimes against property were generally all called *urlïq* in Kazakh.[60] Grodekov found that urlïq meant either vorovstvo/krazha or grabezh. In any case, they were differentiated from barïmta by their punishability, while through the nineteenth century barïmta remained unpunishable. For instance, Valikhanov stated that "after settlement, the confiscated livestock [taken by barïmta] is returned in full, but without any fine [*aïïp*]."[61] Furthermore, in 1863, when Kazakh sultans assembled to respond to the newly drafted "Basic Principles" of legal reform for the empire, they agreed that theft was a punishable offense, but defended barïmta by insisting that it was not theft.[62] By the same token, nineteenth-century records show that theft was subject to a scale of penalties: the fine itself (aiip) was measured in *toghïz* (nine), a combination of sheep, horses, and camels, varying according to the severity of the theft. A particularly bad crime, or one perpetrated against a more respected member of the community, could be punished by fining the accused three toghïz (twenty-seven animals), the number of livestock demanded as payment thus multiplied.

By the beginning of the twentieth century, however, we have evidence that Kazakhs now considered theft unpunishable under certain circumstances. First, in local sayings recorded by Akhmet Baitursynov, we hear voices in defense of theft: "Aitïp istegen urlïqtïng aiïbï joq" (There is no fine for the announced theft) and "Urlïq tübi-qorlïq" (The root of theft is insult/disgrace).[63] Second, in 1907, a committee of Kazakhs argued to their Russian counterparts that cattle theft (skotokradstvo) among Kazakhs was usually not punishable, and for this reason it should fall under the jurisdiction of the narodnyi sud, not of Russian courts.[64] Around the same time, a newspaper article stated that horse thieves were widely protected by aul members from detection by Russian officials seeking to prosecute criminals, pointing to the acceptance among the nomads of theft as a noncriminal act.[65] By arguing against its punishability, these Kazakhs were arguing for its cultural value: they were now willing to consider theft of livestock culturally acceptable; barïmta as theft was nothing more than a daring, youthful deed. In support of this conclusion, one tsarist official noted that "in popular memory the number of batïrs, heroes, is constantly growing, [and they] are glorified not in battle with an enemy, tiger, or boar, but for the successful driving away of cattle."[66]

By the beginning of the twentieth century, barïmta had not left the vocabulary of either Russian or Kazakh, but in practice it now defined the honorable deed of stealing livestock. It was still a crime to Russia, although not as severe a threat, and still a custom to the Kazakhs, but only to the extent that it served as an expression of revenge. Semantically, barïmta was still associated with revenge; in practice, its purpose had shifted from an open demonstration of the consequences of wrongdoing to a secretive act asserting the perpetrator's heroism and glory. While revenge remained the motive, it became an end in itself. The result was that in appearance, barïmta was nothing more than theft. This shift occurred not only in the Russian sources bent on explicating its criminality, but in the Kazakh voices within Russian sources, which sought to justify theft for what barïmta traditionally had been: an unpunished custom, a justified act of revenge. What brought about this shift, and why was theft now acceptable to the Kazakhs?

Under colonial rule, subtle but important changes were brought to Kazakh culture. In the period after 1868, and especially in the last two decades of the century, Kazakhs searching for resolution of disputes among themselves entered a legal arena which was pluralistic, but which was plagued with so many problems that just solutions were difficult to find. Neither adat nor the Russian system functioned effectively, as we will see below.[67] In the Kazakh nomadic cultural setting, where personal and clan honor had to be upheld, Kazakhs continued to rely on revenge by barïmta.

In order to explain the ineffectiveness of adat in the late nineteenth century, we need look no further than the weakening of the authority of the biy. As we have already seen, the questioning of the judgment of a biy often justified the committal of barïmta as legally sanctioned self-justice before colonial times; the questioning of authority itself was nothing new. But with the introduction of Russian legal sensibilities in the 1868 Steppe Statute, this questioning became more common, and arose from all sides. With the enactment of the 1868 Statute, a man was elected to the official post of biy (called "people's judge" [*narodnyi sud'ia*] with the enactment of the 1891 Statute) for a term of three years. He was obligated to uphold tenets and principles of customary law, except when these conflicted with the political and legal principles of the colonial regime. Local Russian administrators had the right to invalidate the election of a judge if they felt that colonial goals (or their own personal powers) were being compromised. Local officials thus tended to support politically malleable biys, who were not necessarily the men who best knew customary law. Increasingly, "the best people . . . withdraw from elected posts, conceding them to people of doubtful reputations."[68] As a result, winning a seat as biy became a battle between the power-hungry, and not an election of the most respected judge.[69] The improprieties of the election system were fully visible to all who tried to use the biy courts; people began to avoid them by appealing to the Russian courts. But appealing to the Russian system was legal only for cases over a certain sum, or for marriage and family law disputes (indeed, women began appealing to the Russian system to aid them in escaping arranged marriages, and inheritance cases were directed toward the colonial administration when litigants complained that a biy did not judge the case fairly, according to Islamic law).[70] Even so, appeals flooded the offices of uezd and oblast' administrators. Many of these cases were sent back to biy courts or congresses, where their outcome is difficult to trace.

However, not all Kazakhs ran to the Russian legal system. Still viable as an alternative for dispute resolution was judgment by a respected elder of the aul or clan. Indeed, we could argue that two courts of the first instance existed for Kazakhs seeking justice: the court of the official biy and the court of the "real" biy,[71] which Russian legal scholars called the court of elders (*sud aksakalov*) or court of arbitration (treteiskii sud).[72] Did this "traditional" form of dispute resolution function properly in the era of colonial rule? If so, we could argue that Kazakhs were able to seek justice and secure restitution within their own community, outside of the colonial framework, regardless of attempts by the local Russian officials to steer them toward "official" courts. It is extremely difficult to speculate on this issue, because we have no records of cases' being heard in the oral "court of elders." We have little evidence that would help us conclude how widespread the reliance on clan elders remained. Given what was widely reported to be an overall breakdown in clan structure as a result of administrative divisions of nomadic lands, it may be that elders were losing their clan power base, and therefore their appeal as knowledgeable, trusted judges. What is certainly clear from archival documents, however, is the steady appeal of Kazakhs to official courts—to the people's court, to the uezd nachal'nik, and even as high as the steppe governor-general in Omsk. But what is also clear from court cases and official observers is the inability of the Russian system to provide Kazakhs with the justice that they sought from colonial institutions.

A. K. Geins, a member of the 1865 Steppe Commission and the governor of Turgai oblast' in the 1870s, wrote a sharp critique in 1878 of the colonial administration and its handling of both Kazakh needs and Russian goals. Although without question writing as a loyal government official who advocated "Europeanizing" the nomads, settling them, and bringing order to the steppe, Geins wanted these goals pursued in a way that would not alienate the nomads from Russian imperial ideals. His essay was a warning to local officials that they were driving Kazakhs to "steppe self-justice, or baranta."[73] The point he was making was echoed in court cases: for instance, a particularly complex land dispute turned into a case of reciprocal barïmta while the opposing parties waited for their complaints to be resolved first by the uezd nachal'nik and then by the military governor.[74] Clearly, Kazakhs did not have any implicit trust in the Russian colonial system. A Kazakh saying goes: "If you tell a lie to a Russian, you will be rid of him" (Orïsqa ötirik aitsang, qutïlasïng). To this Baitursynov remarks, "If Russian officials were just and worked correctly, where would this saying come from?"[75] Kazakhs saw the alternative of appealing to the Russian court as a convenience, often as a last resort (and one that could at times be manipulated to one's benefit), but not as a saving grace in a quest for justice.

Although the 1868 Steppe Statute provided the possibility for Kazakhs to appeal to the Russian legal system on a variety of levels, for a variety of disputes, many cases remained unresolved, and justice for the Kazakh nomad remained elusive. The reasons were several. The steppe was miserably understaffed, and the staff responsible for judicial affairs among the Kazakhs was unfamiliar with the laws of adat that Kazakh plaintiffs wanted upheld.[76] High officials demonstrated an overwhelming lack of concern for the natives under their charge.[77] At the other end of the administrative hierarchy, observers widely charged that local administrators interfered in trials, elections, and sentences, influencing decisions and upsetting the intended legal process. Regardless of attention paid to the system by tsarist officials, the Kazakhs themselves found the Russian judiciary very difficult to approach, because they were unlikely to know either the laws or the procedures, let alone the language.[78] The official Geins even went so far as to allege that the Kazakhs were "denied the possibility of establishing their own viable rights to a well-organized court."[79]

If such a scenario accurately portrays the Middle Horde Kazakhs' efforts to seek justice in the last quarter of the nineteenth century—that is, if most opportunities for resolving disputes were somehow hampered by inefficiencies of the system or lack of legitimacy of officeholders in the eyes of the litigants—then taking justice into one's own hands is a logical alternative. The law did not work, so one had to operate outside the law. However, as I have argued, taking justice into one's own hands, committing barïmta as an act of revenge, making the personal decision to steal someone's sheep because he refused to pay all of the brideprice, did not mean leaving custom behind; rather, it meant reinforcing the customary practice of upholding one's honor and prestige in the larger community. The need to uphold honor transcended the desire to uphold justice in an atmosphere where the system erected to secure justice did not function. Whereas before barïmta was legitimate only if undertaken in a certain way, now it was done simply as the individual (with or without his clan) saw fit.

In this climate of disorder, fueled additionally by dramatic changes in the last decade of the century, when Slavic settlers encroached upon nomadic lands and migratory routes, the image of hero was given new importance. Survival was now key. The nomad who could uphold his and his clan's honor in the face of serious threats to the nomadic existence was glorified, and barïmta as heroic deed found wide resonance in the imaginations of the steppe nomads. One sixty-year-old former barantach described barïmta as "defense of one's clan rights and interests, where 'an eye for an eye, a tooth for a tooth' was the motto, where revenge was considered not only legal but obligatory, where rights of the strong had no limits. . . . Successful baranta brought celebrated glory to the enterprising horseman."[80] Russian observers frequently noted that barïmta was the stuff of heroes. Rumiantsev described batïrs as being "influential thanks to bravery and deftness in raids and robberies (barantas)."[81] Geins compared the respect gained by a successful barantach to that gained by two men engaged in a duel.[82] The legal scholar A. A. Leont'ev observed in 1890 that barïmta was a "product of steppe life." "Still now, . . . [a Kirgiz] considers it his duty to revenge his enemy by 'baranta,' or the driving away of

"Peoples of the Russian Empire: [from left] Kirgiz, Tatars, Bashkirs"
(1900 poster, courtesy of the Russian State Library print collection)

livestock. . . . Baranta today in the eyes of the Kirgiz is something attractive, youthful. The folk song doesn't sing for nothing of the youthful raids of barantachi, and their exploits become widely known in the steppe!"[83]

In a word, even at the end of the century, barïmta was an act that created batïrs and steppe folk heroes; only now those heroes were thieves. Barïmta was still a threat to the stability of the steppe in the eyes of the Russians who were trying to administer it, and now it was undertaken as if to show that Kazakh honor had its place alongside Russian justice. Above all else, barïmta as revenge was a heroic deed, whether in the cultural context of a legitimate alternative for dispute resolution, or in the colonial context of upholding honor when no other alternative would do.

In this chapter, I have argued that while the practice of barïmta survived by adjusting to a new colonial context, the Kazakh cultural understanding of the importance of honor, justice, and revenge remained the same. An examination of barïmta shows that colonization brought new legal structures, but not necessarily new legal sensibilities, to the colonized. Throughout the nineteenth century, the colonial judiciary in the Kazakh steppe represented a separate effort to administer this frontier territory in the most efficient and orderly way. Allowing natives to retain their customary law in a form accommodated in the Russian system was one strategy in this effort. Order could best be maintained if change was brought slowly. On the other hand, the goals of Russification in the legal sphere could not be realized as long as justice within the Russian colonial system was out of reach of the average Kazakh nomad. Thus, the Kazakh custom persisted that if justice could not be obtained from the persons who represented the living law of the land, then it was imcumbent upon the offended to take justice into his own hands.

I have also shown that while "custom" had an enduring value in the nomadic way of life of the Middle Horde Kazakhs, just what that custom meant and how it was practiced in a given period were open to adjustment to a changing social context. Barïmta survived the colonial encounter because it was elevated to the status of protector of honor which required no legal sanction when none was available. In another sense, barïmta survived the colonial encounter because imperial authorities were unable to combat it. Russia could not provide an alternative to self-justice within a system that worked inefficiently at best. Instead it criminalized an act that it really did not understand, and then imposed multiple meanings on that act when discussing the problems of its eradication. Russian administrators tried to make barïmta punishable and bring its perpetrators to trial, but these efforts missed the point that the act had cultural meaning that could not simply be outlawed.

The survival of barïmta as nomadic custom demonstrates both the limits of political power and the power of the colonial context to shape the cultural values of the steppe natives. Semantically, barïmta was colonized by imperial image-makers and was used to represent the nomad as criminal. In practice, barïmta endured as an act which represented for its practitioners the honorable and the heroic—fundamental qualities of the patriarchal nomadic lifestyle. In this colonial encounter, Middle Horde Kazakhs did not allow their cultural identity to be forged by imperial impositions, and yet they were forced to negotiate new ways to express that identity as colonial subjects of the Russian Empire. The encounter over the custom of barïmta demonstrates that the Kazakhs did not passively receive colonial rule, nor violently reject it, but actively worked with it, negotiating for themselves a level of understanding that would ensure the survival of their culture within its confines.

Notes

1. "Ustav o Sibirskikh Kirgizakh," *Polnoe sobranie zakonov,* First Series, no. 29172, vol. 38, 22 July 1822. Text provided in appendix to vol. 3 of A. I. Levshin, *Opisanie Kirgiz-Kazachikh ili Kirgiz-Kaisatskikh ord i stepei* (St. Petersburg, 1832), pp. 243–301.

Under the new administrative framework, "Siberian Kirgiz" was the term used to identify the Kazakhs of the Middle Horde, as opposed to the Little Horde Kazakhs, who were called "Orenburg Kirgiz." After 1868, territorial identifiers were dropped, and all Kazakhs were simply called "Kirgiz" of the Little, Middle, or Great Horde; this label stuck until after the Bolshevik Revolution. I have chosen to focus in this chapter on the Kazakhs of the Middle Horde, defined in accordance with Russian administrative delineations, in order to provide a workable structure for my research. Although not all Middle Horde Kazakhs migrated within borders erected by the colonial regime, most could be found in the territories administered on a regional level from Omsk. Thus almost all archival and most ethnographic sources cited here are from these territories.

2. At least two legal-administrative organs were established for enforcing laws on the steppe in the eighteenth century, although these and other attempts at judicial control of the steppe natives were directed mostly at the Little Horde Kazakhs, whose summer pastures were in close proximity to Russia, and whose frequent interclannic feuds and struggles with the Cossacks (among others) over land and regional power disrupted regional trade. These organs were the Border Court, established in 1784, and the Orenburg Border Commission, established in 1799. Neither of them proved effective for resolving disputes or for ensuring stability and peace. (See Levshin, *Opisanie*, pp. 276–280, and I. I. Kraft, *Sudebnaia chast' v Turkestanskom krae i stepnykh oblastiakh* [Orenburg, 1898], pp. 36–39.) Further legal structures on the territories of the Little Horde were not erected until 1828.

3. 1822 Ustav, article 293. Levshin, *Opisanie*, p. 296; *Materialy po istorii politicheskogo stroia Kazakhstana* (Alma-Ata, 1960), vol. 1, p. 260; Kraft, *Sudebnaia chast'*, pp. 2, 24, and 40–41.

4. B. M. Abdurakhmanov, "Razrabotka M. M. Speranskim 'Ustava o sibirskikh kirgizakh' 1822 g. i sotsial'no-politicheskie instituty Kazakhskogo obshchestva," *Vestnik Moskovskogo universiteta*, seriia 8, istoriia, no. 4 (1991): 49–58; A. Dobromyslov, "Zaboty imperatritsy Ekateriny II o prosveshchenii Kirgizov," *Trudy Orenburgskoi uchenoi arkhivnoi kommissii*, vyp. 9 (Orenburg, 1902), pp. 51–63; and Marc Raeff, *Siberia and the Reforms of 1822* (Seattle, 1956).

5. 1822 Ustav, article 287. In Levshin, *Opisanie*, p. 294.

6. I. I. Ibragimov, "Zametki o Kirgizskom sude," *Zapiski Russkago geograficheskago obshchestva po otdelenii etnografii*, no. 8 (1878): 235.

7. Tsentral'nyi gosudarstvennyi arkhiv Kazakhstana (TsGAKaz), f. 345, op. 1, d. 1608, l. 15.

8. Ch. Ch. Valikhanov, "Zapiski o sudebnoi reforme," *Sobranie sochinenii v piati tomakh* (Alma-Ata, 1985), vol. 4, p. 96.

9. TsGAKaz, f. 15, op. 1, d. 1862, l. 2; Krasovskii, *Oblast' Sibirskikh Kirgizov* (St. Petersburg, 1868), vol. 3, p. 14.

10. Ibragimov, "Zametki," p. 235.

11. N. Maksimov, "Narodnyi sud u Kirgizov (sud biev)," *Zhurnal iuridicheskago obshchestva*, no. 7 (1897): 65.

12. N. Izraztsov, "Obychnoe pravo ('adat') kirgizov Semirechenskoi oblasti," *Etnograficheskoe obozrenie*, no. 4 (1897): 19.

13. I. I. Ibragimov, "Etnograficheskie ocherki kirgizskago naroda," *Russkii Turkestan. Sbornik izdannyi po povodu politekhnicheskoi vystavki*, vyp. 2 (Moscow, 1872), pp. 133–134.

14. Chokan Valikhanov added that barïmta could be done "secretly," but it had to be announced within three days of the act that livestock had been confiscated as barïmta for a particular reason. "Zapiski," p. 97.

15. N. I. Grodekov, *Kirgizi i karakirgizi Syr-Dar'inskoi oblasti,* vol. 1: *Iuridicheskii byt'* (Tashkent, 1889), pp. 170–171.

16. N. S. Smirnova, *Kazakhskaia narodnaia poeziia* (Alma-Ata, 1967), p. 29.

17. T. M. Kul'teleev, *Ugolovnoe obychnoe pravo kazakhov* (Alma-Ata, 1955), p. 248.

18. Ibragimov, "Zametki," p. 236. Also TsGAKaz, f. 15, op.1, d. 85, l. 5.

19. Levshin, *Opisanie,* p. 182.

20. F. I. Leontovich, *Adaty kirgizskikh gortsev. Materialy po obychnomu pravu severnago i vostochnago Kavkaza* (Odessa, 1882), pp. 18f.

21. "The place of first importance is occupied by the law of retaliation: for blood, revenge is in blood, and for mutilation by similar mutilation." English translation in V. A. Riasanovsky, *Customary Law of the Nomadic Tribes of Siberia* (Indiana University Publications, Uralic and Altaic Series 48, 1965), p. 9. For more on the Jeti Jarghï, see T. I. Sultanov, "Sem' ustanovlenii—pamiatnik prava kazakhov XVII v.," in *Strany i narody vostoka* (Moscow, 1980), pp. 252–262.

22. Grodekov, *Kirgizy,* p. 142.

23. Ibid., p. 141.

24. C. Geertz, "Local Knowledge: Fact and Law in Comparative Perspective," in *Local Knowledge: Further Essays in Interpretive Anthropology* (New York, 1983), pp. 167–234; P. Bourdieu, *Outline of a Theory of Practice* (Cambridge, 1977), p. 17. Kazakh customary law compares well with that of other nomadic and rural peoples, including Russian peasants. For recent Western studies of Russian peasant customary law, see, in particular, the series of articles and discussion by M. Lewin, C. Worobec, G. Yaney, and M. Confino in *Russian Review* 44 (1985): 1–43. See also Christine Worobec, "Horse Thieves and Peasant Justice in Post-emancipation Imperial Russia," *Journal of Social History* 21 (1987): 281–293; and Cathy Frierson, "Crime and Punishment in the Russian Village: Rural Concepts of Criminality at the End of the 19th Century," *Slavic Review* 46, no. 1 (1987): 55–69. For an example of the large body of literature by Africanist anthropologists on customary law in a colonial setting, see Sally Falk Moore, *Social Facts and Fabrications: "Customary" Law on Kilimanjaro, 1880–1980* (Cambridge, 1986).

25. Levshin, *Opisanie,* p. 276.

26. Raeff, *Siberia and the Reforms of 1822,* p. 104.

27. *Materialy po istorii,* p. 111.

28. The 1822 Regulations served to separate the Middle Horde Kazakhs from the Little and Great Hordes. However, in reality they were separated only to the extent that Russian administrative divisions coincided with natural divisions between hordes. Furthermore, administrative boundaries identified with horde territories ignored the fact that seasonal migrations took parts of both the Little and Middle Hordes into Syr-Dar'ia oblast' (before 1865 not even part of the Russian Empire), the Great Horde north into Semipalatinsk oblast', and so forth. Administrative boundaries could not possibly represent locations of hordes and clans accurately, given that some traversed huge territories between their summer and winter pastures.

29. S. V. Iushkov, ed., *Materialy po kazakhskomu obychnomu pravu,* sbornik 1 (Alma-Ata, 1948), pp. 29f. It is not entirely clear why this version of adat was neither published nor made available to local officials. However, it is clear from

the 1824 Omsk Committee's comments that it intended to completely rework the Kazakh "code" so as to make it conform to Russian laws of the time. Thus, it seems that providing local Russian officials with a code of Kazakh legal customs would have counteracted the committee's mission of imposing changes to that version of adat. See the committee's comments in Iushkov, *Materialy*, pp. 31–69.

30. 1822 Ustav, article 219. In Levshin, *Opisanie*, p. 282.

31. Valikhanov, "Zapiski," pp. 89, 90, and 97–98.

32. Russkii gosudarstvennyi istoricheskii arkhiv (RGIA), f. 1291, op. 82, year 1865, no. 5a, b, & c.

33. With this statute, the Orenburg krai was divided into Ural'sk and Turgai oblasti, and the oblast' of Siberian Kirgiz was divided into Akmolinsk and Semipalatinsk oblasti. These divisions maintained the former rough separation of Little Horde Kazakhs in the two western oblasti, and the Middle Horde Kazakhs in Akmolinsk and Semipalatinsk. (The Great Horde was found mostly in the Semirech'e oblast', under administrative control of the Turkestan krai until 1882.)

34. "Vremennoe polozhenie ob upravlenii v Ural'skoi, Turgaiskoi, Akmolinskoi i Semipalatinskoi oblastiakh," *PSZ*, third series, vol. 38, no. 46380.

35. *Materialy po istorii*, p. 332.

36. Ibid., pp. 331f.

37. Ibid., pp. 332.

38. In this examination of barïmta as legal alternative, the entire dimension of Islamic law will not be analyzed. However, it is intricately woven into the fabric of customary law. If one were to do a study of adat rules and their application as recorded in the nineteenth century, one would find direct evidence of morals and principles based in an understanding of Shariʿa.

39. *Materialy po istorii*, p. 334.

40. "Polozhenie ob upravlenii Akmolinskoi, Semipalatinskoi, Semirechenskoi, Ural'skoi i Turgaiskoi oblastiami," *PSZ*, third series, vol. 11, no. 7475.

41. A. A. Leont'ev, "Reforma upravleniia i suda v Sibirskikh stepiakh," *Iuridicheskii letopis'*, no. 7 (1892): 22.

42. "Vremennyia pravila o primenenii sudebnykh ustavov k Turkestanskomu kraiu i stepnym oblastiam," *PSZ*, third series, no. 15439 (2 June 1898).

43. Grodekov, *Kirgizy*, p. 22.

44. Valikhanov, "Zapiski," p. 96.

45. TsGAKaz, f. 338, op. 1, d. 302: "Perepiska s general-gubernatorom zapadnoi Sibir, Omskim Oblastnym sudom i dr. o namete tiulengutov i detei khana Valieva na Balta-Kireevskiuiu volost' s tsel'iu baranty."

46. See, e.g., TsGAKaz, f. 4, op.1, d. 3953: "Delo o vzaimnoi barymte mezhdu kazakhami Orenburgskago i Sibirskago vedomstv" (1863); TsGAKaz, f. 369, op. 1, d. 3558: "Po predlozheniiu Stepnago General-Gubernatora o priniatii mer k uderzhaniiu ot barant i grabezhei kazakhov Anakul'skoi volosti, Atbasarskago uezda" (1896–97); and in other archives, including Gos. arkhiv Omskoi oblasti, f. 3, op. 10, d. 16454: "Po predstavleniiu voennogo gubernatora Semipalatinskoi oblasti o barante i grabezhe mezhdu kirgizami Arkatskoi volosti . . . otnial deneg 225 r. i odezhdu . . . loshadei . . . i verbliudov."

47. Levshin, *Opisanie*, vol. 2, pp. 195 and 270.

48. "Korrespondentsiia iz Kokpekty," *Sibirskaia gazeta*, no. 45 (1886): 1309.

49. RGIA, f. Biblioteka, op. 1, d. 91, l. 90.

50. RGIA, f. 1284, op. 69, year 1873, d. 283, l. 86.

51. V. Grigorief, "The Russian Policy regarding Central Asia: An Historical Sketch," Appendix IV in E. Schuyler, *Turkestan* (London, 1876), p. 411.

52. V. Dal', *Tolkovyi slovar' zhivago velikorusskago iazyka* (1880–82; reprint, Moscow, 1955).

53. Ibid., vol. 1, p. 47.

54. *Materialy po istorii*, pp. 183–184.

55. Grodekov, *Kirgizy*, p. 14; P. E. Makovetskii, "Materialy dlia izucheniia iuridicheskikh obychaev kirgizov," in S. V. Iushkov, ed., *Materialy*, p. 275; K. A. Zhirenchin, "Reformy upravleniia 60-ykh godov XIX veka v Kazakhstane i ikh politicheskie i pravovye posledstviia" (Candidate dissertation, Alma-Ata, 1979), p. 46.

56. A. K. Geins, *Motivy k vremennoi instruktsii uezdnym nachal'nikam Turgaiskoi oblasti i soobrazheniia po upravleniiu kirgizami* (Orenburg, 1878), p. 74.

57. RGIA, f. Biblioteka, op. 1, d. 91, l. 90.

58. Makovetskii, "Materialy," p. 283.

59. Levshin, *Opisanie*, p. 170.

60. Kul'teleev, *Ugolovnoe obychnoe pravo*, p. 248

61. Valikhanov, "Zapiski," p. 97.

62. TsGAKaz, f. 345, d.1608, ll. 14–15 and 22–23.

63. A. Baitursïnov, "Mïng bir maqal," *Juldïz*, no. 2 (1993): 31.

64. *Trudy chastnago soveshchaniia, sozvannago 20-go maia 1907 goda Stepnym General-Gubernatorom po voprosam o nuzhdakh kirgizov Stepnago kraia* (Omsk, 1908), p. 47.

65. *Kirgizskaia stepnaia gazeta*, no. 12 (2 April 1900): 3. On the issue of the protection of thieves, this could very well have been done in the context of Kazakhs' stealing horses from Russians in the struggle with new settlers over scarce resources. Horses had market value that other livestock did not have, and the stealing of horses was motivated by economic need. Thus, one could interpret the protection of horse thieves as cultural acceptance of theft only if it was done against Russians; it could be seen as a form of resistance against Russian colonial rule, and not as a form of revenge, which is what motivated barïmta. For instance, Makovetskii discusses "permanent horse thieves" ("Materialy," p. 280). Clearly, two separate types of theft were being committed. A wider examination of changes to Kazakh culture under Russian rule would have to address these issues in more depth.

66. Makovetskii, "Materialy," p. 276.

67. Again, I will defer to a different context an analysis of the importance of Islamic law in the late nineteenth century. I will note only that several observers saw an increase in its application among Kazakhs. Kraft, for instance, argued that Islamic law was becoming strong as a direct result of the ineffectiveness of the narodnyi and Russian courts. *Sudebnaia chast'*, pp. 91–92.

68. Leont'ev, "Reforma," p. 24.

69. A. A. Leont'ev, "Obychnoe pravo Kirgiz. Sudoustroistvo i sudoproizvodstvo," *Iuridicheskii vestnik*, no. 5 (1890): 125.

70. See, e.g., TsGAKaz, f. 345, op. 1, d. 453; TsGAKaz, f. 369, op. 1, d. 1868; GAOO, f. 3, op. 9, d. 14797.

71. "Kirgizskii sud i prisiaga," *Vostochnoe obozreni*e, no. 19 (1884): 8.

72. S. Sabataev, "Sud aksakalov i sud treteiskii u kirgizov Kustanaiskago uezda Turgaiskoi oblasti," *Etnograficheskoe obozrenie*, no. 3 (1900): 66–72.

73. Geins, *Motivy*, p. 64.

74. TsGAKaz, f. 15, op. 1, d. 1862.

75. A. Baitursynov. *Aq jol: Oelengder men taezhimeler, publistikalïk maqalalar jaene aedebi zertteu* (Almaty, 1991), p. 211.

76. Kraft, *Sudebnaia chast'*, p. 64.

77. Zhirenchin, "Reformy," p. 80.

78. Ibragimov, "Zametki," pp. 250–251.

79. Geins, *Motivy*, p. 64.

80. *Sibirskii vestnik*, no. 42 (15 April 1890): 2.

81. P. P. Rumiantsev, *Kirgizskii narod v proshlom i nastoiashchem* (St. Petersburg, 1910), p. 17.

82. Geins, *Motivy*, p. 72.

83. Leont'ev, "Obychnoe pravo," p. 139.

.13.

AGNÈS KEFELI

Constructing an Islamic Identity: The Case of Elyshevo Village in the Nineteenth Century

From the conquest of Kazan in 1552, the Russian state and the Orthodox Church sought to wrest the Tatars from their own Islamic culture through a policy of Christianization. As a result, a small number of them became Orthodox Christians (*Kriashen*). According to Russian law, once an individual had converted to Orthodoxy, neither he nor his descendants could convert back to Islam. Threatened by this policy, Muslim Tatars counterattacked by trying to keep the converts in their community in spite of legal prohibitions on Muslim proselytism. They spread Muslim literacy through clandestine schools and Sufi[1] books, while Russian missionaries enrolled children in parish schools and instructed them in Russian and Slavonic. Consequently zones of competition between two possible identities, two types of knowledge, emerged.

From the beginning of the nineteenth century, the descendants of the baptized Tatars began to apostatize en masse from Orthodoxy as they embraced Islam. These collective apostasies followed one another in 1802–1803, 1827–30, 1865–70, and 1905. They raise an important question: Why did the baptized Tatars choose Islam, the religion of a dominated people, and not remain members of the dominant faith? Eastern Orthodox missionaries, such as the Kriashen Vasilii Timofeev (1836–1895) from Nikiforova (Mamadysh district) and the Russians Nikolai Il'minskii (1822–

1891), Evfimii Malov (1835–1918), and Mikhail Mashanov (1852–1924), generally attributed these mass conversions to two factors. First, most of the baptized Tatars were already Muslim; their "conversion" to Islam was simply an effort to force the Russian authorities to recognize their true faith. Secondly, Christian proselytism was weak and poorly organized. Although these two interpretations contain some truth, they are reductivist and deterministic as if individuals had no control over their identity. Such approaches fail to recognize that the Kriashens faced a real choice between Islam and Christianity. It also fails to explain their choice.

The concept of identity in recent studies of psychologists and sociologists such as Joseph Kastersztein and Isabelle Taboada-Leonetti provides a useful corrective to the traditional historiography of Russian policy toward the Kriashens. For these scholars, identity is a continuous process that is conditioned by a relational conception of the world and not a fixed, stabilized, or idealized entity whose boundaries are defined by history or national heritage. In their approach, identity is not considered as a generic concept that explains collective or individual behaviors. Groups and individuals do not blindly follow the dictates of their so-called national or ancestral identity, but adopt specific strategies to change and develop themselves for specific ends.[2]

Thousands of Kriashens were not attracted to Islam just because they spoke Tatar and most of their ancestors were Muslim. Until the reign of Catherine II, Tatars who converted to Eastern Orthodoxy were excluded from their original community. According to Muslim law, a *murtadd* (renegade) is considered legally dead. Some Kriashens left their native villages to found new ones close by, while others migrated to other Kriashen villages to escape from their Muslim brethren's wrath. Nevertheless, at the end of the eighteenth century, when Catherine II put an end to Orthodox proselytism among the Muslims, mullas and Sufis encouraged Christian Tatars to become familiar with Islamic teaching and writings. The Kriashen response was not uniform. Some remained Christians (though according to missionaries, many of these retained strong ties with pre-Christian animism), while others chose Islam.

This study of the village of Elyshevo will show how Islamicized Kriashens created and maintained cultural and economic networks with the Muslim world, once they perceived themselves as religiously distinct from the Orthodox Church. Furthermore, it will examine how the Kriashens used their Qur'anic and Christian knowledge to define themselves, and how they adapted to the Russian law and resisted colonial imposition.

There were two waves of conversion to Orthodox Christianity. Archbishops Gurii (1555–63) and German (1564–65) of Kazan inaugurated the first wave in the sixteenth century; the Office of New Converts (*Novokreshchenskaia kontora*), which opened in 1740, was responsible for the second. The earlier converts and their descendants came to be known as

Starokriashens, or old converts (*starokreshchennye* in Russian, or *taza-kräshen* in Tatar—literally, "pure converts"); those of the second wave were known as Novokriashens, or new converts (*novokreshchennye* in Russian, or *iangy-kräshen* in Tatar). The Starokriashens were primarily of animist origin and lived in villages separate from both the Orthodox Russians and the Muslim Tatars.[3] By contrast, the Novokriashens had all come from peoples who were originally Muslim, rarely formed isolated villages, and instead generally lived in small numbers in predominantly Muslim villages.[4] This fact greatly increased the risk that these new Christians might return to Islam.

To solve this problem, Russian law had forbidden since the sixteenth century all forms of reconversion and of Muslim proselytism among the animists. In 1593, Tsar Fedor had ordered apostates from Christianity to be thrown into prison, beaten, and placed in chains. Measures were taken to isolate the Christian converts from the Muslims by placing them in special settlements. A Christian convert married to a non-Christian might be legally separated from his or her spouse.[5] Later, in accordance with the Law Code of 1649, any Muslim judged guilty of having turned away a Russian from Orthodox Christianity was condemned to be burned at the stake.[6] In the 1740s, the Office for New Converts punished converts to Islam with fines, beatings, separation from families in cases of mixed marriage, deportation to monasteries, and—for the most rebellious—exile to Siberia.[7]

The Apostasy of 1865–70 and Elyshevo Village

Despite these strictures, the Kriashens began to apostatize en masse beginning in 1802. By 1865, a third wave had begun in Kazan, not only affecting the areas of the previous movements, but also incorporating both Chuvash and (for the first time) Starokriashens in the revolt against Orthodoxy. The increasing mobility of Kriashen society due to improvements in communications in the Russian Empire and to the expanding Tatar market in Central Asia, in particular the growth of the number of seasonal workers, traders, traveling tailors, and even itinerant mullas, helps to explain the ever-increasing geographical extent of the apostate movement. When the Russian government exiled Christian converts to Islam, as it did from the 1830s through the 1850s, it only contributed to this mobility and to the spread of the Muslim religion. These exiles—martyrs of the faith—became the leaders of future apostasies and served as a link between the baptized community and the Muslims.[8]

After the coronation of Alexander II in 1856, these very exiles began to spread rumors of an imperial edict that would permit the Kriashens to profess Islam officially. These rumors may have risen from Alexander II's routine confirmation of his subjects' religious rights (which, of course, did

Mosque in the village of Elyshevo, constructed ca. 1900
(Photo courtesy of Agnès Kefeli)

not include the right of Christians to convert to Islam), or in laws published in 1857 permitting Muslims to open new mosques. Although such laws did not apply to them, the Kriashens interpreted them in their favor and opened their own clandestine prayer houses. More important, in December 1861, the Ministry of Internal Affairs stopped exiling Kriashen apostates because of the practical difficulties of transporting the exiles. In addition, the Crimean War (1853–56), which pitted the Russians against the Ottomans, the major Muslim power in the world, helped to fuel apocalyptic expectations about the final victory of Islam on earth. Probably Alexander's reforms had similar effects.[9]

One of the most important Kriashen communities to apostatize was Elyshevo, whose peasant commune requested official recognition of its Islamic identity in 1866. Located on the road to Ziuri in Mamadysh district, Elyshevo stood fifteen versts from its parish church in Achi village, Laishev district. Its population consisted of Kriashen migrants of various nationalities who had come from neighboring villages and who had been animists or Muslims before their conversion to Orthodoxy.

There is evidence that by the middle of the eighteenth century, the villagers of Elyshevo were genuinely committed to leading an Orthodox way of life. Since their parish church was so far away, the entire commune of Elyshevo successfully petitioned the archbishop to open a chapel. But a century later, in May 1866, the entire village rejected Christianity and embraced Islam. Bashir Valitov (also known as Efrem Kirillov), a Votiak, submitted a petition declaring that the inhabitants of the village had professed Islam for generations. This petition was signed by all but one of Elyshevo's 201 heads of household.[10]

The villagers' official conversion to Islam was not a sudden shift, as the words "conversion" and "apostasy" might falsely imply, but the result of a long exposure to Islamic beliefs, through educational, kinship, and economic networks.

Local Knowledge of Islam

The development of an extensive network of Islamic books and schools had preceded and informed this communal decision to apostatize. The popular knowledge of Islam among the Kriashens of Elyshevo consisted of stories taken from the Qur'an, from the *hadis* (the "traditions" about the practices of the Prophet Muhammad), and from Sufi textbooks that were told and retold in primary Qur'anic schools, at home, and during popular festivals.

Sufism entered the Volga from Central Asia between the tenth and fourteenth centuries. The most popular Sufi orders among the Tatars were the Yasawiya (which arrived in the mid-twelfth century) and the Naqshbandiya (which emerged in the fourteenth century). Both orders played an important role in the conversion to Islam of Mongol and Turkic tribes. They are well known for their flexibility toward local customs, and for their use of native language as a tool of conversion.[11] Although most of these Sufi teachers performed their work anonymously, several pieces of evidence testify to their presence in Elyshevo. First, according to a contemporary epic poem (*bäet*) recorded and published by Malov in 1871, the leader of the apostasy was Iagfar, an *ishan* (Sufi spiritual leader) of Kriashen origin.[12] Second, female descendants of a local dead ishan proselytized among the Kriashens of Mamadysh.[13] Third, the Tatar books that were popular among the Kriashens of Elyshevo were attributed to Sufi saints.

Even an illiterate Tatar or Kriashen could know the content of Sufi books by heart, since most of them were sung as *mönajat* (spiritual songs).[14] Their stereotypical meter and rhythm, which also entered the Volga from Central Asia, helped students to memorize these stories. Originally written in Chaghatai (a literary Turkic language that was widely used by the

Central Asian learned elite), these books made the high tradition of Islamic knowledge available to peasants who had little exposure to Islamic schooling. Their primary function was to gain new converts or to strengthen the faith of Muslim practitioners. They emphasized the belief in one God, the struggle against paganism, the virtue of forgiveness, the importance of literacy, and the thaumaturgical powers of the Prophets, and declared the certainty of the final victory of Islam. Their teachings were particularly appropriate for the Kriashens.

These books concentrated on the cult of the Prophets and often diverged from the Qur'anic narrative to demonstrate their supernatural powers. According to *Qyssa-yi Iosyf* (Tale of Joseph), an epic attributed to the Bulgar poet Qol Gali (b. 1172) and often quoted by the Kriashens, the Prophet Joseph showed signs of his divine calling even as a child. In a fantastic, extra-Qur'anic episode, a wolf who had refrained from attacking the boy explained that God had forbidden him to eat the flesh of the Prophets.[15]

In some cases, the prophets were so powerful that they could change the natural order. In *Qyssa-yi Solomon* (Tale of Solomon), an anonymous tale that was popular among the Tatars, the sun and the moon asked Solomon to pray that God would change their orbit. The narrator implied that Allah would blindly and automatically respond to Solomon's prayers whatever the consequences. This interpretation is quite different from that in the Qur'an, where nature is submitted to God's unique order.[16] By contrast, in *Qyssa-yi Iosyf*, Joseph could change the natural order but only as a passive agent of God; this view is much closer to the doctrine of learned Islam.

The Sufi works also emphasized and validated the cult of dead holy men, whose tombs were thought to be blessed with *baraka* (grace). When Joseph's tomb was removed from his city, which represents the ideal Islamic community, the Muslims endured hardship.[17] Although such doctrines actually contradicted the Qur'an, they pleased a popular audience that looked for magical mediators between man and God.

The Sufi books portrayed Muhammad as a miracle-worker even though the Qur'an explicitly denies this. In *Kisekbash* (The Decapitated Head), Muhammad resurrects both Kisekbash (a Muslim martyr whose head had been cut off) and his son, who had been devoured by the Div, a mythological giant.[18]

The Prophet in Sufi Tatar literature is also extraordinarily compassionate. He weeps for both the martyrs and those weak in faith. At the Last Judgement, he appears to be a mediator between believers and God. For their understanding of the Last Judgment, the Kriashens were heavily dependent on the eschatological writings attributed to Sölaiman Baqyrganyi (d. 1186), a disciple of the Sufi saint Yasawi. Like other Sufi literature, these works emphasized Muhammad's powers as an effective mediator.

In *Akhyr zaman kitaby* (The Book of the End of Time), thanks to Muhammad's entreaties, God forgave the Prophet's pagan parents as well as all Muslims who had failed to keep the law. This is contrary to the Qur'anic ethic of individual responsibility: "a father cannot pay for the sins of his son, nor can the son for his father's" (XXXI, 33). The author likewise attributed extraordinary powers to Muhammad, who could command both the angels and the guardians of hell; in the Qur'an the Prophet had no such authority. Even Adam, Abraham, and Jesus asked for his help. Although the Qur'an specifically declared that Muhammad would face God's judgment like any other man, the author took pains to deemphasize this doctrine, which he mentioned only at the end of his poem.[19] This vision of the Last Judgment promised the apostate Kriashens that as Muslims, they would have a powerful patron before God.

Prophets also taught their faith in a clear vernacular language. Sufi authors such as Qol Gali or the mulla Ishniiaz (fl. 1770s) used Bulgar (the Turkic language of their contemporaries in the Middle Volga) to spread Muhammad's message. Ishniiaz's *Shäraitu'l-iman* (Rules of the Faith), or, as it was known among the Tatars, *Iman sharty* (Principles of the Faith), contains prayers in Turkic language for those who have difficulty reading in Arabic.[20] This greatly favored proselytism among animist peoples, while helping to spread literacy and encourage reading. Unlike popular Sufism in India, Tatar Sufism had no anti-intellectual bias.[21] On the contrary, reading was viewed as a mode of purification.

Finally, Sufi books offered two possible models for living in a world dominated by non-Muslim forces. The first model demonstrated the possibility of cooperation with non-Muslim authorities. For example, in *Qyssa-yi Iosyf*, Joseph, a slave in Egypt, served his infidel masters; by so doing, he rose to a high position and brought many to Islam. But when cooperation demanded abandoning some vital part of Islam, the Sufi ethic offered a second model—complete and total separation from the non-Muslim populace. Thus, when the king of Egypt asks him to stop his proselytism, Joseph instead founds a city where only Muslims can reside. The book of *Bädävam* (Forever) goes further and urges true believers not to drink or eat with non-Muslims.[22] By extension, the Sufi teaching contained in these books encouraged resistance to Russians when the latter tried to impose legal prohibitions on Tatar proselytism, but as the example of Joseph shows, it did not prohibit Muslims from working within the Russian political system.

Sufi Islam in Peasant Discourse

Kriashen and Tatar peasants used these books to resist Russian rule. Before and after their official conversion to Islam, the Kriashens of Elyshevo and other villages of the Mamadysh district recited miracle stories about Jesus and the Prophets from their Sufi books, not from the Bible.[23] Some of the stories were so well integrated into the popular consciousness that they supported arguments against the missionaries. Literate Kriashens familiar with Muslim theology and the Russian language cited the Sufi books to critique Russian Orthodoxy, its scriptures, and missionaries. As one Kriashen pointed out to an Orthodox missionary, *Qyssa-yi Iosyf* recounted the story of Joseph in far greater detail than did Genesis.[24] The apostates also turned to the story of Joseph to attack the Orthodox practice of venerating icons. When Joseph lived with Pharaoh, Pharaoh's wife fell in love with him and fervently prayed to her wooden idols (that is, her icons) so that he would return her passion. When he did not, she broke her idols in a fit of rage.[25]

Muhammad, of course, was the focus of numerous stories. According to some of the Kriashens, Muhammad was born a Greek; to others, a Tatar; and to the most Islamized, an Arab. For the most Islamized Kriashens, Muhammad was the true prophet because his faith was "ancient," by which they understood that his message was the true and immutable religion of Adam, the first man.[26] Even among the Kriashens less advanced in the apostasy, Muhammad, if he was not counted among the prophets, was nonetheless revered as a saint.[27] Returning from Ufa province, the Kriashen traders of Mamadysh district repeated stories such as the account of Muhammad's ascension into heaven, a legend based upon numerous hadis. A great stone had followed the Prophet into the sky and remained suspended in midair from that time on. For those weak in the faith, God had established four pillars under the rock. These four pillars did not touch the suspended stone, but they did protect the Kriashens who struggled in their faith.[28]

Other stories told about Muhammad also emphasized his compassion. One day the Prophet met a poor man without clothes who began to recount all of his troubles. In an act of great compassion, Muhammad offered himself as the poor man's slave and suggested that the man sell him to a wealthy person. After the poor man had completed this transaction and was returning home with his money, he suddenly saw Muhammad praying in a magnificent garden. Frightened, the poor man asked, "Who are you?" The Prophet replied with the words of the Muslim creed, the *shahada*: "Say of me, 'there is no God but God and Muhammad is His Messenger.'"[29]

Islamic eschatology also encouraged the Kriashens to convert by declaring the final victory of Islam as a certainty. "Before the end of the world," said one converted Kriashen *abystai* (a female teacher in a primary Qurʾanic school), "the whole world will become Muslim." The Kriashens of Elyshevo village knew of the messianic (*mahdist*) tradition that Gaisa (Jesus) would return to earth forty years before the end of the world. A

Kriashen tailor thus concluded that Muhammad and Jesus must be equal since believers would pray to both to be saved from hell at the last judgment.[30]

The Carriers of Popular Islam

The principal carriers of popular Islam included itinerant mullas or Sufis, seasonal workers, and women. The seasonal workers constituted a relatively well-to-do segment of the population and were the leaders of the Elyshevo apostasy. They left two by two, master and apprentice. The apprentice was a child old enough to work (between nine and fourteen) and whose presence was not necessary at home. On average, the two tailors earned fifteen to twenty-five rubles (the average price of a cow or horse) during the period from October to March.[31] A large family could count on three or four salaries to increase its income. The carriers of a new type of knowledge, the tailors were living proof of its effectiveness, for their families lacked for nothing. This contrasted favorably with the temporary privileges which the Kriashens' ancestors had received when they were baptized and from which they rarely profited personally.

Women in particular served as a link between communities whose level of Islamization was not necessarily the same. Kriashens as well as Tatars practiced exogamy, which meant that girls rarely stayed in their native villages. Families who were attracted by the teaching of Muhammad tried to find *kilen* (daughters-in-law) in villages that officially apostatized. Those who were illiterate also privileged women with some Qur'anic education. Once married, women sent their children to Qur'anic schools in their own village or in the neighboring one. Finally, after two generations, women in their village or in the village of their husband opened clandestine Qur'anic schools where children could learn their prayers and read Sufi literature. These teachers could not be easily arrested because children, girls very often, would come two by two for short visits. These women pedagogues completed the work of itinerant mullas and helped the Kriashens to have continuous exposure to written Islamic knowledge, despite missionary persecutions.[32]

The *jyens* (popular festivals) served as a common link between itinerant mullas or Sufis, seasonal workers, and women. They represented one of the most important networks for the spread of Islamic knowledge. These festivals began on a Friday at the end of May or the beginning of June and lasted from four to seven weeks. They moved from village to village within an established network; each village hosted the fair for three or four days. These feasts were occasions for merchants to sell their goods and Sufi books, for bards to sing religious and epic poems, and, in this more relaxed atmosphere, for young Tatars to choose a spouse.

Originally, according to Tatar ethnographers, the jyens probably corresponded to the territorial divisions of the Volga Bulgar state. Thus, the village at the center of the jyen network usually contained the oldest cemeteries and other monuments; these villages were often the focus of local pilgrimages. They also served as a point of contact between the Kriashens and the Tatars.

From 1839 through 1849, the Ministry of Internal Affairs and the Holy Synod, not realizing that the Russian village of Blagoveshchenskoe (known as Omara among the Tatars) was a jyen center, exiled some of the apostate leaders there. Instead of being isolated from other Muslims, these apostates found themselves at the center of an important kinship and economic network of the Muslim Tatars. A generation later, during the apostate movement of 1865–70, Muslim Tatars used this strategic position to help spread news of the apostasy of the Chistopol' Novokriashens among the Starokriashens of Mamadysh district, who began to renounce their Christianity for the first time.[33]

The Process of Becoming Muslim

The apostasy in Elyshevo followed a general pattern that can be discerned in Kriashen villages throughout the Volga region. On the eve of the Crimean War, and again in 1865, vagabond Tatars, mullas, and Sufis began to preach in the Kazan region. They reminded believers of their obligation to realize the will of God on earth, the *jihad*, and announced that time would end with the final victory of Islam. Recalling the *hijra* of the Prophet (when opposition to his message forced Muhammad to flee from Mecca to Medina), they encouraged their listeners to go to Turkey and await the day of judgment. They spoke in passionate terms of the coming of the *mahdi*, the "guided one," who, according to Islamic tradition, would reestablish justice on earth at the end of time. The sultan of Turkey, according to them, would take possession of the Muslim lands and restore the khanate of Kazan before the coming of the Antichrist and his defeat by the prophet Gaisa (Jesus).[34]

In their turn, before sending the petition, the leaders of the apostasy spread rumors about the mahdi in order to gain as many adherents as possible. After the petition was sent to St. Petersburg, but before the troops arrived, Kriashens tried to form a distinct community aware of its specific identity. They took the city of Joseph as a model of social exclusiveness, and to mark the passage of Elyshevo to Islam, they performed several symbolic communal acts according to a strict calendar. The leaders of the commune barred all those who refused to profess Islam from participating in the games and dances of the spring feast (jyen). The leaders also ordered them to destroy their icons. Finally, they publicly burned a copy of a recent translation into vernacular Tatar of the Gospel.

Constructing an Islamic Identity

Tombstone in the cemetery of the village of Elyshevo
(Photo courtesy of Agnès Kefeli)

During the apostate movement, the peasant commune put the Muslim religious law (*Shariʿa*) into practice. The village elders established and began to collect both taxes (*zekât*) and voluntary alms (*sadaka*). Everyone in the village was required to give a fixed sum to support the new Muslim community. Wealthier peasants offered larger gifts in return for the promise of a greater reward in the afterlife. They also instituted collective prayer, and sought to fight the jihad by convincing waverers to convert to Islam. They created a separate cemetery for the Muslim dead and forbade fermented drink. Not far from the town tavern, Kriashens publicly shaved their heads, in Muslim fashion, to mark their passage from the world of the Infidels. Finally, they elected an imam to lead them in communal prayer, keep their vital records, arbitrate disputes about inheritance, and teach their children. As an expedient until they could construct a new mosque, they performed their collective prayers in a peasant cottage.

In this way, the peasants of Elyshevo created a society that regulated the relations of its members with God and with one another according to

Allah's revelation in the Qur'an. This new society had nothing in common with the traditional constitution of non-Russian parishes in which a Russian bishop imposed a Russian priest upon the indigenous peoples—a Russian priest who was not chosen by the community and who represented a financial burden on it.[35]

Once the *umma* (the community of believers) was constituted, the undecided no longer had any place in it. In order to encourage them to convert to Islam, the peasant elders confiscated their land. In 1868, in Kibiak-Kozi, a village near Elyshevo, those who remained Orthodox were so badly treated that they tried to form their own village. The apostate movement thus appeared as a living incarnation of the Sufi books.[36]

Islamic Education among the Kriashen

Before and after the apostasy of Elyshevo, Qur'anic education played a primary role in the transmission of Muslim knowledge. It contributed to the formation of a local intellectual elite that constituted the principal cell of resistance. The villages of converts to Islam reflected in every way the different degrees of Islamic knowledge observed in the Tatar villages.

In these village schools the Book (the Qur'an or other Muslim religious work) was first introduced. Children began by memorizing passages from popular primers such as *Iman sharty* or *Qyssa-yi Iosyf*. If all went well, they received a basic Qur'anic education containing all the indispensable elements of the Muslim faith. Finally, a prosperous family might send its son to Central Asia to complete his education in the *madrasa,* the higher theological school.

In Elyshevo, itinerant mullas, who often hid their identity, came to teach the Kriashens. In 1865, a Muslim named Mukhi-ed-din and his wife taught both boys and girls for several months before leaving for another village. An itinerant mulla who spent a summer in one village and a winter in another, Mukhi-ed-din had been among those şakirts (students of the madrasas) who were unable to find a permanent position in a village school or mosque after completing their own education. The state imposed a strict quota on the number of Muslim *mäkhällä* (parishes), and the proximity of Kriashen villages made the opening of new mosques a very delicate question.[37] The work of the mulla was facilitated by the villagers themselves, who, literate or not, taught each other Muslim prayers. For example, one family entrusted its children to an old blind female relative who imparted to them the basics of the Islamic faith.[38] In the 1860s, a Kriashen woman who had studied in Kazan before moving to Elyshevo secretly taught the village girls. After Mukhi-ed-din had left the village in 1865, she continued the work of the itinerant mulla.[39] In 1870, another Kriashen woman replaced her. Some nearby villages such as Tri-Sosny in Mamadysh district, Kibiak-Kozi and Janasal in Laishev district, and Aziak in Kazan district also had clandestine Qur'anic schools whose fragile existence was constantly threatened by the intervention of priest or police.[40] The diffusion of Islam encouraged the formation of an indigenous elite which completed and consolidated the teaching of the mullas and the şakirts.

Mukhi-ed-din's pupils learned to reject all images, drawings, portraits, icons, and crosses—the symbols of the Orthodox world. Their main textbook was the Muslim primer *Iman sharty,* from which the children learned not only reading but also the personal and communal obligations of their faith. Although they could not translate their Arabic prayers into Tatar, Mukhi-ed-din's students mastered the rudiments of literacy and the Muslim faith.[41] These results were comparable to those of the *maktabs* attached to the Tatar mosques.

Literate Kriashens played a crucial role in the 1866 apostasy. One of them could read the *Häfteiak* (the seventh part of the Qur'an) almost without error and was also able to translate two Arabic words, *awwal* and *akhyr* (the First and the Last, one of the Titles of God).[42] Another who was particularly respected by the villagers took the *Häfteiak* and read it with the aid of the *tafsir.*[43] These men narrated numerous stories which were inspired by the qadi Nasiruddin Rabguzi (fifteenth century), such as Solomon's power over the demons and Solomon's ring. Most were tailors or seasonal workers who had left Elyshevo to trade in Ufa and Cheliabinsk district. In these regions, from the age of thirteen or fourteen they had adopted Muslim customs, since Muslims were their most important customers. They went to the mosque and the Qur'anic school.[44] Another tailor who had inspired an apostasy in Kazan had studied in a madrasa there.[45]

The need for a permanent teacher led the villagers of Elyshevo to elect their own imam in 1866. Although we do not know how or where he was trained, his daughter was able to read (slowly but correctly) several verses of the Qur'an.[46]

But the pupils of Qur'anic schools could advance far beyond the mere recitation of certain religious texts. For example, the Efremov brothers, who played a critical role in the apostasy, had an impressive quantity of Islamic works, including the *Häfteiak* and the tafsir. They demonstrated their literacy in court by translating Tatar notes for the judge who was prosecuting the apostates. One of these notes urged the Kriashens to give their children Muslim names and to create a separate Muslim cemetery for their dead. By reading this note, the Efremovs proved their ability to make the connection between the Arabic characters and the Tatar sounds they represented, to decipher a message whose form was not fixed by tradition or dictated by God, and finally to create their own text.[47]

As a general rule, the higher the level of instruction, the more the Kriashens resisted Russification. In 1866, 448 inhabitants of Elyshevo bowed to police pressure and officially repented of their apostasy—except the mulla and the tailors who knew how to read the Qur'an and interpret the commentaries. Among these last, two were deported to Siberia, while the others were able to disappear to Ufa and Menzelinsk, where they were accustomed to trade. To the great embarrassment of the police, the Kriashens of Elyshevo pursued their religious propaganda among the other Kriashens of these regions, even after their official repentance. Other Kriashen villages followed Elyshevo's example and apostatized from Orthodoxy. As a result, the wave of apostasies moved east.[48]

The Russian Response

Nonetheless, if Russian Orthodoxy had become marginalized, the Russian language was not ignored at all. Russian was useful in the world of business and politics. Mikhail Matveev, a Kriashen tailor who during his trip to Cheliabinsk had learned the Russian alphabet to help him in business, had attended the Russian school of Mikhailov, not far from the church of Tikhvin.[49] But he spread only his knowledge of the Qur'an, not his knowledge of Russian, to his home town. Other Kriashens who had been at the parish school of the *volost'* used their linguistic knowledge to demonstrate the superiority of the Qur'an to the Gospel. Knowledge of Russian also permitted the Kriashens to compose and copy drafts of petitions to defend their rights.

In the 1860s, using more peaceful tools than those of the eighteenth century, Orthodox missionaries tried again to convert the Tatars. Professor Il'minskii's school in Kazan introduced a new form of literacy in the countryside, destined to compete not with the sophisticated knowledge of the ulema but with popular Sufi culture. It was posed as a rival to the Qur'anic school, and also to the parish and ministry schools, which had been charged with the religious education of His Majesty's non-Russian subjects.[50] His goal was to create an Orthodox Christian culture in the Tatar language. From 1863 to 1869, Il'minskii's close friend and collaborator, the Kriashen missionary Timofeev, sought out children who had studied in the maktabs.[51]

To demonstrate the superiority of his teaching, he asked the maktab pupils to read in public a page of the Gospel in Tatar in Arabic script and then to paraphrase it. Because it was a new work that they had never seen in the maktab, the children were usually unable to complete the task. They tried to read the text in the way that they had learned at school, by naming each letter (*mim* for *m*, *nun* for *n*), without understanding the sound the letter stood for. Thus, the meaning of the word escaped them. Timofeev then asked them to read one of the books that they had studied in the maktab. The children easily read the text, without spelling out the letters, but often were unable to paraphrase it; the literary calques from Arabic proved too difficult for them.[52]

Timofeev then called upon one of his own pupils, who was usually much younger than his competitors. The young man read the Gospel in Russian, translated it into Tatar, and then opened Il'minskii's primer of popular Tatar, *Book of the True Faith* (*Chyn din kenägäsi*).[53] To the great astonishment of the Tatar and Kriashen adults, for whom the Qur'an remained incomprehensible, the pupil was able to read in both Tatar and Russian.[54]

It goes without saying that Timofeev's testimony was partial. His accounts were designed to win the sympathy of the Holy Synod and the Ministry of Education. Nevertheless, Timofeev's assessment of Muslim education is supported by the Tatars themselves; in the 1880s, Muslim Tatar modernists offered the same critique of maktab education.

To compete with Islamic knowledge, Timofeev introduced three pedagogical practices unknown in the maktab: phonetic reading, immediate comprehension of the text read, and the simultaneous translation of sacred texts into the vernacular. This approach was contrary to the Muslim education, which insisted above all that every character of the text was inviolable, and which did not permit the reader to interpret the text until after many years of study. Thus, Arabic grammar was studied in the madrasa, not in the maktab.

By making Western pedagogy the norm for all forms of scientific and religious knowledge, Timofeev directly attacked the Islam of the Volga Tatars. This popular, magical Islam was dangerous, in his view, because it inspired the Kriashens to apostatize. To struggle more successfully against it, the missionary opposed popular to literate Islam. He criticized the Muslim Tatars and the Kriashens for the faith they placed in healers and for their pre-Islamic animist beliefs that their ignorance of their own sacred texts encouraged. The Tatars, he said, did not know their own religion because the Qur'an is written in a language that they could not understand. For example, the Tatars of Mamadysh district believed that Muhammad worked miracles even though this directly contradicted the Qur'an. Timofeev ended his sermons by claiming that he had studied the scriptures of both Islam and Christianity, compared the two religions, and consciously and scientifically chosen the latter.[55]

Similarly, Timofeev encouraged the Kriashens to pray freely in their own words rather than recite Muslim prayers which meant nothing and which the Tatars themselves did not comprehend.[56] Finally, Timofeev used history, politics, and science to attack Islam. Thus, when the Kriashens alluded to the mahdi, he noted the weakness of the Ottoman Empire. When the Tatars claimed that Islam was the religion of Adam, he showed that historically the Christian faith was older than the Muslim faith, and therefore the true religion. He used globes and maps to prove that the earth was round, contrary to what the Tatars believed.[57]

Yet as impressive as the Il'minskii system of education was, it came too late to attract the intellectual elite of Elyshevo. In 1866, the missionary Evfimii Malov tried to enroll the children of the hamlet in an Orthodox school. However, the most prosperous and educated refused his entreaties. Only those who had never been to the Qur'anic school allowed their children to enter Malov's classroom. But even they were hesitant; as Elyshevo became increasingly Islamized, would their children become outcasts for studying in an Orthodox school?

Because Elyshevo was connected to a wider network of Islamic knowledge outside the village, the missionaries could enjoy only temporary success. Despite the construction of a church[58] and the opening of a school in 1869,[59] despite the presence of a Tatar-speaking priest and then a Starokriashen priest, the apostasies continued.[60] At the end of 1874, 437 parishioners threatened to burn down the church.[61] In 1887, most of the pupils were from neighboring villages and had to live at the school.[62] These pupils were themselves from apostate villages and from the age of eleven years had worked as itinerant tailors in Ufa or Menzelinsk, where, like their fathers, they lived according to the Shari'a.[63] Finally, at the beginning of the twentieth century, when Elyshevo opened its own clandestine prayer house and elected a mulla and muezzin, all the children went to the maktab. In 1912, the school of the Brotherhood was still there, but the Kriashens persevered and finally officially opened a maktab. After the revolution, the village definitively adopted Islam, just like their Novokriashen neighbors of Simbirsk.[64]

Elyshevo was not an isolated case. The Brotherhood of St. Gurii, founded in October 1867 at Kazan under the patronage of Il'minskii, Malov, Rozov, and Petr Shestakov (1826–89), the curator of the Kazan Academy, finished by opening schools on the outskirts of villages which had officially apostatized. In effect, Il'minskii's method knew success only in those regions which Qur'anic schooling had not reached. (Primarily, this was the case only in villages which were completely animist.) Those animists who lived along Tatar trade routes or who lived near a Muslim village were far more inclined to become Muslims themselves.

The case of Elyshevo as a frontier zone between two possible identities illustrates the strength of traditional Islam, too often overshadowed by the jadids (Tatar reformers of the late nineteenth century), in resisting Russian encroachment and developing a Tatar identity. Beginning in the 1880s, the jadids (including modernist Naqshbandi Sufis) contested the Islam at work in Elyshevo because of its eschatological character. They ridiculed the type of Islam the popular Sufi books represented by composing new, mocking words in the stereotyped forms of the mönajat. For instance, in his satirical "The Haymarket or the New 'Decapitated Head'" (*Pechän Bazary, iakhut iaña Kisekbash*), the poet Gabdulla Tukai (1886–1913) wrote that the decapitated head recovered its human body thanks to a satanic ishan and not to the Prophet Muhammad.[65] The jadids also presented traditional Tatar learning as the mere rote memorization of sacred texts, without any understanding on the part of the students. Finally, they described popular Islamic culture as xenophobic.

However, popular Sufi Islam prepared the way for jadidism. Current Tatar historiography has ignored this important continuity, and tends to emphasize the differences between the two movements.[66] Kinship, economic, and popular cultural networks helped the Muslim faith to spread among non-Russian peoples. Sufi books in particular, or peasant discourse originated in Sufi literature, facilitated the extension of literacy to non-Muslim villages such as Elyshevo, despite church and state measures. Traditional popular Islam with its powerful spiritual mediators (such as the Prophet Muhammad) and its magical and initiatory components encouraged peasants to read and develop a clear understanding of their faith. As the Russian missionaries found to their dismay, the Kriashen converts were able to defend their Islam whenever their identity was questioned.

The jadids continued the Sufi practice of using the Turkic language as a tool of moral edification. Qaium Nasyri (1825–1902) and other reformers wrote parables and fables that indeed promoted a new form of Islam, but nevertheless were directly influenced by Sufi texts. For instance, Nasyri recalls one of the most popular miracles attributed to Muhammad, the splitting of the moon. His tale is not different from the itinerant Sufis' stories, except that in his conclusion, Nasyri wrote that Muhammad refused to perform another miracle, since the Faith was not based on supernatural proof.[67]

Jadids also followed their Sufi predecessors in advocating involvement in the dominant society. Traditional Islam was not as xenophobic as the jadids, and in particular Gaiaz Iskhakyi (1878–1954), claimed.[68] Sufi books such as *Qyssa-yi Iosyf* presented Joseph's active involvement in the non-Muslim Egyptian state as an implicit mold for the Kriashen. Moreover, although the spread of Tatar literacy can explain the appeal of Islam to preliterate peasants, the Kriashens also sought to read and write in Russian and used Russian literacy as a powerful tool of resistance to defend their culture.

Finally, in their attempts at reforming Tatar society, the same jadids retained popular Islamic tradition of schooling and literacy in the Turkic language as tools of cultural resistance. Those aspects of popular Islam have been unjustly neglected and demand further study.

NOTES

1. Sufism is a set of mystical movements that had arisen within Islam by the mid-eighth century C.E. Adherents sought to unite themselves with God through a body of ritual practices, spiritual exercises, and ascetic disciplines. Sufis are orga-

nized into different orders and brotherhoods (*tarika*, literally "the way"), each of which was founded by a famous *şeyh* or teacher. The most important of these Sufi orders for the Tatars was the Naqshbandiya, which Muhammad ibn Muhammad Baha[c] ad-Din Naqshband founded in the fourteenth century. Its central characteristic involves the silent ritual invocation of God's names. On Sufism, see Alexandre Bennigsen and Chantal Lemercier-Quelquejay, *Le Soufi et le Commissaire: les confréries musulmanes en URSS* (Paris, 1986).

2. Joseph Kastersztein, "Les stratégies identitaires des acteurs sociaux: approche dynamique des finalités," in Carmel Camilleri et al., *Stratégies identitaires* (Paris, 1990), pp. 27–41; I. Taboada-Leonetti, "Stratégies identitaires et minorités: le point de vue du sociologue," in ibid., pp. 43–83.

3. Many of the Starokriashens probably descended from Sobekullian, Chelmat, and Temtiuzi peoples cited in twelfth-century Russian chronicles who had led an existence separate from that of the Tatars well before the Mongol invasion. See F. S. Baiazitova, *Govory Tatar-Kriashen v sravnitel'nom osveshchenii* (Moscow, 1986), p. 16.

4. When more than three families had accepted baptism, the Office for New Converts had been unable to transfer them to Russian villages as it had originally intended to do. Such a state policy would have rendered baptism a hardship for many potential converts; it also would have cost the state and the church too much. As a result, many of the new converts to Christianity remained a minority in a Muslim world. Evfimii Malov, "O Novokreshchenskoi kontore," *Pravoslavnyi sobesednik* 24, no. 12 (December 1878): 46.

5. A. F. Mozharovskii, "Izlozhenie khoda missionerskago dela po prosveshcheniiu Kazanskikh inorodtsev s 1552 po 1867," *Chteniia v imperatorskom obshchestve istorii i drevnostei rossiiskikh*, bk. 1 (1880): 26–27.

6. M. N. Tikhomirov and P. P. Epifanov, eds., *Sobornoe ulozhenie 1649 goda* (Moscow, 1961), chap. 22, art. 24, p. 291.

7. For example, see the case of the animist Chuvash in Sviazhsk, in Malov, "O Novokreshchenskoi," p. 107.

8. The biography of Egor Fedorov (in Tatar, Gabdul Galim Samigulov), born in 1826, demonstrates the significance of these exiles. In 1843, Samigulov's native village Verkhniaia Nikitkina (in Tatar, Tubulga-tau), situated in the Chistopol' district, apostatized for the first time, during the Ramadan. Six years later, the leaders of the village were deported to the Mamadysh district. In 1856, 1858, and 1859, Samigulov, who was the unofficial mulla of his village, sent petitions to Saint Petersburg, asking the government to allow his exiled countrymen to come back to the village. His requests were denied. Finally, in August 1865, without any authorization, the deported Kriashens came back to their village and founded there a mosque and a Qur'anic school. As for Samigulov, during the month of the Ramadan he traveled to Simbirsk province and Mamadysh district, where Elyshevo is located, and persuaded other villages to follow the example of his own. In January 1866, Samigulov was arrested in Kazan, in the hotel of a Tatar merchant, Khäsän Gafuri, while he was writing petitions for the Kriashens of Laishev and Mamadysh districts. Four years later, the Ministry of Internal Affairs exiled him to Siberia. See *Russkii gosudarstvennyi istoricheskii arkhiv* (abbrev. RGIA), f. 821, op. 8, d. 763, ll. 73ob.–82 and 218–219ob.; Nikolai Il'minskii, ed., *Kazanskaia tsentral'naia kreshcheno-tatarskaia shkola. Materialy dlia istorii khristianskago prosve-*

shcheniia kreshchenykh Tatar (Kazan, 1887), pp. 291–292; Evfimii Malov, "Nyneshnee religioznoe polozhenie kreshchenykh Tatar Zavolzhskago kraia," *Strannik* 7 (1866): 73; *Materialy po istorii Tatarii vtoroi poloviny 19-go veka. Agrarnyi vopros i krest'ianskoe dvizhenie v Tatarii XIX veka* (Moscow-Leningrad, 1936), pp. 233–236 and 250–251 (Samigulov's petitions and police reports).

9. RGIA, f. 821, op. 133, d. 454, ll. 298ob.–299ob. (Kratkaia spravka o pravitel'-stvennykh meropriiatiiakh otnositel'no otpavshikh ot pravoslaviia v magome-tanstvo); *Svod zakonov Rossiiskoi imperii*, vol. 12 (St. Petersburg, 1857), pp. 260–265.

10. Evfimii Malov, "Ocherk religioznago sostoianiia kreshchenykh tatar, podvergshikhsia vliianiiu magometanstva," *Pravoslavnyi sobesednik* 17, no. 11 (1871): 235 and 238; 17, no. 12 (1871): 414; 18, no. 1 (1872): 77; Il'minskii, *Kazanskaia*, p. 280.

11. The best recent study of Sufism in the Middle Volga is Hamid Algar, "Shaykh Zaynullah Rasulaev: The Last Great Naqshbandi Shaykh of the Volga-Urals Region," in Jo-Ann Gross, ed., *Muslims in Central Asia: Expressions of Identity and Change* (Durham, N.C., 1992), pp. 112–133.

12. Malov, "Ocherk," 18, no. 4 (1872): 403–404 (text in Tatar).

13. Mikhail Mashanov, "Zametka o religiozno-nravstvennom sostoianii kre-shchenykh Tatar Kazanskoi gubernii Mamadyshskago uezda," *Izvestiia po Kazan-skoi eparkhii* 9, no. 4 (1875): 113–115.

14. S. I. Raimova, "K voprosu o tatarskom detskom muzykal'nom fol'klore," *Uchenye zapiski Kazanskogo gosudarstvennogo pedagogicheskogo instituta* 104 (1972): 43.

15. Qol Gali, *Qyssa-yi Iosyf* (Kazan, 1880), p. 12.

16. A. Mikhailov, "Kriticheskii razbor i perevod s tatarskago iazyka na russkii broshiury 'Rasskazy o Solomone,'" *Orenburgskie eparkhial'nye vedomosti*, no. 10 (1889): 280–284.

17. Gali, *Qyssa-yi Iosyf*, p. 64.

18. *Kisekbash kitaby* (Kazan, 1846), pp. 15–16. According to Tatar historians, it was composed in the twelfth century.

19. *Akhyr zaman kitaby* (Kazan, 1847).

20. *Shäraitu'l-iman* (Kazan, 1904), pp. 14–15, 17, 26, and 31–32. Ishniiaz's primer speaks favorably of Naqshbandi Sufism.

21. Annemarie Schimmel, "Reflections on Popular Muslim Poetry," in *Islam in Local Contexts*, ed. Richard C. Martin (Leiden, 1982), p. 20.

22. *Bädävam kitaby* (Kazan, 1861). Present-day Tatar scholars attribute this book to an anonymous Bulgar author of the twelfth century.

23. P. B. Znamenskii, "Kazanskie tatary," in *Zhivopisnaia Rossiia. Otechestvo nashe v ego zemel'nom, istoricheskom, plemennom, ekonomicheskom i bytovom znachenii*, vol. 8: *Srednee Povolzh'e i Priural'skii krai*, pt. 1: *Srednee Povolzh'e* (St. Petersburg–Moscow, 1910), p. 140.

24. Vasilii Timofeev, "Dnevnik starokreshchenago Tatarina," in Il'minskii, *Kazanskaia*, p. 72.

25. Timofeev, "Dnevnik," p. 59; Gali, *Qyssa-yi Iosyf*, p. 47.

26. Malov, "Ocherk," 17, no. 12 (1871): 412; 18, no. 1 (1872): 67; 18, no. 5 (1872): 44; Timofeev, "Dnevnik," p. 45.

27. Znamenskii, "Kazanskie Tatary," p. 140.

28. Timofeev, "Dnevnik," p. 52; Malov, "Ocherk," 18, no. 1 (1872): 67. This

legend may refer to the *al-hajar al-aswad*, the sacred black stone in Mecca. See Mikhail Mashanov, *Zametka o religiozno-nravstvennom sostoianii kreshchenykh Tatar Kazanskoi gubernii* (Kazan, 1875), p. 18.

29. Vasilii Timofeev, "Dnevnik starokreshchenago Tatarina, 1865 goda," in Il'minskii, *Kazanskaia*, p. 157.

30. Timofeev, "Dnevnik," pp. 39, 50, and 75; Timofeev, "Dnevnik . . . 1865," p. 157; Malov, "Ocherk," 18, no. 4 (1872): 387.

31. *Materialy dlia sravnitel'noi otsenki zemel'nykh ugodii v uezdakh Kazanskoi gubernii*, vol. 6: *Uezd Mamadyshskii* (Kazan, 1888), p. 61; Iu. G. Mukhametshin, *Tatary-kriasheny. Istoriko-etnograficheskoe issledovanie material'noi kul'tury—seredina XIX–nachalo XX vekov* (Moscow, 1977), p. 54.

32. Agnès Kefeli, "Keräshen kyzy Islam iakly," *Söembikä*, no. 3 (1995): 16–17; Malov, "Ocherk," 18, no. 2 (1872): 126; Il'minskii, *Kazanskaia*, pp. 70–72, 74–75, 132, and 152–154.

33. Evfimii Malov, "Prikhody starokreshchenykh i novokreshchenykh Tatar v Kazanskoi eparkhii," *Pravoslavnoe obozrenie*, no. 12 (1865): 464–466; idem, "Ocherk," 18, no. 3 (1872): 239; *Tatary Srednego povolzh'ia i Priural'ia* (Moscow, 1967), p. 202.

34. Antonii Ivanov, "Otstupnicheskoe dvizhenie kreshchenykh i nekreshchenykh Chuvash Samarskoi gubernii v magometanstvo," *Pravoslavnyi blagovestnik*, no. 1 (1914): 151; S. Bagin, "Ob otpadenii v magometanstvo kreshchenykh inorodtsev Kazanskoi eparkhii i o prichine etago pechal'nago iavleniia," *Pravoslavnyi sobesednik* 56, no. 2 (1910): 227.

35. Gregory Freeze, *The Parish Clergy in Nineteenth-Century Russia: Crisis, Reform, Counter-Reform* (Princeton, 1983).

36. Malov, "Ocherk," 17, no. 11 (1871): 246–247; 17, no. 2 (1871): 410 and 414; 18, no. 5 (1872): 41 and 69.

37. Malov, "Ocherk," 18, no. 1 (1872): 65; 18, no. 4 (1872): 396.

38. Ibid., 17, no. 11 (1871): 243.

39. Timofeev, "Dnevnik . . . 1865," p. 153.

40. RGIA, f. 821, op. 8, d. 763, ll. 288 ob., 289 ob., 299–299 ob., and 301–301 ob.

41. Malov, "Ocherk," 17, no. 11 (1871): 240, 243–244, and 247–248; 17, no. 12 (1871): 406.

42. Ibid., 17, no. 11 (1871): 241.

43. Ibid., 17, no. 11 (1871): 242. In the tafsir, every word, every verse is glossed. It provides grammatical and historical information helpful in understanding the text. Some tafsirs preserve Jewish and Christian traditions. The Volga Tatars overall preferred the tafsir of Jalal al-din al-Mahalli (d. 1459) and his disciple Jalal al-din al-Suyuti (d. 1505). See *Tafsir al-jalalayn*, in Iakov Koblov, "Konfessional'nye shkoly kazanskikh tatar," *Inorodcheskoe obozrenie* 2, no. 1 (1915), supplement to *Pravoslavnyi sobesednik* (January–February 1917), p. 28, fn. 2.

44. Malov, "Ocherk," 17, no. 11 (1871): 250–251.

45. Ibid., 17, no. 12 (1871): 399.

46. Ibid., 17, no. 11 (1871): 246–247; 18, no. 2 (1872): 126.

47. Ibid., 18, no. 1 (1872): 72 and 77–78.

48. RGIA, f. 821, op. 8, d. 763, l. 300.

49. Malov, "Ocherk," 17, no. 11 (1871): 241; 18, no. 4 (1872): 399.

50. Il'minskii, *Kazanskaia*, pp. 80 and 85–86.

51. Ibid., pp. 34–35, 42, 49, and 66.

52. Ibid., pp. 49, 51, 175, and 230–231.

53. In Russian: "Nachal'noe uchenie pravoslavnoi khristianskoi very" (ibid., p. 224).

54. Ibid., p. 132.

55. Ibid., pp. 69 and 148.

56. Ibid., pp. 40, 65, and 134.

57. Ibid., pp. 37–38, 44–46, 59, 61–62, 63, and 162.

58. "Ustroistvo i osviashchenie tserkvei v kreshcheno-tatarskikh mestnostiakh," in Il'minskii, *Kazanskaia*, p. 364.

59. "Godichnoe sobranie Bratstva sv. Guriia 30 oktiabria 1873 g. i otchet o deiatel'nosti soveta sego Bratstva ot 4 oktiabria 1872 g. po 4 oktiabria 1873 g.," *Pravoslavnyi sobesednik* (January 1874), p. 51.

60. Nikolai Il'minskii, *Pis'ma N. I. Il'minskago k ober-prokuroru Sviateishego Sinoda K. P. Pobedonostsevu* (Kazan, 1895), p. 6.

61. *Izvlechenie iz vsepoddaneishego otcheta ober-prokurora sviateishego sinoda grafa D. Tolstogo po vedomstvu pravoslavnago ispovedaniia za 1874* (St. Petersburg, 1876), p. 30; Evstafii Voronets, *Materialy dlia izucheniia i oblicheniia mokhamedanstva* (Orel, 1876), p. 12.

62. *Narodnye uchilishcha v Kazanskoi gubernii. Materialy dlia istorii narodnago obrazovaniia: Mamadyshskii uezd* (Kazan, 1888), pp. 24–25.

63. *Istoriko-statisticheskoe opisanie tserkvei i prikhodov Kazanskoi eparkhii*, vol. 6: *G. Mamadysh i Mamadyshskii uezd* (Kazan, 1904), p. 112.

64. V. M. Gorokhov, *Reaktsionnaia shkol'naia politika tsarizma v otnoshenii tatar Povolzh'ia* (Kazan, 1941), p. 232.

65. Gabdulla Tukai, "Pechän Bazary, iakhut iaña Kisekbash," in *Äsärlär* (Kazan, 1955), vol. 1, p. 199.

66. This has been the case in Western studies of Islam, but recently the works of anthropologists have challenged the existence of a dichotomy between traditional and modernist Islam. See Dale F. Eickelman, *Knowledge and Power in Morocco: The Education of a Twentieth-Century Notable* (Princeton, 1985); idem, ed., *Russia's Muslim Frontiers: New Directions in Cross-Cultural Analysis* (Bloomington, Ind., 1993); and Fanny Colonna, *Savants paysans: éléments d'histoire sociale sur l'Algérie rurale* (Algiers, 1987).

67. Qaium Nasyri, *Mäjmägu'l äkhbar* (Kazan, 1895), pp. 44–45. According to one tradition, Muhammad performed the miraculous "splitting of the moon" (*shaqq al-qamar*) in an unsuccessful attempt to convert the unbelieving citizens of Mecca. However, this enigmatic phrase, which appears in surah 54 of the Qur'an, probably refers to a future apocalyptic sign.

68. Gaiaz Iskhakyi, "Ike iöz eldan soñ inkyiraz," *Kazan Utlary* 69, no. 1 (1990): 110–142; 2 (1990): 109–148. Originally published in 1904.

.14.

BRUCE GRANT

Empire and Savagery: The Politics of Primitivism in Late Imperial Russia

Scholars have long considered imperial Russian society the epitome of authoritarian empire, a land where the imperial court took the definitive role in brokering knowledge and bodies. Indeed, when Jeremy Bentham formulated his utopian nineteenth-century state on the principle of the panopticon, the circular prison where inmates were under constant supervision by an unseen warden, he credited his travels through Russia as inspiration. Yet by dint of sheer expanse alone, we know that the reach of the empire often diminished at its many borders, distant zones where officials relied on missionaries, emissaries, and ethnographers to report on the affairs of social governance.

By examining one imperial borderland history here—narratives of indigenous Giliak (or Nivkh) life on Russia's far eastern Sakhalin Island— my objectives are twofold: first, to consider the stunning range of accounts themselves, reports casting their native subjects as anything from savages to socialists; and second, to ask why only one account, the fledgling evolutionist reading of what it meant to be primitive in a civilizing world, nonetheless rose to the fore.[1] Indeed, although nineteenth-century Giliaks were as likely to address foreign visitors in Japanese or Chinese as in the Giliak language, they emerged in popular ethnographic discourse of the late empire as exemplars of both European evolutionary theory and Russian populist values.

Sakhalin Giliaks are unusual here precisely because of their seeming obscurity. A diminutive population of some twenty-five hundred hunters and fishermen living ten thousand versts from the imperial capital, they were unlikely candidates to become the subject of debate in the cultural politics of a massive empire. Yet over the course of the nineteenth century, they became the centerpiece of a movement among Russian anthropologists to redefine primitivism along socialist lines, inspiring further reports from sources as diverse as Japanese intelligence agents to the eminent playwright Anton Chekhov.

A close look at these accounts reveals contentious images of Sakhalin as an Asian island, as well as Giliaks integrated into a transnational orbit almost too oriental for the comfort of the Russian court. What role, then, did a discourse of primitivism play in drawing the hinterland and its native inhabitants back into the Russian imperial fold? To this end, I begin with one of Russia's most prominent ethnographers of the last century, Lev Shternberg.

Exile Ethnography

Much folklore surrounds the work of Shternberg, the idealist revolutionary who was arrested in 1886 for his participation in the populist movement Narodnaia Volia (People's Will), and who went on to spend eight years among the native Giliaks of Russia's distant penal colony, Sakhalin Island. Through the publication of one of his earliest articles, Shternberg's description of Giliak kinship rites caught the attention of Frederick Engels, who saw in the Giliak system of levirate—the sharing of wives among designated brothers—proof that group marriage was alive and well in the Siberian hinterlands. Engels's endorsement not only raised Shternberg's stock in socialist circles, but it linked the latter's work, in a way that became almost legendary, to the belief that primitive life revealed communism as mankind's original state. A reluctant Marxist but an ardent materialist, Shternberg rose with the aid of his political credentials to be the eventual dean of Soviet ethnography in the new order, and his early death in 1927 left him as a relatively clean slate for Soviet hagiographers.

The lengthy field stays prompted by Shternberg's involuntary journey to Sakhalin and the simultaneous exile to Chukotka of his Narodnaia Volia colleague Vladimir Bogoraz set new standards for protracted cultural immersion in ethnographic study. Indeed, exile defined the fledgling discipline of Russian ethnography in ways that set it apart from its counterparts in western Europe, at least preempting the better-known banishment of anthropologist Bronislaw Malinowski from Australia to the Trobriand Islands by some thirty years. Shternberg and Bogoraz entered the group in its twilight phase, through its "Central Student Circle." In the fall of 1882, however, after only his first year at St. Petersburg University, Shternberg was exiled from the capital for having taken part in a student demonstration. He moved to Odessa to study law at the University of Novorossiisk, but continued his work as a youth-wing organizer and sometime editor of the movement's journal, *Vestnik narodnoi voli*. For his continued activities, authorities arrested him in April 1886 and held him for three years in an Odessa prison.[2] In 1889, a court sentenced him to ten years of exile on Sakhalin Island.[3]

The Sakhalin of Shternberg's day bore the marks of a somewhat recent territorial acquisition by Russia. Both Russia and Japan had made claims to the island since the 1850s, and only the Treaty of St. Petersburg in 1875 formally put Sakhalin into Russian hands. Yet its staggering distance from the Russian center slowed settlement. Indeed, where so many visions of Siberia were predicated on distance, Sakhalin entered the ranks as one of the most distant outposts of them all. At some sixty-five hundred kilometers and eight time zones from the Russian capital, Sakhalin remained farther from Petersburg than Newfoundland. Despite the fact that its most northerly tip was at the same latitude as Hamburg or Dublin, the island was (and is) routinely thought of as being Arctic; despite being only fifty kilometers north of Japan, it is thought of more often not as the Far East but as "the Uttermost East," or more commonly, "the end of the world."[4]

Given these impediments to more rapid colonization, the island's indigenous Giliaks initially fared somewhat better than, for example, their counterparts in northwestern Siberia such as the Nentsy or the Khanty, mainly because they were so much less accessible. However, these literal and metaphoric distances turned against the local island populations in the latter half of the century when the tsarist administration saw in Sakhalin the perfect outpost for its growing exile population. Officials began considering the penal colony idea in 1870, and by 1881 the island prison system was established. The tsar accorded Sakhalin its own governor, and from 1884 onward more than one thousand exiles were shipped to the island each year. "By 1888 Sakhalin had become," in the words of George Kennan, "the largest and most important penal establishment in Siberia."[5] Indeed, although exiles were banished all across Siberia during the tsarist and Soviet periods, often to places much farther than Sakhalin (such as Chukotka or Kamchatka), the island's choppy seas and perceived isolation made it one of the most dreaded of exile destinations. Any man with a sentence of more than two years and eight months qualified for Sakhalin exile; any woman under the age of forty with a sentence of two years or more could go; and political exiles of any stripe qualified automatically.[6] The writer James McConkey concurs that by the end of the nineteenth century, Sakhalin had become synonymous with hopelessness, bestial callousness, moral depravity, obliteration of the self, despair, and miasma.[7]

Upon Shternberg's arrival in 1889, his status was that of a political rather than criminal exile, which permitted him to reside in special housing in the small administrative town of Aleksandrovsk and perform physical labor during the days. However, by March of 1890, penal officials cited Shternberg's harmful ideological influence over other local exiles, and they relocated him to the remote community of Viakhta some hundred kilometers north of Aleksandrovsk on the Tatar Strait. That the playwright Anton Chekhov was known to be en route to Sakhalin at the same time, and that authorities were likely fearful of having Shternberg brief Chekhov on the finer points of the tsarist penal system, were additional factors often later observed in Soviet writings.[8] Viakhta consisted of five houses for exiles who had finished their prison terms, and it was a way station for Giliaks in the surrounding area. "It was here," Shternberg wrote, "that I was ethnographically baptized."[9] In his "Russian Palestine," a "grim land" where the sea was "eternally stormy," and where the true inhabitants were "bears, powerful winds, punishing hellish blizzards and destructive hurricanes," Shternberg had greater access to investigations of local Giliak life, and by February 1891 he was allowed to undertake what would be the first of dozens of excursions to Giliak communities across North Sakhalin.[10]

Shternberg arrived at a time when outside influences were deeply restructuring Giliaks' access to fishing and hunting grounds. Giliaks had long been integrated into trade networks with neighboring indigenous groups and the Amur mainland Manchurians; however, they were clearly under new pressure to define their rights to resources when Russian and Japanese fishing fleets began sparring over the prime waters. The arrival of fishing industrialists introduced the additional draw of paid seasonal labor, by which many Giliaks were lured into taking disadvantageous salary advances and fell into considerable indebtedness.[11]

Although by the late nineteenth century some Giliaks had begun to build Russian-style houses, the majority still lived a seminomadic life between summer and winter homes, offering access to seasonal fishing and hunting grounds. The traditional Giliak summer dwelling was a large one-room wooden cabin perched on posts four to five feet above the ground, whereas winter dwellings were partly underground to ensure warmth. On Sakhalin, both shores of the northern portion of the island as well as the banks of the central Tym' River were lined with Giliak villages approximately every five kilometers. Anywhere from one or two to ten families constituted a village, with the maximum number of residents usually around fifty. Almost every family kept a team of dogs for winter transport, and shared narrow wooden boats carved from logs for navigating the famously hazardous coastal waters.

Fishing dominated the Giliak economy in almost all respects. Summer was the busiest period, given the intensity of the fish runs and the volume of salmon to be dried into *iukola*. Winter, by contrast, was set aside for periodic hunting and, as Shternberg wrote, *"dolce far niente,"* sweet doing nothing, and almost constant socializing.[12] The Giliak diet consisted of fresh or dried salmon, a variety of wild berries prepared plain or in custards, and a range of products adopted from Japanese and Manchu traders, such as the low-grade brick tea, millet, potatoes, sugar, alcohols, and tobaccos. Traditional Giliak clothing, in the form of tunics and pants for men and long tunic-style dresses for women, was made from a variety of textiles, including complexly crafted salmonskin jackets. As with the clothing of other indigenous peoples of the Amur area, Giliak designs borrowed heavily from local Chinese influences. Few if any Giliaks were known to be lettered, though many had practical knowledge of Chinese, Japanese, Russian, and other indigenous languages for trading purposes. Though Shternberg expressed surprise at the number of Giliaks who knew Russian, he worked largely in Giliak, a language noted for a grammatic complexity which includes twenty-six ways of counting from one to ten based on the spiritual and material qualities of the objects being counted, and considered to be so distinct as to have no known linguistic affiliations with any other language.

Despite the fact that Giliaks, as both Shternberg and later anthropologists observed, came the closest of any Far Eastern peoples in the nineteenth century to adopting Russian ways, there was generally little effort made to convert them to the Russian Orthodox faith. Through to the early twentieth century, reports suggested a Giliak worldview that remained deeply animistic, recognizing four spirit masters presiding in turn over the Sky, the Hills, the Water, and Fire. Giliaks recognized each of these figures through feeding rituals, such as a ritual feeding of the sea with tobacco and *mos'* (a potato and whortleberry puree) before commencing a fishing expedition. By the same token, Giliaks had a complex symbolic relationship with the animal world: Bears in particular were regarded as ritual kin, and would often be kept in pens inside or alongside family homes for several years as visiting guests, culminating in a carnivalesque bear festival which marked the high point of the winter social season. And across the spiritual spectrum, shamanic spirit mediums negotiated healing rituals pertaining to a variety of what were perceived to be spiritually based illnesses.[13] In short, from the Russian point of view, they were among the empire's more unconventional constituents.

By virtue of language, clothing, systems of counting, or sheer physical appearance, there was much to set Giliaks apart from the gradually expanding Russian community around them. Between bear sacrifice, shamanic healing rituals, and Giliak forest feedings, there was much fodder for the nascent practice of ethnography, which my briefest description only begins to touch upon here, and which has been so excellently treated elsewhere.[14] What is again so striking about the corpus of literature on Giliak life—and here we return to the crux of this chapter—are the shifting tides of what was considered to be useful or important knowledge from one political era to another. This was perhaps most evident in the Soviet period, when Shternberg's careful work on the clan system, for example, was published posthumously to ensure "the liquidation of patriarchal clan survivals."[15] But with the regnant intellectual trends at the time of Shternberg's field research, it was Giliak kinship structure, and its implications for burgeoning socialist theory, that rose to the fore.

By the time Shternberg arrived on Sakhalin in 1889, the American scholar Lewis Henry Morgan had already published his pathbreaking book *Ancient Society* (1877), and Frederick Engels had responded to Morgan in the influential *Origin of the Family, Private Property and the State* (1884). Shternberg had first read Engels while in prison in Odessa, and wrote of relaxing with Engels's book in his tent at night during his first trip through Giliak villages in 1891.[16] Here a short intellectual exchange between Engels and Shternberg began.

Engels's book had been fashioned as a response to Morgan's sweeping comparative investigations of kin terminologies. After meeting with Darwin, Morgan had begun to think of family structures as evidencing different stages in human social evolution: To the stage of savagery, Morgan located group marriage—the rights of sexual access among all husbands and wives of a designated group.[17] To the more advanced period of barbarism, he traced a loose pairing arrangement between husband and wife; and to the more recent period of civilization, he tied the monogamy we are more familiar with today.

While Morgan concentrated primarily on the first two stages of savagery and barbarism, Engels focused more on the civilizing process and how family relations intersected with the rise of private ownership. Whereas in savagery and barbarism descent was often marked through the female line, Engels argued, civilization saw the rise of male descent rights through monogamy and the perceived facility for identifying a hold over private resources. When descent was traced through the female line, Engels reasoned, paternity, or more specifically precise rules of material inheritance, could not be firmly held. "Once it had passed into the private possession of families and there rapidly begun to augment, this wealth dealt a severe blow to the society founded on pairing marriage and the matriarchal gens," Engels wrote. "Monogamous marriage comes on the scene as the subjugation of the one sex by the other."[18] While modern states presented themselves as products of natural social evolution—"the image and reality of reason," as Hegel set forth—Engels countered that states were products of society that bound up specific interests in the accumulation of private wealth by a few, and families governed under a patriarchal system of monogamy structured to serve that end.[19] Nonetheless, in order to demonstrate that the bourgeois state form was a temporary one, Marx and Engels were in need of examples of something different. For this they prized Morgan, but it was clear that the farther back their examples went, the more their reliance on him was total.

Where did Giliaks fit into all of this? As with many indigenous peoples across Siberia, clan affiliation prescribed a great deal of Giliak political, economic, social, and religious life. There were roughly a dozen active clans among Sakhalin Giliaks at the turn of the century. While only one clan or lineage traditionally prevailed in a given village, mixed settlements had made the system more variegated by the late 1800s. Shternberg's descriptions of the Giliak kinship system were famously labyrinthine: Giliaks were exogamous, in that they married only outside their lineage in a complex system of reciprocities that bound together, in Giliak terms, the wife givers and the wife takers.[20] But what made Giliaks unique, Shternberg claimed, was a triangulated system of marital exchange, based on a tri-clan phratry or alliance group (from the Giliak *pandf*) which underwrote a complex web of mutual social and economic obligations. Following Morgan's terminology, Shternberg charted Giliak kin relations under the heading of "group marriage," since he found the Giliak kin system to be remarkably similar to the Punaluan system in Hawaii that Morgan had documented. According to the classificatory nature of Giliak kin terminology, any married man or woman had several "husbands" or "wives" from his or her marrying generation. As a result, "all men of a given lineage had rights of sexual access to women of their own generation in the wife-giving lineage," and by the same token, women had the same access to men of their own generation in the wife-taking lineage.[21] In practice the system was a loose kind of monogamy: Many Giliak men and women initiated discreet but permissible affairs, particularly with visiting guests; and under more formal circumstances of levirate, a widow often married her husband's younger brother. Public displays of affection were uncommon, and most Giliaks considered it indiscreet to discuss extramarital activities in public.[22] The crucial moment here is the reference to group marriage, for according to Morgan's taxonomy, any group still practicing group marriage could fall under only the category of savagery.

When Engels came upon this first article of Shternberg's in the Moscow newspaper *Russkie vedomosti* in 1892, he seized upon the case as an example of group marriage still extant, and had it translated into German for reprinting within days.[23] Shternberg's report was important for Engels not only because it suggested the existence of group marriage in general, but because the perceived backwardness of Giliak life resonated so well with Marx and Engels's evolutionary frame. The proven existence of group marriage, which Engels reported had recently been under attack, validated Morgan's theory of developmental stages.[24] What made the Giliak case interesting is that "it demonstrates the similarity, even their identity in their main characteristics, of the social institutions of primitive peoples

Exemplars of "Natural Communism"
Group portrait of Nivkh (Photograph by Lev Shternberg, courtesy of the Arkhiv
Akademii Nauk [St. Petersburg], f. 282, op. 1, d. 161, l. 19)

at approximately the same stage of development."[25] What was good for Morgan, by association, was good for Marx and Engels's evolutionist theory of class struggle. Hence, that Giliaks were proven to be a primitive people with backward customs became, in its own way, a necessary building block in the edifice of Russian socialism.

For Giliaks, the die was cast. Their role as the quintessential savages of Engels's favor made them famous in Russian ethnographic literature. Moreover, although he would contradict himself on this point many times, Shternberg also provided a portrait of a people with "virtually no sense of land ownership," for whom "communism and individualism coexist without tension."[26]

What was lost in the process is that the article that found its way into *Russkie vedomosti* was one of Shternberg's first, and one outlining a clan system that Shternberg would later come to recognize as far less fixed than he first perceived it. Looking back once, he reflected, "I took them all for pure-blooded aristocrats."[27] Given the swell of non-Giliaks into the area, increasing dislocations through travel and trade, and the demographic havoc wrought by disease, he realized that much of what he had been presented was an ideal system. The Soviet ethnographer Anna Smoliak also pointed out that intermarriage with Nanai, Evenk, and Manchurian

Chinese prefigured the character of many Giliak settlements in a way that made close adherence to the marriage rules described by Shternberg somewhat difficult; while Chuner Taksami noted that actual examples of Shternberg's labyrinthine systems were few.[28]

That the clan system may not have functioned as methodically as suggested, that group marriage was not as licentious as it sounded, that Shternberg himself was not wholly loyal to the Marxian strain of materialism for which Engels had imported him (Shternberg once called Marxism "a hackneyed reworking of the Hegelian triad")[29]—or that Giliaks at the turn of the century were far from an isolated tribe waiting to be discovered—were moments that soon came to be lost in a handful of popular and scholarly accounts that entrenched Giliaks in an edifice of evolutionary theory. To appreciate how and why the evolutionary frame might have been so readily embraced in the Russian context, we need to turn to the fuller range of literatures on the indigenous peoples of the Russian Far East to which Shternberg was contributing.

From Playwrights to Patrons

Shternberg's focus on Giliak kinship and social structure, following in the evolutionist tradition of Tylor and Morgan, argued a socialist strain of humanism that set in line a new Russian tradition of ethnographic thought. Yet while Shternberg made his mark in academic circles, his story was preempted in all respects by the more famous restless pilgrimage made by Anton Chekhov to the island shortly after Shternberg's own arrival. Chekhov's unexpected 1890 journey puzzled his friends in Moscow as to why he would impose such exile and danger upon himself at the height of his career. Whether he went out of altruism ("In our time a few things are being done for the sick, but nothing at all for the prisoners"), to enlist public consciousness ("I'm sorry I'm not sentimental or I'd say that we ought to make pilgrimages to places like Sakhalin the way the Turks go to Mecca"), or to supplicate anomie ("Granted, I may get nothing out of it, but there are sure to be two or three days that I will remember with rapture and bitterness"),[30] Sakhalin clearly met his requirements of distance and difference. In the words of literary critic Cathy Popkin,

> Chekhov viewed Sakhalin as "separated from the entire world by 10,000 versts," so remote that it would take "a hundred years to get home again." "This is where Asia ends"; "This is the end of the world"; "you can't go any farther than this" (45). That Sakhalin is "far, far away" (42) to the very edge (41), to elsewhere.... It is the exotic Orient, where people seem to exchange greetings by waving geese (45), that the climate is "fierce" and the inhabitants are fiercer still (41), that it is "not Russia," "not Russian," "not ours" (42–43), not Europe, not continent and most saliently not known.[31]

Alterity embodied, Sakhalin was, if not a blank slate, an imperfect slate waiting to be fixed.

Despite his efforts to have the book be a chronicle of humanity and the victory of the human will, Chekhov's *Sakhalin Island* is more a testimony to the constant struggle between the alternating visions of Siberia as heaven and as hell.[32] Of the arduous sixty-five-hundred-kilometer journey across tundra and through forest, Chekhov wrote to a friend that he saw "prose before Lake Baikal and poetry afterwards."[33] But in other accounts, he wrote of the fabulous tedium and depressions he endured, passing town after town inhabited by people "who manufactured clouds, boredom, wet fences and garbage."[34] The prospect of describing Sakhalin upon his arrival was less vexing since, in its pre-redeemed state, Chekhov expected the island to be horrible. As his boat neared the Sakhalin shores for the first time, "I could not see the wharf and buildings through the darkness and the smoke drifting across the sea, and could barely distinguish dim lights at the post, two of which were red. . . . On my left, monstrous fires were burning. . . . It seemed that all of Sakhalin was on fire."[35] Early into the trip, the horrors of Sakhalin were not just the vales of suffering, but the trauma of senselessness that pervaded the prison administration.

Absurdities and inversions abounded. Chekhov had wondered what became of exiles after sentencing, but even on Sakhalin this was not clear. There was an almost complete failure to distinguish prisoners; the warden could not be bothered to sort out the sick from the well; the forced labor and the free labor could not be told apart from each other.[36] Chekhov ignored the northern half of the island, but referred to the center of the island as northern. "By the end, after countless claims that the south is more 'x' than the north, and the north is more 'y' than the south, Chekhov concedes that they are probably just the same. North, which is really center, is the same as south."[37] The strait that insulated Sakhalin and was supposed to render it the impenetrable island of the damned froze over in the winter, thus negating the insularity. In sum, nothing on Sakhalin was quite what it seemed. Sakhalin, Chekhov ruminated, evinced a "vague mood" (*febris sachaliensis*).[38]

Chekhov's odyssey through the island's heavenly and hellish qualities extended to the Giliaks. The native population on Sakhalin was intended by Chekhov to contrast the errors of the man-made environment. Giliaks were "a wonderful and cheerful people . . . always intelligent, gentle, naively attentive,"[39] yet they were also dirty, repulsive and prone to lying.[40]

Other, non-Russian gentlemen travelers made their way to Sakhalin around the same time and were less constrained by the *noblesse* that bound Chekhov. All claimed to be the first of their kind (the first Englishman, the first Frenchman, the first American); all met beautiful young women on the boat going over whose tragic fates had sent them in search of meaning;

and all had disparaging things to say about Giliaks. B. Douglas Howard, an Englishman traveling to Sakhalin just before Chekhov in 1889–90, brought with him trinkets that he wagered would be "pleasing to savages anywhere,"[41] but found the Giliak food repulsive, the women's hair like horse rakes, and the clothing grotesque.[42] The Frenchman Paul Labbé, traveling to Sakhalin ten years later in 1899, might well have concluded that Howard had spoiled things for him: In efforts to enrich his private collection at the Trocadero, Labbé complained that Giliaks charged for being photographed, evidence of the corrupting influence of the Russians living around them.[43] Harry de Windt echoed the same theme when he traveled to Sakhalin in 1896. Giliaks, with their "repulsive mask-like faces [which] leered out at us like evil spirits . . . may be summed up in three words: dirt, drink and disease, the two latter having been greatly augmented since their intercourse with Europeans."[44] Only the Englishman Charles Hawes, who traveled to Sakhalin in 1901, ventured a more sympathetic portrait. After visiting Giliaks in the northern interior, he wrote at length on problems of Giliak-Russian contact: Native hunting preserves had been overtaken, the best fishing spots had been appropriated, increases in clearings had chased off game, and Giliak dogs could no longer be left to roam and feed themselves since they frequently attacked Russian cows; once tied, they had to be fed, further depleting Giliak fish supplies.[45] Nor had the exile community added any good, for "if a purse is almost indispensable in Regent Street, a revolver is absolutely so on Sakhalin."[46]

While Shternberg and his popular contemporaries may have differed in their accounts of Giliak life, what they shared was a notable oversight of the Asian setting, everywhere conspicuous by its absence. We find a particular contrast here by considering the earlier work of the Japanese official Mamiya Rinzo (1776–1844), which provides one of the most detailed portraits of Giliak life from the Manchu period. Rinzo was an intelligence officer from Hokkaido who was instructed in 1807 to make a study of Karafuto, the Japanese name for Sakhalin. He set off in June 1808 at the age of twenty-six and remained until November 1809. In the interim he spent a good deal of time among Ainu, Orokko (Orok), and Sumerenkuru (Giliak) communities.[47]

Rinzo's remarks about North Sakhalin Giliak/Sumerenkuru life are remarkable for the level of sophistication they convey, contrasting so starkly with the travelogues of Russian explorers of the same period. Rinzo reported active trade and tribute conducted between Giliaks and the Manchu administration, facilitated not only by dog sledges over the frozen Tatar Strait in the winter season, but via seven ferries that traversed the strait regularly at seven different points between contemporary Pogibi (Japanese, Noteto) and Moskal'vo (Tamurao). On the northwestern shore to the north of Pogibi, Rinzo wrote of a Sumerenkuru community more refined than the reindeer-herding Oroks. They wore Manchurian-made cotton clothes, washed their mouths and faces every day "to keep their looks clean and handsome," and were amiable to strangers. Their diet consisted mainly of fish, but included also millet, buckwheat flour, wheat flour, and beans imported from the mainland, although these were expensive and not eaten as staples. Japanese lacquerware was present in most homes, as were wine bottles, tin cups, and earthenware brought over from Manchuria. The Sumerenkuru did their own forging, but the dearth of ironware was a continual problem.[48]

By the same token, we get a markedly international portrait of Sakhalin life from Leopold von Schrenk, the German ethnographer whom the Russian Imperial Academy of Sciences had commissioned in 1859 during its territorial disputes with Japan. His assignment was part ethnography and part foreign policy: Schrenk's express mandate was to understand the influence of non-Russian interlopers among the local populations of Sakhalin and the Amur. In what became a weighty three-tome report, Schrenk's research confirmed what imperial officials conscious of their tiny presence throughout the area likely expected: As of 1860, Schrenk wrote, Amur peoples had far greater ties with Chinese and Japanese traders than with Russians, and many Amur peoples, including Giliaks on Sakhalin, were apparently ill disposed to the Russian administration.[49] In the same spirit, the Russian scholar P. Tikhmenev observed in 1863 that, for whatever reasons—Japanese intimidation or distrust of the Russians—Sakhalin Giliaks preferred to purchase goods at Japanese stores, even when the same products from the Russian-American Company were less expensive.[50] On the other hand, as a tsarist representative traveling with no small contingent, it seems clear that Schrenk met mainly with the Giliaks already best inserted into the north Asian networks of the day: Though most of his Giliak interlocutors spoke to him in Russian, they addressed him by the Chinese *dzhangin'*, a vocative term reserved for well-placed bureaucrats; and on the whole, he found Giliaks to be active traders of fish and fur, with a love of wealth and a strong predilection for gambling at cards.[51]

Although Schrenk noted divisions between rich and poor among all Amur peoples, he was struck in particular by what Shternberg too would come to remark upon as "natural communism" among the Giliaks: The rich, he contended, lent charitably to the poor, and there were few disputes over access to fishing and hunting territories.[52] Schrenk's ruminations on this particular aspect of Giliak life set in motion what would become a long debate over the inherent appropriateness of socialist government to primitive communities across Siberia.

Between Schrenk and Rinzo, Rinzo in particular likely erred on the side of courtesy when he described certain aspects of the Giliak/Sumerenkuru way of life. His illustrations of Sumerenkuru interiors, for example, suggest a far greater degree of good housekeeping than any other prerevolutionary account. It was also salient that he spent time with Giliaks from central and northwest Sakhalin, who had a history of much greater contact with their Asian colonizers. Had he fraternized with Giliaks from the eastern shore, whom Russian administrators would refer to later as Sakhalin's "Dark Giliaks," the portrait might have been different.[53] But his matter-of-fact renderings of Sumerenkuru commerce, industriousness, and affability provide, however briefly, a rare portrait of Sakhalin aboriginals outside the conventional nature-culture continua. It lays the groundwork in turn for questioning the politics of backwardness and isolation so often ascribed to Sakhalin Giliak communities upon the arrival of the Soviets. How could one small group be so many to so few?

Why Evolutionism?

There are numerous examples in anthropology of different scholars working with the same group of people and arriving at fundamentally different conclusions. A recent example can be seen in Alcida Ramos's review of literature on the Yanomami, where we find three scholars respectively determining the Yanomami to be cold-blooded warriors, star-struck Latin lovers, and ersatz Viennese intellectuals. The point here is that representations, of course, are political, and it was not surprising that the Brazilian government made frequent reference to the scientific reports on "the fierce people" when they stepped up relocation programs in order to mine Yanomami lands in the 1970s and 1980s.[54]

Our first task here is to consider how and why so many divergent accounts were produced. Rinzo's account is the most striking in its exception to the others for its halcyon visions of native life. We are tempted to speculate on Rinzo's romantic motives or to question the nature of his lengthy stay, but little evidence from the rest of the career would seem to merit this skepticism. After his work on Sakhalin, Rinzo distinguished himself as among the most rigorous of the intelligence officers in the service of the Tokugawa shogunate, gathering information on the foreign presence in Japan. In spirited ethnographic fashion, he became well known for his ability to assimilate into alien environments, often disguising himself as a beggar or journeyman.[55]

In Rinzo's Giliak writings, the more likely divergence comes from the very time period itself. Despite the "Manchu yoke" that held Giliaks under sway politically at the outset of the 1800s, the foreign presence on north Sakhalin was a vastly more limited one by contrast with the naval traffic to the island brought on by the sparring territorial claims. When the Russian admiral Gennadi Nevel'skoi sailed up the Amur in 1851, Giliaks on the mainland complained of the British and American vessels constantly sailing up and down the Tatar Strait. "The Giliaks," Nevel'skoi wrote, "not knowing whom to turn to for aid and protection, and having not a single means of defending themselves, do not know how to repulse and punish the intruders."[56] Scores of Soviet accounts would later point to the mayhem brought on by the Russian and Japanese merchant traders fast settling the area, dislocating the native population, and creating patterned indentured labor.[57] In short, the many Russian accounts give darker portraits than Rinzo's because circumstances had markedly worsened in the half-century that intervened.

We look, then, to the internal variations among the Russian accounts themselves, and here it becomes key to understand the ideological role that the Far East played in the Russian imperial imaginary of the day. In his essay on nineteenth-century Russian geographers in the Far East, Mark Bassin reminds us that by the 1830s there was widespread frustration that the Petrine path to Europe had failed Russia, and that the empire's real destiny lay east.[58] Alexander Herzen was among many who looked to the Pacific as "the Mediterranean of the future," and given the particular instability of claims made to the Amur and Sakhalin regions, it was clear that the empire needed an ideological as well as an infrastructural hold on the indigenous populations there. It was likely of little comfort to Russia's overseers, as it was to Nevel'skoi and Schrenk when they traveled among the Giliak populations in midcentury, to realize the hold of the Manchu and Japanese populations in the area. Nevel'skoi's ready intervention on behalf of the native populations set the stage for a new native sovereign: "In order to protect you poor indigenous peoples who are his subjects from the offenses of foreigners, the Great Tsar . . . has decided to erect military posts in the Bay of Hope . . . and on the mouth of the Amur, a decision which I, as the emissary of the Great Tsar, solemnly declare to you."[59] But could it have been encouraging to Nevel'skoi, as to Schrenk who followed him, that the Giliak translation of Great Tsar was "Pili-Pili-Djanguine," meaning "very big Chinese official"?[60]

The most common response by Russian explorers to native lands was to lament the unclean surroundings and pagan ways, a discourse of impurity that was common to the civilizing, and Christianizing, mission that had brought these reformers to the empire's distant borders. Nevel'skoi's wife, Catherine, accompanying her husband, wrote of the "ugly faces of the Giliaks lurking about us," but, "overcoming her disgust," she fed the "filthy, stinking, bloodthirsty Giliaks in their hovels."[61] Like Mikhail Veniukov, who followed the Nevel'skois to the Nanai regions of the Amur in the 1850s, or Nikolai Przheval'skii, who compared the native Orochei of the Ussuri valley to dogs during his 1866 voyage, the imperative to overcome their disgust was a moral if not religious one.[62] Yet for all the clear civilizing mission to which the reports of Schrenk and Chekhov alike spoke, almost any report of impurity or the defilement of natives by foreign interlopers matched the task.

For Shternberg, by contrast, the socialist pedigree he cultivated from his student activism and his readings in evolutionary theory made the debates over purity and pollution somewhat irrelevant. If we recall that the linchpin of Engels's argument was that the origin of family, private property, and the state was indeed one, family or kin relations became the necessary starting point in understanding the relational infrastructure that prefigured broader forms of economic and political exploitation. Shternberg's education in evolutionism began with Engels, and here we can assume a linkage with Shternberg's eventual legendary writings on kinship structures at large. Engels's resonance with the populist and socialist movements of the late imperial period needs little underscoring here, yet one need not have been a socialist to craft a future through the evolutionary writings of the day. The very telos of evolutionary thinking, from at least Edward Tylor's 1871 *Primitive Culture* on, spoke equally to the inferiority of non-European peoples as it did to European preeminence in all matters of social development. Like Christianity, evolutionism offered an explanation that united all peoples of the empire under one ideological arc; for scholars in the service in the empire, it also professed a clear doctrine of European ascendance. It was a theoretical stance that reached out to writers of all political stripes.

For Giliaks of a century ago, Shternberg's chance reading of Engels on the eve of his Sakhalin exile produced much of consequence. The irony is that for someone who set out to produce a sympathetic portrait of Giliak life, one of the results of his path through evolutionism was to scientifically buttress the broader vision of savagery held by so many of his contemporaries. Many Russian ethnographers besides Shternberg followed the terminology of the day by making similar claims to group marriage in Siberia in the later 1800s; however, as the anthropologist Peter Schweitzer has shown, few if any of the cases actually corresponded to Morgan's criteria. What so many scholars and travelers salaciously documented as group marriage more closely approximated extensive extramarital liaisons and, in some cases, prostitution. The process of Morganian classification was itself awkward in Siberia since, as in Chukotka, for example, there were a handful of cases of virtually neighboring ethnic groups, effectively at the same "stage" of social development, with widely divergent kinship systems.[63] One wonders, then, how the Giliaks' life might have been perceived differently had their social organization not been foregrounded so prominently.

In her famous preface to Engels's *Origin of the Family, Private Property and the State*, Eleanor Burke Leacock explained that modern materialists substitute the terms "food gathering" and "food production" for "savagery" and "barbarism." This offers an improvement, but still demonstrates how arbitrarily one can classify certain groups. Giliaks, who considered it a transgression to plow the land, did not grow their own potatoes or millet, but rather purchased them from the Manchus and Japanese. Would their status have improved if they grew their own foodstuffs rather than buying them? One wonders, by another example, how much less communal Giliak life might have appeared if Bakunin, writing in the 1870s, had not so energetically popularized the idea of the Russian peasant as "a born socialist," thus inclining his followers to politicize rural life everywhere.[64] One wonders how much less primitive Giliaks might have seemed even to Shternberg had their Asian affiliations not been occluded by presumptions of the virtues of Russian sovereignty.

In the final reading, the import of socialist philosophy on ethnographic writing at this time calls into question the more rigid notions of late nineteenth century Russian ethnography under tsarist censorship. As the eminent historian of Russian ethnography Sergei Tokarev reminded us, by the 1890s a motley assemblage of all ideological types, from Marxists to missionaries, from proto-Trotskyites to proto-tourists, was undertaking the bulk of ethnographic work in Russia.[65] This makes for a discipline that challenges our expectations of ideological homogeneity in colonial societies, and asks whether nineteenth-century Russian ethnography may indeed have been less statist than is often presumed. We open up in turn the possibility of a borderland history that is perhaps less empirical, but also less imperial, than we might normally imagine.

NOTES

1. Giliak is an ethnonym that Russians borrowed from the indigenous Tungusy (Evenki) on Sakhalin. Since the 1920s, Giliaks have become more commonly known by the ethnonym from their own language (Nivkhgu), Russianized as Nivkhi.

2. For more on Narodnaia Volia, see V. A. Malinin, *Filosofiia revoliutsionnogo narodnichestva* (Moscow, 1972), pp. 100–180 and 312–331; "Narodnichestvo," in *Great Soviet Encyclopedia* (New York, 1974), vol. 17, pp. 339–342; "People's Will," in ibid., pp. 617–618; Franco Venturi, *Roots of Revolution: A History of the Populist and Socialist Movements in Nineteenth Century Russia* (New York, 1960), chap. 21.

3. For a range of biographical works on Shternberg, see the prefaces by Ian Petrovich Al'kor in the three following Shternberg collections: *Giliaki, orochi, gol'dy, negidal'tsy, ainy* (Khabarovsk, 1933), pp. iii–xxxvi; *Sem'ia i rod u narodov severovostochnoi Azii* (Leningrad, 1933), pp. iii–xix; *Pervobytnaia religiia v svete etnografii* (Leningrad, 1936), pp. iii–xv; also Vladimir Bogoraz, "L. Ia. Shternberg kak chelovek i uchenyi," *Etnografiia* 2 (1927): 269–282; N. I. Gagen-Torn, *L. Ia. Shternberg* (Moscow, 1975); Sergei Kan, "The Mystery of the Missing Monograph, or Why Boas Did Not Include Shternberg's 'The Social Organization of the Gilyak' in the Jesup Expedition Publications" (Paper presented at the 92nd Annual Meeting of the American Anthropological Association, 1993); S. Ol'denburg, ed., *Pamiati L'va Iakovlevicha Shternberg* (Leningrad, 1928); Chuner Mikhailovich Taksami, "Issledovatel', drug i uchitel' nivkhov," in *Issledovateli Sakhalina i Kuril*, ed. Ivan Andreevich Senchenko (Iuzhno-Sakhalinsk, 1961), pp. 108–131.

4. C. H. Hawes, *In the Uttermost East* (London, 1904), p. 269.

5. Kennan, in John Stephan, *Sakhalin: A History* (Oxford, 1971), p. 68.

6. Hawes, *In the Uttermost East*, p. 337.

7. James McConkey, *To a Distant Island* (New York, 1986), p. 154. For another of many examples, see also A. A. Panov, *Sakhalin kak koloniia* (St. Petersburg, 1905), p. 1.

8. Gagen-Torn, *Shternberg*, pp. 28–30.

9. Lev Shternberg, *The Social Organization of the Gilyak* [Translation Manuscript] (Archives of the Dept. of Anthropology, American Museum of Natural History [hereafter AMNH], New York), p. 1.

10. Shternberg, *Social Organization*, p. 5; idem, *Giliaki*, pp. 22 and 23.

11. Anna V. Smoliak, *Etnicheskie protsessy u narodov Nizhnego Amura i Sakhalina* (Moscow, 1975), pp. 161–182; "Zametki po etnografii nivkhov Amurskogo Limana," in *Sovremennoe khoziaistvo Severa* (Moscow, 1960), pp. 96–98.

12. Shternberg, *Giliaki*, p. 27.

13. Ibid., pp. 49–79.

14. Prior to Shternberg, the German ethnographer Leopold von Schrenk initially conducted a lengthy survey of Nivkh life for the Imperial Academy of Sciences in 1859. The Polish scholar Bronislaw Pilsudskii (older brother of the Polish leader Iuzef) was a coeval in exile with Shternberg on Sakhalin. At the outset of the Soviet period, one of Shternberg's graduate students, Erukhim Kreinovich, began what would become decades of research on Nivkh life; in the 1960s, 1970s, and 1980s, there were considerable contributions by Anna Smoliak, the Nivkh ethnographer Chuner Taksami, and the collective of the Sakhalin Regional Museum. In the English language, Lydia Black put the nineteenth-century materials to excellent use in her monographs on Nivkh social organization and symbol systems. The Nivkh language has been the subject of many studies, including studies by Robert Austerlitz, Roman Jakobson, Claude Lévi-Strauss, Galina Otaina, and Vladimir Panfilov.

15. Al'kor, "Predislovie," in Shternberg, *Giliaki*, p. xxxvi.

16. Gagen-Torn, *Shternberg*, pp. 57–58; Shternberg, "Dnevnik," in *Peterburgskii filial arkhiva Akademii nauk Russkoi federatsii* [hereafter *PF AAN rf*], f. 282, op. 1, d. 190, l. 59.

17. Darwin's role in the work assumed by Morgan and later Engels was nonetheless a passive one. Reeling from the social arguments being drawn from his work, Darwin reacted in horror when Marx proposed dedicating *Das Kapital* to him. See Maurice Bloch, *Marxism and Anthropology* (London, 1983), p. 5; Alexander Vucinich, *Darwin in Russian Thought* (Berkeley, 1988).

18. Frederick Engels, *The Origin of the Family, Private Property and the State: In Light of the Researches of Lewis H. Morgan* (New York, 1972), pp. 119 and 128.

19. Ibid., p. 144.

20. Shternberg's cardinal writings on Nivkh kinship are in *Giliaki*, pp. 30–45 and 81–246, and *Sem'ia i rod*, passim; the clearest summaries in English are in Lydia Black, "Dogs, Bears and Killer Whales: An Analysis of the Nivkh Symbolic System" (Ph.D. diss., University of Massachusetts, Amherst, 1973), chap. 4, and "Relative Status of Wife Givers and Wife Takers in Gilyak Society," *American Anthropologist* 74, no. 5 (1972): 1244–1248. Smoliak, *Etnicheskie protsessy*, pp. 76–88, 150–167, and 222, is an excellent Russian review.

21. Black, "Dogs, Bears and Killer Whales," p. 34.

22. Shternberg, *Giliaki*, p. 169; idem, *Social Organization*, chap. 6.

23. *Russkie vedomosti*, 14 October 1892. Reprinted in German in *Die Neue Zeit* 11 (12), bd. 2 (1892): 373–375; and in English in Engels, *Origin*, pp. 238–241.

24. Engels, *Origin*, p. 78.

25. Ibid., p. 239.

26. Shternberg, *Giliaki*, pp. 110 and 113. In *Social Organization* Shternberg wrote, "Contrary to the old view that the life of primitive man is largely communistic, we find now the primitive household, at least in providing shelter, and the preparation of food and clothing, in the main, individual" (AMNH, p. 71). Shternberg's writings on property among the Nivkhi are widely disputed in Kreinovich, "Perezhitki rodovoi sobstvennosti i gruppovogo braka u giliakov," *Trudy Instituta antropologii, arkheologii i etnografii* 4, pp. 711–754; Smoliak, *Etnicheskie protsessy*; and Taksami, *Osnovnye problemy etnografii i istorii nivkhov* (Leningrad, 1975).

27. Shternberg, in Smoliak, *Etnicheskie protsessy*, p. 86.

28. Ibid.; Taksami, *Osnovnye problemy*, pp. 86 and 110.

29. From Al'kor, in Shternberg, *Giliaki*, p. xxi.

30. These three Chekhov quotations are from McConkey, *To a Distant Island*, p. 15.

31. Cathy Popkin, "Chekhov as Ethnographer: Epistemological Crisis on Sakhalin Island," *Slavic Review* 51, no. 1 (1992): 36. Page references in parentheses are from Anton Chekhov, *Ostrov Sakhalin (Iz putevykh zapisok)*, in *Polnoe sobranie sochinenii i pisem. Sochineniia*, vols. 14–15 (Moscow, 1978). The English version has been published in two separate editions under the title *The Island: A Journey to Sakhalin*, trans. Luba and Michael Terpak (New York, 1967), and *A Journey to Sakhalin*, trans. Brian Reeve (Cambridge, 1993).

32. I borrow the phrase from the collection of the same name: Galya Diment and Yuri Slezkine, eds., *Between Heaven and Hell: The Myth of Siberia in Russian Culture* (New York, 1993).

33. Quoted in McConkey, *To a Distant Island*, p. 119.

34. Quoted in Robert Payne, "Introduction," in Chekhov, *The Island*, p. xxi.

35. Quoted in McConkey, *To a Distant Island*, p. 141.

36. Popkin, "Chekhov as Ethnographer," p. 44.

37. Ibid., p. 42.

38. Ibid., p. 47.

39. Chekhov, *The Island*, p. 146.

40. Popkin, "Chekhov as Ethnographer," p. 47. See also Joseph L. Conrad, "Anton Chekhov's Views of the Ainu and Giljak Minorities on Sakhalin Island," in Rolf-Dieter Kluge, ed., *Anton P. Cechov: Werk und Wirkung* (Wiesbaden, 1990), vol. 1, pp. 433–443.

41. B. Douglas Howard, *Life with Trans-Siberian Savages* (London, 1893), p. 21.

42. Ibid., pp. 37, 59, and 63.

43. Paul Labbé, *Ostrov Sakhalin. Putevye vpechatlenii*, trans. from French (Moscow, 1903), p. 228.

44. Harry de Windt, *The New Siberia* (London, 1896), pp. 112–113.

45. Hawes, *In the Uttermost East*, p. 274.

46. Ibid., p. 355.

47. I am grateful to Rika Sato of Princeton University for her work on Rinzo in

Japanese historiography entitled "Authorship and Possession: The Hidden Agenda of 'Discovery'" (unpublished manuscript).

48. John A. Harrison, "*Kito Yezo Zusetsu* or a Description of the Island of Northern Yezo by Mamiya Rinzo," *Proceedings of the American Philosophical Society* 99, no. 2 (1955): 111–113.

49. Leopold von Schrenk, *Ob inorodtsakh Amurskago kraia*, 3 vols. (St. Petersburg, 1883–1903), vol. 1, p. 3, and vol. 3, p. 277.

50. P. Tikhmenev, *Istoricheskoe obozrenie obrazovaniia Rossiisko-Amerikanskoi kompanii i deistvii ee do nastoiashchego vremeni* (St. Petersburg, 1863), vol. 2, p. 128.

51. Schrenk's Russian transliteration of *dzhangin'* somewhat obscures the Chinese address, which may have been a version of the words now romanized as *zhangren* (pinyin system of transliteration) or *chang-jen* (Wade-Giles system), which would be a traditional address along the lines of "my elder" but not indicative of an official status; *zhangguan* (pinyin) or *chang-kuan* (Wade-Giles) may have been closer to an address to an official of status. I am grateful to my colleague Alan Berkowitz for sifting through the variants.

52. Schrenk, *Ob inorodtsakh*, vol. 3, pp. 34–41.

53. TsGADV, f. 1133, op. 1, d. 2031 (1900), l. 11.

54. Alcida Ramos, "Reflecting on the Yanomami: Ethnographic Images and the Pursuit of the Exotic," *Cultural Anthropology* 2, no. 3 (1987): 284–304.

55. Donald Keene, *The Japanese Discovery of Europe* (Stanford, 1969), pp. 154–155, cited in Sato, "Authorship and Possession," p. 9.

56. Nevel'skoi, cited in Mark Bassin, "Russian Geographers and the 'National Mission' in the Far East," in *Geography and National Identity*, ed. David Hooson (Oxford, 1994), pp. 112–133.

57. Taksami, "Issledovatel', drug," p. 116.

58. Bassin, "Russian Geographers," p. 114.

59. Ibid., p. 122.

60. From the Giliak verb *pil'd*, "to make big"; see note 51 above on Schrenk's recording of *dzhangin'*.

61. Bassin, "Russian Geographers," p. 123.

62. Ibid., pp. 125–127.

63. Peter Schweitzer, "Spouse-Exchange in North-eastern Siberia: On Kinship and Sexual Relations and Their Transformations," *Vienna Contributions to Ethnology and Anthropology* 5 (1989): 17–38. Maurice Bloch expands on general misconceptions held by Morgan in *Marxism and Anthropology*, passim.

64. "Narodnichestvo," in *Great Soviet Encyclopedia*, vol. 17, p. 340.

65. Sergei A. Tokarev, *Istoriia russkoi etnografii* (Moscow, 1966), p. 374.

Conclusion

There are many stories of the Russian Empire revealed in this volume. They unfold on the borders among the subject peoples and in the writing cabinets of naturalists and travelers, in the chancelleries of central ministries and among provincial administrators, in the imaginations of poets and in the weekly markets in the Caucasian foothills. Our version of imperial history will be successful if it attests the richness and diversity of a subject too long neglected in favor of the grand historical panorama seen from St. Petersburg.

But beyond the interest in discovering borderland histories lie issues of historical significance that this conclusion must address. Our volume, intended to raise new questions and stimulate further research, cannot propose a new theory or paradigm of Russian imperial history. But it can put forward possible outlines for significant reinterpretation of that history. Three perspectives helpful in rethinking Russia's imperial past are suggested by the terms, employed abundantly in studies of all Western empires, "imperialism," "Orientalism," and "colonialism."

Large parts of the vast territory governed by the Russian tsars were as remote, until the coming of the railroad, as the Asian and African lands of the Western empires. Yet our chapters uncover only sporadic, uncoordinated efforts by the state to lay the foundations for a coherent colonial rule. Until the late nineteenth century, there is little evidence of the organization of well-trained personnel to govern those distant regions. A cohort of army generals with extensive borderlands experience, including A. N. Kuropatkin and N. I. Grodekov, emerged in the late tsarist period. Did it constitute a protocolonial administration? The subject must await further study.

Our volume does suggest the broad outlines of policies of imperial rule. The confusion of labels attached to the subject peoples, discussed in

Michael Khodarkovsky's chapter, reveals a long-standing dilemma for tsarist rulers: how to reconcile their basic goal of imperial integration with the enormous ethnic and religious diversity within the population. Austin Jersild's chapter argues persuasively that administrators in the Caucasus long accepted and at times welcomed the departure, forced or voluntary, of conquered peoples whom they considered unfit to become submissive, orderly subjects. One might think of the pattern of forced integration of new territories and assimilation of the elite of newly absorbed frontier populations as a rudimentary imperial ideology. Yet it drew far more from Muscovite practices of constructing an autocratic state than it did from recognizing and accommodating the diversity of a multi-ethnic, multi-religious empire.

Acknowledgment of the importance of ethnic differences came at the same time that the empire's leadership became champions of progress. Signs of a new approach to imperial rule and a new claim to imperial legitimacy emerged clearly in Catherine II's reign. Her particular attention to her empire's non-Christian peoples bore a strong resemblance to the "curiosity" that Yuri Slezkine's chapter argues was at the heart of the Russian naturalists' efforts to put together an ethnographic taxonomy of empire. But her new policies also included official tolerance of the once-persecuted Muslims and attempts to implement progressive policies to construct a new type of citizen-subject. Integration of all the empire's peoples remained the goal; short-term accommodation of ethnic and religious differences represented the civilized method of getting there.

In some respects this Catherinian compromise marked the beginning of a new period of imperial borderlands policy. Dov Yaroshevski's chapter emphasizes the tortuous process by which the legal formula of republican citizenship found its way into borderlands policy. By the last half of the nineteenth century, a new set of imperial priorities had emerged in both Caucasia and Turkestan. There, groups of administrators made serious efforts to understand the religion and way of life of their subject peoples, who were, as both Jersild and Daniel Brower point out, the subject of extensive official and semi-official study. Repression and exile were in disfavor; "otherness" was, in a manner of speaking, in favor, or at least recognized to be an inescapable reality. Virtuous citizen-subjects became the new hope of a unified, mighty empire.

But there is a fine line between ideology and myth. The advantages of technology, medicine, education, and secular law constituted in theory the ingredients of a new imperial vocation. It rested, as in the British and French empires, on the expectation that the natives were amenable to collective and individual improvement on the Western model. Some did respond accordingly, as Edward Lazzerini and Adeeb Khalid show for Crimea and Central Asia. But Jo-Ann Gross makes us aware of the other voices, as exemplified by one Muslim scholar as opposed to Western values as he was disillusioned by the weakness of his Bukharan rulers. And even when non-Russians welcomed Western-type innovations in public life, they fixed their own objectives for civic action. In doing so, their activities provoked opposition among Russian officials to the very principles of the Catherinian compromise. The Russian educational program, as Robert Geraci suggests, had by the early twentieth century reached an impasse. Political leaders such as P. A. Stolypin deemed citizen-subjects participating in public life in Muslim territories a more threatening presence than conservative Muslims. Perhaps the empire's proclaimed progressive vocation resembles less an imperial ideology than a myth buttressing imperial authority.

That conception of empire included a complex set of images of peoples. Among them the Russians (and their Western scholarly collaborators) had pride of place, defining and representing both themselves and everyone else. Their ethno-linguistic map of the southern and eastern borderlands did not include a term to designate a distinct exotic region in a manner corresponding to the French and British "Orient." They confronted an enormous diversity among the empire's peoples, whose study attracted and confounded the naturalists whom Slezkine discusses. But his and Susan Layton's chapters, each in its own way, point out the extent to which this project implicated Russia as well. Traits attributed to the civilized West surfaced, in mirror image, in the scholarly and soon literary portraits of peoples of the empire (at least those beyond the western borderlands), among whom Russians at times counted also as "natives." Russian servility found its idealized antithesis in Caucasian valor. To describe the natives was to depict Russia, and it was not necessarily a flattering picture.

These images of ethnic "others" implied very dissimilar scenarios of imperial rule. The future of the borderlands peoples was inscribed in their representations. Islam remained a dominant preoccupation for a militant Orthodox Church and tsarist leaders intent on making Orthodoxy the foundation of the empire. Later, imperial administrators voiced great apprehension at political subversion radiating outward from the Ottoman Empire and inspiring their Muslim subjects to revolt. In a very different, secular perspective, the "savagery" attributed to Sakhalin Island tribes was, to the Russians discussed in Bruce Grant's chapter, a phase in the progressive march of humanity. By uncovering primitive society on the distant borders of the empire, they reaffirmed their own confidence in progress (and reassured themselves that Russia could continue, somehow, its own advance). In the Russian imperial context, these collective portraits of peoples, each with a unique, relatively backward way of life, sustained an exotic, "orientalist" stereotype of the inferiority of the population in the borderlands. But at the same time they tended to undermine the combative conception of otherness that so deeply imbued Russian notions of militant Islam.

The message that ethnic differences were malleable reemerged among Muslim writers who subscribed to a faith in progress. Adeeb Khalid's chapter reveals that Central Asian reformers themselves employed disdainful images of backwardness in calling for improvement in the lives of their people. The terms by which they measured the inferior condition of the Muslim population—filth, disease, ignorance—echoed the language of Russian observers. Similarly, the future to which they aspired bore the imprint of Russian cultural traits. For the jadids, modernism held out an alluring image of the future of peoples who could preserve their own distinct way of life and identity and yet commit themselves to profound rejuvenation. Muslim reformers such as Gasprinskii, as Lazzerini makes clear, relied on its promise both to call fellow Muslims to action and to reassure Russians. When the "Orient" talked back to its Russian rulers, at least some of its voices constructed a generous image of the Occident.

The conditions in which the empire and its borderlands peoples managed their everyday relations were as dissimilar as the ethnic features attributed to the inhabitants of the empire's frontiers. As those borders expanded farther east and south, the individual stories of local encounters multiplied and diversified. Everywhere the terms of those relations were set (at least in theory) by imperial decrees and official actions. But as the word "borderland" suggests, the edges of empire were places where everyday reality bore little resemblance to idealized bonds of subjects and rulers. Dov Yaroshevski's chapter contains clues to the deftness of local peoples to turn to their advantage (or to diminish the hardships of) tsarist efforts to alter their traditions and conditions of life. Just how unpredictable were these local modes of negotiation and adaptation appears clearly in Virginia Martin's chapter. Customary practices of conflict resolution among Kazakh nomads were altered dramatically by the intrusion of tsarist legal procedures. The social custom of raiding reemerged in a new guise, no longer capable of settling disputes and sustained by the greater freedom of young Kazakhs to demonstrate in their own manner their valor and manliness.

The autonomy of local agents of colonial rule in turn created the occasion for social and economic adaptation on both sides of ethnic boundaries. Where Cossack settlements materialized near Caucasian mountain tribes, their inhabitants proved as adept at trading as at fighting. In his chapter Tom Barrett discloses that their daily needs, and presumably those of the tribes, created bonds in the eighteenth and early nineteenth century between the two groups in the very midst of sporadic raiding and fighting. Russians in one way or another "went native" even while natives adopted Russian ways. Crimea, as Edward Lazzerini points out, witnessed similar mingling of customs.

Conclusion

The proximity of Russian-speaking and non-Russian peoples grew steadily in the era of Russian colonial rule. Conditions of life within those territories were irreversibly altered. Increasingly the Russian language penetrated subject communities, for reasons of both necessity and choice; yet loyalties to local communities and the perception of profound interethnic differences remained and may even have strengthened. Agnès Kefeli's chapter offers a vivid reminder that where vital markers of community identity mixed with religious piety, the power of the past was greater than autocratic edict. The resurgence of Islam in the nineteenth century in the area of the former Tatar principality of Kazan, the oldest of Russia's colonial territories, revealed how fragile had been the conversions to Orthodoxy in previous centuries. The villagers of Elyshevo did not threaten the stability of the empire by their efforts to return to the Muslim faith. They did defy tsarist claims to impose their conditions of colonial rule. The empire was more, not less, multiethnic by the turn of the twentieth century. Beneath the apparent autocratic uniformity of imperial domination, cultural and ethnic fault lines were splintering the borderlands in ways that the empire was powerless to control.

Bibliography

Representations

Orientalism

Alatas, Syed Hussein. *The Myth of the Lazy Native*. London, 1977.

Austin, Paul M. "The Exotic Prisoner in Russian Romanticism." *Russian Literature* 16, no. 3 (1984): 217–274.

Azim, F. *The Colonial Rise of the Novel*. London, 1993.

Ballhatchet, K. *Race, Sex and Class under the Raj: Imperial Attitudes and Policies and Their Critics, 1793–1905*. New York, 1980.

Bassin, Mark. "Inventing Siberia: Visions of the Russian East in the Early Nineteenth Century." *American Historical Review* 96 (1991): 763–794.

———. "Russia between Europe and Asia: The Ideological Construction of Geographic Space." *Slavic Review* 50, no. 1 (1991): 1–17.

Batunsky, Mark. "Islam and Russian Culture in the First Half of the 19th Century." *Central Asian Survey* 9, no. 4 (1990): 1–27.

———. "Racism in Russian Islamology: Agafangel Krimsky." *Central Asian Survey* 4 (1992): 75–84.

———. "Russian Clerical Islamic Studies in the Late 19th and Early 20th Centuries." *Central Asian Survey* 13, no. 3 (1994): 213–235.

Becker, Seymour. "The Muslim East in Nineteenth-Century Russian Popular Historiography." *Central Asian Survey* 5, nos. 3–4 (1986): 25–47.

Breckenridge, Carol A. "The Aesthetics and Politics of Colonial Collecting: India at World Fairs." *Comparative Studies in Society and History* 31, no. 2 (1989): 195–216.

Brower, Daniel. "Imperial Russia and Its Orient: The Renown of Nikolai Przhevalsky." *The Russian Review* 53, no. 3 (1994): 367–381.

318

Çelik, Zeynep. *Displaying the Orient: Architecture of Islam at Nineteenth-Century World's Fairs*. Berkeley, 1992.

Clammer, John. "Colonialism and the Perception of Tradition." In *Anthropology and the Colonial Encounter*, ed. T. Asad, pp. 199–222. London, 1975.

Cohn, Bernard S. "Representing Authority in Victorian India." In *The Invention of Tradition*, ed. Eric Hobsbawm and Terence Ranger, pp. 165–209. Cambridge, 1983.

Diment, Galya, and Yuri Slezkine, eds. *Between Heaven and Hell: The Myth of Siberia in Russian Culture*. New York, 1993.

Frye, Richard N. "Oriental Studies in Russia." In *Russia and Asia*, ed. Wayne S. Vucinich, pp. 30–51. Stanford, 1972.

Hokanson, Katya. "Literary Imperialism, Narodnost' and Pushkin's Invention of the Caucasus." *The Russian Review* 53, no. 3 (1994): 336–352.

Hourani, Albert. *Islam in European Thought*. Cambridge, 1991.

Jersild, Austin Lee. "Who Was Shamil? Russian Colonial Rule and Sufi Islam in the North Caucasus, 1859–1917." *Central Asian Survey* 14, no. 2 (1995): 205–223.

Kabbani, R. *Europe's Myths of Orient*. Bloomington, Ind., 1986.

Layton, Susan. "The Creation of an Imaginative Caucasian Geography." *Slavic Review* 45, no. 3 (1986): 470–485.

———. "Eros and Empire in Russian Literature about Georgia." *Slavic Review* 51, no. 2 (1992): 195–213.

———. "Marlinsky's 'Ammalat-Bek' and the Orientalisation of the Caucasus in Russian Literature." In *The Golden Age of Russian Literature and Thought*, ed. Derek Offord, pp. 34–57. London, 1992.

———. "Primitive Despot and Noble Savage: The Two Faces of Shamil in Russian Literature." *Central Asian Survey* 10, no. 4 (1991): 31–45.

———. *Russian Literature and Empire: Conquest of the Caucasus from Pushkin to Tolstoy*. Cambridge, Mass., 1994.

Longzi, Z. "The Myth of the Other: China in the Eyes of the West." *Critical Inquiry* 15, no. 1 (1988): 108–131.

Lowe, L. *Critical Terrains: French and British Orientalisms*. Ithaca, N.Y., 1991.

Mitchell, Timothy. *Colonising Egypt*. Cambridge, Mass., 1988.

———. "The World as Exhibition." *Comparative Studies in Society and History* 31, no. 2 (1989): 217–236.

Obeidat, M. "Lured by the Exotic Levant: The Muslim East to the American Traveler of the Nineteenth Century." *The Islamic Quarterly* 31, no. 3 (1987): 167–193.

Poujol, Catherine. "Les Voyageurs russes et l'Asie Centrale: Naissance et declin de deux mythes, les réserves d'or et la voie vers l'Inde." *Central Asian Survey* 4, no. 3 (1985): 59–73.

Powers, David S. "Orientalism, Colonialism, and Legal History: The Attack on Muslim Family Endowments in Algeria and India." *Comparative Studies in Society and History* 31, no. 3 (1989): 535–571.

Riasanovsky, Nicholas V. "Asia through Russian Eyes." In *Russia and Asia*, ed. Wayne S. Vucinich, pp. 3–29. Stanford, 1972.

Rydell, Robert. *All the World's a Fair: Visions of Empire at American International Expositions, 1876–1916*. Chicago, 1984.

Said, Edward W. *Culture and Imperialism.* New York, 1993.
———. *Orientalism.* New York, 1979.
———. "Representing the Colonized: Anthropology's Interlocutors." *Critical Inquiry* 15, no. 2 (1989): 205–225.
Soltykoff, Alexandre. "L'Orient et l'Occident et Russie." *Le Monde slave* 1, no. 3 (1934): 348–369.
Todorov, T. *The Conquest of America.* New York, 1984.
Vaughan, A. "From White Man to Redskin: Changing Anglo-American Perceptions of the American Indian." *American Historical Review* 87, no. 4 (1982): 917–953.
Visnanathan, G. *Masks of Conquest: Literary Study and British Rule in India.* New York, 1989.
Vostokov, P. "L'Extreme-Orient et la science russe." *Le Monde slave* 10, no. 4 (1937): 134–160.
Woods, S. "Images of the Orient: Goldsmith and the Philosophes." *Studies in Eighteenth-Century Culture* 15 (1986): 257–270.

Ethnography and the Sciences of Empire

Anuchin, D. N. "O zadachakh russkoi etnografii." *Etnograficheskoe obozrenie,* no. 1 (1889): 1–35.
Berelowitch, Wladimir. "Aux origines de l'ethnographie russe: La Société de Géographie dans les années 1840–1850." *Cahiers du monde russe et soviétique* 3, nos. 2–3 (1990): 265–274.
Çelik, Zeynep, and Leila Kinney. "Ethnography and Exhibitions at the Expositions Universelles." *Assemblage* 13 (1990): 35–59.
Clay, Catherine Black. "Ethos and Empire: The Ethnographic Expedition of the Imperial Russian Naval Ministry, 1855–1862." Ph.D. diss., University of Oregon, 1989.
———. "Russian Ethnographers in the Service of Empire, 1856–1862." *Slavic Review* 54, no. 1 (1995): 45–61.
Clifford, James. "On Ethnographic Authority." *Representations* 1, no. 2 (1983): 113–146.
Clifford, James, ed. *The Predicament of Culture: Twentieth-Century Ethnography, Literature, and Art.* Cambridge, Mass., 1988.
Comaroff, John, and Jean Comaroff. *Ethnography and the Historical Imagination.* Boulder, 1992.
Dantsig, B. M. *Blizhnii vostok v russkoi nauke i literature.* Moscow, 1973.
Desmond, Ray. *The India Museum, 1801–1879.* London, 1982.
Geraci, Robert P. "Window on the East: Ethnography, Orthodoxy, and Russian Nationality in Kazan, 1870–1914." Ph.D. diss., University of California, Berkeley, 1995.
Pypin, N. N. *Istoriia russkoi etnografii.* 2 vols. St. Petersburg, 1890–91.
Semenov (Tian-Shanskii), Petr Petrovich, ed. *Istoriia poluvekovoi deiatel'nosti Imperatorskago Russkago geograficheskago obshchestva 1845–1895.* 3 parts. St. Petersburg, 1896.
Slezkine, Yuri. "The Fall of Soviet Ethnography, 1928–1938." *Current Anthropology* 32, no. 4 (1991): 476–484.

320

Bibliography

Stepanov, N. N. "Russkoe geograficheskoe obshchestvo i etnografiia (1845–1861)." *Sovetskaia etnografiia,* no. 4 (1946): 187–206.
Stocking, G., ed. *Colonial Situations: Essays on the Contextualization of Ethnographic Knowledge.* Madison, Wis., 1991.
Thomas, Nicholas. *Colonialism's Culture: Anthropology, Travel and Government.* Princeton, 1994.
Tokarev, S. A. *Istoriia russkoi etnografii.* Moscow, 1966.

Looking at the Colonizer

Abu-Lughod, Ibrahim. *Arab Rediscovery of Europe.* Princeton, 1963.
al-ʿAzm, Sadiq Jalal. "Orientalism and Orientalism in Reverse." In *Forbidden Agendas: Intolerance and Defiance in the Middle East,* ed. Sadiq Jalal al-ʿAzm, pp. 349–376. London, 1984.
Lewis, Bernard. *The Muslim Discovery of Europe.* New York, 1982.
Louca, Anaouar. *Voyageurs et écrivains égyptiens en France au XIXe siècle.* Paris, 1970.
Miller, S., ed. *Disorienting Encounters: Travels of a Moroccan Scholar in France in 1845–1846.* Berkeley, 1992.
Rorlich, Azade-Ayşe. "'The Temptation of the West': Two Tatar Travellers' Encounters with Europe at the End of the Nineteenth Century." *Central Asian Survey* 4, no. 3 (1985): 39–58.

Studies of the Western Empires

Anderson, Benedict. *Imagined Communities: Reflections on the Origins and Spread of Nationalism.* 2nd rev. ed. New York, 1991.
Asad, Talal. "Two European Images of Non-European Rule." In *Anthropology and the Colonial Encounter,* ed. Talal Asad, pp. 103–120. London, 1975.
Beck, L., and N. R. Keddie, eds. *Women in the Muslim World.* Cambridge, Mass., 1980.
Bender, Donald. "The Development of French Anthropology." *Journal of the History of the Behavioral Sciences* 1 (1965): 139–151.
Burke, Edmund. "The Image of the Moroccan State in French Ethnological Literature: A New Look at the Origin of Lyautey's Berber Policy." In *Arabs and Berbers: From Tribe to Nation in North Africa,* ed. Ernest Gellner and Charles Micaud, pp. 175–199. London, 1972.
———. "The Sociology of Islam: The French Tradition." In *Islamic Studies: A Tradition and Its Problems,* ed. Malcolm Kerr, pp. 73–88. Malibu, 1980.
Chatterjee, Partha. *Nationalist Thought and the Colonial World: A Derivative Discourse?* London, 1986.
Cole, Juan R. I., ed. *Comparing Muslim Societies: Knowledge and the State in a World Civilization.* Ann Arbor, 1992.
Danziger, Raphael. *Abd al-Qadir and the Algerians: Resistance to the French and Internal Consolidation.* New York, 1977.
Das, Veena. "Gender Studies, Cross-Cultural Comparison and the Colonial

Organization of Knowledge." *Berkshire Review* 21 (1986): 58–76.

DelPlato, Joan. "Eugene Delacroix's Women of Algiers of 1834: Colonialism and the French View of Muslim Women." Ph.D. diss., University of California at Los Angeles, 1980.

Denning, Greg. *Islands and Beaches: Discourses on a Silent Land—Marquesas, 1774–1880.* Honolulu, 1980.

Dirks, Nicholas B., ed. *Colonialism and Culture.* Ann Arbor, 1992.

Handler, Richard. "On Having a Culture." In *Objects and Others: Essays in Museums and Material Culture,* ed. George W. Stocking, Jr., pp. 192–217. Madison, Wis., 1985.

Harrison, Christopher. *France and Islam in West Africa, 1860–1960.* Cambridge, 1988.

Keddie, N. R., ed. *Scholars, Saints and Sufis: Muslim Religious Institutions in the Middle East since 1500.* Berkeley, 1972.

Landau, Jacob M. *The Politics of Pan-Islam: Ideology and Organization.* Oxford, 1990.

Mani, Lata. "Contentious Traditions: The Debate on Sati in Colonial India." *Cultural Critique* 7 (1987): 119–156.

Martin, B. G. *Muslim Brotherhoods in Nineteenth Century Africa.* Cambridge, Mass., 1976.

Metcalf, Barbara Daly. *Islamic Revival in British India: Deoband, 1860–1900.* Princeton, 1982.

Metcalf, Thomas A. *An Imperial Vision: Indian Architecture and Britain's Raj.* Berkeley, 1989.

Mills, Sarah. *Discourses of Difference: An Analysis of Women's Travel Writing and Colonialism.* London, 1991.

Moore, Sally Falk. *Social Facts and Fabrications: "Customary" Law on Kilimanjaro, 1880–1980.* Cambridge, 1986.

Prakash, Gyan. "Writing Post-Orientalist Histories of the Third World: Perspectives from Indian Historiography." *Comparative Studies in Society and History* 32, no. 2 (1990): 383–408.

Richards, T. *The Imperial Archive: Knowledge and the Fantasy of Empire.* New York, 1993.

Schneider, William. *An Empire for the Masses: The French Popular Image of Africa, 1870–1900.*Westport, Conn., 1982.

Spurr, David. *The Rhetoric of Empire: Colonial Discourse in Journalism, Travel Writing, and Imperial Administration.* Durham, N.C., 1993.

Stoler, Ann Laura. "Rethinking Colonial Categories: European Communities and the Boundaries of Rule." *Comparative Studies in Society and History* 31, no. 1 (1989): 134–161.

Suleri, Sara. *The Rhetoric of English India.* Chicago, 1992.

Vatin, Jean-Claude. *L'Algérie des Anthropologues.* Paris, 1982.

———. *Connaissances du Maghreb: Sciences sociales et colonisation.* Paris, 1984.

Voll, John Obert. *Islam: Continuity and Change in the Muslim World.* Boulder, 1982.

Williams, Elizabeth A. "Anthropological Institutions in Nineteenth-Century France." *Isis* 76 (1985): 331–348.

Bibliography

Colonial Strategies

General

Enteen, George M.; Tatiana Gorn; and Cheryl Kern, eds. *Soviet Historians and the Study of Russian Imperialism.* University Park, Pa., 1979.

Geyer, Dietrich. *Russian Imperialism: The Interaction of Domestic and Foreign Policy, 1860–1914.* Trans. Bruce Little. New Haven, 1977.

Huttenbach, Henry R. "The Origin of Russian Imperialism." In *Russian Imperialism from Ivan the Great to the Revolution,* ed. Taras Hunczak, pp. 18–44. New Brunswick, N.J., 1974.

Kolarz, Walter. *Russia and Her Colonies.* New York, 1952.

Mosely, Philip E. "Aspects of Russian Expansion." *American Slavic and East European Review* 7, no. 3 (1948): 197–213.

Nolde, Boris. *La Formation de l'Empire russe.* 2 vols. Paris, 1952–53.

Pearson, Raymond. "Privileges, Rights, and Russification." In *Civil Rights in Imperial Russia,* ed. Olga Crisp and Linda Edmondson, pp. 85–102. Oxford, 1989.

Raeff, Marc. "Patterns of Russian Imperial Policy toward the Nationalities." In *Soviet Nationality Problems,* ed. Edward Allworth, pp. 22–42. New York, 1971.

Sarkisyanz, Emanuel. "Russian Imperialism Reconsidered." In *Russian Imperialism from Ivan the Great to the Revolution,* ed. Taras Hunczak, pp. 45–81. New Brunswick, N.J., 1974.

Shteppa, Konstantin F. "The 'Lesser Evil' Formula." In *Rewriting Russian History,* ed. Cyril E. Black, pp. 107–120. New York, 1956.

Starr, S. Frederick. "Tsarist Government: The Imperial Dimension." In *Soviet Nationality Policies and Practices,* ed. Jeremy R. Azrael, pp. 3–38. New York, 1978.

Tillett, Lowell R. *The Great Friendship.* Chapel Hill, 1969.

Velychenko, Stephen. "Identities, Loyalties and Service in Imperial Russia: Who Administered the Borderlands?" *The Russian Review* 54 (1995): 188–208.

Caucasia

Atkin, Muriel. *Russia and Iran, 1780–1820.* Minneapolis, 1980.

———. "Russian Expansion in the Caucasus to 1813." In *Russian Colonial Expansion to 1917,* ed. Michael Rywkin, pp. 139–186. London, 1988.

Barratt, Glynn R. "A Note on the Russian Conquest of Armenia (1827)." *Slavonic and East European Review* 50, no. 120 (1972): 386–409.

Barrett, Thomas M. "The Remaking of the Lion of Dagestan: Shamil in Captivity." *The Russian Review* 53, no. 3 (1994): 353–366.

Bennigsen, Alexandre. "The Qadiriyah (Kunta Haji) Tariqah in North-east Caucasus: 1850–1987." *Islamic Culture* 62, nos. 2–3 (1988): 63–78.

———. "Un Témoignage français sur Chamil et les guerres du Caucase." *Cahiers du monde russe et soviétique* 7, no. 3 (1966): 311–322.

Bibliography

Boratov, Pertev. "La Russie dans les archives ottomanes: un dossier ottoman sur L'Imam Chamil." *Cahiers du monde russe et soviétique* 10, nos. 3–4 (1969): 524–535.

Brooks, E. Willis. "Nicholas I as Reformer: Russian Attempts to Conquer the Caucasus, 1825–1855." In *Nation and Ideology,* ed. Ivo Banac, John G. Ackerman, and Roman Szporluk, pp. 227–263. New York, 1981.

Broxup, Marie Bennigsen. *The North Caucasus Barrier: The Russian Advance towards the Muslim World.* New York, 1992.

Dubrovin, Nikolai F. *Istoriia voiny i vladychestva russkikh na Kavkaze.* St. Petersburg, 1871.

Dzidzariia, G. A. *Makhadzhirstvo i problemy istorii Abkhazii XIX stoletiia.* Sukhumi, 1982.

Gammer, Moshe. "Prince Bariatinskii: The Conqueror of the Eastern Caucasus." *Central Asian Survey* 13, no. 2 (1994): 237–247.

Gregorian, Vartan. "The Impact of Russia on the Armenians and Armenia." In *Russia and Asia,* ed. Wayne S. Vucinich, pp. 167–218. Stanford, 1972.

Henze, Paul B. "Circassia in the Nineteenth Century." In *Turco-Tatar Past, Soviet Present,* ed. Chantal Lemercier-Quelquejay, Gilles Veinstein, and S. Enders Wimbush, pp. 243–273. Louvain-Paris, 1986.

Jones, Stephen F. "Russian Imperial Administration and the Georgian Nobility: The Georgian Conspiracy of 1832." *Slavonic and East European Review* 65, no. 1 (1987): 53–76.

Kazemzadeh, Firuz. "Russian Penetration of the Caucasus." In *Russian Imperialism from Ivan the Great to the Revolution,* ed. Taras Hunczak, pp. 239–263. New Brunswick, N.J., 1974.

———. *The Struggle for Transcaucasia.* New York, 1951.

Kravtsov, I. S. "Kavkaz i ego voennonachal'niki." *Russkaia starina* 50 (1886): 563–592.

McKay, John P. "Baku Oil and Transcaucasian Pipelines, 1883–1891: A Study in Tsarist Economic Policy." *Slavic Review* 43 (1984): 604–623.

Ortabaev, B. Kh., and F. V. Totoev. "Eshche raz o kavkazskoi voine: o ee sotsial'nykh istokakh i sushchnosti." *Istoriia SSSR,* no. 4 (1988): 78–96.

Rhinelander, L. Hamilton. "The Creation of The Caucasian Vicegerency." *Slavonic and East European Review* 59, no. 1 (1981): 15–40.

———. *Prince Michael Vorontsov: Viceroy to the Tsar.* Montreal, 1990.

———. "Russia's Imperial Policy: The Administration of the Caucasus in the First Half of the Nineteenth Century." *Canadian Slavonic Papers* 17, nos. 2–3 (1975): 218–235.

———. "Viceroy Vorontsov's Administration of the Caucasus." In *Transcaucasia: Nationalism and Social Change,* ed. Ronald Grigor Suny, pp. 87–104. Ann Arbor, 1983.

Rieber, Alfred J., ed. *The Politics of Autocracy: Letters of Alexander II to Prince A. I. Bariatinskii, 1857–1864.* Paris, 1966.

Tarran, Michel. "The Orthodox Mission in the North Caucasus: End of the 18th–Beginning of the 19th Century." *Central Asian Survey* 10, nos. 1–2 (1991): 103–117.

Tillett, Lowell R. "Shamil and Muridism in Recent Soviet Historiography." *American Slavic and East European Review* 20, no. 2 (1961): 253–269.

Bibliography

Totoev, M. S. "K voprosu o pereselenii Osetin v Turtsiiu (1859–1865)." *Izvestiia Severo-Osetinskogo nauchno-issledovatel'skogo instituta* 13, vyp. 1 (1948): 24–46.

Whittock, Michael. "Ermolov: Proconsul of the Caucasus." *The Russian Review* 18, no. 1 (1959): 53–60.

Zisserman, A. L. *Fel'dmarshal Kniaz' Aleksandr Ivanovich Bariatinskii, 1815–1879*. Moscow, 1888.

Central Asia and the Volga

Allworth, Edward, ed. *Central Asia: 130 Years of Russian Rule*. Durham, N.C., 1995.

Bacon, Elizabeth. *Central Asians under Russian Rule*. Ithaca, N.Y., 1966.

Baumann, F. Robert. "Subject Nationalities in the Military Service of Imperial Russia: The Case of the Bashkirs." *Slavic Review* 46 (1987): 489–502.

Becker, Seymour. *Russia's Protectorates in Central Asia: Bukhara and Khiva, 1865–1929*. Cambridge, 1968.

Blank, Stephen J. "National Education, Church and State in Tsarist Nationality Policy: The Il'minskii System." *Canadian-American Slavic Studies* 17 (1983): 466–486.

Demko, George J. *The Russian Colonization of Kazakhstan, 1896–1916*. Bloomington, Ind., 1969.

Donnelly, Alton. *The Russian Conquest of Bashkiria*. New Haven, 1968.

Kappeler, Andreas. *Russlands erste Nationalitäten: Das Zarenreich und die Völker der Mittleren Wolga vom 16. Bis 19 Jahrhundert*. Cologne, 1982.

Khalfin, N. A. *Prisoedinenie Srednei Azii k Rossii (60–90-e gody XIX veka)*. Moscow, 1965.

Khodarkovsky, Michael. "Uneasy Alliance: Peter the Great and Ayuki Khan." *Central Asian Survey* 7, no. 4 (1988): 1–45.

———. *Where Two Worlds Meet: The Russian State and the Kalmyk Nomads in the 17th and 18th Centuries*. Ithaca, N.Y., 1992.

Kreindler, Isabelle. "Educational Policies toward the Eastern Nationalities in Tsarist Russia: A Study of Il'minskii's System." Ph.D. diss., Columbia University, 1969.

MacKenzie, David. "Kaufman of Turkestan: An Assessment of His Administration (1867–1881)." *Slavic Review* 26 (1967): 265–285.

———. *Lion of Tashkent: The Career of General M. G. Cherniaev*. Athens, Ga., 1974.

McCarthy, Frank T. "The Kazan Missionary Conference." *Cahiers du monde russe et soviétique* 14 (1973): 308–332.

Morris, Peter. "The Russians in Central Asia, 1870–1887." *Slavonic and East European Review* 53, no. 133 (1975): 521–538.

Pierce, Richard. *Russian Central Asia, 1867–1917: A Study in Colonial Rule*. Berkeley, 1960.

Semenov, A. "Pokoritel' i ustroitel' Turkestanskago kraia." In *Kaufmanskii sbornik*. Moscow, 1910.

Siscoe, Frank G. "Eugene Schuyler, General Kaufman, and Central Asia." *Slavic Review*, no. 1 (1968): 119–124.

Williams, D. S. M. "Native Courts in Tsarist Central Asia." *Central Asian Review* 14, no. 1 (1966): 6–19.

Crimea

Druzhinina, E. I. *Iuzhnaia Ukraina 1800–1825 gg.* Moscow, 1970.
———. *Iuzhnaia Ukraina v period krizisa feodalizma, 1825–1860 gg.* Moscow, 1981.
———. *Severnoe Prichernomor'e v 1775–1800 gg.* Moscow, 1959.
Fisher, Alan W. *The Russian Annexation of the Crimea, 1772–1783.* Cambridge, Mass., 1970.
Lynch, Donald F. "The Conquest, Settlement and Initial Development of New Russia (the Southern Third of the Ukraine), 1780–1837." Ph.D. diss., Yale University, 1965.
Potichnyj, Peter J. "The Struggle of the Crimean Tatars." *Canadian Slavonic Papers* 17, nos. 2–3 (1975): 302–319.
Vozgrin, V. E. *Istoricheskie sud'by krymskikh tatar.* Moscow, 1992.

Siberia

Coquin, François Xavier. *La Sibérie: Peuplement et immigration paysanne au 19e siècle.* Paris, 1969.
Marks, Steven G. *Road to Power: The Trans-Siberian Railroad and the Colonization of Asian Russia, 1850–1917.* Ithaca, N.Y., 1991.
Raeff, Marc. *Siberia and the Reforms of 1822.* Seattle, 1956.

Administering Muslims

Dowler, Wayne. "The Politics of Language in Non-Russian Elementary Schools in the Eastern Empire, 1865–1914." *The Russian Review* 54, no. 4 (1995): 516–538.
Fisher, Alan W. "Enlightened Despotism and Islam under Catherine II." *Slavic Review,* no. 4 (1968): 542–553.
Fon-Kaufman, Konstantin P. *Proekt vsepoddanneishego otcheta General-ad"iu-tanta K.P. fon-Kaufmana po grazhdanskomu upravleniiu i ustroistvu v oblastiakh Turkestanskago general-gubernatorstva 7 noiabria 1867–25 marta 1881 g.* St. Petersburg, 1885.
Lemercier-Quelquejay, Chantal. "Les Missions orthodoxes en pays musulmans de Moyenne et Basse-Volga, 1552–1865." *Cahiers du monde russe et soviétique* 8, no. 3 (1967): 369–403.
McCarthy, Frank T. "The Kazan Missionary Congress." *Cahiers du monde russe et soviétique* 13 (1973): 308–322.
Malov, E. A. *O Novokreshchenskoi kontore.* Kazan, 1873.
Palen, K. K. *Otchet po revizii Turkestanskago kraia, proizvedennoi po vysochaishemu poveleniiu Senatorom Gofmeisterom Grafom K.K. Palenom.* 19 vols. St. Petersburg, 1909–10.
Yaroshevski, Dov B. "Imperial Strategy in the Kirghiz Steppe in the Eighteenth Century." *Jahrbücher für Geschichte Osteuropas* 39, no. 2 (1991): 221–224.

Bibliography

Studies of Western and Eastern Empires

Barfield, Thomas. *The Perilous Frontier: Nomadic Empires and China.* Cambridge, Mass., 1989.

Betts, Raymond F. *Assimilation and Association in French Colonial Theory, 1890–1914.* New York, 1961.

Bidwell, Robin. *Morocco under Colonial Rule.* London, 1973.

Burke, Edmund P. "A Comparative View of French Native Policy in Morocco and Syria, 1912–1925." *Middle Eastern Studies* 9 (1973): 175–186.

Christelow, Allan. *Muslim Law Courts and the French Colonial State in Algeria.* Princeton, 1985.

Cohen, William. *Rulers of Empire: The French Colonial Service.* Stanford, 1971.

Collins, Robert O. *Land beyond the Rivers: The Southern Sudan, 1898–1918.* New Haven, 1971.

Creagh Coen, Terence. *The Indian Political Service: A Study in Indirect Rule.* London, 1971.

Fletcher, Joseph. "China and Central Asia, 1368–1884." In *The Chinese World Order: Traditional China's Foreign Relations,* ed. John K. Fairbank, pp. 206–224. Cambridge, Mass., 1968.

Heussler, Robert. *Yesterday's Rulers: The Making of the British Colonial Service.* Syracuse, N.Y., 1963.

Kanya-Forstner, Alexander S. *The Conquest of the Western Sudan: A Study in French Military Imperialism.* London, 1969.

Mann, Kristin, and Richard Roberts, eds. *Law in Colonial Africa.* Portsmouth, N.H., 1991.

Mommsen, W. J. and J. A. DeMoor, eds. *European Expansion and Law: The Encounter of European and Indigenous Law in 19th- and 20th-Century Africa and Asia.* New York, 1992.

Perkins, Kenneth J. *Qaids, Captains, and Colons: French Military Administration in the Colonial Maghrib, 1844–1934.* New York, 1981.

Prochaska, David. *Making Algeria French: Colonialism in Bone, 1870–1920.* Cambridge, Mass., 1990.

Rossabi, Morris. *China and Inner Asia from 1368 to the Present Day.* London, 1975.

Frontier Encounters

General Frontier Studies

Axtell, James. *The Invasion Within: The Contest of Cultures in Colonial North America.* New York, 1985.

Bitterli, Urs. *Cultures in Conflict: Encounters between European and Non-European Cultures, 1492–1800.* Stanford, 1989.

Clancy-Smith, Julia. *Rebel and Saint: Muslim Notables, Populist Protest, Colonial Encounters (Algeria and Tunisia, 1800–1904).* Berkeley, 1994.

Bibliography

Clendinnen, Inga. *Ambivalent Conquests: Maya and Spaniard in Yucatan, 1517–1570*. Cambridge, 1987.

Comaroff, John, and Jean Comaroff. *Of Revelation and Revolution: Christianity, Colonialism, and Consciousness in South Africa*. Vol. 1. Chicago, 1991.

Cronon, William; George Miles; and Jay Gitlin, eds. *Under an Open Sky: Rethinking America's Western Past*. New York, 1992.

Edwards, David B. "Mad Mullahs and Englishmen: Discourse in the Colonial Encounter." *Comparative Studies in Society and History* 31, no. 4 (1989): 649–670.

Greenblatt, Stephen. *Marvelous Possessions: The Wonder of the New World*. Chicago, 1991.

Guha, Ranajit, and Gayatri Chakravorty Spivak, eds. *Selected Subaltern Studies*. New York, 1988.

Hess, Andrew C. *The Forgotten Frontier: A History of the Sixteenth-Century Ibero-African Frontier*. Chicago, 1978.

Kicza, John E., ed. *The Indian in Latin American History: Resistance, Resilience, and Acculturation*. Wilmington, Del., 1993.

Lane, Christopher. *The Ruling Passion: British Colonial Allegory and the Paradox of Homosexual Desire*. Durham, N.C., 1995.

Limerick, Patricia Nelson; Clyde A. Milner; and Charles E. Rankin, eds. *Trails: Towards a New Western History*. Lawrence, Kans., 1991.

Nandy, Ashis. *The Intimate Enemy: Loss and Recovery of Self under Colonialism*. Delhi, 1983.

Powell, James M., ed. *Muslims under Latin Rule, 1100–1300*. Princeton, 1990.

Reilly, Bernard F. *The Contest of Christian and Muslim Spain, 1031–1157*. London, 1992.

Sahlins, Marshall. *Islands of History*. Chicago, 1985.

Schwartz, Stuart B., ed. *Implicit Understandings: Observing, Reporting, and Reflecting on the Encounters between Europeans and Other Peoples in the Early Modern Era*. Cambridge, Mass., 1994.

Sider, Gerald. "When Parrots Learn to Talk, and Why They Can't: Domination, Deception and Self-Deception in Indian-White Relations." *Comparative Studies in Society and History* 29, no. 1 (1987): 3–23.

Stoler, Ann. "Perceptions of Protest: Defining the Dangerous in Colonial Sumatra." *American Ethnologist* 12, no. 4 (1985): 642–658.

———. *Race and the Education of Desire: Foucault's "History of Sexuality" and the Colonial Order of Things*. Durham, N.C., 1995.

Usner, D. *Indians, Settlers, and Slaves in a Frontier Exchange Economy: The Lower Mississippi Valley before 1783*. Chapel Hill, 1992.

White, Richard. *The Middle Ground: Indians, Empires, and Republics in the Great Lakes Region, 1650–1815*. New York, 1991.

The Russian Empire

Abaev, V. D. *Tbilisi i Osetiia*. Tbilisi, 1959.

Allen, W. E. D. *A History of the Georgian People*. London, 1932.

Allworth, Edward. *The Modern Uzbeks: From the Fourteenth Century to the*

Present. Stanford, 1990.

Altstadt, Audrey L. *The Azerbaijani Turks: Power and Identity under Russian Rule.* Stanford, 1992.

Altstadt-Mirhadi, Audrey. "Baku." In *The City in Late Imperial Russia,* ed. Michael F. Hamm, pp. 282–318. Bloomington, Ind., 1986.

Baddeley, John F. *The Russian Conquest of the Caucasus.* London, 1908.

Barrett, Thomas M. "Lines of Uncertainty: The Frontiers of the North Caucasus." *Slavic Review* 54, no. 3 (1995): 578–601.

Bassin, Mark. "Turner, Solov'ev, and the 'Frontier Hypothesis': The Nationalist Signification of Open Spaces." *Journal of Modern History* 65 (1993): 473–511.

Bliev, M. M. *Osetiia v pervoi treti XIX veka.* Ordzhonikidze, 1964.

Chichagova, M. N. *Shamil' na Kavkaze i v Rossii: Biograficheskii ocherk.* St. Petersburg, 1889.

Fisher, Alan W. *The Crimean Tatars.* Stanford, 1978.

Gvosdev, Nikolas K. "The Russian Empire and the Georgian Orthodox Church in the First Decade of Imperial Rule, 1801–30." *Central Asian Survey* 14, no. 3 (1995): 407–423.

Henze, Mary L. "The Religion of the Central Caucasus: An Analysis from 19th Century Travellers' Accounts." *Central Asian Survey* 1, no. 4 (1983): 45–58.

———. "Thirty Cows for an Eye: The Traditional Economy of the Central Caucasus—An Analysis from 19th Century Travellers' Accounts." *Central Asian Survey* 4, no. 3 (1985): 115–129.

Khodarkovsky, Michael. "Russian Peasant and Kalmyk Nomad: A Tragic Encounter in the Middle of the Eighteenth Century." *Russian History* 15, no. 1 (1988): 43–69.

———. "War and Politics in Seventeenth-Century Muscovite and Kalmyk Societies as Viewed in One Document: Reinterpreting the Image of the 'Perfidious' Nomad." *Central and Inner Asian Studies* 3 (1989): 36–56.

Lang, David M. "A Century of Russian Impact on Georgia." In *Russia and Asia,* ed. Wayne S. Vucinich, pp. 219–247. Stanford, 1972.

———. *A Modern History of Soviet Georgia.* New York, 1962.

Lantzeff, George V., and Richard A. Pierce. *Eastward to Empire: Exploration and Conquest on the Russian Open Frontier to 1750.* Montreal, 1973.

Lazzerini, Edward J. "The Debate over Instruction of Muslims in Post–1905 Russia: A Local Perspective." In *Religious and Secular Forces in Late Tsarist Russia,* ed. Charles E. Timberlake, pp. 230–241. Seattle, 1992.

Magomedov, R. M. *Shamil v otechestvennoi istorii.* Makhachkala, 1990.

Narochnitskii, A. L., ed. *Istoriia narodov severnogo Kavkaza (konets XVIII v.–1917g.).* Moscow, 1988.

Olcott, Martha Brill. *The Kazakhs.* Stanford, 1987.

Rorlich, Azade-Ayşe. *The Volga Tatars.* Stanford, 1986.

Slezkine, Yuri. *Arctic Mirrors: Russia and the Small Peoples of the North.* Ithaca, N.Y., 1994.

Suny, Ronald Grigor. *Looking toward Ararat: Armenia in Modern History.* Bloomington, Ind., 1993.

———. *The Making of the Georgian Nation.* Bloomington, Ind., 1988.

———. "Transcaucasia: Cultural Cohesion and Ethnic Revival in a Multinational Society." In *The Nationalities Factor in Soviet Politics and Society*, ed. Lubomyr Hajda and Mark Beissinger, pp. 228–252. Boulder, 1990.

Swietochowski, Tadeusz. *Russian Azerbaijan, 1905–1920: The Shaping of National Identity in a Muslim Community*. Cambridge, Mass., 1985.

Wieczynski, Joseph L. *The Russian Frontier*. Charlottesville, Va., 1976.

Zisserman, A. L. *Dvadtsat' piat' let na Kavkaze (1842–1867)*. 2 vols. St. Petersburg, 1879.

Native Resistance

Algar, Hamid. "Shaykh Zaynullah Rasulev: The Last Great Naqshbandi Shaykh of the Volga-Urals Region." In *Muslims in Central Asia: Expressions of Identity and Change*, ed. Jo-Ann Gross, pp. 112–133. Durham, N.C., 1992.

Allworth, Edward. "The Arguments of Abdalrauf Fitrat, the Bukharan." *Central and Inner Asian Studies* 5 (1991): 1–21.

Altstadt, Audrey. "The Baku City Duma: Arena for Elite Conflict." *Central Asian Survey* 5, nos. 3–4 (1986): 49–66.

Arsharuni, A., and Kh. Gubaidullin. *Ocherki panislamizma I pantiurkizma v Rossii*. Moscow, 1931.

Bennigsen, Alexandre, and Ch. Lemercier-Quelquejay. *La Presse et le mouvement national chez les Musulmans de Russie avant 1920*. Paris, 1964.

Bliev, M. M. "K probleme obshchestvennogo stroia gorskikh (vol'nykh) obshchestv severo-vostochnogo i severo-zapadnogo Kavkaza XVIII– pervoi poloviny XIX veka." *Istoriia SSSR*, no. 4 (1989): 151–168.

Carrère d'Encausse, Hélène. *Réforme et révolution chez les Musulmans de l'empire russe: Bukhara 1867–1924*. 2nd ed. Paris, 1981.

Cole, Juan R. I. "Of Crowds and Empires: Afro-Asian Riots and European Expansion, 1857–1882." *Comparative Studies in Society and History* 31, no. 1 (1989): 106–133.

Fisher, Alan W. "Ismail Gaspirali, Model Leader for Asia." In *Tatars of the Crimea: Their Struggle for Survival*, ed. Edward Allworth, pp. 11–26. Durham, N.C., 1988.

Gammer, Moshe. *Muslim Resistance to the Tsar: Shamil and the Conquest of Chechnia and Daghestan*. London, 1994.

Georgeon, François. "Yusuf Akçura: Les Années de Formation." *Central Asian Survey* 5, no. 1 (1986): 15–28.

———. "Yusuf Akçura: Le Mouvement national des Musulmans de Russie (1905–1908)." *Central Asian Survey* 5, no. 2 (1986): 61–71.

Guha, Ranajit. *Elementary Aspects of Peasant Insurgency in Colonial India*. Delhi, 1983.

Henze, Paul B. "Circassia in the Nineteenth Century: The Futile Fight for Freedom." In *Turco-Tatar Past, Soviet Present*, ed. Chantal Lemercier-Quelquejay, Gilles Veinstein, and S. Enders Wimbush, pp. 243–273. Louvain-Paris, 1986.

———. "Fire and Sword in the Caucasus: The 19th-Century Resistance of the North Caucasian Mountaineers." *Central Asian Survey* 2, no. 1 (1983): 5–44.

Karimullin, Abrar. *Tatarskaia kniga nachala XX veka*. Kazan, 1974.

———. *Tatarskaia kniga poreformennoi Rossii: Issledovanie*. Kazan, 1983.

Bibliography

————. *U istokov tatarskoi knigi (ot nachala vozniknoveniia do 60-kh godov XIX veka)*. Kazan, 1971.

Khalid, Adeeb. "Muslim Printers in Tsarist Central Asia: A Research Note." *Central Asian Survey* 11, no. 3 (1992): 113–118.

————. "The Politics of Muslim Cultural Reform: Jadidism in Tsarist Central Asia." Ph.D. diss., University of Wisconsin–Madison, 1993.

Kirimli, Hakan. "National Movements and National Identity among the Crimean Tatars (1905–1917)." Ph.D. diss., University of Wisconsin–Madison, 1990.

————. "The 'Young Tatar' Movement in the Crimea, 1905–1909." *Cahiers du monde russe et soviétique* 34, no. 4 (1993): 529–560.

Kreindler, Isabelle. "Ibrahim Altynsarin, Nikolai Il'minskii and the Kazakh National Awakening." *Central Asian Survey* 2, no. 3 (1983): 99–116.

Lazzerini, Edward J. "Beyond Renewal: The Jadid Response to Pressure for Change in the Modern Age." In *Muslims in Central Asia: Expressions of Identity and Change*, ed. Jo-Ann Gross, pp. 151–166. Durham, N.C., 1992.

————. "From Bakhchisarai to Bukhara in 1893: Ismail Bey Gasprinskii's Journey to Central Asia." *Central Asian Survey* 3, no. 4 (1984): 77–88.

————. "Gadidism at the Turn of the Twentieth Century: A View from Within." *Cahiers du monde russe et soviétique* 16, no. 2 (1975): 245–277.

————. "Ismail Bey Gasprinskii (Gaspirali), the Discourse of Modernism, and the Russians." In *Tatars of the Crimea: Their Struggle for Survival*, ed. Edward Allworth, pp. 149–169. Durham, N.C., 1988.

————. "Ismail Bey Gasprinskii and Muslim Modernism in Russia, 1878–1914." Ph.D. diss., University of Washington, 1973.

————. "Ismail Bey Gasprinskii's *Perevodchik/Tercüman*: A Clarion of Modernism." In *Central Asian Monuments*, ed. Hasan B. Paksoy, pp. 143–156. Istanbul, 1992.

Manz, Beatrice Forbes. "Central Asian Uprisings in the Nineteenth Century: Ferghana under the Russians." *Russian Review* 46 (1987): 261–281.

McKenzie, Kermit E. "Chokan Valikhanov: Kazakh Princeling and Scholar." *Central Asian Survey* 8, no. 3 (1989): 1–30.

Murad, Sultan. "The Jihad of Said Shamil and Sultan Murad for the Liberation of the Caucasus." *Central Asian Survey* 10, nos. 1–2 (1991): 181–187.

Murphy, Christopher. "Abdullah Qadiriy and the Bolsheviks: From Reform to Revolution." In *Muslims in Central Asia: Expressions of Identity and Change*, ed. Jo-Ann Gross, pp. 190–202. Durham, N.C., 1992.

Nart. "The Life of Mansur." *Central Asian Survey* 10, nos. 1–2 (1991): 81–92.

Oraltay, Hasan. "The Alash Movement in Turkestan." *Central Asian Survey* 4, no. 2 (1985): 41–58.

Robinson, David. *The Holy War of Umar Tal*. Oxford, 1985.

Sheehy, Ann. "The Andizhan Uprising of 1898 and Soviet Historiography." *Central Asian Review* 14, no. 2 (1966): 139–150.

Shorish, M. Mobin. "Traditional Islamic Education in Central Asia Prior to 1917." In *Turco-Tatar Past, Soviet Present*, ed. Chantal Lemercier-Quelquejay, Gilles Veinstein, and S. Enders Wimbush, pp. 317–343. Louvain-Paris, 1986.

Sokol, E. *The Revolt of 1916 in Russian Central Asia*. Baltimore, 1954.

Zenkovsky, Serge A. "*Kulturkampf* in Pre-revolutionary Central Asia." *American Slavic and East European Review* 14 (1955): 14–52.

———. *Pan-Turkism and Islam in Russia*. Cambridge, Mass., 1960.

Bibliographic Guides

Alektorov, A. E. *Ukazatel' knig, zhurnal'nykh i gazetnykh statei i zametok o kirgizakh*. Kazan, 1900.

Allworth, Edward. *Central Asian Publishing and the Rise of Nationalism: An Essay and a List of Publications in the New York Public Library*. New York, 1965.

———. *Soviet Asia: A Compilation of Social Science and Humanities Sources on the Iranian, Mongolian, and Turkic Nationalities, with an Essay on the Soviet Asia Controversy*. New York, 1985.

Bregel, Yuri, comp. and ed. *Bibliography of Islamic Central Asia*. 3 vols. Bloomington, Ind., 1995.

Drabkina, E. L. *Natsional'nyi i kolonial'nyi vopros v tsarskoi Rossii*. Moscow, 1930.

Gammer, Moshe. "Shamil and the Murid Movement, 1830–1859: An Attempt at a Comprehensive Bibliography." *Central Asian Survey* 10, nos. 1–2 (1991): 189–247.

Kharuzin, A. N. "Bibliograficheskii ukazatel' statei kasaiushchikhsia etnografii kirgizov i karakirgizov." *Etnograficheskoe obozrenie* 2 (1891): 1–68.

Kozlov, Viktor. *The Peoples of the Soviet Union*. Bloomington, Ind., 1988.

Mezhov, V. I. *Turkestanskii sbornik sochinenii i statei, otnosiashchikhsia do Srednei Azii voobshche i Turkestanskago kraia v osobennosti*. 3 vols. St. Petersburg, 1878–88.

Pierce, Richard. *Soviet Central Asia: A Bibliography*. Berkeley, 1966.

Sinor, D. *Introduction à l'étude de l'Eurasie Central*. Wiesbaden, 1963.

Vitkind, N. Ia. *Bibliografiia po Srednei Azii (Ukazatel' literatury po kolonial'noi politike tsarizma v Srednei Azii)*. Moscow, 1929.

Edited Collections Previously Cited

Allworth, Edward, ed. *Soviet Nationality Problems*. New York, 1971.

———. *Tatars of the Crimea: Their Struggle for Survival*. Durham, N.C., 1988.

Asad, Talal, ed. *Anthropology and the Colonial Encounter*. London, 1975.

Gross, Jo-Ann, ed. *Muslims in Central Asia: Expressions of Identity and Change*. Durham, N.C., 1992.

Hobsbawm, Eric, and Terence Ranger, eds. *The Invention of Tradition*. Cambridge, 1983.

Hunczak, Taras, ed. *Russian Imperialism from Ivan the Great to the Revolution*. New Brunswick, N.J., 1974.

Lemercier-Quelquejay, Ch.; G. Veinstein; and S. E. Wimbush, eds. *Turco-Tatar Past, Soviet Present*. Louvain-Paris, 1986.

Rywkin, Michael, ed. *Russian Colonial Expansion to 1917*. London, 1988.

Suny, Ronald Grigor, ed. *Transcaucasia: Nationalism and Social Change*. Ann Arbor, 1983.

Vucinich, Wayne S., ed. *Russia and Asia*. Stanford, 1972.

Contributors

THOMAS M. BARRETT completed his Ph.D. dissertation, "The Terek Cossacks and the North Caucasus Frontier, 1700–1860," at Georgetown University. He has published articles on the history of Russia and the North Caucasus.

DANIEL BROWER is Professor of History at the University of California–Davis. Most recently, he is author of *The Russian City between Tradition and Modernity.*

ROBERT GERACI is Assistant Professor of History at the University of Virginia. He is currently completing a study of ethno-cultural assimilation of eastern peoples in prerevolutionary Russia, and is coediting a collection of essays on religious conversion and tolerance in the Russian Empire.

BRUCE GRANT is Assistant Professor of Anthropology at Swarthmore College. His recent book *In the Soviet House of Culture: A Century of Perestroikas* examines Russian state policy toward Siberian indigenous peoples.

JO-ANN GROSS is Associate Professor of History at the College of New Jersey. She has written a number of articles on the social history of the Naqshbandi Sufi order in Timurid Central Asia, has edited a book entitled *Muslims in Central Asia: Expressions of Identity and Change,* and is presently working on a joint project with Asam Urunbaev of the Institute of Oriental Studies in Tashkent to publish a book on the correspondence of Khwaja ʿUbaydullah Ahrar and his associates.

AUSTIN LEE JERSILD is Assistant Professor of History at Old Dominion University in Norfolk, Virginia. He recently completed his dissertation, "Colonizing the Caucasus: Muslims, Mountaineers, and Russification, 1845–1917."

AGNÈS KEFELI teaches Tatar at the Critical Language Institute of Arizona State University. A former student of Alexandre Bennigsen, she has studied at the University of Paris (Sorbonne) and the Institut des Langues et Civilisations Orientales (Paris), and is currently completing her doctoral work at Arizona State University.

ADEEB KHALID is Assistant Professor of History at Carleton College. His research interests focus on cultural change in Muslim societies. He is currently working on a book on debates over culture and identity in tsarist Central Asia.

MICHAEL KHODARKOVSKY is Associate Professor at Loyola University of Chicago. He is the author of *Where Two Worlds Met: The Russian State and the Kalmyk Nomads, 1600–1771.*

SUSAN LAYTON has taught Russian and comparative literature at Columbia University and the American University of Paris. Now a research associate at the Centre d'études sur la Russie and the Institut d'études slaves, she recently published *Russian Literature and Empire: Conquest of the Caucasus from Pushkin to Tolstoy.*

EDWARD J. LAZZERINI is Professor of History at the University of New Orleans. He has published extensively on the history of European Russia's major Turkic peoples (Volga Tatars, Crimean Tatars, and Azerbaijanis), particularly as regards their cultural and intellectual evolution since the eighteenth century and their problems of adaptation to Russian/Soviet dominance. He is presently completing a study of Ismail Bey Gasprinskii, the nineteenth-century Tatar social activist.

VIRGINIA MARTIN is Assistant Professor of History at the University of Alabama–Huntsville. She recently earned her Ph.D. at the University of Southern California with a dissertation entitled "Law and Custom on the Steppe: Kazakh Judicial Practices and Russian Colonial Rule in the Nineteenth Century."

YURI SLEZKINE is Associate Professor of History at the University of California–Berkeley. He is the coeditor of *Between Heaven and Hell: The Myth of Siberia in Russian Culture* and the author of *Arctic Mirrors: Russia and the Small Peoples of the North.*

DOV YAROSHEVSKI is a senior research associate at the Cummings Center for Russian and East European Studies at Tel-Aviv University. He is currently completing a book on the *inorodtsy,* and editing for publication the memoirs of Natan Davidov, a cotton merchant from tsarist Turkestan.

Index

Abduragim, 102
Adyge, 102. *See also* Cherkess
Afghans, 58
Aivazovskii, I. K., 172
Al-Ahad, ʿAbd, 205–208, 214–18
Al-Malik Türa, ʿAbd. *See* Türa, ʿAbd al-Malik
Alexander II, 65, 273–74
Alexander III, 206
Altynsarin, Ibrahim, 180
Amur River, 303
Anatolia, 170
Arakcheev, 92
Aristotle, 60, 62, 67
Armenians, 59, 104, 235, 237, 241–43
Assimilation (*sliianie*), 20, 25n.34, 182. See also *Sliianie*
Astrakhan, 11, 229–30
Ayni, Sadriddin, 206–207
Azerbaijan, 102, 108–10

Bacon, Roger, 3
Badmaev, P. A., 72
Bakhtin, Mikhail, 81
Bakunin, Mikhail, 307
Balkans, 170
Baqyrganyi, Solaiman, 276
Bariatinskii, Aleksandr, 105–107
Barïmta, 249–65
Barth, Frederic, xv

Bartol'd, Vladimir, 154, 157
Bashkirs, 10, 13, 16, 19, 21–22, 31, 69, 116, 128
Batyrev, 227
Behbudi, Mahmud Khoja, 188, 191–200
Bennigsen, Alexandre, xii–xiii
Bentham, Jeremy, 292
Berezin, Il'ia, 88
Berlin, Isaiah, 109
Berzhe, Adol'f, 109
Bestuzhev, V., 63
Bestuzhev-Marlinskii, 91–93, 96
Bobrovnikov, N. A., 142–43, 149, 153
Bogdanov, Anatolii, 123–24, 129
Bogoraz, Vladimir, 293
Bourdieu, Pierre, 169, 204
British Empire, 89, 115, 122, 312–13
Broca, Paul, 128
Bronevskii, Semen, 86, 233
Bukhara, Amirate of, 210–19
Bukharans, 166, 169, 190–91, 196, 199–201, 313
Buriats, 70–73
Byron, Lord, 85

Catherine II, 4–6, 29, 43, 62, 65–67, 80, 85, 102, 116–20, 131–32, 139, 145, 156, 172, 179, 232–33, 249, 254, 272, 312–13
Caucasians, 82–96, 101–11, 115, 165, 312–14
Caucasian wars, 61, 103, 116–17, 119, 122–23

Index

Central Asia, 188–200, 203–21, 313–14. *See also* Turkestan
Chateaubriand, 87
Chechens, 103–109, 227–28, 233–41
Chekhov, Anton, 293, 295, 300–302
Cheremis, 19–20, 46–47. *See also* Mari
Cherkess, 95, 103. *See also* Circassians
Cherniaev, General, 118
Chinggis Khan, 22
Chukchis, 34, 38, 41
Chuvash, 19–20, 22, 42, 46–47, 141
Circassians, 14, 44, 48, 83–90, 93, 95, 230, 239–42. *See also* Cherkess
Citizenship. See *Grazhdanstvennost'*
Clifford, James, xviii
Colonialism, xv–xvii, 132–33, 171–72, 244, 314–15
Congress of Orientalists, 125
Cossacks, 42, 69, 83, 86, 89–91, 103, 105, 165, 227–44, 314
Crimea, 41, 102, 166, 169–85, 313–14
Crimean War, 69, 274, 280
Cuvier, Georges, 128

Dagestan, 102–109, 228, 241
Dal': *Dictionary of Russian Language,* 75, 258
Danish, Ahmed, 207–208
Darwin, Charles, 297
Davidson, Basil, 182
Dening, Greg, xvi
Derzhavin, 65–66, 80, 84
Divaev, 71
Dukhovskoi, General, 132

Eco, Umberto: *Name of the Rose,* 3
École des hautes Études en Sciences Sociales, xii–xiii
Economic activity, borderland trade of, 227–44, 295–96, 303
Elyshevo, 271–87, 315
Encyclopedia of Law, 67–70
Engels, Frederick, 293, 297–300, 306
Epifanova, L. M., 207
Ermolov, General, 84, 87–88, 237
Ethnicity: defined, xv–xvi; ethnic identity, 14–15, 272; gender differences, 42, 92, 261, 279, 297–98, 306; in Crimea, 174–76; in Sakhalin, 295–96; in Turkestan, 122, 128–31; and languages, 46–48
Ethnography, xv–xvii; eighteenth century, 30–47; nineteenth century, 123–25, 128–30, 134n.28, 251–52, 293, 297–300, 306–307, 308n.14

Fadeev, Rostilav, 94
Fedchenko, Aleksei, 123–24
Fedor, Tsar, 273
Finns, 31, 47, 50
Fisher, Johann, 30, 34
Fitrat, Abdurrauf, 190–91, 196–99, 206–207
Foucault, Michel, 81
French Empire, 106, 115, 313

Gali, Qol: *Tale of Joseph,* 276–77
Gasprinskii, Ismail Bey, 110, 139, 145–46, 153–54, 166, 176–85, 198, 207, 314
Geins, Aleksandr, 70, 123, 262–63
Gender. See Ethnicity. See also Islam, and gender
Georgians, 34, 38–43, 46, 82, 92, 102, 108, 110
German, Archbishop, 272
Germogen, Bishop, 174
Giliaks (Niukhs), 292–307
Gmelin, Johann, 44
Golden Horde, 11, 22
Gosudarstvennost' (statist principle), 74
Grazhdanstvennost' (citizenship): defined, 60–61, 101–102; in borderlands, 65–71, 101, 106–11, 131, 312; in West, 60, 67–68. *See also* Russian Empire
Great Reforms, 61, 69, 255
Grebentsy, 227–44. *See also* Cossacks
Grech, Nikolai, 85
Greenblatt, Stephen, 6
Griboedov, Aleksandr, 81, 88
Grodekov, N. I., 311
Gurii, Archbishop, 272

Habermas, Jürgen, 75
Hawes, Charles, 302
Hegel, G. W. F., 297, 300
Herzen, Alexander, 305
Howard, B. Douglas, 302
Hume, David, 44

Iagfar, 275
Iakuts, 31, 40, 47
Iasak (fur levy), 15–17
Ibragimov, I. I., 251–52
Igel'strom, O. I., 66
Il'minskii, Nikolai, 107, 123, 139, 144, 153, 180, 271, 284–86
Imperial School of Jurisprudence (*Uchilishche pravovedeniia*), 64–65
Inaq, Shir 'Ali, 212, 217
Ingesh, 103–104, 232
Inorodtsy (native populations), 9, 15

Index

Inovertsy (non-Orthodox populations), 15, 21

Inozemtsy (non-Russian populations), 15

Iskhakyi, Gaiaz, 287

Islam: conversion from Orthodoxy, 139–40, 271–72, 280–81, 283–84; and gender, 197, 279; in Caucasia, 102–103; in Russian literature, 84; in Turkestan, 116–20, 204–206; jadidist criticism of, 177, 190–91, 195–99, 285–87; literary response to Russian conquest, 203–204, 206–21; schooling, 144–46, 149, 152–53, 204, 275, 279, 282–83, 285; subjects of Muscovy, 17–18, 20; Sufi teachings, 275- 79, 287–88n.1. *See also* Jadidism

Iurkovskii, General, 106–107

Ivan III, 10

Ivan IV, 11, 17, 169

Ivanov, A., 174

Izhors, 37, 40

Jadidism (modernism in Islam), 110, 139–40, 145–47, 150–54, 177–79, 181–83, 188–90, 193–200, 201n.3, 205–206, 287, 314; in literature, 190–97

Japan, 302–303, 307

Jerome, Jean-Leon, 126

Jews (in Caucasus), 241

Kabardians, 13–14, 104, 230–40

Kadets (Constitutional Democrats), 140

Kalmyks, 10, 13, 21, 38, 69, 116, 233–34, 242

Kamchadals, 31, 40–44, 48

Karaims, 176, 184

Karakalpaks, 19

Karamzin, Nikolai, 84–85, 87

Kartsov, General, 103–104

Kaspii (newspaper), 109–10

Kaufman, Konstantin von, 6, 115–33, 212–14

Kazakhs, 10, 16, 19, 31, 141, 166, 197, 314; Lesser Horde, 13; Middle Horde, 249–65; people's courts, 255–57, 261–62

Kazan, 11, 14–15, 17–18, 20, 22, 107, 139- 46, 150–54, 280, 215

Kazas, Il'ia, 176, 184–85

Kazi-Magom, 104

Khanty, 11, 14, 294

Kharuzin, Aleksei, 142–43, 148–50, 155–56

Kirgiz, 69, 122, 129–30. *See also* Kazakhs

Kirgiz-Kaizakh steppe, 40, 66–67, 70–72, 249

Kishenskii, P., 236, 242–43

Kisliar, 231, 233, 235–36, 239, 241–42

Klements, Dimitri, 73

Klevetskii, 38, 45

Klimovich, Liutsian, 150

Koran. *See* Qur'an

Koriaks, 32, 34

Kriashens, 271–87

Krol, M., 73

Kruzhenshtern, A. O., 106

Krymskii, Agafangel, 154

Kryzhanovskii, General N. A., 118–19

Kulomzin, A. V., 72–73

Kumyks, 104, 230–41

Kundukhov, Mussa, 104

Kuropatkin, General A. N., 58–59, 311–12

Labbe, Paul, 302

Leacock, Eleanor, 306

Leibniz, G. W., 27–29, 39, 47

Leont'iev, A. A., 263–64

Leontovich, F. I., 253

Lepekhin, 43, 45

Lermontov, Mikhail, 82, 88, 90–96

Leushin, 253, 259

Linnaeus, Carl, 4, 45, 47

Lomonosov, Mikhail, 50

Lorer, Nikolai, 93

Loris-Melikov, Mikhail, 63, 104–108

Madrasa (Islamic school), 144, 146–47, 149. *See also* Islam, schooling

Maev, N. A., 123–24

Mahdum, Sharif Muhammmad, 208

Maine, Sir Henry, 121–22

Makhtab (Islamic school), 143–44, 159n.44, 177, 283. *See also* Islam, schooling

Maksudi, Sadruddin, 151

Malinowski, Bronislaw, 293

Malov, Evfimii, 154–55, 272, 275, 286

Manchuria, 302–305, 307

Mansi, 11, 14

Mari, 22, 141. *See also* Cheremis

Marquesas Islands, xvi

Marx, Karl, 297–300

Mashanov, Mikhail, 272

Melikov-Zardobi, Hasan, 109–10

Merjani, Shihabeddin, 145

Mikhail, Grand Duke, 104

Mikhailovich, Aleksei, 230

Mikheev, General, 106, 111

Military service: on borderlands, 69, 106-107

Miliutin, Dimitri, 69–70, 103, 105, 118

Ministry of Education, 144–51

Modernism. *See* Jadidism

Moldavians, 34, 38, 43–44

Index

Mongols, 11–12
Montesquieu, Comte de, 85, 116
Mordva, 19, 22, 41
Mordvinov, N. S., 63, 66
Morgan, Lewis Henry, 297–300, 306
Moroshkin, Fedor, 64
Mukhi-ed-din, 282–83
Müller, Gerhard, 28–30, 47, 49
Munzim, Abdulwahid, 206
Muscovy, 10–13, 15–18, 27–28, 229–30
Muzaffar al-Din (amir), 203, 205–206, 208-20

Nash, Manning, 7
Nasr Allah (amir), 205
Nasyri, Qaium, 281
Nation. *See* Ethnicity
Nemivorich-Danchenko, Vasilii, 95
Nevel'skoi, Catherine, 305
Nevel'skoi, Gennadi, 304–305
Nevolin, 67–68, 70
Newspapers, 109–10, 123, 183–85
Nicholas I, 64, 88, 96, 117
Nicholas II, 111
Niva, 95
Noble savage, literary images, 82–86, 88- 89, 94, 96
Nogais (Tatars), 12, 14, 17, 19, 234, 238, 242
Nomads, pastoral, 129–30, 249–65, 266n.1, 267n.28

Oirats, 12, 14
Orientalism (*vostokovedenie*), xi–xiii; and borderlands, xviii, 138, 155–56, 313; defined, xviii, 81–82; in art, 126- 27; in Russian literature, 81–82
Orthodoxy: conversion to, 17–21, 24n.30, 25n.42, 138–39, 271–73; missionaries, 107–109, 139, 141, 143, 284–86; and Russian ethnicity, 32, 35–36; struggle against Islam, 141–43, 152–53, 271–73, 284–86
Ossetians, 34, 37, 104, 109, 232
Ostiaks (Khanty), 31–33, 40–41
Ostroumov, Nikolai, 123, 153–55
Ottoman Empire, 18–19, 104, 116, 142, 147, 280, 285, 313

Pallas, P. S., 172
Pan-Islamism, 116, 118–19, 142–43, 150–52
Pan-Turkism, 142–43, 151–52, 189–90
Persians, 43, 45, 58, 229–30
Peter the Great, xix, 19, 28, 39, 181
Pletnev, Petr, 89

Pnin, I., 63
Pobedonostsev, Konstantin, 152–53
Pocock, J. G. A., 60
Pogodin, Mikhail, 88–89
Pososhkov, Ivan, 19
Potemkin, Grigorii, 102
Primitive society, xvii, 43–45; in Russian literature, 80–83, 94–95; in borderlands, 102–103, 116, 297–300, 304–307, 313. *See also* Noble savage
Pushkin, Aleksandr, 63, 80, 82–91, 93, 95–96, 172

Qari, Munawwar, 193–94
Qur'an (Koran), 191, 275–77, 284–85. *See also* Islam
Qushbegi, Ya'qub, 213

Rabguzi, Nasiruddin, 283
Radishchev, 44–45, 63
Radlov, Vasilii, 145
Razin, Stenka, 91, 229
Regulations on the Administration of Indigenous Peoples, 254
Regulations on the Siberian Kirgiz, 249–51
Renan, Ernst, 121, 153
Rinzo, Mamiya, 302–305
Rogger, Hans, 80–81
Romanovskii, Colonel Dimitri, 94
Rousseau, Jean-Jacques, 88
Russian Empire: citizenship (*grazhdanstvennost'*), 61–65, 73–75, 101, 106–11; colonial policies, xiii, xix, 65–71, 103–105, 116- 19, 122–24, 131–32, 142–43, 150, 231–32, 249–50, 254–59, 266n.2, 273, 304–305, 311- 13; colonial wars, 84, 90–93, 103, 210–14, 228, 237–38; exile of Muslim subjects, 102–104, 170–71; religious tolerance, 116, 118- 20, 132, 138–39, 179; study of borderlands, 28–29, 122–24; travel literature, 301–304. *See also* Muscovy
Russians: ethnic traits, 38–39, 48–50; literary self-image, 81, 88–92, 313
Russo-Japanese War, 140–41, 216

Sadr, Ishan Baqa-Khoja, 210
Said, Edward, xi, xviii, 81–82, 138, 155–56
Sakhalin, 167, 292–307, 313
Samarqand, 212–14, 217–19
Sami, 'Abd al-'Aziz, 193, 203–221
Sarts, 129–30, 132
Savagery. *See* Primitive society
Sblizhenie (accommodation), 180–83, 233

Scaliger, Joseph, 46
Schlozer, August, 28–29, 37, 47–48, 62–63
Schooling, 107–108, 110, 143–48; Russo-Tatar (Russo-native), 144–45, 148, 153, 159n.37, 204. *See also* Islam, schooling
Schrank, Leopold von, 303, 305
Shamil, 92, 94–95, 102–103, 115, 228, 241
Shariʿa (Islamic law), 120, 122, 281, 286. *See also* Islam
Shcherbatov, Mikhail, 21, 63
Shert' (peace treaty), 12–13, 23n.6
Shidlovskii, I., 236
Shternberg, Lev, 293–307
Siberia, 11, 15, 22, 41, 66, 70
Slavs, 49–50
Sliianie (administrative integration), 102, 116, 230. *See also* Assimilation
Smirnov, Vasilii, 152, 184–85
Smoliak, Anna, 299–300
Society for Amateurs of Natural Science (OLAAE), 124
Society for the Restoration of Orthodoxy in the Caucasus, 109
Soviet Union, 297, 304
Special Conference on Islam, 140–42
Speranskii, Mikhail, 66–67, 69–70, 249, 254
Spiro, Mikhail, 176, 184
Stalin, Joseph, 110
Stanislavskii, 108
Steppe Statute (1868), 255–56
Stolypin, P. A., 6, 71, 74, 142, 149–51, 313
Struys, Jan, 229
Subalterns, theory of, 171–72, 175–76
Sufi, 279, 282, 286–87, 287–88n.1. *See also* Islam, Sufi teachings
Sumarokov, P., 172
Svanetiia, 102

Tajiks, 207–208, 218
Tale of Joseph (Qol Gali), 276–77
Tatars, 6, 14–19, 22, 31, 34, 41, 47, 49, 107, 116, 139–57, 166, 169–85, 199, 207–208, 271–87, 315
Tatishchev, 28, 33, 40, 45, 47
Tauke, Khan, 253
Terek region, 103–108, 165, 227–44
Terskii gorod, 229–30
Teukelev, Mehmet, 13
Thompson, E. P., 209

Tiflis Theater, 108
Timkovskii, 66–67
Timofeev, Vasilii, 271, 284–85
Tokarev, Sergei, 307
Tolstoi, Lev, 90, 93, 96
Tumanov, Aleksandr, 107
Tungus, 31, 33, 38, 44–45
Türa, ʿAbd al-Malik, 209, 216–20
Turgenev, Aleksandr, 88
Turgenev, Nikolai, 64
Turkestan, 115–20, 166, 312. *See also* Central Asia
Turkey. *See* Ottoman Empire
Turkmens, 169, 218
Tylor, Edward, 300, 306

Udmurts. *See* Votiaks
Ukhtomskii, Prince E., 73
Ukrainians, 92
Ulykhanova, Anna, 92
Uslar, Petr, 107–108
Uvarov, Sergei, 108
Uzbeks, 129, 205, 207–208, 213–14, 218

Valitov, Bashir (Efrem Kirillov), 275
Vel'iaminov, Aleksei, 91, 239
Vereshchagin, Vasilii, 123, 126–27, 200
Viazemskii, Petr, 87–89
Voloshin, Maksimilian, 172
Voltaire, 116
Vorontsov, Prince Mikhail, 116–17, 119, 123
Votiaks (Udmurts), 47, 141

Weber, Eugen, 106
White, Hayden, 209
Windt, Harry, 302
Witte, Sergei, 132

Yakuts, 14
Yanomani, 304
Yaʿqub-Qushbegi, 213

Zenkovsky, Serge, 151–52
Zhukovskii, Vasilii, 84, 86
Zhuze, P. K., 155
Zisserman, Arnold, 93, 108
Zolotarev, Captain, 103
Zubov, Platon, 232–33